The Rise and Fall
of the Man of Letters

THE RISE

A Study of the Idiosyncratic

AND FALL OF THE
MAN OF LETTERS

and the Humane in Modern Literature

JOHN GROSS

COLLIER BOOKS

The Macmillan Company
866 Third Avenue, New York, N.Y. 10022
First published in Great Britain in 1969
by Weidenfeld and Nicolson, London
The Rise and Fall of the Man of Letters
is also published in a hardcover edition by
The Macmillan Company.
Library of Congress Catalog Card Number: 69-12939

First Collier Books Edition 1970

Printed in the United States of America

TO MIRIAM

CONTENTS

ILLUSTRATIONS

FOREWORD

In the course of his unfinished autobiography, *A Little Learning*, Evelyn Waugh describes his father as a Man of Letters, someone belonging to 'a category, like the maiden aunt's, that is now almost extinct'. There was a time when 'man of letters' meant something very different from the kind of elderly bookman Waugh had in mind. Originally the term denoted a scholar; then it gradually came to be applied to authors in general. By 1840 Carlyle was able to talk about the Hero as Man of Letters, acclaiming him as 'our most important modern person'. After this, however, the meaning began to be narrowed down. A generation later, it was still possible to call a new series of books about poets, playwrights and novelists English Men of Letters, but only just: the idea already seemed faintly pompous or absurd. By this time a man of letters was very definitely coming to suggest a writer of the second rank, a critic, someone who aimed higher than journalism but made no pretence of being primarily an artist. Up until the First World War men of letters in this sense were a familiar part of the literary landscape; then the term fell into disrepute.

It was a useful term, and nothing has really taken its place. 'Literary journalist' is cumbersome, 'critic' doesn't mean quite the same thing. But if the phrase is obsolete, it is largely because the concept it describes is obsolete too. As Waugh put it, 'today that broad, smooth stream has divided'. Instead of men of letters, there are academic experts, mass media pundits, cultural functionaries.

In the following pages I have tried to sketch some of the main changes which have taken place in the world of the man of letters since the beginning of the nineteenth century. I have mostly dealt with individual authors, which in a crowded field inevitably means being highly selective, sometimes arbitrarily so. I have also interpreted 'man of letters' fairly broadly, so that it covers a major figure like Carlyle, as well as one or two poets and novelists in the less familiar role of critic. It seems to me that any picture of the literary world which concentrated exclusively on minor figures would be as unnatural as one which left the minor figures completely out of account. For the most part, however, I am concerned with journalists and reviewers, teachers and interpreters – and, more generally, with the role of literature in public life, and the social context of criticism; with the rise of English studies, and the extension of the reading public; with the shaping of nineteenth-century literary culture, and with its gradual disintegration.

1

THE RISE OF
THE REVIEWER

I

In 1831, writing – not without a sense of irony – in the *Edinburgh Review*, Thomas Carlyle instanced the growth of reviewing as a characteristic symptom of unhealthy modern self-consciousness, one more sign of the vertiginous times:

Far be it from us to disparage our own craft, whereby we have our living! Only we must note these things: that Reviewing spreads with strange vigour; that such a man as Byron reckons the Reviewer and the Poet equal; that at the last Leipzig Fair, there was advertised a Review of Reviews. By and by it will be found that all Literature has become one boundless self-devouring Review ...

Complaints about the parasite-proliferation of criticism were nothing new: seventy years earlier, Goldsmith had compared the literary world of his day to a Persian army, in which the men who actually did the fighting were heavily outnumbered by slaves, camp-followers and hangers-on. With the rise of the professional author came the rise of the professional critic. The first successful reviews, the *Monthly* and the *Critical*, were both established in the reign of George II, and by the end of the eighteenth century other competitors had taken the field. At their worst these periodicals were little more than thinly-disguised publishers' catalogues, at their best they carried competent, respectable, even original work. (Quite apart from its Toryism, Dr Johnson preferred the *Critical* to the *Monthly* because its contributors, though they often only skimmed the books which they wrote about, knew how to 'lay hold of a topic, and write chiefly from their own minds'. The

Monthly Reviewers were 'duller men, and glad to read the books through'.) Despite the pioneers, however, it was only at the beginning of the nineteenth century that the review emerged as a really powerful institution, a major social force. The ground may have been laid earlier, but no one has ever doubted that essentially the revolution which Carlyle describes dates from the launching of the *Edinburgh Review* in 1802.

The founders of the *Edinburgh* – Brougham, Jeffrey, Horner, Sydney Smith – created a demand which took them by surprise: initially only 750 copies of the first number were printed. All kinds of local, short-term considerations have been advanced to account for the review's subsequent success; but the primary reason, as Jeffrey's biographer Lord Cockburn wrote in his memoirs, was 'the irrepressible passion for discussion which suc-ceeded the fall of old systems on the French Revolution' – and beyond that, the stirring-up of fundamental social questions by the steady advance of industrialism. The *Edinburgh* might be fitful and tepid in its liberalism; the *Quarterly*, its chief rival from 1809, might hew to a rigid Tory line. Yet both, by their very existence, testified to the need for reassurance in the face of looming un-certainties, and also to the growing importance of public opinion. Since they sold at the generally prohibitive price of five or six shillings, the 'public' in question was a limited one, but not as limited as all that. In the years around Waterloo the two reviews achieved between them a combined circulation of well over 20,000, and there were of course several readers for every copy bought. Élie Halévy reckoned that at their peak they had a reader-ship of something like 100,000.

The man who more than any other helped to usher in the age of the Reviewer was Francis Jeffrey (1773–1850). A reluctant pioneer, he slipped into the editorship of the *Edinburgh* as unobtrusively as possible. It was no job for a gentleman; in fact at first he doubted whether it was any kind of job at all, prophesying that the *Review* would fold within a year. After the third number he was per-suaded to become permanent editor, on a fixed salary. For a struggling young lawyer without private means the extra income (£300 a year) was a godsend; even so, given the chance he would much rather have earned the money at the bar. He ran the

Review for nearly thirty years, investing the whole notion of an editor with a dignity which had been unheard-of at the outset of his career. Lengthy articles – over two hundred of them – streamed from his pen. And all the while he toiled away at his legal practice, insisting that politics and the law were his real vocation, and that journalism was only a sideline. When the Whigs came back to power, he got his reward. But somehow public honours were less gratifying than they should have been. It was the editor, not the M.P. or the Lord Advocate, who enjoyed a European reputation.

Jeffrey was quick-witted, fluent, and (even by the standards of an age when reviewers were expected to know everything about everything) exceptionally versatile. Less than half his contributions to the *Edinburgh* were on literary topics; the very last he wrote, for instance, was an attempt to establish who first discovered the composition of water. A well-drilled child of the Scottish Enlightenment, a debater trained to argue back to first principles, he was admirably equipped to play the schoolmaster to an audience looking for sound views and predigested information.

For posterity, though, he is the man who told Wordsworth that *The Excursion* would never do. In a way he was right, but he signed his own death-warrant. Extenuating pleas are sometimes entered on his behalf: he was generous to Byron, he praised Keats (partly to spite the *Quarterly*), he spurred on the revival of interest in the Elizabethans. With all his grumbling he rated the gifts of the Lake Poets more highly than those of their Augustan predecessors, while he was perfectly capable, when he chose, of seeing fashionable tinsel for what it was. But the verdict must stand. Undoubtedly the chief use he made of his prestige was to uphold the conventional, the anaemic, the decorously second-rate, while trying to crush potential enthusiasm for Wordsworth and Coleridge. It could hardly have been otherwise. His whole success as an editor depended not only on the skill but on the positive zeal which he brought to his role of spokesman for the approved view of things, the polite consensus. He saw himself as a public watchdog sniffing out heretics, an official observer (his own phrase) representing traditional values which – or so he announced in the first number of the *Edinburgh* – it was 'no longer lawful to question'.

He protested too much. The neo-classic tones ring confidently out, but one soon learns to recognize the romantic tremor they are meant to conceal. There is no reason to suppose that Jeffrey was being a humbug when he claimed, off the record, that he knew most of the *Lyrical Ballads* by heart. His natural sympathies tugged him in that direction. Only there were feelings it was safer not to admit to in company. Wordsworth may have had genius, but he lacked an even more desirable social asset – the *savoir-faire* which warns us that in civilized drawing-rooms 'many things, which we still love, and are moved by in secret, must necessarily be despised as childish, or derided as absurd'. The idea of secrecy is highly characteristic. Again and again Jeffrey insists on drawing a veil round the furtive individual pleasures of literature in the name of universally acceptable standards. (For practical purposes a Whig salon may be said to constitute the universe.) This obviously makes criticism an uncomfortable occupation. An ordinary reader merely has to keep his more specialized enthusiasms to himself, but a critic, as soon as he goes on parade, may well have to actively disavow them. His wisest course, under the circumstances, is to have '*two* tastes – one to enjoy, and one to work by'.

The notion is perhaps not quite as fantastic as it looks at first sight. In common with everyone else, critics are more inconsistent than they usually care to admit. Still, plainly Jeffrey pushed his doctrine to preposterous extremes: his ideal man of letters would have been a thoroughgoing Jekyll and Hyde. And even before the *Edinburgh* was planned, he could write to a friend that 'every man who appears before the public appears before a company to whom he owes respect and on whose sympathies he ought not to reckon too securely . . .' A baleful prospect: the public was a stony-faced tribunal, and the author who presumed too far was asking for a merciless rebuke.

With all his pretence of severity, Jeffrey was basically rather timid and apprehensive. No doubt he recognized that it helped the *Edinburgh*'s circulation for him to hit out. Arguably, too, a critic, however disinterested he claims to be, is always something of an aggressor at heart. But Jeffrey, unlike his bludgeoning contemporaries on the *Quarterly* and *Blackwood's*, seldom gives the impression of simply letting his hatreds go on the rampage. He is too obviously afraid – of ridicule, of unpopularity, above all of seeming childish. His key terms of rejection are 'silly', 'babyish', 'puerile' – as though he felt obscurely threatened by Wordsworth's recognition of how far the sources of poetry lay embedded in childhood. Romanticism which dug as deep as that represented a challenge to hard-won adult values which had to be laughed out of court as briskly as possible.

All the more so, when the judge himself had once nursed crypto-romantic ambitions. There, but for the grace of native prudence and insufficient talent, went Jeffrey. In his early twenties his hopes were set on a poet's career, although only his family were allowed to inspect his first shy efforts: an 1,800-line fragment of blank verse on 'Dreaming', a handful of lyrics and landscape-sketches. Lacking faith in his gifts, he confided to his sister that if he could bring himself to give up the struggle he would be a happier man. But it took time. Eventually he is supposed to have submitted a poem to an Edinburgh bookseller and fled from the city, returning only when he heard that publication had been held up. It had been a close shave. He retrieved the manuscript, and never again ran a comparable risk. He did subsequently come up to London, though, when he was twenty-five, armed with introductions and hoping to break into the literary world. If he had succeeded, and if the *Edinburgh* had been set up without him, it would probably have devoted far less space to discussing poetry than it did. On the principle that any publicity is good publicity, even the poets he attacked owed him something – as Coleridge sarcastically acknowledged in *Biographia Literaria*.

In his more disconsolate moments Jeffrey blamed his failure to grow into a poet on his education and his social background. There is a heartfelt passage in his essay on Burns, where he describes the plight of a not-very hypothetical young man whose ambitions have been fired and at the same time dampened by reading all the right books and talking to all the best people. The classics haunt and oppress him. He knows the kind of comparison to which friends, so-called, will subject anything he writes, he can already hear the jeers which wait on failure. In a word, he is paralysed. A man of the people like Burns, on the other hand, was a free spirit who could let his powers develop to the full, without having to keep glancing nervously over his shoulder. And then immediately Jeffrey back-pedals. Fortunately Burns was unhampered by good breeding, but this also meant, alas, that he wasn't well-bred. His satires could be deplorably acrimonious, his love-poetry displayed 'a fervour that is sometimes indelicate, and seldom accommodated to the "sweet austere composure" of women of refinement'. (Mrs Grundy, one recalls, came to the throne long before 1837.) He was stubborn, wayward and hot-tempered; and there is a good deal of pious clucking over his fecklessness and lack of restraint. When it came to the everyday rules of conduct, genius didn't enjoy any special privileges. Commonplace enough in themselves, these strictures are notable for the retort which they provoked from Wordsworth, in his 'Letter to a Friend of Robert Burns', with its proud reaffirmation of the poet's right 'to catch a spirit of pleasure wherever it can be found'. But the Wordsworthian concept of pleasure, of 'trusting to primary instincts', lay beyond Jeffrey's psychological grasp. If anything it cut across the simpler notion of happiness which he rather plaintively urged was the most important thing in the world – happiness as conceived of by a twinkling old lawyer who flirted with his friends' wives and prided himself on cultivating the art of living. Sometimes he regretted ever having allowed himself to become involved with writers in the first place. On the whole they were trouble-makers, diseased specimens. Ordinary folk were really much more agreeable.

Jeffrey lived long enough to shed notorious tears over Dickens, and to correct the proofs of the first volume of Macaulay's *History*. Macaulay, the one really invaluable contributor whom he bequeathed to his successor Macvey Napier, went on dazzling readers of the *Edinburgh* down to the early 1840s; during the same period the *Quarterly* retained its near-biblical status in the eyes of staunch Tories. But by mid-century events had left both publications lagging behind. The whole ground of political debate was shifting, while the quickening tempo of the railway age favoured dailies and weeklies. (On his death-bed in 1850 Jeffrey had a dream in which he was surrounded by proof-sheets and struggling with an article on free trade in a paper which looked like an amalgam of *The Times*, the *Economist* and the *Daily News*.) The true era of the quarterlies was over. The *Edinburgh* kept going until 1929, the *Quarterly* until 1968. From early Victorian times onwards, however, they were useful receptacles for miscellaneous essays rather than significant battering-rams of public opinion. The days in which (despite formal anonymity) they could confer a reputation on a contributor were past; Lytton Strachey, for instance, wrote for the *Edinburgh*, but nobody ever thought of him as an *Edinburgh* Reviewer.

It is hard for a modern reader not to feel in two minds about the reviews. They presupposed widespread public interest in many topics which have since been handed over almost exclusively to students and specialists; they offered serious writers an enviable amount of space, to say nothing of handsome rates of pay; they set a precedent for the solid journals of opinion – what the Russians called the 'thick journals' – which were to play such a central role in the intellectual life of nineteenth-century Europe and America. On the other hand they were unashamed vehicles for party propaganda, often of the narrowest kind, and generally too overbearing and coarse-grained in their approach to encourage criticism of much depth. They were not even particularly well written. In the mid-Victorian period Leslie Stephen was startled, turning up the early volumes of the *Edinburgh*, to find how much padding and slack workmanship they contained, how threadbare they seemed in comparison with the best journalism of his own day. John Morley and Walter Bagehot said much the same thing; and at least as far as the *Review*'s literary coverage went, their attitude was justified.

Jeffrey himself paid a heavy price for his literary sins. When Cockburn opened the official biography in 1852 by asserting that he was 'the greatest of British critics', younger readers treated it as a joke in doubtful taste; and a generation later, his reputation had completely ebbed away. He remains a classic instance of the critic who comes unstuck through trying to play safe. He was also, in the view of Carlyle, a man whose real gifts had gone to waste:

I used to find in him a finer talent than any he has evidenced in his writing. This was chiefly when he got to speak Scotch, and gave me anecdotes of old Scotch Braxfields and vernacular (often enough but not always cynical) curiosities of that type; which he did with a greatness of gusto quite peculiar to the topic, with a fine and deep sense of humour, of real comic mirth, much beyond what was noticeable in him otherwise; not to speak of the perfection of the mimicry, which itself was something. I used to think to myself: 'Here is a man whom they have kneaded into the shape of an Edinburgh Reviewer, and clothed the soul of in Whig formulas and blue and yellow; but he might have been a beautiful Goldoni too, or something better in that kind, and have given us *comedies* and aerial pictures true and poetic of human life in a far other way!'

It is very much to the point that the anecdotes which brought Jeffrey to life were 'Scotch and vernacular'. As a young man he was determined to get rid of his native burr – or, as Cockburn put it, 'bent on purifying himself of the national inconvenience'. Only partially successful, he came back from Oxford with a queer hybrid accent which astonished his friends and delighted his enemies. The problem of 'correct' speech was a serious one for educated Scotsmen even before the Act of Union, and one need go no further than Boswell to see how it nagged at them in the eighteenth century. In principle most Edinburgh lawyers and *philosophes* deferred to standard English usage, rejecting Scotticisms as provincial and uncouth. Paradoxically this helped them to escape from English domination, by bringing them into closer contact with European culture as a whole – with brilliant results, as everybody knows. But at the same time, repressed patriotic feelings were always liable to rise to the surface. Jeffrey, who usually writes a flavourless courtroom prose, can be absurdly touchy on this score. He reproached Scott for introducing the marauding bands

> *Who sought the beeves that made their broth*
> *In Scotland and in England both*

into *The Lay of the Last Minstrel*: 'The ancient metrical romance might have admitted these homely personalities; but the present age will not endure them; and Mr Scott must either sacrifice his Border prejudices, or offend all his readers in other parts of the Empire.' Please don't embarrass us by being so Scottish in front of the neighbours. Yet when it comes to the novels Jeffrey has nothing but praise for Scott's mastery of colloquial idiom, which only a fellow-countryman, he maintains, can properly appreciate. There is an unfeigned warmth and spontaneity about his enthusiasm which confirms Carlyle's impression of how deeply it went against his innermost nature for him to try to anglicize his speech as thoroughly as he did.

On one issue he remained as staunch a patriot as any Burns-Nighter could have asked. His pride in the achievement of Scottish education, at the level of parish school and college alike, was immense. He paid tribute to the hard-won intellectual attainments of the labouring poor; while when he gave evidence to the first of the Royal Commissions set up to look into Scottish universities, in 1826, he vigorously defended the existing order, with its un-English emphasis on general studies and philosophical dispute. In particular he cherished the traditions of the Humanity class, which encouraged students to argue excitedly about the basic questions of 'history, literature, physics, metaphysics, and everything . . . '

Which turned them, one might say, into fledgeling reviewers. Bagehot thought that teaching in Scotland could have been deliberately designed in order to train men to write authoritative articles, and certainly it would be hard to exaggerate the part played by Scotsmen in the development of the English periodical press. They helped to create not only the great quarterlies and monthlies, as is well known, but the weeklies as well: the first editors of the *Spectator*, the *Economist* and the *Saturday Review*, for example, were all Scotsmen. And right through the nineteenth century critics and essayists made their way south across the border. Lockhart, Masson, Andrew Lang, William Archer are a few random instances. The list could easily be extended – and it would become positively daunting if one were allowed to include the second generation of the diaspora: men like Ruskin, who still spoke with traces of a Scots accent, or Macaulay, whose features in repose struck Carlyle as those of 'an honest good sort of fellow, made out of oatmeal'.

II

For much of the nineteenth century the distinction between a review and a magazine, which has since become so blurred, still held firm. A review consisted of nothing but reviews, while a magazine was a *magasin*, a general store. At first magazines were seldom in any real sense literary: following the pattern set by the venerable *Gentleman's Magazine*, which hired Samuel Johnson to write up parliamentary debates (and which lingered on, incredibly, until 1907), they were usually miscellanies stuffed with news, public announcements, pastimes, notes and queries, extracts from books or from other magazines.* Only with the founding of *Blackwood's* in 1817 did they come to be thought of principally as collections of original articles, fiction and poetry; but from that date onwards they bulk much larger in literary history than the reviews. For as well as printing imaginative work, they were concerned with manners rather than doctrine, with social attitudes rather than political theory; their tone was intimate, their aim to make the reader feel at home. The editor of a review might see himself, ideally, as bringing the encyclopaedia up to date (and, indeed, Macvey Napier was in charge of revising the *Britannica* before he took over the *Edinburgh*). Conducting a magazine was an altogether less austere occupation, more like running a theatrical troupe.

The men who put *Blackwood's* on the map, John Gibson Lockhart and John Wilson ('Christopher North'), were an unattractive pair – although one must discriminate. Within the limits of his resolute conservatism Lockhart was a shrewd, workmanlike writer, who outgrew his worst faults; his *Life* of Scott is a book which survives, even if the comparisons which used to be made with Boswell won't bear much examination. Wilson, on the other hand, was a pest, lashing out viciously at friends as well as enemies under cover of anonymity, and then trembling in case they penetrated his disguise. Often he sounds half-cracked; and the famous *Noctes Ambrosianae*, the semi-fictitious 'Nights at Ambrose's Tavern' over which he presided together with James Hogg, the 'Ettrick Shepherd', are (to my mind at least) so much unreadable rigmarole. As for the abuse which surged through the early numbers of *Blackwood's*, much of it was there for its own sake; but the social animus behind the most sustained of the

---

* Carlyle might have been less struck by the literary cannibalism of his Review of Reviews if he had recalled that a *Magazine of Magazines* existed as early as 1750.

magazine's invective is unmistakable. When Lockhart and Wilson ran their campaign against the Cockney School, they were not so much waging a literary feud as sneering at a whole range of middle-class aspirations. A *Blackwood's* reviewer, confronted with a new work by Leigh Hunt, felt like

a man of fashion when he is invited to enter, for a second time, the gilded drawing room of a little mincing boarding-school mistress, who would fain have an *At Home* in her house. Everything is pretence, affectation, finery and gaudiness. The beaux are attorneys' apprentices, with chapeaux bras and Limerick gloves – fiddlers, harp-teachers and clerks of genius; the belles are faded fan-twinkling spinsters, prurient vulgar misses from the school, and enormous citizens' wives. The company are entertained with lukewarm negus, and the sounds of a paltry pianoforte.

In modern terms, for 'cockney' read 'suburban'. We are in the area where lofty cultural judgements shade into everyday class-prejudice, debatable territory later to be occupied by deceased wives' sisters and small house-agents' clerks. With Arnold or Eliot the underlying assumptions are naturally far more complex; here the snobbishness is naked and unashamed. It must be conceded, however, that the picture is sufficiently vivid to strike a chill: in real life an invitation to a gathering of the type indicated would not be something to accept in a hurry. What ought to be said by way of redressing the balance is that the prospect of a night out with Christopher North and his cronies, a boozy *Nox Ambrosiana*, would scarcely be more alluring. The mere thought of 'Maga' in full spate, with its hoaxes and rib-poking and learned tomfoolery, is enough to induce a headache. By comparison Cockney suburbia seems like a bastion of civilization – even if the negus is lukewarm.

The arch-Cockney, Leigh Hunt, was a far more enterprising editor than any of his Tory assailants. A timeless setter-up of periodicals, at one time or another he provided a platform for most of the outstanding anti-establishment poets and critics of the age. Byron and Shelley collaborated with him on the *Liberal*; Lamb, not yet masquerading as Elia, wrote some of his finest essays for the *Reflector*; Hazlitt worked as theatre critic and essayist-in-residence on the *Examiner*, the paper in which Keats first appeared in print. Most of Hunt's ventures were short-lived (there were only four numbers of the *Liberal*, for instance), but the *Examiner* was an exception: the first of the major nineteenth-century weeklies, it was run by Hunt and his brother from 1808 to 1825, and under subsequent editors, John Forster among them, it survived into the 1880s. Primarily a political paper, it was famous in its early days for its hard-hitting radicalism. The *Liberal*, too, was as controversial as its name implied at a time when liberals were commonly regarded as dangerous subversives, and regularly referred to by their opponents (as Halévy pointed out) as *les libéraux* and *los liberales*, no better than Jacobins or foreign agitators.

The first editor of the *London Magazine* (1820–9), John Scott, took a more cautious political line than Hunt, but his paper was nevertheless Wilson and Lockhart's most effective rival, explicitly designed, according to the original prospectus, as a metropolitan counterblast against journals emanating from 'secondary towns of the Kingdom', i.e. Edinburgh. (Scott himself, incidentally, came from Aberdeen.) After half a dozen unsparing attacks on *Blackwood's* the feud boiled over, and within a year of founding the *London* Scott was dead, killed in a duel by one of Lockhart's henchmen. He had already had time, however, to make the magazine a brilliant success. Subsequently it changed hands, began to decline, changed hands again, and eventually expired in the shape of a minor Benthamite propaganda-sheet; but in its heyday it set a standard which has rarely been approached. Apart from *The Confessions of an English Opium Eater* and the essays of Elia, it published work by Keats, Hazlitt, Clare, Landor, George Darley. Stendhal supplied comments on the French scene (under the pseudonym of 'Grimm's Grandson'); Tom Hood was a member of the editorial staff; Carlyle contributed a series of articles on Schiller which he later turned into his first full-length book.

In its early years the *London* lived up to its name, and to its metropolitan pretensions. For one thing, it marked the beginning of a new romantic interest in London folklore. City types and curiosities – the more smoked in antiquity the better – were wistfully delineated. Lamb commemorated the old South Sea House; Barry Cornwall followed suit with a sketch of the Cyder Cellar; Tom Hood made his debut with 'A Sentimental Journey from

Islington to Waterloo Bridge'. And at a time when London was starting to lose its shape, sprouting in all directions, there was a conscious attempt to keep alive the eighteenth-century idea of the Town, the small compact centre of things. The Londoners jostled one another like coffee-house wits; and while most contributions were theoretically anonymous, there was a vigorous cult of assumed personality. Hazlitt, writing on theatre, became 'Mr Drama'. Everyone had a kind word for Elia. Thomas Wainwright transformed himself into the ubiquitous coxcomb 'Janus Weathercock', flaunting his diamonds, his cambric handkerchief and his lemon-coloured gloves.* It was less like a magazine than a club – and John Scott's successor, the publisher John Taylor, tried to keep up the illusion by inaugurating a series of regular monthly dinner-parties for his contributors.

At the same time the atmosphere of the *London* was intensely bookish. The magazine was a great promoter of literary revivalism: new editions of the older English classics were greedily seized on, while Lamb's were by no means the only contributions to be laced with archaisms, hand-picked quotations, artful Jacobethan echoes. A determined effort was made to popularize antiquarian anecdotes of the Isaac D'Israeli variety: John Taylor, for instance, ran a series called, uninvitingly, 'Facetiae Bibliographicae, or Old English Jesters'. The Londoners' poems, where they were not pastiches, tended to have costume-drama themes (e.g. 'Milton Visits Galileo in Prison'). And appropriate mottoes were extracted from the Family Shakespeare for such regular features as the loquacious editorial column, 'The Lion's Head' ('Valiant as a lion, and wondrous affable') and the notes-and-queries section ('I will make a prief of it in my notebook').

Today much of this sounds intolerably cosy, pointing forward as it does to the whole carpet-slippered, wondrous affable era of

---

* An early admirer of Blake, Wainwright was a writer of real originality, but deeply neurotic. As a young man, like Mill and so many others, he turned to Wordsworth for guidance, using the poetry as a kind of sedative to calm the turmoil of a 'giddy, flighty disposition'. Later, however, he went over the edge, achieving notoriety (and transportation to Tasmania) as 'Wainwright the Poisoner', an authentic *critique maudit*. Oscar Wilde wrote an essay on him, 'Pen, Pencil and Poison', celebrating among other things his 'curious love of green, which in individuals is always the sign of a subtle artistic temperament'.

bookmen who made Lamb one of their patron saints and worked
his charms to death. The taste for Old English Jesters is not what
it was – nor the taste for old books, old logs, old wine. In its day,
however, the bibliolatry of the Londoners was a humanizing force,
and their catholicity (the 'anti-critical spirit' which Leigh Hunt
so admired in Lamb) the sign of determined liberalism rather
than lazy-mindedness. It was something, in a world of sermons,
prohibitions, juggernaut ideologies, to throw away the book of
rules, to assert so tenaciously the individual's right to his own
unsystematic preferences. To his own idiosyncrasies, for that
matter: the personality-mongering to which modern readers
object in the Romantic essayists deserves to be seen at least in part
as an understandable shying-away from the myth of the critic as a
disembodied voice of authority, an anonymous examining
magistrate. Renounce 'private' inclinations with the thoroughness
of a Jeffrey, and you are inviting someone like Lamb to cultivate
his foibles as ostentatiously as possible.

It must be conceded that in a quiet way Lamb practises his own
brand of intolerance. No one did more to narrow down the very
meaning of 'literature' to *belles-lettres*,* and even professed
admirers often sound secretly irritated by the banter and affectation. Fortunately there were times when he knew how to rise
above his mannerisms – in the essay on Shakespearian tragedy, for
instance, which is a really eloquent piece of work (and which
incidently contains the first half-way adequate praise of *King Lear*
in English, two hundred years after the play first appeared). He
was capable, too, of keen psychological insights – into night fears,
into the tortured spirit of a Malvolio, into 'the sanity of true
genius'. But the quintessential Lamb, the winsome Elia, no longer
casts much of a spell.

Hazlitt presents a more paradoxical case, He was a full-blown
Romantic egoist and a byword for obstinacy, ready at a moment's

---

* The shift can be observed taking place in Hazlitt's famous essay 'Of Persons
one would wish to have seen', where Lamb is shown teasing his friend Ayrton,
who is solemn enough to have cast his vote for Newton and Locke, and old-
fashioned enough to describe them as 'the two greatest names in English literature'.
Lamb himself nominates Fulke Greville, and Sir Thomas Browne – a connoisseur's
choice, but it is possible to feel a gleam of sympathy for the straightforward
prosaic Ayrton.

notice to start unwinding the thread of reminiscence or prejudice. Yet despite the peremptory judgements, despite the abrupt masculine style, the personality behind his essays remains curiously fluid. At his best he is plain, transparent, aphoristic, a man who knows how much there is to be said for travelling incognito, for trying to shuffle off the burden of 'importunate, tormenting, everlasting personal identity'. And there is more to this than the natural enough wish of someone who has taken a battering from life to get beyond praise and blame. As a critic, too, he believed that 'the largest hearts have the soundest understandings, and he is the truest philosopher who can forget himself'. The greater the artist, the deeper he will submerge himself in his material, without ramming home the moral or otherwise advertising his presence: hence the supremacy of the protean Shakespeare. These are views which were to receive their classic formulation in Keats's letters, but Keats, who once walked seven miles to hear Hazlitt lecture, never made any secret of how much he owed to the older man's 'fiery laconicism'.

An unsuccessful painter and a failed metaphysician, Hazlitt was in his mid-thirties when he first 'declined into a journalist'. In the fifteen years or so which were left to him he managed to churn out over three million words, but even so he was harassed by debts to the last: as he lay dying in his Frith Street lodgings he was forced to write to Jeffrey asking for a loan of £10. (He received £50 by return of post.) Inevitably he ran through his stock of ideas and started repeating himself; much of his work, written against the clock, is slovenly and diffuse. But if his bad habits were those of a freelance, so were his virtues. The goad of a deadline stung him into spontaneity, and the Hazlitt who survives is the reporter, the weather-beaten moralist, the student of human nature whose most trenchant judgements – notably in *The Spirit of the Age* – have the weight of a lifetime's experience behind them.

As literary historians Hazlitt, Lamb and Hunt were amateurs ranging freely in a field in which there were as yet very few professionals. Their aim was to inform as well as to stimulate: slapdash as they were, for instance, Hazlitt's lectures on English literature added up to the most comprehensive sketch-map of the subject yet available. It was only a matter of time, however, before the experts got to work on their ordnance survey. Already there were signs of what was to come. Henry Southern, the last editor of the *London Magazine*, was also the founder of the *Retrospective Review* (1820–8), a periodical devoted to learned critiques of the literature of the past – a first primrose on the road which eventually led to the *Review of English Studies*, *PMLA*, *Dissertation Abstracts on Microfilm* and the *Journal of English and Germanic Philology*.

III

Lockhart left Edinburgh for London to take up the editorship of the *Quarterly* in 1825. Christopher North stayed on, but by the early 1830s *Blackwood's* had been outflanked. The new stamping-ground for riotous Tory bohemianism was *Fraser's Magazine*, founded in 1830 and dominated during its early years by William Maginn (1793–1842), who as 'Sir Morgan O'Doherty' had been one of the rowdiest participants in the *Noctes Ambrosianae*. Maginn borrowed many features from *Blackwood's*, in particular the idea of an editor (there was a fictitious one, called Oliver Yorke) as a Lord of Misrule. The magazine was crammed with doggerel, innuendo, burlesque, furious insults, scholarship run mad. The Fraserians usually collaborated on their lampoons: they presented themselves to the world as a collective entity, a gang of inseparable, insatiable boon-companions. It was a reasonably accurate picture. Carlyle, who had once spent an unhappy evening at 'Ambrose's Tavern', awkwardly sipping diluted port, felt even more out of place dining with the Fraserians at their Round Table. He was repelled by the brutishness of their conversation – and it must have particularly sickened him to think that they had hastened the final crack-up of his friend, the preacher Edward Irving, by claiming him as one of their own. ('Oft of a stilly night he quaffed glenlivat with the learned editor.') As for the magazine itself, it seemed to him 'a chaotic, fermenting dung-hill heap of compost'. But during his leanest years he also found it a valuable source of income. Unlike the staid men of the *Edinburgh*, at least the Fraserians were prepared to take a risk. It was in the pages of the magazine that *Sartor Resartus* first appeared, as a serial, not without a good many protests from irate subscribers: Carlyle alludes to the outcry in the closing paragraph of the book, as he takes ironical leave of Oliver Yorke and his 'all-too Irish mirth and madness'.

Like several of his satellites – the folklorist Crofton Croker, for instance, and F. S. Mahoney, the learned ex-Jesuit who wrote comic verse under the name of Father Prout – William Maginn originally came from Cork. A child prodigy, he was already fluent in Latin, Greek and Hebrew when he entered Trinity College, Dublin, at the age of eleven. He went on to master an extraordinary number of languages, ancient and modern, and to graduate as a precocious LL.D. – to the Fraserians he was inevitably 'the Doctor'. After ten years as a school-teacher in his home town, he decided to settle (if that is the right word) in London; by this time he was an accredited member of the *Blackwood's* team, having initially clambered aboard the magazine behind a smokescreen of facetious mystification which must have bewildered even Christopher North. His stamina was prodigious: he scribbled incessantly, everything from scurrilous paragraphs of political gossip to notes for his projected editions of Homer and Shakespeare. And as Dr Johnson said of Richard Savage, 'at no time of his life was it any part of his character to be the first of the company that desired to separate'. In the end drink got the better of him, and his last few years were a reckless plunge downhill into gin-sodden obscurity. He intimidated contemporaries: one can get some idea both of his learning and of his misplaced polemical vigour from his slashing attack – a small book in itself – on the eighteenth-century Shakespearean scholar Dr Farmer. But nothing he wrote has lasted, not even the once-popular Homeric ballads which Matthew Arnold rated much higher than Macaulay's *Lays of Ancient Rome*. If he and his henchmen can be said to survive anywhere, it is in the elegant, slightly mocking outline portraits by Daniel Maclise, another exile from Cork, which were the most popular single feature in *Fraser's*, and which remained collectors' items for years afterwards – greatly admired, among others, by Goethe.

Maginn's career is a reminder that economic conditions are

never quite enough in themselves to account for the calamities of Grub Street. A man of his stamp would have come to grief in any period, and all the patronage in the world would hardly have sufficed to damp down his talent for self-destruction. In a sense, though, he was the last of his breed. By the 1840s the kind of raffishness which he represented was being driven steadily underground. *Fraser's* quietened down and eventually re-emerged as an eminently respectable publication edited by J. A. Froude; within a year or two of Christopher North's death *Blackwood's* was serializing *Scenes of Clerical Life*. And amid all this sobriety 'the Doctor' began to seem like a figure from the mercifully remote past. Only Lockhart's spirited epitaph – 'Here, early to bed, lies kind William Maginn' – kept alive the legend of the brilliant might-have-been:

> *For your Tories his fine Irish brains he would spin,*
> *Who received prose and rhyme with a promising grin,*
> *'Go ahead, you queer fish, and more power to your fin!'*
> *But to save from starvation stirred never a pin. . . .*

It wasn't quite as simple as that, but an epitaph is an epitaph; and Lockhart was determined to make Maginn out as a cast-off Falstaff who had tried to put on a brave front for as long as he could:

> *But at last he was beat, and sought help of the bin,*
> *(All the same to the Doctor, from claret to gin),*
> *Which led swiftly to gaol, with consumption therein;*
> *It was much, when the bones rattled loose in his skin,*
> *He got leave to die here,* out of Babylon's din.*
> *Barring drinks and the girls, I ne'er heard of a sin,*
> *Many worse, better few, than bright broken Maginn.*

IV

The average Victorian reader, if he had heard of Maginn at all, probably thought of him simply as the original of Captain Shandon in *Pendennis*. Thackeray, who was nearly twenty years

---

* In Walton-on-Thames, where he is buried.

his junior, had first got to know him as a very young man, in 1832. He roamed around the West End with him, lent him several hundred pounds, bought control of a paper, the *National Standard*, and appointed him editorial consultant. Before long, however, the boot was on the other foot: Thackeray's fortune had disappeared, and he was reduced to asking Maginn for help finding work as a journalist. In time he became a leading Fraserian, specializing in squibs aimed at Bulwer Lytton and the cult of the dandy. (His most celebrated contributions to the magazine were the *Yellow-plush Papers*.) He acknowledged Maginn as his master; as late as 1839 he could propose a toast to him as a writer who adorned everything he touched, 'even Homer'. But five years later, having transferred his loyalties to *Punch* and the *Morning Chronicle*, he was already tut-tutting over the wild men of *Fraser's* and their shameful antics. The success of *Vanity Fair* rounded off the transformation of middleweight humorist into illustrious man of letters. Ready at last to take stock of Youth and all its follies, he embarked on *The History of Pendennis*.

At the outset of his foray into journalism Arthur Pendennis is taken to the Fleet to meet Charley Shandon, who together with his family has been imprisoned for debt. An infant Shandon is pattering round the room; the Captain himself is sitting on his bed in a ragged dressing-gown, dashing off the prospectus for a new paper, the *Pall Mall Gazette*, which is to be 'written by gentlemen for gentlemen: its conductors speak to the classes in which they live and were born'. As soon as he has handed over the manuscript he pockets his publisher's five guineas and hurries off to spend it at the prison tavern; by the end of the day there is nothing left for his long-suffering wife except some small change. Tradition has always assumed that the Captain is meant to stand for the Doctor, and Maginn's friends were quick to accuse Thackeray of treachery. Certainly the portrait would be highly misleading taken at face-value; Miriam Thrall, the historian of *Fraser's*, has no trouble in drawing up a list of glaring disparities, and flatly denies that any direct reference to Maginn was ever intended. She suggests instead that Thackeray may have had in mind an obscure Fraserian hanger-on called Jack Sheehan. But the point is rather that Shandon is Maginn tidied up, toned down, and generally rendered fit for Victorian domestic consumption. The conventions of the time didn't allow Thackeray to begin to do justice as a novelist to the man who had once spent a whole morning reciting Homer to him and then dragged him off to a cheap brothel in the afternoon. Maginn at least blazed away for all he was worth, and there was a lurid pathos about his final downfall. Shandon by contrast is a mere commonplace pantomime scamp, who is bundled into the wings as soon as he has said his piece and who dies off-stage without a murmur. He has none of the bounce with which elsewhere in *Pendennis* Thackeray was able to endow a scapegrace like the old sponger Captain Costigan. Nor have any of the other 'literary' characters in the book: they represent an area of the author's experience which he is clearly anxious to laugh off as lightly as possible. Contemporary readers may possibly have enjoyed a mild shock of recognition encountering Mr Wagg the wit and Mr Bludyer the critic, or following the antics of the rival publishers Bacon and Bungay and the interchangeable leader-writers Hoolan and Doolan. But there can never have been much edge to the satire even when it was topical: those routine joky names tell their own dismal story.

In the preface to *Pendennis* Thackeray complains that since Fielding 'no writer of fiction among us has been permitted to depict to his utmost power a MAN'. He was thinking chiefly of the limitations imposed by prudery, but he spoke more truly than he knew. Whatever may have been the case a hundred years earlier, by 1850 it was no longer feasible for a serious novelist to make an epic hero out of an average healthy Tom Jones. Society had grown too complex, too unsettled, too nakedly competitive, and the effective hero tended increasingly to be either a careerist or a misfit, a rebel or (combination of all three) an artist. Like *David Copperfield*, which was written at the same time, *Pendennis* can be seen as a first faltering step towards the *Künstlerroman*, the novel about the making of a novelist. This was a *genre* with an immense future, but neither Dickens nor Thackeray was equipped to explore its possibilities. David Copperfield's literary triumphs have to be taken on trust – and after the splendour of the childhood scenes one is grateful, on the whole, not to be told anything about books written with Agnes at his side as an ever-present inspiration, 'pointing upwards'. Arthur Pendennis becomes a journalist and even perpetrates a novel, *Walter Lorraine*, but first and last he remains a representative gentleman, 'no better nor worse than most educated men'. The result is an uncomfortable hybrid, a portrait of the artist as a basically sound young chap – and consequently not too much of an artist. (Clive Newcome five years later is a variation on this theme.) With a little more nerve and a longer social perspective Thackeray might conceivably have written a masterpiece, an English equivalent to *Les Illusions Perdues*. But well-cushioned sentimentality won the day, and there is nothing in *Pendennis* to compare with the gang of literary sharks and squalid journalistic wire-pullers who drag down Lucien de Rubempré. For Balzac, corruption is more than a lighthearted romp with Bacon and Bungay and Hoolan and Doolan: it really dirties the spirit. And if his incorruptibles, the group of high-principled intellectuals gathered around Daniel d'Arthez, are unduly idealized, at least the ideals which they embody are genuinely ennobling ones – and altogether preferable to the housemasterly wisdom doled out by Arthur Pendennis's mentor, the gruff pipe-smoking George Warrington.

Ultimately Thackeray lacks faith in the literary vocation itself. He was too anxious about losing caste; and indeed, he would probably have been a better novelist if he had had the courage of his snobbish convictions, instead of trying to conceal them behind a façade of good-fellowship. When *Pendennis* appeared he was attacked by John Forster, who accused him of libelling his fellow-authors and truckling to the upper classes. Naturally he rejected the charge, but his disclaimer (in the shape of a letter to the *Morning Chronicle* on 'The Dignity of Literature') doesn't ring entirely true. He had little sense of professional solidarity with other writers, and when Dickens and Bulwer Lytton launched the Guild of Literature and Art in 1851 he let fly a barrage of dubious objections. It was degrading to accept charity, a lot of humbug was talked about the special privileges of genius, Grub Street in the old sense had as good as disappeared, literature was a trade like any other, etcetera. He sounded the same note a few weeks later at the conclusion of his lectures on *The English Humourists*: 'Hearts as brave and resolute as ever beat in the breast of any wit

or poet sicken and break daily in the vain endeavour and un-
availing struggle against life's difficulty. . . . The great world, the
great aggregate experience, has its good sense, as it has its good
humour. . . .' All nicely calculated to soothe the great world's
vanity – and Thackeray's lectures were in fact one of the fashionable events of the season. (He had to interrupt them during Ascot
week so that the ladies-in-waiting in the audience could go down
with the Court to the races.) Behind his pose of relaxed fireside
geniality lay a cool professionalism, and after twenty uphill years
he was ready to exploit his newly-acquired fame while he could.
The English Humourists brought him in £500 in London alone,
and several times that sum when he went on tour in the provinces
and America; subsequently he managed to squeeze over £5,000
out of his second, flimsier lecture-series, *The Four Georges*.

With all his acumen, however, he had little of Carlyle's insight
into the sheer explosive potentialities of journalism. Carlyle might
despise newspapermen as a breed, but he saw unhesitatingly that
whether or not they were acceptable in Mayfair, they were the
agents of profound social change – and had been since the previous
century. The cameo in *The French Revolution* of the Parisian bill-
stickers with their *Journaux Affiches*, for instance, is as heady as a
newsreel of Red Guards plastering the walls of Peking. By comparison Thackeray usually seems hopelessly superficial, bogged
down in the minutiae of drawing-room protocol. Yet he too sometimes has his solemn moments, when he marvels at the power of
the Fourth Estate. One night as Pendennis and Warrington are
strolling back to their rooms in the Temple, Warrington suddenly
lets slip his secret: he is a member of 'the Corporation of the
Goosequill – of the Press, my boy'. Then, as they pass a newspaper
office in the Strand, its lights ablaze, he permits himself an un-
characteristic lyrical outburst: 'Look at that, Pen. There she is –
the great engine – she never sleeps. She has her ambassadors in
every quarter of the world – her couriers upon every road. . . .'
We have reached the Street of Adventure; and as far as his picture
of journalism went, Thackeray's occasional flights of enthusiasm
seem to have made a stronger impression on the succeeding generation than his muted satire. Over the next fifty years more than one
hardened newspaperman was to reveal that it had been a boyhood

reading of *Pendennis* which had fired him with his first romantic dreams of a Fleet Street career.

V

In *Les Illusions Perdues*, when Lucien de Rubempré is instructed in the finer points of that useful journalistic standby, blackmail, he is told that it is *une invention de la presse anglaise*, recently imported. At the beginning of the nineteenth century the English press as a whole was still notoriously virulent and corrupt. Newspaper proprietors were in the habit of augmenting their profits with 'contradiction' and 'suppression' fees (John Walter I, the founder of *The Times*, is supposed to have been particularly adept at collecting hush-money), and there would have been every reason for the Thackerays and Warringtons to look down on journalism as a degrading business. Only the reviews were wholly above suspicion. As late as 1829 Sir Walter Scott warned Lockhart that it would be socially ruinous for him to become a newspaper editor, although he had been perfectly happy to see him go to the *Quarterly* (at a salary of £1,000 a year, which was as much as Thomas Barnes initially received for running *The Times*). Scott's attitude was that of a true-blue Tory, however, and by this date somewhat antiquated. A handful of editor-proprietors had in fact already begun to emerge as men to be reckoned with in the 1800s. James Perry, the self-made owner of the *Morning Chronicle*, was a minor political luminary on friendly terms with many of the Whig leaders; Daniel Stuart (a Scotsman, as was Perry) transformed the ramshackle *Morning Post* into a powerful journal of opinion; John Walter II cleaned up *The Times*, modernized its plant, and paved the way for Barnes by securing its complete editorial independence. Barnes's own reign at Printing House Square lasted from 1817 until his death in 1841. He was an editor who 'required civility' from politicians, and usually got it: by the time of the 1832 Reform Bill the thunderous reputation of his paper had been firmly established, and he was acknowledged to be one of the most influential men in England.

Perry, Stuart and Walter all had numerous literary connections.

The *Morning Chronicle* gave Hazlitt his start in journalism; the *Morning Post* hired Coleridge, published Wordsworth, and brought jokes from Lamb at sixpence a time. (There is an amusing glimpse of Stuart, with his rosewood desk and his silver inkstand, in Lamb's essay on 'Newspapers Thirty-five Years Ago'). John Walter, before appointing Barnes, had originally offered the editorship of *The Times* to Southey. As for Barnes himself, as a young man he was considered a promising man of letters in his own right. A loyal friend of Leigh Hunt, who had been one of his classmates at Christ's Hospital, he stood in as theatre critic of the *Examiner* during Hunt's imprisonment (and was incidentally one of the first to acclaim the genius of Kean); while under the pen-name of 'Strada' he wrote intelligent, unsentimental profiles of contemporary authors for the *Champion*, a paper run by John Scott prior to the founding of the *London Magazine*. Combative, widely read, bohemian in his tastes, a generation earlier Barnes might well have ended up as a literary nomad, a less illustrious Hazlitt. But once settled in as editor he became almost entirely engrossed in day-to-day politics, and neither he nor his successor, the celebrated Delane, had much time to spare for literature. Naturally they published reviews – a favourable notice in *The Times* could make all the difference to a book's sales – and they could hardly help employing one or two interesting critics. Eneas Sweetland Dallas, the author of that curious foray into the psychology of inspiration, *The Gay Science*, was a member of Delane's staff for many years. Occasionally, too, by virtue of its unique position, *The Times* was able to publish a review of great historical importance: Huxley on *The Origin of Species* is the best-known example. Nevertheless the paper at its nineteenth-century zenith deserves a much smaller place in purely literary history than Perry's *Chronicle* or Stuart's *Morning Post*, and the same is equally true of its immediate competitors. The Continental tradition of the *feuilleton* was virtually unknown in early Victorian England, while English newspapers of the period can certainly show nothing remotely comparable to the *Lundis* of Sainte-Beuve. After Barnes, the world may have been a safer place for leader-writers, but critics and essayists still had to depend on the periodical press for their living.

The field remained a very restricted one, although a partial improvement can be dated from 1828, the year in which two celebrated weeklies both appeared for the first time: the *Athenaeum* (which only really got going when it was taken over by Charles Wentworth Dilke in 1830) and the *Spectator*. Under Dilke the *Athenaeum*, which had many links with members of the old *London Magazine* set, especially Hood, kept up a fierce campaign against the dishonest puffing of new books, in a manner which John Scott would have appreciated. Later the emphasis rather shifted from literature to scholarship, science and antiquarianism. *Notes and Queries*, which Dilke helped to found in 1849, can be seen as an off-shoot; and it was in the *Athenaeum* that Leslie Stephen published his regular lists of candidates for admission to the *Dictionary of National Biography*, asking readers to suggest additional names. The *Spectator*, during its first thirty years, was not primarily known as a literary review, either. Under the editorship of R. S. Rintoul it concentrated on politics, from a radical standpoint, and by far its most important feature was a long, detailed summary of the week's news.

Both these papers were to become hallowed Victorian institutions, but they were not enough in themselves to raise the status of the professional reviewer. Among the upper classes, at least, Thackerayan doubts as to whether journalism, even literary journalism, was really an occupation for gentlemen persisted into the second half of the century. Sir Walter Besant, whose very stodginess makes him a particularly credible witness on such matters, recalls in his autobiography the prevalent attitude of Cambridge undergraduates in the middle 1850s: 'As for the profession of letters, that, in any shape, we regarded with pity and contempt. ... The only journalism accounted worthy of a gentleman and a scholar was the writing of leaders for *The Times*.' But this prejudice was soon to melt away. Besant also records the stir made in Cambridge by the early numbers of the *Saturday Review*, and the *Saturday* was only the first of a whole new crop of intellectually ambitious monthlies and weeklies. By the 1860s, as outlets continued to multiply, literary journalism was at last becoming a secure enough profession for it to attract a steady flow of talent from the universities. By the 1870s, the novelty of the journalist with a degree in his pocket had completely worn off.

2

HEROES AND MEN OF LETTERS

I

Journalism is a career; literature is, or ought to be, a vocation. Few major nineteenth-century writers would have gone quite as far as Ruskin, who dismissed the entire output of Fleet Street as 'so many square leagues of dirtily printed falsehood', but most of them viewed the growth of the press as a very mixed blessing indeed. It gave them a powerful new platform, and at the same time drowned out what they were trying to say with triviality and claptrap. Nor could they take the same unalloyed pleasure that lesser men did in the improved position of authors as a social group. This kind of petty haggling over status was the epitome of half the ignoble things they were fighting against. In principle, at least, they saw themselves as witnesses to the truth, or nothing.

Of all the Victorians, none had a loftier conception of his calling than Carlyle, and none came to despise the whole trade of authorship more thoroughly. In 'Characteristics', written as early as 1831, he could already treat as self-evident the proposition towards which Matthew Arnold was still edging his way fifty years later. Literature was ultimately a branch of religion: moreover, 'in our time, it is the only branch that shows any greeness; and as some think, must one day become the main stem'. But experience was to teach him that words alone will never save us; and having pitched his claims too high, he was correspondingly bitter in his revulsion. By the time he published *Latter-Day Pamphlets*, in 1850, the bough no longer blossomed. Instead, he now looked on literature as a morbid substitute for reality, 'the haven of expatriated

spiritualisms, and also alas of expatriated vanities and prurient im-
becilities: here do the windy aspirations, foiled activities, foolish
ambitions, and frustrate human energies reduced to the vocable
condition, fly as to the one refuge left . . .'

The notorious set of lectures *On Heroes and Hero-Worship* (1840)
mark as clear a turning-point as any in Carlyle's shifting outlook.
After considering in turn the Divinity, the Prophet, the Poet, the
Priest – antique varieties of hero, all of them pretty well extinct –
he comes in his fifth lecture to their one true modern counterpart,
who is not surprisingly 'our most important modern person', the
Hero as Man of Letters. An ideal type, admittedly, and only very
imperfectly embodied by the actual examples whom Carlyle cites,
the oddly-assorted trio of Dr Johnson, Rousseau and Robert Burns.
Yet even this hypothetical paragon doesn't altogether satisfy him.
Action was what the times required, unflinching leadership, blood
and iron. His sixth and final lecture, misleadingly entitled 'The
Hero as King', is a celebration of the Strong Man which sounds the
first menacing chords of what was soon to be the dominant theme
in his work.

There was no one clean break in his development, however.
His radical impulse never entirely spent ¡ self, while his misgivings
about literature as a way of life date from long before *Heroes and
Hero-Worship* – date from the very outset of his career, in fact.
Nothing in his early background had prepared him for the role of
romantic artist: quite the reverse. As a student, he flatly denied
having literary ambitions. He was expected to become a preacher,
or failing that a teacher: if he showed a special bent, it was towards
mathematics. His earliest recorded composition was a sermon,
written as a college exercise at the age of fourteen, on the text
'Before I was afflicted I went astray'; his first appearance in print
was in a geometry book, as 'the ingenious young mathematician'
who had solved a problem which had been baffling the author.
After a few years he turned his back on teaching and abandoned
mathematics, except as a pastime; but a preacher he remained. No
literary form had a more obvious influence on the structure and
rhythm of his essays than the sermon; and if he gradually came to
use a more audacious rhetoric than any he could have heard in the
pulpit, it was only, he insisted, as a means to a moral end. When

John Stuart Mill, in the first unclouded days of their friendship, spoke of him enthusiastically as a true artist, he was quick with his disclaimer: the future would show that he was simply 'an honest artisan', an unassuming craftsman – like his father, he might have added, the village stonemason from whom he had inherited his Calvinistic suspicions of artifice and make-believe.

Eventually, in middle age, those suspicions completely got the better of him. But as a young man he had cast them aside: the Romantic currents which came flooding in had beaten down the sternest resistance that puritanism could offer. In his *Reminiscences* he admits that in his mid-twenties, when he finally gave up school-mastering in Kirkcaldy and returned to Edinburgh, he was 'intending darkly towards potential "literature", if I durst have said or thought so'. And by literature he certainly had in mind something more than the expository criticism with which he initially made his name, more than interpreting Schiller or playing second fiddle to Goethe. For fifteen years he struggled to find the appropriate medium for his own creative gifts. There were some laborious false starts, abandoned novels and abortive poems; the gradual mastery in his essays of a dynamic new style; and then, in *Sartor Resartus*, an elaborate gothic fantasia which defies classification, but which belongs on the Fiction shelf rather more plausibly than anywhere else. Even so, until he was well into his forties Carlyle was known principally as a man of letters in the unheroic sense, a commentator on other men's books.* Outside all but a very restricted circle it took *The French Revolution* (1837) to establish his reputation as a primary force, an artist in his own right.

He was an artist in spite of himself, with the artist's power of transforming private neurosis into meaningful public myth, and the artist's delight in the sheer virtuoso possibilities of his medium. The old joke (John Morley's) about him managing to compress his Gospel of Silence into thirty-five volumes makes a serious point. If words were treacherous, they were also inexhaustibly beguiling;

---

* It seems curious in retrospect, though it made much better sense at the time, against the background of the *Quarterly* or *Blackwood's*, that Thackeray in 1839 should have singled out for special praise Carlyle's detachment, his refusal to subordinate critical judgement to political bias: 'Pray God we shall begin ere long to love art for art's sake. It is Carlyle who has worked more than any other to give it its independence.'

while the gloomy stakhanovite message of *Sartor* ('Produce! Produce!') is given the lie by the purely playful element in Carlyle's art, his wanton picturesque extravagance. At the same time, no English prose of his period, apart from Dickens's, has more body – or, on occasion, greater delicacy. Legend suggests otherwise: what has come to be the stock notion of Carlylese takes far too little account of all the really subtle, quicksilver effects at his command, to say nothing of his genius for serio-comic caricature. That he frequently descends into bombast, no one is likely to dispute. His teutonic contortions are often unsightly, his bible-thumping repetitiousness can be maddening. But he has been made to pay altogether too heavy a price for such verbal excesses. Strip away the rant, and what remains is a daring chiaroscuro prose, flecked with satire, opening up vistas which still have the power to startle.

A mere propagandist could never have devised so potent a style. But neither could a mere stylist. Although there were times when Carlyle apologized half-jokingly for his expletives and his syntactic oddities, he knew what he was doing when he sent the words swarming over the barricades of conventional usage. 'The whole structure of Johnsonian English breaking up from its foundations – revolution there as visible as anywhere else!' Unprecedented social realities called for new modes of speech. From 'Signs of the Times' (1829) onwards Carlyle strove to make sense of the disordered condition of England – through images rather than reasoned arguments, but, at least until *Past and Present* (1843), with a degree of penetration which his subsequent blusterings shouldn't be allowed to obscure. It is dodging the issue to write him off as an intellectual luddite. He may have used the medieval past (more compellingly, in my view, than any of his successors) as a yardstick for gauging the troubled present, but he recognized that there could be no going back. Abbot Samson was in his grave, and 'the gospel of Richard Arkwright once promulgated, no Monk of the old sort is any longer possible in this world'. His quarrel in *Past and Present* was not with machinery as such, but with mechanized thinking; his anger was directed against political cash-registers unable to reckon the cost in human terms, against a factory system which ripped up traditional loyalties without having anything to

put in their place. Mortality rates spoke louder than trade-figures –
and even statistics, however doleful, only scratched at the surface
of things:

Who shall compute the waste and loss, the obstruction of every sort,
that was produced in the Manchester region by Peterloo alone! Some
thirteen unarmed men and women cut down, – the number of the slain
and maimed is very countable: but the treasury of rage, burning hidden
or visible in all hearts ever since, more or less perverting the effort and
aim of all hearts ever since, is of unknown extent.

Nevertheless, revolution was not the answer: Carlyle had enough
insight into the rage smouldering in his own heart to apprehend
that 'violence does even justice unjustly'. Instead, he called for
strong government – which in the immediate context of the
period meant calling for factory inspectors, public parks, sanitary
reform. He saluted Shaftesbury and Chadwick, and the first freedom which he proposed curtailing was the freedom to starve.
There are some ugly moments in *Past and Present*, but on the whole
the tone is humane; and if Carlyle had died at fifty, he would
almost certainly be thought of today, with a few qualms and reservations, as having been on the side of the angels.

As it is, the diatribes of his later years have inevitably tended to
bring the rest of his work into disrepute – and after Hitler, it is
impossible to brush them aside (although professional campus
Carlyleans still sometimes try). No doubt accusations of Nazism
by anticipation get bandied about rather too freely nowadays, and
even in Carlyle's case they are not entirely apt: there are usually a
few home truths to be winnowed from all but his most frantic
outbursts, while (chiefly, perhaps, on account of his dedication to
the Goethean ideal of a 'World Literature') he never quite lost a
certain distaste for the more cramping varieties of chauvinism.
The Nazis themselves, though they found much to admire in him,
were disappointed that he had not arrived at a full appreciation of
Nordic supremacy. On the other hand it is clear that he didn't
have very far to go. His hateful views on 'the Nigger Question'
are well known, and his conduct during the Governor Eyre case
shows that he was ready, given half a chance, to put his prejudices
into practice. The same is equally true of his anti-semitism. One of

the less attractive medieval customs recorded, with a grim satisfaction, in *Past and Present* was the habit of extorting money from
Jews by pulling out their teeth; and a vivid passage in Froude's
biography describes Carlyle standing on the edge of Hyde Park,
gazing at the Rothschild mansion and miming the same operation
with an imaginary pair of pincers. More directly ominous is the
letter which he sent to the German ideologue Paul Lagarde, an
indubitable forerunner of the Nazis, congratulating him on 'the
fine spice of satire' in his attacks on the Jews. Curiously enough, in
the *Life of John Sterling* (1851) he uses the actual word 'anti-semitic',
which is generally supposed to have been coined in Germany some
twenty years later: in a religious rather than a racial context, but
still . . .

The psychological origins of his rancour and of his infatuation
with power are well worth exploring: the clues are sown thick all
over *Sartor* in particular. What would be a mistake would be to
stop there, to write him up as an isolated special case. On the
contrary, he was very much a portent. He points forward, not
indeed to fascism itself, since after all he never crossed over into
the realm of active politics, but to the *trahison des clercs*, the long
procession of artists and intellectuals whose hatred of the modern
world has led them to flirt with brutally authoritarian regimes or
to clutch at obscurantist dogma. And, as with so many of his successors, the infected areas of his work cannot simply be cordoned
off from the healthy. Both are the product of the same fundamentally imperious approach to social complexities, of an imagination naturally drawn to clear-cut diagnoses and drastic solutions,
impatient of hedging and compromise. It is to the credit of such a
man that he should nevertheless have been willing to prescribe
unromantic short-term palliatives (organized emigration, elementary schools, etc.), but this was hardly his first claim on the consideration of his contemporaries, any more than it is on ours. His
most enduring distinction as a social critic is to have brought into
dramatic focus the ruthlessly disruptive effects of unrestrained
laissez-faire industrialism. Trying to describe the larger forces at
work in his society, he fell back on metaphors of homesickness,
uprooting, disharmony. As metaphors, they are brilliantly suggestive; but as the point of departure for any kind of comprehensive

political programme, they need to be handled with care. Like many other romantics, Carlyle ultimately seems to be judging society as though it were an unsuccessful work of art. The analogy is dangerous, since social cohesion can never be as absolute as artistic unity; it will always be easy for those who dream of restoring an organic society to despair, and tempting for them to assume that a deliberately imposed uniformity will come to much the same thing in the end. A romantic is properly concerned with integrity – the integrity of a personality, the integrity of a poem. But politics is the art of rough, very rough approximations; and ever since Plato, the desire and pursuit of the whole has usually turned out, taken far enough and translated into political terms, to be a first-class recipe for totalitarianism.

In Victorian England, needless to say, Carlyle's preaching had no such dire consequences. He was admired and applauded. By tens of thousands, hungering for a religion with the theology left out, he was revered. His moral strenuousness and missionary fervour helped to colour the mood of an entire generation. But if his influence was immense, it was also vague, a something-in-the-air rather than an ideology; and as his political opinions hardened, it grew more diffuse than ever. The violently reactionary views expressed in *Latter-Day Pamphlets* found very few takers. Among the rank and file, his fame as a spiritual teacher continued to spread. The sixpenny edition of *Sartor*, for instance, published the year following his death, and nearly fifty years after the book's first appearance, sold 70,000 copies: few works as esoteric can ever have enjoyed such genuinely wide popularity. But from around 1850 he was no longer a leader of advanced opinion. Younger writers, when they paid their respects, began to insist on treating him less as an intellectual guide than as an exhilarating spectacle. George Eliot's tribute of 1855 can stand as one of many:

It is not as a theorist, but as a great and beautiful human nature, that Carlyle influences us. You may meet a man whose wisdom seems unimpeachable, since you find him entirely in agreement with yourself; but this oracular man of unexceptionable opinions has a green eye, a wiry hand, and altogether a *Wesen*, or demeanour, that makes the world look blank to you, and whose unexceptionable opinions become a bore; while another man, who deals in what you cannot but think 'dangerous paradoxes', warms your heart by the pressure of his hand, and looks out on the world with so clear and loving an eye, that nature seems to reflect the light of his glance upon your own feeling. So it is with Carlyle.

We may feel that this is both letting Carlyle off rather lightly and undervaluing him at the same time, conveniently disposing of his more subversive insights. In the milder climate of the 1850s, however, apocalyptic politics inevitably no longer evoked as keen a response as they had in the crisis-torn England of the Chartists. And it surely says a good deal for the soundness of Victorian liberalism that, with all his prestige, Carlyle's 'dangerous paradoxes' should have gained so few out-and-out adherents. He played an indirect part, admittedly, in fostering the spirit of *fin-de-siècle* imperialism, but at least as significant was his impact on Ruskin and William Morris, and through them on the course of English socialism. The strands of influence were tangled. Ruskin, one might add, had his jingoistic spasms: the proclamations of imperial destiny in his inaugural lecture as Slade Professor at Oxford are supposed to have made a lasting impression on the young Cecil Rhodes. It was one of the privileges of a Victorian Sage to send his troops marching off in all directions at once.

Certainly Carlyle succeeded, down until the early years of the twentieth century, in exciting the admiration of the most diverse types, from Thomas Hardy to Havelock Ellis, from T. H. Huxley to Proust. Even those who couldn't bear him were often ready to concede, like Gerard Manley Hopkins, that his genius was 'gigantic'. And he had a way of meaning all things to all men: to go no further than the House of Commons, at different times Lloyd George, Bonar Law and Keir Hardie all claimed that his writings had had a decisive effect in reshaping their lives. A full-scale history of his reputation would cut right across accepted party lines in every sense: it would contain a strong element of pathos – since he promised innumerable hard-pressed readers more spiritual consolation than he could deliver – and an equally sizeable element of farce. In a fallen world the prophet who, so to speak, makes good is inevitably liable to end up in an anomalous position, flattering while he fulminates, cheered on by the very people he originally set out to denounce. When Carlyle substituted one brand of aggressive individualism for another, the difference wasn't always apparent to his middle-class audience. He scolded the arche-typal businessman, Plugson of Undershot, and soothed his vanity in the next breath: 'Poor Plugson – he was a Captain of Industry, born member of the Ultimate genuine Aristocracy of this Universe, could he have known it!' A few strokes of the pen, and for 'Plugson of Undershot' read 'Sir Andrew Undershaft'. The captains of industry went away duly gratified, and Carlyle was assured of a niche in the self-made man's pantheon. Samuel Smiles salutes him at the beginning of *Thrift*. Samuel Barmby, the up-and-coming tradesman in Gissing's novel *In the Year of Jubilee* who is meant to embody everything complacent, half-baked and inane *circa* 1887, swears by 'Carlyle and Gurty' ('those two authors are an education in themselves'), though he isn't often shown actually reading them. Inch by inch the tremendous exhortations were whittled down to editorial talking-points, slogans for the Chamber of Commerce. And these penalties of fame were not altogether unmerited: there was a platitudinous, boosterish side to Carlyle crying out for the kind of exploitation which he underwent.

In retrospect, it is tempting to see the myth of the Hero as Man of Letters as a fairly transparent exercise in self-glorification. The clouds of Immensities and Infinitudes roll away, and there is Thomas Carlyle alone on the rostrum, his fashionable audience 'all sitting quite mum, and the Annandale voice gollying at them'. An indomitable pride kept him from cashing in on his success as a lecturer, as he so easily could have done, especially when the invitations started to arrive from America. But whatever his pro-testations to the contrary, he had all the instincts of a spell-binder: in their original spoken form the *Hero-Worship* lectures, which read so uninspiringly in cold print, were a dramatic performance rather than an intellectual discourse, with listeners moved to tears, or to shouts of 'Splendid!' and 'Devilish fine!', or, occasionally, to cries of protest, as when a white-faced John Stuart Mill rose to his feet, calling out 'No!', after Bentham had been unfavourably contrasted with Mohammed. (A moment later Islam was described as a more effective faith than modern Christianity, but although there were half-a-dozen bishops in the auditorium, everyone sat tight.) The atmosphere was as heady as that of an opera-house; and today, certainly, nothing in the actual content of the lectures

seems as gripping as the account of their reception which Carlyle
sent back home to his mother. Nor, for that matter, can one
readily imagine even the most benighted of modern readers turning to *Sartor* for the sake of its yea-saying message: such fascination as the book retains, other than as an historical document, is
that of a surrealist, many-layered autobiography. The essays in
social criticism are another story – and, given Carlyle's current
reputation, the intelligence and humanity of his early radicalism
are what need to be stressed. But, even here, his doctrines are too
disjointed to be worth considering for very long in the abstract,
apart from the man himself. All said and done, he survives most
compellingly in what ought by rights to be his secondary works –
in his *Reminiscences*, in the semi-autobiographical *Life of Sterling*,*
in his letters, which Henry James thought were the most remarkable in the language – and though a fair amount has to be allowed
for suave Jamesian hyperbole (he was writing to Carlyle's editor,
Charles Eliot Norton), there are times when such a judgement
doesn't seem all that extravagant.

As for the literary essays, leaving aside those where Carlyle was
largely content to act as an intermediary for the Germans,† they
were too violent and subjective to have much effect on the actual
course of critical opinion, in spite of their undoubted merits. The
sketch of Dr Johnson (1832), for example, is much superior to
Macaulay's firework-display of the previous year. (Both men
were ostensibly reviewing Croker's edition of Boswell.) Carlyle
responds to the tragic depths of Johnson's character, and compels
the reader to take them seriously, in a way that Macaulay never
could. But he only sees as much as he wants to see; a rugged
Carlylean hero beating a solitary path through the wilderness of
unbelief. He was too passionately involved in dramatizing his own
conflicts to keep the Dr Johnson of history steadily in view, and

* When Mrs Carlyle was asked by a friend what Sterling had ever done in his
life, that he should rate a biography, she replied: 'Induced Carlyle somehow to
write him one.'

† This is putting it too casually: he was an interpreter as well as an intermediary,
and an independent-minded one. On such matters I can merely repeat what I read,
but the evidence looks impressive. See, for example, the comments on the
originality of his insight into Goethe's moral character in Ernst Cassirer's *The
Myth of the State* (1946).

despite his vehemence – or because of it – his essay failed to count-
eract the standard nineteenth-century tradition of Johnson as
lumbering eccentric, half-genius half-buffoon, which Macaulay
more than anyone else had helped to establish.

Criticism in the Arnoldean sense was in fact foreign to Carlyle's
nature; he lacked the necessary patience for a sustained effort 'to
see the object as it really is'. This may well imply that his creative
drive was more urgent than Arnold's: an analogous comparison
between D. H. Lawrence and T. S. Eliot as critics suggests itself.
But who can doubt that Arnold, although he owed him a heavier
debt than he would willingly admit, was right to turn his back on
him? Or that he was justified when he described his gospel of
Earnestness as bringing coals to Newcastle? Victorian England
already had all the fanatics it needed, and Carlyle's potent example
made it that much more difficult to discuss literature calmly,
flexibly, without crippling moral preconceptions.

His influence can, however, be read in another light. The great
Romantic critics left no immediate successors, and René Wellek
speaks for most historians of the subject when he says that 'around
1850 English criticism had reached a nadir'. This was more than a
chronological fluke: it reflects the same breakdown of standards
which can be seen, more familiarly, in the hideous bric-à-brac of
the 1851 Exhibition. Under the circumstances, one could argue
that Carlyle's literary practice counted for a great deal more than
his philistine precepts. The tone of the age was harsh, and many
of his audience must have learned from him for the first time that
art was something more than a luxury. With all his snarls, in fact,
no writer of his generation can have done more to raise the whole
moral prestige of literature.

II

The main reason why a satisfactory history of journalism will
never be written is that journalism itself is such an elastic term. In
the 1830s it could have been stretched to cover the activities of the
editor of the *Edinburgh Review* and the editor of the *Eatanswill
Gazette*, the writings of a William Maginn and of a John Stuart

Mill. These men were all journalists only in the sense that, say, St Augustine, Talleyrand and Dr Proudie were all bishops: the form tells one nothing about the function. It goes without saying, for instance, that a man of Mill's stature had no more use than Carlyle for journalistic success as an end in itself, any more than he did for vague literary aspirations conceived, like Arthur Pendennis's, in a moral and intellectual vacuum. When the committee of the Neophyte Writers' Society optimistically applied to him for support, they were firmly slapped down. 'There is already,' he told them, 'an abundance, not to say superabundance of writers who are able to express in an effective manner the mischievous commonplaces which they have got to say' – and he was utterly opposed to encouraging scribble for its own sake. He might perhaps have been expected to look a little more kindly on the idea of the press being at any rate a *carrière ouverte aux talents*. His own father had originally come to London to try his luck as a journalist (and had incidentally devised and edited the first true literary-cum-political weekly, the *Literary Journal* [1803–6], a forerunner of the *Examiner* and the *Athenaeum*). Still, it is hard to imagine either of the Mills describing himself, in however mellow a moment, as a member of the Corporation of the Goosequill. When James Mill helped to set up the *Westminster Review* in 1824 it was solely in order to propagate his Benthamite beliefs, and his son was equally indifferent to personal advancement when he ran the *London Review* (which amalgamated with the *Westminster* after its fourth number) from 1835 to 1840, editing it in his spare time and at a substantial loss which during the latter stages he made good out of his own pocket.

The *London and Westminster* was as closely identified in the public mind with Utilitarianism as the original *Westminster* had been. But it was Utilitarian with a difference. As an editor John Stuart Mill's express aim was to soften the harsher features of his father's creed, 'to give a wider basis and a more free and genial character to Radical speculation'. The Radicals – the Philosophical Radicals, that is – were, in effect, to be liberalized: to be instructed about poetry, shown that the Coleridgeans had a case, given a remedial dose of Carlyle.

An admirable policy, but one not always appreciated as it

should have been – least of all by Carlyle, who ended up showering characteristic insults on the *Review*, although he had every reason to feel grateful to a paper which besides printing his own articles, in the teeth of objections from the Benthamite old guard, also published Mill's enthusiastic notice of *The French Revolution* and Sterling's generous appraisal of his work as a whole. Initially, however, he was well-disposed, and he even offered Mill a word of friendly advice. It was entirely commendable, he told him, to struggle against Falsehood and Cant –

yet there is a kind of Fiction which is not Falsehood, and has more effect in addressing men than many a Radical is aware of. This has struck me much of late years in considering Blackwood and Fraser; both these are furnished as it were with a kind of theatrical costume, with orchestra and stage-lights, and thereby alone have a wonderful advantage, perhaps almost their only advantage . . . The Radicals, as you may observe, appear universally *naked* (except so far as decency goes!); and really have a most prosaic aspect . . .

Mill was unable to comply. He could claim, with justice, that he had genuinely widened the scope of the *Westminster*, but he was not the man to provide orchestra and stage-lights. His own writing was singularly unadorned: it is curious to hear him advocating the virtues of independence and eccentricity in level, restrained tones, while the prose of the disciplinarian Carlyle grows increasingly freakish and idiosyncratic. He believed that it was important to 'establish a character for strangeness', but he could no more have become an eccentric himself, in the flamboyant sense, than he could have joined the Mormons, whose right to live as polygamously as they chose he went out of his way to defend in his essay *On Liberty*. If he had been pressed, he might well have agreed with his adversary Fitzjames Stephen that in practice eccentricity is less likely to be a sign of strength than of weakness. The 'strangeness' which meant so much to him was a question of inward integrity, not of superficial oddities. He was arguing out of his own experience: *On Liberty* is a personal testament as well as a political tract, the work of a man who has had to fight all the way to achieve autonomy, and who still feels in danger of being thwarted or hemmed in. The work, in short, of James Mill's dutiful, overburdened son. Not that this necessarily invalidates his arguments; on the contrary, it helps to account for the moral passion which keeps them fresh, even where they are lop-sided or incomplete. The essay shows how little a great writer, if not a working editor, need have recourse to the theatrical props which Carlyle recommended. It may be 'prosaic', but its heavy cadences are more moving than all the odes to Liberty in the anthologies.

Whatever deprivations Mill may have suffered in childhood, it would be quite wrong to suppose that poetry played no part in his education. His father was much less of a Gradgrind than he tried to make out, or wanted to believe. 'He cared little for any English poetry,' Mill says of him in his *Autobiography*, and then grudgingly lists a few exceptions: Milton (whom he idolized), Spenser, Dryden, Gray, Goldsmith, Cowper, Beattie, Burns, Walter Scott. Something to be getting on with, at any rate. As a child, Mill was set to write imitations of Pope and James Thomson, as well as having an entire book of *The Faerie Queene* read aloud to him; in adolescence he went through a phase of trying to compose tragedies, under the inspiration of Joanna Baillie (whose *Constantine Paleologus* he loyally describes in the *Autobiography* as 'one of the best dramas of the last two centuries'). Many poets have had a less strenuously literary upbringing. But where James Mill thought of poetry as nothing more than versified eloquence, his son learned to look deeper. In his early twenties, recovering from the first of his breakdowns, he discovered in Wordsworth 'the very culture of the feelings'. Here at last was a writer who made the inner life seem as significant and substantial as the external world of action and calculation. The ice began to thaw; and no passage in the *Autobiography* is more justly celebrated than Mill's account of how Wordsworth helped him to recover his emotional equilibrium.

The crisis he describes took place in 1828. Five years later, in an essay written for his friend W. J. Fox's magazine the *Monthly Repository*, he set out to define the essential nature of poetry, and decided that it was 'feeling confessing itself to itself', without the distraction of an audience. Eager to sort out the authentic poets from the rhetoricians, he maintained that all poetry was 'of the nature of soliloquy' – which if strictly true would limit its role to that of a therapeutic process conducted purely for the benefit of the poet. (Cf. Ernst Kris, *Psychoanalytic Explorations in Art*: 'The artist identifies himself with his public in order to invite their participation. . . . No such intention prevails in our patient. He does not produce in order to communicate with others any more than he converses with others. Basically his speech is soliloquy.') In a companion-piece written a little later, 'The Two Kinds of Poetry', Mill took up a less extreme, one might say a less neurotic position. The essay is built around an alleged contrast between Wordsworth, the thinker slowly and deliberately schooling himself to become a poet, and the spontaneous, exuberant Shelley, a poet by nature. Mill's admiration for Shelley, though it may have been originally implanted by Harriet Taylor, was real enough: in old age, reading his poetry to Bertrand Russell's parents, he choked with emotion and could scarcely go on. But Wordsworth touched a deeper chord, and he was uneasy about the distinction he had drawn. He could not help regretting that Shelley's intellectual development had been so uneven: the finer a poet's natural gifts, he insisted, the more imperative it was for him to ripen into a philosopher. Writing about Tennyson in 1835 he preached on the same text. At that date most readers knew of the future Laureate, if at all, as the butt of the orthodox reviews, and Mill's first aim was to display Tennyson's virtues as straightforwardly as possible. Along with other lengthy extracts from his work, he quotes 'Mariana' and 'The Lady of Shalott' in their entirety. (For reviewers, at least, those were spacious days.) His enthusiasm is plainly sincere – it was balm to the poet's wounds – and his generosity puts to shame the fault-finding of *Blackwood's* and the malevolence of the *Quarterly*. One or two of his comments also reveal an alert response to the precise tints and shades of Tennysonian verse. But he can't resist a final schoolmasterly admonition. Tennyson must guard against the temptation of merely luxuriating in beautiful imagery, since the only poets who count in the end are those who have taken care to stock their minds with thoughts derived 'from trains of reflection, from observation, analysis and generalization'.

Mill was anxious to reconcile the artist and the philosopher, to heal the breach between thought and feeling. If it came to a choice, though, he was on the side of the philosophers, as his severely abstract language suggests, and he preferred to deal with poets as types rather than individuals. Take his essay on Alfred de Vigny (1838), the last and, in his own opinion, the best of his purely literary studies. It contains some conscientious paraphrasing and plot-summary (as well as what must be one of the earliest English tributes to 'the sober and impartial Sainte-Beuve'), but basically de Vigny is used as a peg on which to hang a consideration of the aristocratic temperament and its fate in an irrevocably bourgeois world. He is explicitly compared to de Tocqueville, and the liveliest passages in the essay really belong with Mill's other writings on culture and democracy, the series of papers which culminated in 1840 with his essay on Coleridge and his review of the second part of *Democracy in America*. These early studies are among Mill's most durable work, unlike his essays on poetry, which are only curiosities. He was not, after all, particularly well-equipped to theorize about poetry as such. (One handicap, as his disciple Alexander Bain pointed out, was that he had inherited his father's inability to understand why people made so much fuss about Shakespeare.) His true strength as a critic lay elsewhere, in what must be called, for want of a less daunting term, cultural criticism. The effect of the mass market on traditional values, the spread of conformism, the abuses of literacy, the estrangement of the intellectual: these were the kind of problems exercising him most strongly from around 1830. He was not the first to confront them – many of his best ideas were pieced together from the work of more original minds – but he brought to the task exceptional reserves of courage and lucid honesty. Few Englishmen of his time were able to discern more clearly or to describe more un-flinchingly some of the key aspects of life as it was coming to be lived in a modern industrial society.

Some aspects, not all. He isolates cultural questions too thoroughly from political ones: he was more humane than Carlyle, but he would have been a better man still if he had had it in him to write as Carlyle did about the legacy of Peterloo. And if his society was in some ways even worse than he makes out, in other respects it was not nearly as bad. The neutral tone he adopts can lull one into overlooking just how subjective much of his pessimism really was. What were the criteria which enabled him to decide that 'books, of any solidity, are almost gone by', or that 'over the whole class of gentlemen in England there has crept a moral effeminacy, an inaptitude for every kind of struggle'? Both these judgements come from his essay on 'Civilization', written in 1836, while he was undergoing the second and more serious of his major breakdowns (which he passes over in silence in the *Autobiography*), and they surely reveal at least as much about his own troubled state of mind as they do about the life of the period. Time lends perspective, even to the *laudator temporis acti*: few people today would contend that early nineteenth-century literature was especially insubstantial, or that Englishmen of Mill's generation, whatever their faults, were notably lacking in masculine vigour. Or again, when Mill complains that literature has become a trade, he talks as though nothing of the kind had ever been seen before. It is easy – and convenient – to forget, for instance, that an Elizabethan playgoer's staple diet was in large measure provided by hacks like Chettle and Munday. Critics of mass culture have a trick of weighing the worst of the present against the best of the past, and for all his usual scrupulousness Mill is by no means immune. It is tempting, indeed, to take his insights for granted, and to concentrate on picking holes in his more dubious assertions. Since his time we have had more than our fill of critics ready to smother us with blanket denunciations of the modern world, critics who talk as though the over-all quality of life in a society were an easy thing to assess. There is a bad, false tradition which has grown up among literary men of assuming that it is permissible to measure a culture in terms of, say, advertisements but not of anaesthetics. (A banal consideration? Anyone who thinks so would do well, before protesting, to ponder some of the evidence: the quality of life depicted, for example, in Rowlandson's drawing of an eighteenth-century gentleman having his leg sawn off.) However, it would be patently unfair to blame Mill for the heresies of his less enlightened successors. Unlike them, he is never facile, and his indictment of the debasing effects of commercialism has lost none of its relevance. It is particularly interesting because it comes from a man who refused to give up his belief in democratic ideals. On paper, at least, he would have had an easier time of it if he had simply surrendered to romantic conservative dreams of putting the clock back. By trying to combine liberalism in politics with cultural *élitism*, he found himself plunged into difficulties from which there is still no obvious way out.

Like all good liberals, he pinned his ultimate hopes on education. Meanwhile, he came to urge that the progress of democracy should be slowed down by the application of what were in effect meant to be a number of *élitist* brakes, such as plural voting. One doesn't have to be a Marxist to feel that he was often inconsistent or unrealistic. As far as the social basis of literature went, at one stage – in 'Civilization' – he was capable of taking over from Carlyle the view, or rather the fantasy, that the era of the commercial publisher was in some mysterious way drawing to a close:

The resource must in time be, some organized co-operation among the leading intellects of the age, whereby works of first-class merit, of whatever class, and of whatever tendency in point of opinion, might come forth with the stamp on them, from the first, of the approval of those whose names would carry authority.

This was at the height of his Carlylean phase; later the idea seems to have been shelved, understandably. A small-scale authors' co-operative might have been feasible, and might have done valuable work, but it would be hard to say whether Mill's comprehensive scheme reveals more unwarranted optimism about economics or about human nature. Even assuming it had somehow been possible to fence off publishing from the rest of the capitalist system, his vision of a compact ministry of all the talents would have proved a mirage the moment he started naming names. Did he seriously expect to see Wordsworth and Jeffrey, Shelley and Maginn, Carlyle and Lamb working together in close harmony? And supposing his publication committee had been dominated, as it probably would have been in practice, by heads of colleges, *Quarterly* reviewers, pillars of the Establishment? Matthew Arnold, after making out a strong case for the corrective influence of Academies, took care to add that an actual English Academy might not turn out to be quite what was needed. ('One can see the happy family in one's mind's eye as distinctly as if it were already constituted. Lord Stanhope, the Dean of St Paul's, the Bishop of Oxford, Mr Gladstone, the Dean of Westminster, Mr Froude, Mr Henry Reeve, – everything which is influential, accomplished, and distinguished . . . !') By comparison, Mill was lacking in common sense; or rather, in this particular case, as at other awkward moments, he chose to ignore the widening gap which had opened up between intellectuals and the traditional educated classes. An *élitist*'s first problem is to decide who exactly qualify for his *élite*; and the more fluid and pluralistic a society has become, the less hope there can be of a definitive answer.

Mill's retreat back towards a stricter utilitarian position after 1840 involved a measure of disenchantment with the possibilities of imaginative literature. As a young man, he had been content to describe himself, in his role of critic, as 'logician in ordinary' to the poets: his job was to expound and clarify the truths which they had obscurely intuited, for the benefit of the general reader. Advancing years brought a sharp reversal of attitude; it was now the artist's turn to subordinate himself to the logician. In the journal which he kept during the early months of 1854, Mill accused Carlyle and 'the Germans' of committing intellectual treason by trying to enthrone the poet-seer as the highest type of thinker. Art must never be allowed to usurp the position of philosophy: the poet should be satisfied with the secondary task of clothing given truths in expressive and eloquent symbols. (Back to James Mill!) Nor was this really claiming very much for poetry, even at the level of rhetoric, since at an earlier point in the journal Mill had come to the conclusion that in an age of crisis like his own it was mere foppery to waste time cultivating 'beauty of form in the conveyance of meaning'. For anyone with a message to deliver, the short direct route was best.

This was not his last word on the subject. He continued to stress the educational significance of literature, and he assigned a much more honourable place to the arts in general in his inaugural address as Lord Rector at St Andrews in 1867 than Carlyle had done in *his* inaugural address at Edinburgh the previous year. The 'aesthetic branch' of education, he told the St Andrews students, though 'subordinate and owing allegiance' to the two other main branches, the moral and the intellectual, was 'barely inferior to them, and not less needful to the completeness of the human being'. It was a grievous loss that this should have been obscured from us by 'the two influences which have chiefly shaped the British character since the days of the Stuarts: commercial money-getting business and religious Puritanism'. The average Englishman, unlike a Continental, had to struggle to recognize that art – 'the endeavour after perfection' – was not just a pastime, but a primary agent of civilization. All this is very much in the spirit of Arnold, who in fact put on record his admiration for the lecture. Mill argues strenuously on behalf of a fully-rounded and harmonious ideal of culture. But what he lacks is Arnold's style, his verve. Presented with such unremitting solemnity, the 'aesthetic branch of education' can sound a poor genteel schoolmarmish affair, a thing of guided tours and plaster casts. The irony is that Mill, after setting out to expound the essential unity of culture, should have thrust the arts so firmly into their own special airtight compartment. Whatever his ultimate goal, he remained wedded to Utilitarianism in practice. But so, in a very loose sense, do most of us: the problems which vexed him have still to be solved, and the emphasis ought to fall on what he hoped to achieve, rather than on his partial failures or imperfections. The fine words of the inaugural address were more than transient speechday pieties: his entire career was marked by a constant effort to keep alive the idea of a complete human being, and with it the idea of a liberal education, in which all the elements 'conspire to the common end, the strengthening, exalting, purifying, and beautifying of our common nature'.

III

If the Neophyte Writers' Society had approached Matthew Arnold, they would probably have drawn down on their heads an even more freezing rebuke than they received from Mill. At no stage in his life was Arnold a full-time man of letters; he had a low opinion of literature as a profession, and it could reasonably be said of him, as he himself said of Clough, that 'in the saturnalia of ignoble personal passions, of which the struggle for literary success, in old and crowded communities, offers so sad a spectacle, he never mingled'. To turn to his work from that of the lesser magazine-writers of the age is at once to breathe a cleaner air, to have a re-newed sense of that relative disinterestedness which is one of the main reasons why he speaks so directly to us today. He can make almost all his contemporaries seem parochial by comparison. And yet nothing is more misleading than the fairly widespread legend of an impersonal Arnold, eternally detached, eternally aloof. He was immersed in the affairs of his own time, and even his most olympian judgements take on a slightly different colouring as soon as they are looked at in their immediate Victorian context.

He was, to begin with the obvious, a critic of society at least as much as a critic of literature – and of the outward demeanour of society, its nuances and mannerisms, rather more than of its under-lying structure. In 'The Function of Criticism at the Present Time', which is the nearest he ever came to a manifesto, it is striking how quickly he moves away from discussing the difficulties facing the poet in the modern world to talking, not just about middle-class civilization at large, but about Mr Roebuck and Sir Charles Adderley and the British College of Health in New Road, with its lion and its statue of the Goddess Hygeia. The comic detail is all-important: what makes Arnold's arraignment of Philistinism so much more effective than, say, Mill's is that he is so much more precise, that he quotes chapter and verse and pinpoints his targets with a novelist's accuracy. Some of the grotesques in *Friendship's Garland*, for instance, sound as though they might have stepped straight out of the pages of Dickens: a character like the stock-broker Job Bottles – 'a man with black hair at the sides of his head, a bald crown, dark eyes and a fleshy nose, and a camellia in his button-hole' – was surely a regular dinner-guest *chez* Podsnap and *chez* Veneering. On the other hand there are times when Arnold's satire is far too narrowly-based to deserve being labelled Dicken-sian; I agree with Mr Raymond Williams that it is often no more than 'a kind of witty and malicious observation better suited to minor fiction'. He is never coarsely contemptuous; his taunts against the Philistines never boomerang back on him in the same way as those of *Blackwood's* against the Cockneys. But he does make too much turn on mere questions of taste. I write 'mere' with some hesitation, since I am uncomfortably aware that one of his great virtues is to show, perhaps more forcibly than any previous English critic, that questions of taste are also questions of morality, symptoms of the values which men live by. We have all learned something from him in this respect, and he still has something to teach us. Yet one doesn't have to go to melodramatic extremes, and fall back on the stock example of the S.S. man playing classical music for relaxation (though such types were common enough), to feel that taste and morality can nevertheless operate on utterly different levels, and that there is a danger in equating them too insistently. Arnold himself provides some curious instances of mis-placed emphasis, even at his best. No single moment in 'The Function of Criticism at the Present Time' is more telling than the one where he suddenly introduces the newspaper report of the workhouse girl called Wragg, who has been charged with the murder of her illegitimate child. A grim little story: those four con-cluding words – 'Wragg is in custody' – are enough to puncture all the inflated patriotic sales-talk of the Roebucks and Adderleys. Let them say what they liked, Wragg was in custody. (She eventually got twenty years' penal servitude.) What is odd, however, is that the first aspect of the case which Arnold sees fit to comment should be the ugliness – the alleged ugliness – of the name Wragg:

Has anyone reflected what a touch of grossness in our race, what an original shortcoming in the more delicate spiritual perceptions, is shown by the natural growth among us of such hideous names – Higginbottom, Stiggins, Bugg! In Ionia and Attica they were luckier in this respect, etc., etc.

It is as though, momentarily, he were more affronted by the sheer squalor of the newspaper item than by the depths of misery which its threadbare language conceals. True, he goes on to consider the episode as a whole, and by the time he has finished no one could doubt his moral revulsion from the harshness of a society where such things are permitted to happen. But that initial piece of snobbery – and snobbery seems to me the right word for it – leaves an unpleasant taste behind. Putting aside the problem of Stiggins and Bugg, would Arnold have found Wragg so objection-able a name if it had had other, less poverty-stricken associations for him? To some people, as the Victorian critic J. M. Robertson remarked, it seems no more inherently unmusical than Hinksey, Bagley, and the other evocative place-names of 'The Scholar-Gipsy'.

Snobbish or not, Arnold was deeply committed to the values of his own class, that of the university-educated gentleman – a social stratum lying somewhere between the Barbarians and the Philistines. Not rigidly or savagely committed: the romantic and the dandy were too much alive in him for that, while the skill with which he managed to needle such powerful upholders of the *status quo* as Fitzjames Stephen and the rest of the *Saturday Review* set is a sufficient index of his ability to rise above narrowly partisan considerations. The 'culture' which he took as his watchword was in the first place a state of mind, a literary ideal into which many elements from Homer to Wordsworth had been fused. But often it stood for something more tangible as well – for the particular way of life in which he himself had been raised, a way of life which can be conveniently, if not literally, summed up as 'Oxford'. Even the famous aria about the last enchantments of the Middle Age, so often quoted out of context, is in effect part of his judgement on the middle classes. It occurs at the very end of his preface to the first series of *Essays in Criticism*, and arises directly out of the previous paragraph, in which he has been contemplating that as yet unhackneyed embodiment of urban middle-class man, the commuter. A sensational murder has recently been committed on the North London Railway; Arnold often uses the near-by Woodford Branch of the Great Eastern himself, and it sets him thinking:

'Suppose the worst to happen,' I said, addressing a portly jeweller from Cheapside; 'suppose even yourself to be the victim; *il n'y a pas d'homme nécessaire*. We should miss you for a day or two upon the Woodford branch; but the great mundane movement would still go on, the gravel walks of your villa would still be rolled, dividends would still be paid at the Bank, omnibuses would still run, there would still be the old crush at the corner of Fenchurch Street.'

A few bantering reflections on the high hopes of Utilitarianism follow – perhaps, after all, the man is not travelling up to his shop, or to buy shares, but 'on a pious pilgrimage, to obtain from Mr

Bentham's executors a secret bone of his great, dissected master'; and only then does Arnold launch into his Oxonian purple patch.

However 'barbarous' the upper classes might be, however rashly over-confident a man like Fitzjames Stephen, the main practical threat to Culture seemed to Arnold, especially in the 1860s, to come from the more aggressive of the Philistines, and from further left still, from the turbulent working-class masses who were being stirred up by Liberals of the John Bright persuasion. *Culture and Anarchy* (originally published in the *Cornhill*, 1867–8) contains a good many subtle concessions to the Barbarians, and some not so subtle slurs on the Populace. Arnold makes no real attempt, for instance, to distinguish adequately between democratic and violent trade-unionism; he pays one or two rather back-handed compliments to the moderate union leader George Odger, but it would be impossible to guess from his references to the Sheffield 'rattening' outrages how bitterly they were condemned by the entire reputable leadership of the labour movement. The fear of revolution coloured much of his political thinking, and at the first threat of civil disorder he tended to revert to his father's authoritarianism. He had caught a glimpse of the Hyde Park riots of July 1866 from the balcony of his house in Chester Square, and in *Culture and Anarchy* one can still hear the reverberations:

I remember my father, in one of his unpublished letters written more than forty years ago, when the political and social state of the country was gloomy and troubled, and there were riots in many places, goes on, after strongly insisting on the badness and foolishness of the government, and on the harm and dangerousness of our feudal and aristocratical constitution of society, and ends thus: 'As for rioting, the old Roman way of dealing with *that* is always the right one; flog the rank and file, and fling the ring-leaders from the Tarpeian rock!' And this opinion we can never forsake....

By 1875, when he prepared the second edition of the book, Arnold's temper cooled, and he cut this passage out. As many of the Liberals he made sport of could have told him at the time, he had completely misjudged the situation. Hooliganism may be hateful, but it is also the duty of a civilized commentator to enquire into its causes, and indeed to try to ascertain how far it *is* just hooliganism. The leaders of the Reform League, who had organized the Hyde Park demonstration, were neither cut-throats nor fanatics; they were ready to listen, when Mill argued that it would be folly to attempt a second assault on the Park. Instead, they contented themselves with a peaceful protest rally, with Mill as the main speaker, at the Agricultural Hall in Islington – that same borough which had been good for an automatic jibe when Arnold was assailing the Philistine's notion of Progress in *Friendship's Garland* ('. . . the trains only carry him from an illiberal, dismal life at Camberwell to an illiberal, dismal life at Islington . . .'). Given the nature of their grievances, the common people of England were extraordinarily patient and open to reason: I doubt whether Arnold would have heard many of the speakers at the Agricultural Hall blithely invoking the Tarpeian Rock. There was a lot which he still had to learn about the society in which he lived – or rather, a lot which he preferred to ignore.

At home, he called for a greater show of authority; abroad, for strong policies to match strong words. It was largely on account of middle-class stupidity, he complained, that England had lost that secret of success which she had enjoyed in 1815 – by which he chiefly meant, when it came down to it, that she was no longer indisputably the foremost military power in the world, since he can hardly have supposed the government of Lord Liverpool and Castlereagh remarkable for any other kind of occult political wisdom. He disliked Palmerstonian bluster; but eventually, in the closing years of his life, his own brand of 'realistic' patriotism was to lead him into courses which can only be described as illiberal, and at worst as dismal. From 1880 onwards he was preoccupied, even more than most Englishmen, with the problem of Ireland: his brother-in-law, W. E. Forster, was Chief Secretary during the renewed disturbances of 1880–2, and both he and his family were able to see something of the crisis at first hand on private visits to Dublin. His reaction was a harsh one: he supported Forster's Coercion Bill to the hilt, called for sterner measures still (including, by 1887, the virtual imposition of martial law), and described Home Rule as 'the nadir of Liberalism', a first step which could well lead on inexorably to the break up of the entire Empire. Gladstone, the principal object of his wrath, he repeatedly described as a latter-day Cleon, a self-deluding demagogue. Today the articles in which he argued his case make sorry reading. It was Cleon who displayed real imagination, not his critic – and real eloquence, too. Indeed, a career like Gladstone's forces one to reconsider the conventional modern assumption that oratory is invariably a poor relation of literature. He has been plausibly presented by Conor Cruise O'Brien as a poet-tribune, the nearest thing to a Victor Hugo that the England of his time had to offer; and certainly his more volcanic speeches make Arnold's strictures on his Irish policy show up by contrast as both short-sighted and ungenerous.*

To anyone who values Arnold, this is a sad conclusion, all the more so in that his attitude to Ireland was not the result of a fit of elderly petulance, but the logical outcome of a political philosophy which was very far from sterile or repressive in its original intent. At the end of *Culture and Anarchy* he reiterates that he has faith in 'the progress of humanity towards perfection', but insists that such progress will come about only as

we grow to have clearer sight of the ideas of right reason, and of the elements and helps of perfection, and come gradually to fill the framework of the State with them, to fashion its internal composition and all its laws and institutions conformably to them, and to make the State more and more the expression, as we say, of our best self, which is not manifold, and vulgar, and unstable, and contentious, and ever-varying, but one, and noble, and secure, and peaceful, and the same for all mankind....

For ever and ever, amen. This is essentially a vision of the Kingdom of Heaven, of a paradise which is unlikely to be established on earth in any foreseeable secular future. Yet it is not quite that either, since apparently, and incongruously, our mortal imperfections are going to survive into the Millennium. When the State truly embodies our best self, Arnold continues,

---

* The full story of Arnold's views on the Irish question is a long and complicated one: in the 1870s, for instance, he had come out strongly in favour of official government backing for a Catholic university, and there were enlightened or unconventional elements in his thinking to the last. For a thorough examination of his involvement with Ireland, to which I am much indebted, see Patrick J. McCarthy's *Matthew Arnold and the Three Classes* (New York, 1964), which also gives an admirable account of his politics generally.

with what aversion shall we not *then* regard anarchy and with what firmness shall we not check it, when there is so much that is so precious which it will endanger!

Utopia is not only going to be a better world than the one we know today, it is also going to be much better policed. Such are the contradictions which can arise from too strenuous an attempt to translate religious concepts into political terms. A Marxist persuades himself that the State is withering away with the active collaboration of 750,000 members of the K.G.B.; a certain type of conservative thinker comes to regard the inherited structure of the State as utterly inviolable – and although Arnold never went as far as this, there were times when he was capable of seriously obscuring the issue. The paragraph from which I have just been quoting opens with the asseveration that 'in our eyes, the very framework and exterior order of the State, whoever may administer the State, is sacred . . .' Coming from a man who took his religion in earnest, this is highly ambiguous language: once one starts using words like 'sacred', there is a strong temptation to identify existing social arrangements with the general principle of the Rule of Law, and beyond that to make the perfection towards which the State is supposedly labouring an excuse for not interfering with the very far from perfect *status quo*.

What must be emphasized, however, is that Arnold tended to talk like this only during periods of crisis, when rightly or wrongly he believed that the very foundations of society were threatened. In calmer times his thoughts were steadily directed towards social reform, and much of what was best in his thinking sprang from his willingness to contemplate a far higher degree of state intervention in everyday life than most of his contemporaries were ready to accept. If he laughed at the British College of Health in New Road, he also went on to observe:

In England, where we hate public interference and love individual enterprise, we have a whole crop of places like the British College of Health: the grand name without the grand thing. Unluckily, creditable to individual enterprise as they are, they tend to impair our taste by making us forget what more grandiose, noble, or beautiful character properly belongs to a public institution.

It was the welfare state, not the servile state, that he wanted to call into being. The area where he laboured most persistently to improve conditions was, of course, his chosen field of education – I say 'of course', although his efforts in this direction are still not nearly as well known as they ought to be. People talk of the poet being sacrificed to the Inspector of Schools, and there is something in that; yet I don't know that, even as literature, one would willingly forgo his reports on elementary schools for the sake of another 'Thyrsis'. These reports (they were collected and published after his death, in 1889) must be read in the light of his long and disheartening struggle against Robert Lowe's Revised Code of 1862, with its brutal insistence on 'payment by results', which he didn't live long enough to see finally done away with. But he is perhaps even more impressive on points of detail than on broad issues of policy. Whether he is discussing needlework or parsing, textbooks or examinations, his views are marked by the same breadth, sanity and thoroughness. He is equally himself quoting Comenius on the ultimate aims of education or berating school managements who make inadequately-lit classrooms even worse by economizing on whitewash. And his fundamental respect for children comes out repeatedly in small but significant ways, such as his disapproval of the habit 'of culling in an official report absurd answers to examination questions in order to amuse the public with them'. It isn't possible to read very far in his work, in fact, without being struck both by his kindliness and by his attention to mundane detail. He might inveigh against those who blindly put their faith in 'machinery', but when the cause was one in which he believed he was never ashamed to soil his own hands. Again and again he addresses himself to practical considerations. Writing about copyright, where he might have been expected to confine himself to advancing authors' claims, he touches illuminatingly on a dozen different aspects of publishing, above all on the need for cheap books – not 'the hideous and ignoble things with which, under this name, England and America have made us familiar', but attractive duodecimo volumes, selling at half-a-crown, along the lines pioneered in France by Michel Lévy: 'books shapely, well printed, well margined; agreeable to look upon and clear to read'. Expressing pleasure at the visit of Sarah Bernhardt's company to London (not without the reservations of a middle-aged man who had seen Rachel when he was young), he takes the opportunity to urge the establishment of a National Theatre in the West End, together with a drama school. Nor does he forget to add: 'When your institution in the West of London has become a success, plant a second of like kind in the East' – in Stepney or Bethnal Green, 'whither my avocations often lead me'. His attitude may smack somewhat of paternalism; what he would have made of Joan Littlewood, one can only surmise. But the great thing is that he recognized a basic hunger for the theatre, and wanted to see it properly satisfied, just as he wanted better playgrounds and better schools. Without being able to enter at all deeply into the life of the working class, by his own lights he was genuinely and consistently anxious for their opportunities to be radically enlarged.

His dealings with the Philistines were more complicated. In a sense he succeeded too well in exposing 'the bad civilization of the middle classes': modern readers are liable to take his assessments of specific individuals and institutions on trust, as though they were beyond serious dispute. Someone ought to write a thesis setting out the achievements of all the various figures whom he uses as whipping-boys in *Culture and Anarchy* and elsewhere. I am not suggesting that in every case his estimate would have to be favourably revised; on the contrary, some of his victims were even more deserving of punishment than one could readily gather from his references to them. Sir Charles Adderley, for instance, whom he quotes in 'The Function of Criticism' holding forth to the Warwickshire farmers about 'the old Anglo-Saxon race, the best breed in the whole world', was also Robert Lowe's predecessor on the Council on Education, in which capacity he maintained that 'any attempt to keep children of the labouring classes under intellectual culture after the very earliest age at which they could earn their living, would be as arbitrary and improper as it would be to keep the boys at Eton and Harrow at spade labour'.* Lowe himself could hardly have gone further. On the other hand it would be a pity if, say, Sir Daniel Gooch were thought of by readers of *Culture and Anarchy* simply as the man who regaled his assembled workmen at Swindon with the sentence which his mother had repeated to

* Quoted by Asa Briggs, *Victorian People*, Chapter IX.

him every morning before he set out to work: 'Ever remember, my dear Dan, that you should look forward to being someday manager of that concern!' There was another Gooch, the boy whom Brunel appointed locomotive superintendent on the Great Western Railway at the age of twenty-one, and who took advantage of the G.W.R.'s broad gauge to design locomotives on strikingly original lines. 'His engines,' according to the *D.N.B.*, 'attained a speed and safety not previously deemed possible'; in particular the 'North Star', constructed when he was only twenty-three, was 'a marvel of symmetry and compactness'. This may not make his speechifying any less fatuous; but I don't think Arnold's little jokes about 'Mrs Gooch's Golden Rule' quite meet the case either. Or again, while Frances Power Cobbe was no doubt as tiresome a woman as Arnold more than once hints, she was also a selfless campaigner for many excellent causes, such as the humane treatment of juvenile offenders; and though I don't suppose that I shall ever read her essay on 'Dreams as Illustrations of Involuntary Cerebration' (1872), I am interested to learn from Philip Rieff (in *Freud: The Mind of the Moralist*) that it contains some bold anticipations of psycho-analytic theory. Middle-class civilization was very far from being all of a piece, and there were many things to be said in its favour. In underlining this elementary fact, one is arguing not so much against Arnold as against those of his successors who assume that he damned the middle classes unreservedly, and forget that he was at pains to insist on the presence of 'a soul of goodness' in Philistinism itself. To his credit, he was incapable of emulating Flaubert's total contempt for the nineteenth century as the age of *muflisme*, or of reducing his opponents to the level of a sub-human booboisie. Nor was he content merely to take for granted the comforts of a middle-class existence; in at least one passage (in *Celtic Literature*) his sense of reality prompted him to spell them out: 'Doors that open, windows that shut, locks that turn, razors that shave, coats that wear, watches that go, and a thousand more such good things, are the invention of the Philistines.' Coming from a company chairman or a Liberal candidate, this would have been a sufficiently trite reflection; coming from Matthew Arnold, it was something which needed to be said.

The familiar charges that Arnold was a kid-gloved aesthete and a prig will hardly bear a minute's serious examination, either of his writings or of his public career. With the dandified element in his work of which some critics complain, we are on rather different ground: it is undeniably there, but it seems to me one of his positive virtues. As a young man he had indulged, in the words of Lionel Trilling, 'in a kind of mild Byronism of conduct to preserve imagination and self from the corroding effects of his society that he might still be a poet'. Later on this instinct was to show itself less in his poetry than in his prose – in the rapier-work with which he fended off obtuse critics, the irony which saved him from lapsing into preachiness. His comic flourishes were a necessary form of artistic self-assertion, his 'insolence' a way of guarding against platitude – and I hope enough has already been said to demonstrate how little this was a matter of cutting himself off from social concerns and social responsibilities. The touches of dandyism simply give the rest of his work added savour. And yet if he is seldom precious or over-fastidious himself, it must be conceded that he was often the cause of preciosity and over-fastidiousness in others. To contemporaries he was above all the apostle of Culture; and Culture is a manifold concept, which easily lends itself to misinterpretation. What it had come to suggest in everyday speech a generation after Arnold's death is handily summarized by the American anthropologist Edward Sapir, in an essay written in 1924. Sapir is contrasting the sense in which ethnologists talk about culture with a second, much more widespread use of the word, which

refers to a rather conventional ideal of individual refinement, built up on a certain modicum of assimilated knowledge and experience but made up chiefly of a set of typical reactions that have the sanction of a class and of a tradition of long standing. Sophistication in the realm of intellectual goods is demanded of the applicant to the title of 'cultured person', but only up to a certain point. Far more emphasis is placed upon manner, a certain preciousness of conduct which takes different colours according to the nature of the personality that has assimilated the 'cultured' ideal. At its worst, the preciousness degenerates into a scornful aloofness from the manners and tastes of the crowd; this is the well-known cultural snobbishness. At its most subtle, it develops into a mild and whimsical vein of cynicism, an amused scepticism that would not for the world find itself betrayed into an unwonted enthusiasm; this type of cultured manner presents a more engaging countenance to the crowd, which only rarely gets hints of the discomfiting play of its irony, but it is an attitude of perhaps even more radical aloofness than snobbishness outright. Aloofness of some kind is generally the *sine qua non* of the second type of culture.*

It is difficult to believe that Sapir does not have Arnold specifically in mind, although he is referring in a more general way to that whole genteel tradition, incubated in Oxford and Cambridge and their Ivy League counterparts, which found Arnold so acceptable a prophet. How had this distortion of Arnold's teaching come about? For much of the time, as we have seen, he tends to identify his cultural *élite* with the older universities, the learned professions, the more highly educated sections of the upper middle class. But paradoxically, the explanation also lies in those aspects of his thinking which led him to maintain that culture in its truest sense must always transcend class-boundaries. There was another, alternative kind of *élite* in which he believed, one made up of scattered individuals bound together only by the common 'love and pursuit of perfection' which they shared, irrespective of their origins. As he wrote in *Culture and Anarchy*:

> Natures with this bent emerge in all classes, -- among the Barbarians, among the Philistines, among the Populace. And this bent always tends to take them out of their class, and to make their distinguishing characteristic not their Barbarianism or their Philistinism, but their *humanity*. They have, in general, a rough time of it in their lives; but they are sown more abundantly than one might think. . . .

They are the leaven in the lump, the righteous minority on whom the continuing health of society finally depends; and in one of Arnold's later essays, 'Numbers', he makes the religious analogy quite explicit, falling into the language of the Hebrew Prophets: 'Though thy people Israel be as the sand of the sea, only a remnant of them shall return.' Now it is one thing for Isaiah to talk like this, and another for Matthew Arnold. The Prophets speak in the name of a God who is zealous to save, and they believe – *really*

* From 'Culture, Genuine and Spurious', reprinted in *Culture, Language and Personality* (Berkeley, California, 1964).

believe – that salvation lies only through the paths of righteousness. But if there is one lesson to be learned from *Culture and Anarchy*, it is that righteousness alone – 'Hebraism', indeed – is not enough. No one who knows Arnold's work at all well will be predisposed to underrate the importance which he attached to questions of morality as the term is commonly understood. 'Conduct,' he announced bluntly in the opening chapter of *Literature and Dogma*, 'is three-fourths of our life and its largest concern', and it went without saying that the members of his unofficial *élite* were to be upright honourable men. But they were to be distinguished by another, more elusive set of qualities as well: urbanity, informed judgement, delicacy of perception, sweetness and light. They were intended, in other words, to constitute both a spiritual *and* a cultural aristocracy, to combine the roles of Isaiah's righteous remnant and Stendhal's Happy Few. From here it would have been only a short step, had Arnold followed his basic assumptions through, to treating sensitivity or heightened sensibility as the indefinable, unarguable equivalent of divine grace. The quandary in which he found himself was a genuine one, not to be resolved by a few hopeful egalitarian incantations: if he was 'undemocratic' in his commitment to austere critical standards, then comparatively few serious artists are democrats. But he ought at least to have recognized more clearly than he did the snares against which any self-elected *élite* has to guard. There is a sin of what might be called cultural pride as well as one of spiritual pride: it comes from subordinating all other virtues to an ideal of artistic excellence, and, though it has taken many different shapes since, in Arnold's time its most conspicuous result was the kind of languid affectation which Sapir outlines in his Identikit sketch. A direct line of descent, as T. S. Eliot argued in his essay on 'Arnold and Pater', runs from the Culture of *Culture and Anarchy* to the Art for Art's Sake of the 1880s, and beyond that to the more rarefied or anaemic varieties of subsequent aestheticism. Inadvertently, by appearing to surround the idea of culture with a devotional hush, Arnold helped to give it a bad name – and we are still paying the price, not least in terms of that dismal glorification of the *nyekulturny* which is stamped over so much of our recent art and entertainment.

With the passage of time, however, it has become easier to do justice to the complexities of Arnold's position than it was when Sapir and Eliot were writing, forty-odd years ago, easier to appreciate the wisdom of his attempt to strike a balance between the cultural claims of the community and those of the individual. We may sigh over lost pre-industrial innocence, but in a highly developed society culture *must* remain to a considerable degree a matter of random personal interests and attainments – assuming that individual freedom of choice continues to be prized, that is to say: the only real alternative is the drill-sergeant's *Kultur*, systematically imposed from above. Yet at the same time a merely personal, merely selfish culture, whatever its exotic possibilities or short-term satisfactions, will invariably end in sterility and affectation. This is something which Arnold, at least, never doubted: the conviction that any culture worthy of the name is bound to promote what he called 'the social idea' runs through every major phase of his work, from the literary essays, with their rejection of pedantry and caprice, to his admirable lecture on 'Equality' (1878), with its unequivocal reminder that 'no individual life can be truly prosperous, passed in the midst of men who suffer'. And if he is sometimes rightly to be reproached with having tried to fit secular square pegs into theological round holes, one must also acknowledge how firmly his 'social idea' was grounded on traditional Christian conceptions of charity and loving kindness.

Not that one can readily imagine anyone today turning to him as a religious thinker. Even those who regret that he lost the rearguard action which he fought in works like *St Paul and Protestantism* and *Literature and Dogma* must surely agree that by comparison with – shall we say? – a Kierkegaard, his weapons were hopelessly inadequate. It is true that nowadays there is a risk of our misunderstanding him *as a man* by playing down his religious concerns and concentrating too exclusively on his social and literary criticism. His poetry alone, both in its wistfulness and in its frequent arid patches, bears sufficient witness to how desolate he could find a world from which, as Professor Hillis Miller would put it, God had withdrawn. Yet it nevertheless seems to me plain that his final court of appeal is always what he conceives of as human nature itself. The men and women whom he valued most highly, it will be recalled, were characterized in his eyes not so much by piety or intellectual distinction as by their full untrammelled *humanity* (his italics): they formed an *élite*, that is to say, defined in terms which were incompatible with any permanent or absolute philosophy of *élitism*. In literature, too, he could recognize and respond to a note which he was content to describe simply as 'the truly human'. He uses the phrase in connection with Chaucer, but he might just as easily have applied it to the *Iliad*, or Shakespeare, or *Anna Karenina*, about which he published a remarkable essay in the last year of his life (remarkable given that it appeared at a time when the great majority of English critics still looked on Tolstoy with suspicion or hostility).* There are certain authors, he wrote in his *Encyclopaedia Britannica* article on Sainte-Beuve, who come so close to perfection in their own ways that 'the human race might willingly adopt them as its spokesmen'. Homer, for example, Plato, Shakespeare, Voltaire and, 'in his line of literary criticism, Sainte-Beuve'.

And at this point one pulls up short. Homer and Shakespeare, yes; Plato and Voltaire, perhaps. But Sainte-Beuve? With all his merits, how many members of the human race would really be willing to adopt that rather chilly figure as their spokesman? One is reminded that he was Arnold's particular hero; one is also reminded of how local and subjective any one man's definition of the truly human is liable to be. Some highly unlikely people, after all, have styled themselves humanists; in America forty years ago, for instance, Humanism was usually taken to mean the thin-lipped reactionary dogmatism of Irving Babbitt (*lucus a non lucendo*). And even far more democratic versions of humanism tend to be impossibly high-minded and genteel, to put abstract Humanity on a pedestal. In *The Armies of the Night* Norman Mailer describes how he came to love 'what editorial writers were fond of calling the democratic principle with its faith in the common man. He found that principle and that man in the Army, but what none of the editorial writers ever mentioned was that

---

* It is also mildly remarkable for the way in which Arnold, exactly fifty years after Pushkin's death, manages to commiserate with the Russians for not yet having produced a great poet. Tolstoy himself, incidentally, admired both *Culture and Anarchy* and *Literature and Dogma*. He was particularly taken with the phrase 'sweet reasonableness'.

that noble common man was obscene as an old goat, and his obscenity was what saved him.' Not only in America, either.

Today humanism seems little more than a word, and a rather unhelpful word at that. We are too aware of the obscenities (both humorous and otherwise) which it conceals, of the facts of life which it ignores, of the class-divisions and cracks which it can be used to paper over. Yet judged in its mid-Victorian context it was a plausible ideal, one of the great sustaining ideals of Victorian literature. Mill spoke of the strengthening and exalting of our common nature; Arnold might have said exactly the same thing. And Carlyle, in his younger days at least, went furthest of all, dreaming of literature as a means of completely transcending social conflicts and differences of belief. It was a dream which led him, for example, to describe Goethe – fancifully, but movingly – as the perfect writer, and therefore as the perfect citizen: 'He is neither noble nor plebeian, neither liberal nor servile, nor infidel nor devotee; but the best excellence of *all* these, joined in pure union, "a clear and universal Man".' The Hero as Man of Letters was a humanist, too.

3

THE HIGHER
JOURNALISM

I

In the 1850s the whole tempo of journalism accelerated sharply. Among newspapers *The Times* still led the field, never more so than in the epoch of the Crimean War: Trollope's caricature of Delane as Tom Towers in *The Warden* (1855) shows him at the undisputed height of his influence, apparently without a rival anywhere. Powerful new competition was at hand, however. The same year, 1855, also saw the final abolition of the newspaper tax (the tax on advertisements had been lifted two years previously), and the successful launching of the *Daily Telegraph*, a penny paper which by the end of the next decade was able to boast of the biggest circulation in the world – and boast is what it did, much to Arnold's disgust. Other popular dailies soon sprang up in its wake, still fairly ponderous by subsequent Fleet Street standards, but beginning to exploit the kind of garish possibilities which in France had already been seized on a generation earlier by adventurers like Emile Girardin of *La Presse*. Although the days of its full splendour were still to come, the cheap mass-circulation daily was a living reality by the mid-1860s, before Northcliffe was born.

It is misleading, then, to talk as the historian R. C. K. Ensor does of a 'dignified phase of English journalism' which 'reigned unchallenged' until the 1880s; and Raymond Williams is fully justified when he objects, in *The Long Revolution*, to this widely accepted version of events, with its implication of standards having been dragged down wholesale as a result of Forster's Education Act. The dignity of the *Telegraph* and its competitors was all too often only skin-deep. Nevertheless, the myth does have its foundations in fact: the quality of the best Victorian journalism was exceptionally high, especially as far as the periodical press is concerned. In the 1850s and 1860s an unprecedented number of serious journals of opinion managed to strike root and prosper. With the founding of the *Saturday Review* (another 1855 landmark) and the transformation of the *Spectator* under Hutton and Townsend, the weeklies took on a new literary significance. Monthly reviews, an innovation, increasingly supplanted the quarterlies – the incongruously-named *Fortnightly* was a pioneer here, soon to be followed by the *Contemporary* and later, with more of a flourish, by the *Nineteenth Century* and the *National Review*. Another new departure was the shilling monthly magazine offering a mixture of 'family' reading and miscellaneous essays, which while overlapping with the reviews also succeeded in largely ousting the part-issue as a means of serializing fiction. The most notable periodicals of this type were *Macmillan's*, founded in 1859, and the *Cornhill*, which began publication the following year with Thackeray in command and an initial sale of 120,000.

It was the *Saturday Review* which marked most decisively the advent of a new era, although the first editor, John Douglas Cook, was, in the words of Leslie Stephen, 'a survivor of the old Shandon or Maginn race', a pugnacious veteran notorious for hurling insults (and ink-bottles) at his subordinates. Reputedly he never opened a book; but, rather like Harold Ross, he was a lowbrow who knew how to pick the right highbrows, and he built up a formidable editorial team. With men like Henry Maine and Fitzjames Stephen among its regular contributors, the *Saturday* could fairly claim to speak for the university-bred class of scholarly gentlemen and gentlemanly scholars. *Saturday* reviewers, mostly recruited direct from Oxford or Cambridge (especially Cambridge), assumed an imposing degree of cultivation among their readers, and specialized in enthusiastic exposures of shoddy thinking or defective scholarship. Contemptuous of the age in which they lived as one 'of vapours and smelling-bottles', their pet victims were hot-gospellers, demagogues, sentimental novelists. Undeniably they provided a bracing corrective to a great deal of nonsense which up till then had gone pretty much unchallenged. But where they deluded themselves was in supposing that 'the educated class' as they defined it could somehow stand permanently aloof from party interests. Not for the first time a nominal independence turned out, when it came to the test, to mean unorthodox conservatism. The *Saturday* had no love for Disraeli, but by the 1860s it was unmistakably showing its colours. Contributors raged against trade unions, vied with *The Times* in their hostility to the North in the American Civil War, jeered at the campaign to bring in a secret ballot; they reserved their heaviest ammunition of all for John Bright, who retaliated by christening them the 'Saturday Revilers', a nickname which they cherished as a compliment. The forthrightness on which they prided themselves was often no more than an excuse for un-restrained brutality. Nor was their astringent 'realism' the wholly commendable policy which it may sound in the abstract. Many of the attitudes which they derided as mawkish might better be described as humane, while the fact that they took for granted the conventional taboos of the age only makes their deliberate callousness seem that much more distasteful. M. M. Bevington, in his history of the *Saturday's* early years, cites a characteristic exercise in well-bred sadism: an editorial defending the death-penalty for women, entitled 'The Strangulation of Females', which goes out of its way to pillory sentimentalists who advocated a reprieve where the condemned woman was pregnant. Yet it was the same paper which, reviewing *Adam Bede*, took exception to Hetty Sorrell's pregnancy being described in what it regarded as excessive detail: 'a decent author and a decent public may surely take the premonitory symptoms for granted'. Decency, it will be seen, is a highly flexible concept.

Where the *Saturday* held out against the spirit of the age it did so in the name of entrenched upper-class standards rather than those of a hypothetical *élite*. It especially deplored the idea of a separate literary caste which presumed to stand aside from affairs and pass judgement on society. When Dickens, in his obituary notice for the *Cornhill*, taxed Thackeray with not having taken his vocation as a novelist seriously enough, the *Saturday* was quick to reply, denouncing 'this feeling of the honour and nobleness of being a writer apart from the interest in particular compositions' as so much self-intoxicated cant:

> It is the creation of writers who have written upon writing. It has been suggested by those who have seen a hero in the 'Man of Letters' and who have spoken of the higher kind of composition as of something godlike and divine.

The thrusting young barristers and politicians of the *Saturday* had no patience with this tendency: they sensed in the rise of an independent literary intelligentsia a threat to the supremacy of the compact Oxford-and-Cambridge 'educated class'. And this suspicion died hard. It was the historian Freeman, one of the most regular of the original *Saturday* revilers, and one of the most vituperative, who a generation later spurred on the resistance to the introduction of English studies at Oxford with his warnings against 'chatter about Shelley'.

Arnold, who had some brisk exchanges with the *Saturday*, was always careful to distinguish it from the common run of English journalism. By comparison it was 'a kind of organ of reason' in matters of literature and taste, an advocate of civilized standards which had put serious readers heavily in its debt. But at the same time it also had a decided tinge of the boastful, insular 'newspaper-spirit' from which it prided itself on being immune. Its tone was too assertive, its views too closely bound up with those of the propertied classes, for it to serve as the bastion of urbane, disinterested intelligence which Arnold called for in 'The Literary Influence of Academies'.

As its name implies, the *Academy*, a weekly founded in 1869, was a deliberate attempt to answer this need, although the guiding spirit behind it was not so much Arnold as Mark Pattison. The first editor, Charles Appleton, was a young Oxford don who had taken to heart Pattison's view that it was the role of a university to remedy the aimless confusion of current literature, to supply 'the harmonising hand of liberal culture'. In practice this came close to treating culture as the province of professional savants, and the select audience which the *Academy* was originally intended to serve was unashamedly erudite, academic in the strict sense of the word. Appleton campaigned vigorously for the endowment of university research, and hoped that he would be able to put his paper on the same footing as the major learned journals which had already been firmly established in Germany and France. A project of this kind was scarcely an enticing commercial proposition. After a few months Appleton quarrelled with his publisher, John Murray, and took over the management of the paper himself (turning it into a fortnightly), while retaining his fellowship at St John's. Most of the *Academy's* shareholders were also fellows of Oxford colleges. It proved impossible, however, to run a paper on the exclusively scholarly lines which Appleton had laid down, and at the time of his death in 1879 the *Athenaeum* was able to point out that the *Academy* had long since evolved into a general literary review with aims very similar to its own. The amateur spirit in England was still too strong for purely academic journals of the Continental type to find much support, and while this may argue backwardness in the English universities of the period, it had its compensations for the educated general public. Scholarly topics which might otherwise have been buried in the files of specialized publications were aired in the major reviews, and a tradition of lucid *haute vulgarization* was kept alive. But ultimately, as knowledge multiplied, there was to be no resisting the process of intellectual fragmentation, and the last quarter of the century saw the setting up of many of the most notable English learned journals (*Mind* in 1876, the *English Historical Review* in 1886, the *Classical Review* in 1887, etc).

Among those who deplored the partisan ferocity of the Victorian press (and here Arnold was by no means alone) it became a commonplace to hold up the supposedly impartial *Revue des Deux Mondes* as a model to emulate. The *Fortnightly Review*, which began publication in 1865 with G. H. Lewes as editor, was explicitly inspired by the French journal, but it had a liberal slant from the first, and after John Morley took over in 1867 it rapidly developed into the acknowledged mouthpiece of advanced, free-thinking radicalism. The *Nineteenth Century*, founded by James Knowles in 1877, was more eclectic. An architect by training – responsible among other things for the Grosvenor Hotel and the lay-out of Leicester Square – Knowles had the exceptionally wide range of interests which one comes to take for granted in the upper reaches of Victorian journalism.* In 1869 he had been instrumental in setting up the Metaphysical Society, the famous dining-and-debating club which counted Gladstone, Tennyson and Manning among its members, and which he conceived of as a potential English Academy. (With the example of the Académie Française in mind, he proposed limiting the membership to the magic number of forty.) The *Nineteenth Century* was to some extent the Metaphysical Society translated into print; it also had the stamp of the Establishment all over it. The first number, like the first meeting of the Society opened with a poem by Tennyson, a close friend of Knowles (who designed Aldworth for him); it also contained an essay by Arnold, who was to be a frequent contributor to the paper in its early years. Among older readers the *Nineteenth Century* soon enjoyed unrivalled prestige as an intellectual forum, and incidentally earned Knowles a handsome annual profit. But if it aspired to be open-minded it was also incorrigibly right-thinking, and though it published a few rebels such as Kropotkin the wider-post Victorian reaction against Victorianism left it trailing behind. In time it became the *Nineteenth Century and After* – 'but it ought to call itself the Middle Ages', Arnold Bennett remarked.

In addition to being lavishly supplied with periodicals, from 1865 the cultivated well-to-do public was also catered for by an evening paper, the *Pall Mall Gazette*, which was owned by George Smith of Smith Elder, publisher of the *Cornhill*, and edited by Frederick Greenwood. For readers of *Pendennis*, the choice of the name *Pall Mall* must have seemed like a clear case of nature catching up with art, but it was selected without undue irony, and indeed without any precise topographical significance: it was simply meant to conjure up a reassuring leathery atmosphere of clubs and clubmen. The paper – which was really more like a miniature review – consisted of a short résumé of the morning's news, followed by political comment and solid articles on literature and topics of the day. Greenwood himself was a strong

---

* His versatility pales, however, by comparison with that of a man like George Grove, who edited *Macmillan's* from 1868-83. An engineer, Groves began his career by building a lighthouse in Jamaica at the age of twenty-two, and crowned it by editing his famous *Dictionary of Music* (a subject in which he was entirely self-taught).

Tory, and many of his staple contributors were orthodox *Saturday* Reviewers, but he also opened up his columns to less vehemently partisan points of view. It was in the *Pall Mall*, for instance, that Arnold first published *Friendship's Garland*. And while a younger man like Leslie Stephen, who contributed a series of 'Letters from Cambridge', might disagree with the paper's politics, socially he felt thoroughly at home in its pages. The *Pall Mall* occupied a unique position among English newspapers, and for fifteen years it managed to retain its original character. Then George Smith made a present of it to his son-in-law, who was a Liberal; Greenwood resigned and John Morley took over, to be succeeded in his turn three years later by the sensation-mongering W. T. Stead. By the mid-1880s, with Stead getting into his stride, exposing 'The Maiden Tribute of Modern Babylon' and hounding Sir Charles Dilke, the paper which had been explicitly designed 'by gentlemen for gentlemen' was paving the way for the yellow journalism of the following decade, a clear harbinger of un-gentlemanly things to come. But the ironies of history are seldom quite as neat as that; the *Pall Mall* retained some of its distinction, and regained more after Stead had gone. His successor, Sir Edward Cook, was one of the best of the old type of scholarly Victorian journalists: he particularly deserves to be remembered for his life of Florence Nightingale, which even Lytton Strachey was compelled to praise, and for the magnificent thirty-nine-volume Cook and Wedderburn edition of Ruskin, which he worked at in his spare time. (The index alone would be worth a Ph.D.) And though Cook's successor, the wayward aristocrat Harry Cust, was not made of quite such stern stuff – he once printed a leading article under the heading 'Can't Think of a Title' – he ran a lively paper, with Kipling, H. G. Wells and a dozen other outstanding writers among his contributors.

II

The *Saturday Review*, the *Nineteenth Century* and the other papers at which we have glanced had a limited appeal, but essentially they served the interests of the most powerful section of the community, and they reflected the prosperity of their readers. Running a journal of genuine intellectual dissent, on the other hand, remained as chancy a business as it has always been. Between the severing of Mill's connection with the *Westminster Review* and the founding of the *Fortnightly* twenty-five years later there was no adequate established platform for advanced opinion in the period-ical press, although for a few years in the 1850s a rejuvenated *Westminster* under John Chapman came close to providing one. Chapman had at one stage been the English agent for the American *Dial*, and when it folded he tried to start a paper on the same lines, to be published simultaneously in London and Boston, but with-out success. Instead, he took over the *Westminster*, with financial backing from Edward Lombe, one of those useful wealthy eccentrics who did so much to leaven the conformism of Victorian culture. Lombe's particular fad was the peculiarly nebulous cause of 'organic change', which Chapman understandably felt free to interpret more or less as he chose, publishing work by authors with as little in common, on the face of it, as Herbert Spencer, Mazzini and Froude.

It was through the *Westminster* that George Eliot was first drawn into the London literary world. She was a heavily overworked assistant editor from 1851 to 1854, and then, in the early days of her alliance with George Henry Lewes, an indispensable outside contributor, running the department of 'Belles Lettres' single-handed and keeping Chapman supplied with a succession of lengthy critical essays. George Eliot's criticism is important because it is by George Eliot, although in itself it would have been enough to have guaranteed her a modest immortality. It has its undeniably lumpish moments. But the same qualities which shine through her fiction are already discernible, the same blend of soaring idealism and placid common sense, charitableness and severity. Severity not least: aspiring wherever possible to praise rather than condemn, she none the less manages to temper her mercy with a discon-certing amount of justice. The two most memorable of her longer essays are both withering attacks – on Dr Cumming, a deplorable fire-and-brimstone evangelist then at the height of his popularity, and on the eighteenth-century poet Edward Young, author of the sepulchral *Night Thoughts* and assiduous social climber. Rather flimsy targets for so much heavy artillery, it might be thought: few readers of the *Westminster* can have lost much sleep over Dr Cumming's bodeful prophecies, while Young's reputation had long since begun to fade. To George Eliot, however, they represented not so much errors to be calmly disposed of as aspects of her own past which still needed to be exorcized: the bigotry which she had encountered as a girl, the pious rhetoric (Young's specifically) by which she had once been enthralled. Her passions were as fully engaged as her critical intelligence: she had a moral vision of her own to put across. And it was in fact the paper on Cumming which finally persuaded Lewes that he was dealing, not just with an exceptionally gifted bluestocking, but with a woman of genius – genius which he made it the main business of his life to encourage and promote.

Lewes himself (1817–78) was one of the most agile intellectual journalists of his time. His heterodox views never stopped him from getting on well with more conventional colleagues, and in the annals of the mid-Victorian press his name turns up again and again – as a prolific freelance, as the editor of the weekly *Leader* and of the *Fortnightly*, as editorial adviser to the *Cornhill* and the *Pall Mall Gazette*. Today, apart from his connection with George Eliot he figures in the reference books chiefly as the biographer of Goethe, and as a representative standard-bearer for Victorian positivism, materialism, mechanistic thinking, etc. His personal acquaintances found him a less daunting figure than this may suggest. 'Witty, French, flippant' was one contemporary summing-up; 'the ugliest man in London' was another. His early inclinations were theatrical as much as literary; both his father and grandfather had been actors, and he himself made a number of sporadic appearances on the professional stage, the last of them (as Shylock, in Edinburgh) when he was already in his thirties, an established man of letters and the author of a voluminous *Biographical History of Philosophy*. As 'Slingsby Lawrence' and – with a bow to one of his favourite novelists – as 'Frank Churchill', he also turned out a succession of pot-boiling farces and melodramas for London managements. He was a keen patron of the best-known bohemian haunts of the day: in his otherwise mediocre early novel *Ranthorpe* there are some lively glimpses of the Cyder Cellar, the Coal Hole, and their *habitués*. And all this while he was energetically pursuing his interest in philosophy, which had first been aroused in his teens when he used to attend an informal discussion group which met at a tavern in Red Lion Square. It was here that he discovered the works of Spinoza, which were expounded to the club (at the rate of a proposition a night) by a watchmaker called Cohn – an episode which years later was to find an echo in the Jewish section of *Daniel Deronda*. Subsequently he became a disciple of Mill, and through him of Comte, whose teachings he probably did more than anyone except Mill to make known to the English public, although in the end his reservations about the religious aspects of Positivism led to his being denounced by the Master as an arch-heretic. If a longing for intellectual certainty predisposed him towards the secular messiahs and utopian conventicles thrown up by the age, his native wit usually saved him from toppling over into complete extravagance. On the other hand there was often the strong odour of a crank's kitchen about the circle in which he moved. He and his wife were especially friendly with the Thornton Hunts, who tried to run their household in Bayswater on co-operative lines as a 'phalanstery' – although it was hardly as revolutionary an establishment as Fourier, from whom they borrowed the term, had envisaged. Thornton Hunt was Leigh Hunt's son: Lewes thought highly of him, and the two of them acted together as joint-editors of the *Leader* when it was started in 1850. The most lasting consequence of their friendship, however, was a liaison between Hunt and Mrs Lewes, and the break-up of Lewes's marriage. Naturally this also created difficulties for the editorial partnership. But both men continued writing for the *Leader*, and it remained the liveliest of the weeklies until the success of the *Saturday Review* lured away its public and drove it out of business. Hunt, his Fourierist days behind him, eventually joined the staff of the *Daily Telegraph*.

One of the *Leader's* most popular features was a bantering semi-satirical column which Lewes conducted under the pseudonym of 'Vivian', a name with suitably dandyish overtones which he also took to using for his work as the paper's theatre critic. The persona of Vivian was carefully elaborated; he was presented as a sprightly young man about town with an unaccountable enthusiasm for the writings of the Church Fathers, alternately preening himself on his conquests and poring over the works of St Gregory Nazianzen and Tertullian. A good deal of Lewes's frustrated histrionic ambitions clearly went into the role. The theatricality of the theatre has a way of infecting everyone concerned with it, inducing even otherwise staid critics to make an exhibition of themselves. Mincing around as Vivian brought out a tiresomely flashy side of Lewes; but it also released his liveliest qualities as a writer. He was an admirable theatre critic, one of the most intelligent of the nineteenth century: certainly none of his English contemporaries could match his combination of wide reading in European dramatic literature and intimate knowledge of stage technique. He was witty, provocative, direct, and, despite the persiflage, altogether in earnest when it came to lamenting the debased condition of the English theatre at the time, or suggesting improvements. The remedy lay, as usual, in a return to nature, but naturalness on the stage was an effect which could be achieved only through strict artistic discipline and economy of means: the actor's art, like any other, was a 'representative', not an 'imitative' process. Although he is supposed to have been the earliest English critic to have talked (approvingly) of realism, Lewes had no more use for niggling photographic accuracy than he did for barn-storming exaggeration. Another of his aversions was the Chamber-of-Horrors element in Jacobean tragedy, which he blamed Lamb and his followers for having glossed over. At times, especially on this theme, he can sound distinctly Shavian, and Shaw readily acknowledged him as a predecessor. Another posthumous admirer was William Archer, who edited a selection of his contributions to the *Leader*. Lewes himself, twenty years after giving up regular reviewing, had distilled his experiences of the theatre into a fine retrospective study, *On Actors and the Art of Acting*, but the Archer volume is useful because it preserves more of the hit-or-miss spontaneity of his original weekly journalism. As Vivian, he had taken a certain pride in the hectic conditions under which he was compelled to work. The 'grands seigneurs of criticism' might look down their noses at daily or weekly reviewers, but he could not help wondering how a Quintilian would have acquitted himself if he had had to rush straight from a first night to a printing office and jot down his impressions in half an hour. Whatever the virtues of academic theory, there was no substitute for the sharp immediate impact of the dramatic event.

Lewes's dealings with fiction are much less illuminating, although they had their importance at the time. He was one of the first Victorian critics to try to introduce a little order into the chaos of novel-reviewing. His watchwords – truthfulness, coherence, plausibility – were unexceptionable ones, but they didn't take him very far, and they were a positive hindrance when he came to consider the foremost imaginative writer of the age. In his essay on 'Dickens in Relation to Criticism' (1872) he has no difficulty in demonstrating to everybody's satisfaction that Dickens exaggerates and distorts, and no means of accounting for this except as a symptom of immaturity, or worse. At several points he even talks as though he were diagnosing an actual mental disorder. A cautionary tale: the 'advanced' critic plods along miles behind the unintellectual artist. But the essay is plainly the work of a clever man, and far superior to most attacks made on Dickens from the standpoint of inflexible realism. It still has the power to irritate.

The mid-1850s marked the decisive turning-point in Lewes's career. After joining forces with George Eliot, and with the Goethe biography safely behind him, he began to devote more and more of his time to scientific reading and research. In particular, he was drawn to marine biology: his first publication following *Goethe* was a collection of scientific papers, *Seaside Studies at Ilfracombe, Tenby, the Scilly Isles and Jersey*. But he struck out confidently in many other directions as well. He lectured at the British Association on the functions of the spinal cord, wrote popular zoological studies for the *Cornhill*, became engrossed in the possibilities of putting psychology on a firmer physiological basis – a refinement, as it were, of his early enthusiasm for phrenology. Without professional training, the original contributions which he was able to make to research were necessarily limited. But as a scientific popularizer he enjoyed a distinguished reputation, and not only in the English-speaking world. It was while reading the Russian translation of one of his books that Pavlov, then a fifteen-year-old pupil in a theological seminary, first resolved to take up the study of physiology.

Amid the molluscs and the anemones Lewes still found time to write a certain amount of literary criticism. Indeed, in *The Principles of Success in Literature* (originally serialized in the *Fortnightly* in 1865) he calmly offered to expound the immutable psychological laws holding good in all ages and under all circumstances for successful creative writing of every description. It could hardly be claimed that the book itself is much of a triumph. There are some sensible observations scattered through it, but the actual Principles – moral, aesthetic, intellectual – boil down to little more than a stern demand for sincerity. And Lewes's science is less in evidence than his scientism. At one stage he even takes over Herbert Spencer's analogy between an effective piece of writing and an efficient piece of machinery ('It is the writer's art so to arrange words that they shall suffer the least possible retardation from the friction of the reader's mind . . .'), laboriously clanking his way through the iron laws of style: Economy, Simplicity, Sequence, Variety, Climax. Then his natural spirits revive, and he is reminded of Edward Lear's recipe for making an Amblongus pie, with its impossible list of ingredients and its final instruction to 'serve up in a clean dish, and throw the whole out of the window as fast as possible'. He may have had more than his share of brassy self-confidence – that title, *The Principles of Success*, is rather a give-away – but he was incapable of being taken in by his own dogmatizing for very long at a stretch.

Nor was he under any illusion about the dangers of setting up as a literary jack of all trades. 'For the most part,' he once wrote in an irritable moment, 'literary men have no *raison d'être*, have no justification in their talents for the career they stumble through. . . . How few men of letters *think* at all!' The problem of the false vocation was one which deeply exercised George Eliot: her conception of Will Ladislaw in *Middlemarch* is a case in point. Although Ladislaw is commonly thought of as a hopelessly idealized curly-haired hero, he is meant to have very definite limitations: Lydgate's mildly contemptuous dismissal of him as 'miscellaneous and bric-à-brac' is allowed to carry a good deal of weight. When he first appears in the novel he is quickly marked down as a dilettante, merely trifling with the idea of how agreeable it would be to become a painter. He is contrasted, rather too forcibly perhaps, with the genuine article, his friend Adolf Naumann, an uncompromising single-minded artist who makes him wince by sardonically (and Teutonically) pronouncing his doom: 'O, he does not mean it seriously with painting. His walk must be *belles lettres*. That is wi-ide.' Too wide to lead anywhere in particular, we are meant to conclude; and although at the very end of the book we hear about Ladislaw's exploits as an M.P. and a doughty social reformer, effectively he is shown subsiding into just another journalist. Not everyone has it in him to produce masterpieces. George Eliot found her true vocation as a novelist; G. H. Lewes might be said to have found a vocation in George Eliot. With the partial exception of his theatre criticism, most of what he wrote is now little more than research-fodder. But he was no Ladislaw, and his versatility deserves a kinder name than dilettantism. It would be truer to speak of disinterested curiosity, of a many-sidedness which makes the biography of Goethe a monument to its author, at his own level, as well as to his subject. A monument, also, to Lewes's public, to a generation which wanted to be instructed, and which took it for granted that in their separate ways the philosopher and the historian, the man of science and the man of letters, were all adding to the stock of a common culture.

III

The public hungered for intellectual guidance. Still, how had it come about that so many men of real literary ability were willing to devote their best energies to commenting on other men's books? Walter Bagehot (1826–77), the most brilliant journalist of Lewes's generation, addressed himself to the problem with mock-bewilderment. The growth of reviewing had often been put down, especially by aggrieved authors, to sheer indolence, and undoubtedly it was easier to review a book than to write one. But whether it was easier to review hundreds of books, which is what actually happened, was quite another question. No, the reason must lie deeper, Bagehot reasoned, in the whole disjointed character of modern life, and the corresponding scrappiness of modern literature. The ponderous quarto was as much a relic of the past as the stage-coach. Reviewers merely exemplified the hustling spirit of the age: people everywhere were now eager for packaged information, casual entertainment, reading-matter which they could get at in a hurry, 'like sandwiches on a railway journey'. Bagehot was prepared to be as quizzical about his own trade as he was about most things. But if it came to a serious dispute between ancients and moderns he was firmly on the side of the moderns. His account of the characteristic modern writer is, by his usual standards, exceptionally warm: he sees him

glancing lightly from topic to topic, suggesting deep things in a jest, unfolding unanswerable arguments in an absurd illustration, expounding nothing, yet really suggesting the lessons of a wider experience [than that of the older type of systematic scholar], embodying the results of a more finely tested philosophy, passing with a more Shakesperian transition, connecting topics with a more subtle link, refining on them with an acuter perception, and what is more to the purpose, pleasing all that hear him . . . fragmentary yet imparting what he says, allusive yet explaining what he intends, disconnected yet impressing what he maintains.

This is hardly an accurate description of the kind of writing which confronted the average Victorian reader leafing through the average Victorian periodical. But it is a fair summary of Bagehot's own personal ideal, and even (after one or two of the adjectives have been toned down) of his own personal practice. More than any of his contemporaries he excelled in the art of informal criticism – of what it would be tempting to call talkative criticism, if that didn't suggest the maundering velvet-jacketed causerie of a later date. His occasional excursions into the uplands of literary theory, such as his well-known tripartite division of poetry into the Pure, the Ornate, the Grotesque, are the least rewarding part of his work. Luckily they *are* only occasional. For the rest, he generalizes cheerfully but undogmatically: he is a master of the disposable aphorism, the working classification which he knows when to jettison. It is characteristic that in *Physics and Politics* he should have put forward 'the instinct for discussion' as the great dissolvent without which all early societies would have set as hard as plaster, in the way that most of them actually did. No advanced civilization without conversation: talk was not only enjoyable, it was liberating. As a critic Bagehot was content to address himself to 'the natural reader'. Natural reading, he freely admitted, was often superficial, but it was the only kind which really stuck in the end. He had very little use for card indexes: 'what truly indicates excellent knowledge, is the habit of constant, sudden, and almost unconscious allusion, which implies familiarity, for it can arise from that alone. . . .' The immediate reference here is to Shakespeare, but once again Bagehot might plausibly have been stealing a glance at the mirror, discreetly congratulating himself on his own intellectual dexterity and presence of mind.

No themes were more congenial to him than the ignorance of the learned, the cramping effects of too exclusive a devotion to literature. The reason why so few good books got written, he maintained, was because so few people who could write knew anything; and he was fond of drawing a contrast between the alleged sluggishness of authors and what he liked to think of as the characteristic cheerful resilience of humanity at large. Naturally he felt that he could afford to indulge his irony in this direction. His own career brought him into daily contact with bankers and senior officials; his views were respectfully sought out by cabinet ministers. Far more than most commentators, he knew what really made the wheels go round. It is true that the bulk of his purely literary essays were written in his twenties and early thirties, before he joined the *Economist*, before he wrote *The English Constitution*. But his acumen and self-possession were apparent from the first: it seems entirely appropriate that he should actually have been born in a bank (his father's, which was also the family residence). And yet one can make too much of Bagehot the level-headed realist; if that were the whole story, after all, his criticism would hardly be worth lingering over for very long a hundred years later. He had an imagination as well, and a dry, insinuating wit; he took care to distinguish between his own philosophy and the short-sighted shrewdness which passed for wisdom among the common run of practical men; he recognized that a broad experience of life, invaluable literary asset though it might be under favourable circumstances, would do very little for an author who hadn't also been granted (useful concept) 'an experiencing nature'. No single formula will sum him up. There was a businesslike Bagehot, and an introspective, half-romantic Bagehot, and a Bagehot who played one side off against the other and then came to the conclusion that, 'taken as a whole', the universe was absurd. The comfortable money-making universe, at any rate:

> There seems an unalterable contradiction between the human mind and its employments. How can *a soul* be a merchant? What relation to an immortal being have the price of linseed, the fall of butter, the tare on tallow, the brokerage on hemp? Can an undying creature debit 'petty expenses' and charge for 'carriage paid'?

Another kind of writer addressing another kind of audience might have muttered something about Alienation. Bagehot was content to use less metaphysical language: 'The soul ties its shoes; the mind washes its hands in a basin. All is incongruous.'

How did one find an anchorage in such a universe, how did one, so to speak, keep body and soul together? By maintaining a decent respect for tradition, and by not worrying too much about first causes. Ideologies could be dangerous things: 'great and terrible systems of divinity and philosophy lie round about us, which, if true, might drive a wise man mad'. Fortunately most people were too well-balanced – or too 'stupid' – to be seriously affected by them. Bagehot is of course famous for talking about stupidity as though it were virtually synonymous with instinctive wisdom. On the same principle, he was a connoisseur of prosaic temperaments: when he starts summing up the character of Sir Robert Peel by asking whether there can ever have been as dull a man, his readers can be pretty sure that they are in for a eulogy, and a persuasive one. The paradox doesn't work quite as well with poets, however, as it does with politicians, and for all its virtues Bagehot's literary criticism remains obstinately earthbound. An essay like his much-praised 'Shakespeare the Individual' brings out very clearly both his strength and his limitations. In his eagerness to get away from the stock romantic idea of an inscrutable, super-human Shakespeare, out-topping knowledge, he stumbles more than once into bathos; while there is a note of complacency in his picture of the poet as prosperous freeholder which recalls nothing so much as the soothing after-dinner tones of Bishop Blougram –

> *He leaves his towers and gorgeous palaces*
> *To build the trimmest house in Stratford town . . .*

We can learn more from him about Shakespeare the sound judge of dogs, the 'out-of-door sporting man', than about the author of *King Lear*. Yet there are some fine passages in the essay as well. In particular, what might be called the intellectual aspects of Shakespeare's feeling for common humanity have never been better caught: his refusal to condemn 'narrow intelligence' when it was the product of narrow circumstances, his sympathetic insight – very Bagehotish, this – into the erratic thought-processes of 'the illogical classes'. ('He felt, if we may say so, the force of their bad reasoning.') Bagehot is deliberately putting forward a one-sided case, and no one in their senses would go to him – or, for that matter, go anywhere else – in order to hear the last word on Shakespeare. Like almost all Victorian critics, he is especially inclined to over-emphasize the dramatist's geniality. But much of what he maintains, even on this score, is substantially true – and no less so for being out of tune with the cruelties and absurdities of current theatrical practice. As a rough likeness, I would say, 'Shakespeare the Individual' fits the facts at least as well as *Shakespeare Our Contemporary*.

One point at least is beyond dispute – Bagehot was more at home with Shakespearian comedy than he was with the tragedies. A bias in the other direction would have been emphatically out of character. In his own writings the violence and horror of life tend to get pushed firmly to the edge of the picture; as a critic, certainly, his finest strokes were comic ones, and the comedy was of the kind which depends on a predominantly mellow atmosphere for its effect. The world was there to be enjoyed. Often in his essays he seems to be arguing by implication against an invisible antagonist, a puritan or malcontent, urging the counter-claims of an enlightened hedonism. Not all that enlightened, either – what hedonism is? 'A slight daily unconscious luxury is hardly ever wanting to the dwellings in civilization; like the gentle air of a genial climate, it is a perpetual minute enjoyment.' As a thrust at the whole romantic cult of the primitive, this may have been amply justified; as the expression of a purely personal *bonhomie*, it may have been healthy-minded and commendably free from humbug. But as a generalization about life in early Victorian England, it was appalling – or would have been, if Bagehot had been thinking of the civilized dwellings in which most of his fellow-countrymen actually dwelt. Naturally no such reference was intended. When he spoke about civilization, it was overwhelmingly the affluent classes whom he had in mind – the other side of the coin being his curt insistence (apropos of Dickens, whom he disliked) that poverty was 'an unfit topic for continuous art'.

He was not usually as explicit as this, and, once under his spell, it is easy to forget how narrow his horizons in fact were, how strong an element of wishful thinking there was in his picture of mid-Victorian stability. The comparison with Trollope, which has often been made, cuts both ways: if the novelist, within his limits, was a penetrating student of political behaviour, the political journalist had more than a touch of the myth-maker. This is almost as true of Bagehot's criticism as it is of his other writings. In an undogmatic, easy-going way, he looked to literature for confirmation of his views on the English character, and what he took to be its essential moderation and respect for law and order. At the most funadmental level, subsequent events have vindicated him: one of the more attractive features of English life remains, as Orwell put it, our habit of not killing one another. But a law-abiding country is not necessarily the same thing as a country at peace with itself. Even within Bagehot's own comparatively short lifetime it became obvious how many of the forces making for social conflict or social change he had glossed over during the 1850s and 1860s. The England of the Palmerstonian era was neither as tranquil nor as pleasant a society as he implies, or as some of his admirers would like to suppose: in the words of the historian W. L. Burn, he represents 'a standing temptation to indulge in selective Victorianism'. Certain major aspects of his age he understood clearly and described brilliantly. But there were many others which were a closed book to him – not least on account of his equanimity and self-assured wit, of qualities which also give his work much of its lasting appeal.

Most of Bagehot's literary essays originally appeared in the leading Unitarian journal of the day, the *Prospective Review*, and in its successor, the *National Review*,* which he founded together with R. H. Hutton (1826–97) in 1855 and edited throughout the nine years of its existence, Hutton acting as co-editor until 1862, when he joined the Church of England. The two men had been close friends since their student days at University College (the one in Gower Street); and it was through Hutton, who preceded him briefly as editor there, that Bagehot first got the idea of offering his services to the *Economist*. Hutton's future lay elsewhere, in more secluded pastures. The son and grandson of Unitarian ministers, he had originally trained for the ministry himself, but after deciding that he lacked a true vocation had switched to journalism instead. For a number of years, in spite of his heavy editorial commitments, he was also professor of mathematics at Bedford College. It was not until 1861, however, that he really came into his own, when together with Meredith Townsend, who had already made his mark as a political journalist in India, he acquired control of the *Spectator*, taking charge of the literary pages while Townsend looked after the front half of the paper. The partnership, which lasted until Hutton's death nearly four decades later, was one of the success-stories of Victorian journalism. After initially losing readers by coming out for Lincoln and the Union against the South, the new *Spectator* quickly established a reputation for blameless sobriety. For thousands of readers it was *the* respectable weekly – a fact much resented by the *Saturday Review*, which scoffed at its public as one sheltering from the boisterous realities of life in leafy rectories and somnolent villas. Cautiously Liberal, the editors gave their blessing to Gladstone (who reciprocated by calling the paper 'one of the few written in the fear and

---

* Not to be confused with the Conservative review of the same name established in 1883 under the editorship of Alfred Austin, later famous for his verses on the Jameson Raid ('*They rode across the veldt/As fast as they could pelt*') and as Poet Laureate. In spite of Austin, and largely thanks to the efforts of the assistant editor, W. J. Courthope, the second *National Review* published some excellent literary material – e.g. most of Leslie Stephen's *Hours in a Library*. Subsequently it became a purely political review, of the most stridently right-wing variety, under the editorship of Leo Maxse, son of Meredith's radical friend Frederick Maxse (see below, p. 102).

love of God'), but broke with him over Home Rule. On the literary side, *Spectator* reviewers, all of them still anonymous, tended to be clergymen, headmasters, dons. An occasional piece from, say, Swinburne might add a touch of unexpected colour, but if one wanted to examine a representative contributor one would have to unearth someone like the Hertfordshire parson and classical scholar the Rev. Alfred Church, whose ruminations appeared in the paper week after week for almost fifty years.

Hutton himself, while much admired as a critic by Tennyson and other eminent contemporaries, was known to the general public primarily as a Christian apologist. He had his worldly interests – he could hardly have been Bagehot's closest friend without them – and his worldly wisdom: in the 1860s, for instance, he wrote a series of clever and distinctly non-mystical parliamentary profiles for the *Pall Mall Gazette*. But religion was beyond all question the overriding concern of his life. His beliefs had not been arrived at lightly. As a young man he had suffered a serious breakdown following the death of his first wife, shortly after their marriage. This in turn led to a prolonged crisis of faith, from which he was finally extricated by the influence of Frederick Denison Maurice, who more than anyone else helped to win him over to the Church of England. Maurice, another former Unitarian, was a liberal theologian and one of the leaders of the Broad Church movement. In his later years, however, Hutton shifted his ground; he came more and more to be regarded as a High Churchman, and towards the end it was often whispered that he was about to convert to Catholicism, chiefly on account of his intense admiration for Newman.

Much of his writing was directly polemical: he kept up a running fight against scientific materialists on the one hand and (with rather more success) against ersatz religions like Positivism on the other. It was inevitable, too, that his theology should spill over into his criticism, especially since he largely confined himself in his literary essays to those contemporary or fairly recent English writers from Wordsworth to Arnold who had set up shop as spiritual preceptors, guides to the perplexed. His actual critical verdicts, however, rarely seem to have been distorted by doctrinaire bias: he might hammer away, for example, at the 'ardent

agnosticism' of George Eliot and her associates, but there was no
novelist whom he rated more highly or wrote about more
perceptively. If fairmindedness and integrity, indeed, were enough
to make a major critic, he would have been one of the most
notable of the nineteenth century. Not that his approach was
exclusively, thumpingly moralistic. He had a feeling for the finer
shades as well: he could trace a writer's shifts of mood with
precision, or fasten on to a striking line of poetry and show in
some detail how it 'worked'. (From such innocent acorns as these
the great oak of Practical Criticism was one day to spring.) In
short, he was the sensitive, sympathetic reader whom authors
dream about. Yet when all his merits have been totted up, he
remains an obstinately uninspiring figure: there is no bite to his
judgements, nothing to lay hold of in his lack-lustre prose. The
comparison with Bagehot is inescapable, and it must always tell
against him. Admittedly of the two it was Hutton who came
closer to being a representative spokesman for educated mid-
Victorian critical opinion; but then in literature, at least, a representative spokesman is surely a rather dismal thing to be.

IV

To turn from Hutton to Leslie Stephen (1832–1904) is a bracing
experience. Although Stephen himself took it for granted that
after his death posterity would quickly consign him to the learned
footnotes, few Victorian prose-writers of the second rank have
in fact worn as well. His accomplishments as editor, biographer,
historian of ideas, essay-writing alpinist are still fairly common
knowledge, while his criticism has a tart flavour which recommends it to modern tastes, and marks him off from all but a tiny
handful of his contemporaries. It is true that latter-day admirers
have sometimes paid too much attention to his purely negative
virtues as a critic, but it must also be conceded that these are an
essential part of his appeal. He knew how to make short work of
mawkishness or affectation. He was expert at showing up im-
postors for what they were. In an age of histrionics he kept a cool
head, and his lack of enthusiasm can be infectious.

Stephen's astringency has often been put down to the intellectual nip in the Cambridge air. He himself was proud to belong to a university which favoured mathematics rather than mysticism, a university where a Newman, let alone a Jowett, would have been judged by the dry light of reason – and found wanting. A follower of John Stuart Mill, in a looser way he can also be thought of as a product of Cambridge rationalism. It is possible, however, to make too much of the *genius loci*. One of Stephen's most ardent modern defenders, Q. D. Leavis, has even gone as far as to label him 'Leslie Stephen, Cambridge Critic'. There seems to be some question of faking a pedigree here, so it is perhaps worth pointing out that 'London critic' would be at least as appropriate a description. If Stephen had remained a don, pushing generations of students through the Tripos, coaching the college eight, presiding over bump suppers, he might never have become a writer at all. As it is, he shouldered the burdens of journalism without complaining – deliberately opted for them, in fact, after his loss of faith had led to him resigning his fellowship. And journalism in turn was able to offer a man of his calibre far better openings than would have been the case twenty years earlier.

His first important connection, secured for him by Fitzjames, was with the *Saturday Review*, which according to Mrs Leavis 'seems to have been a congenial extension of the Cambridge ethos'. Bearing in mind Female Strangulation and much else, we may well feel that if this were altogether true, so much the worse for Cambridge. Fortunately, however, Stephen found the *Saturday* a good deal less congenial than Mrs Leavis suggests. He may have caught the superficial tone of the paper, but he disapproved of most of its policies, and like another dissident contributor, his friend John Morley, he was barred from writing about politics or religion in its pages. Nor was he a reviler by nature. It is true that on one side of his character he was rather impressed by what he praised Bagehot for demonstrating – 'the real value of good, sweeping, outrageous cynicism'. When he first began writing for the *Cornhill*, he chose to sign himself 'A Cynic'. But no one can have been taken in for very long. At heart he was an affectionate man, easily bruised, with none of his brother's truculence. His agnosticism, too, gave him a certain dry detachment, which kept him from committing himself too belligerently to the common assumptions of his class. For a Victorian moralist he was tactful, even circumspect. But whatever his private misgivings may have been, he was not prepared to fly in the face of established convention, and his literary work was to some extent a means of gently disengaging himself from the fray. Starting out as an energetic Liberal, by the 1870s he was ready to settle for political quietism. He did not expect to change the world by writing essays, and there was nothing particularly heroic, in his view, about being a man of letters. Rather, it was a career which called for a decent regular dose of humorous self-depreciation.

The writers who meant the most to him – the only writers, one sometimes feels, who really touched him deeply – were those like Dr Johnson or Wordsworth who offered, as he saw it, fairly direct lessons in fortitude and stoical wisdom. For the rest, he was content with the role of judicious biographer. The one modern critic whom he praised unreservedly was Sainte-Beuve, but he himself approached authors less as a 'naturalist of souls' than as a seasoned judge of character. His curiosity was hemmed in by orthodox taboos, and the deeper riddles or contradictions of a personality were liable to strike him as merely irritating and perverse. However, he was far from being the head prefect which his concern with character-building may make him sound. The judgements are worth having; the clear, effortless style, with its beautifully marshalled detail and glancing ironies, represents in itself a notable mastery of experience.

Furthermore, Stephen's interest in biography goes well beyond that of the miniaturist: his figures are always firmly set down in a landscape. Primarily a historian of ideas, he also pioneered the sociological study of literature in England. Today this method can hardly be considered a blinding novelty: every A-level candidate knows how to examine Tom Moore's slightest lyric in the light of the Industrial Revolution. There is still something to be learned, though, from Stephen's flexibility and natural caution. He might refer to literature as 'the noise that the wheels make as they go round', which sounds as mechanistic an image as anything in Taine, but he was keenly aware of the dangers lurking in oversimplified analogies and monocausal explanations. His long review of Taine's *History of English Literature,* which appeared in the *Fortnightly* in 1873, is one of the most devastating things he ever wrote: on page after page he shows how brutally the Frenchman had had to torture the facts in order to make them fit his pre-ordained theories. The demonstration is all the more convincing in view of his complete agreement with Taine's fundamental doctrine, that 'we ought to study the organism in connection with the medium'. Scientific literary history was both possible and desirable, but to get very far it would require precision instruments which still had to be developed. What was objectionable was Taine's brash assumption that his home-made gadget – *race, milieu, moment* – was already fully adequate to the task.

A contemporary reader who accepted Stephen's detailed criticisms of Taine might nevertheless quite reasonably have felt that his overall severity was out of place. By being so resolutely hostile, he was in effect trying to stifle a new subject in its infancy.* What, after all, were the alternatives? How would *he* have set about relating writers to their social background? Thirty years later, in *English Literature and Society in the Eighteenth Century,* he took up the challenge. The lectures which make up this book – they were delivered at Oxford on his behalf by his nephew H. A. L. Fisher, while he himself lay dying – are modest and tentative in their conclusions, but admirably clear-headed; they sketch out, as no previous English criticism had done, the right lines on which to explore the literary consequences of changes in the economic status of authors and the composition of the reading public. Admittedly this is as far as Stephen ventures. He had very little sense of the subtler ways in which consciousness might be transformed by environment; compared with a modern account like Ian Watt's, for instance, his treatment of the eighteenth-century novel seems two-dimensional. But at least he provided foundations on which others could build.

If the book were no more than a scholarly blueprint, however,

* A similar charge could be levelled against his essay on 'The Cosmopolitan Spirit in Literature' (1899), in which he politely takes apart a pioneering study in Anglo-French literary relations by the French scholar Joseph Texte. He has little trouble in convicting Texte of dubious arguments and faulty parallels. No doubt he is right. Only somehow, by the time he has finished, he has managed to throw cold water over the whole idea of comparative literature as well.

it would have been superannuated long ago. What keeps it alive is Stephen's essential sympathy with his material. Ostensibly the only point he sets out to prove is that the literary history of any period gains by being seen as one strand in a complex social tissue; he does not offer to revise established rankings or pass judgement on the phenomena which he studies. No one could read him for long, though, without detecting a strong undercurrent of regret for lost virtues. He admires the dominant temper of eighteenth-century civilization, and looks back with nostalgia on its relative homogeneity. Where he really warms to his theme is discussing Dr Johnson and the Club. Educated society in Johnson's day had still been compact enough for him to be accepted as literary dictator in the tradition of Ben Jonson, Dryden, Pope. But he was the last of his line – 'men like Carlyle and Macaulay, who had a similar distinction in later days, could only be leaders of a single group or section in the more complex society of their time, though it was not yet so multitudinous and chaotic as the literary class has become in our own'. Stephen believed in facing the facts. He was a modern man, who lectured to Ethical Societies and tried to keep up with modern thought. But his heart lay in the past. Maitland, in his biography, recalls seeing a list of books which Stephen ordered from the London Library during his last illness:

It begins with the names of Réville, Martineau, Brunetière, Flint, Vauvenargues, Vandal, Sabatier, Chateaubriand, Sorel, Pater, Ostrogorski, W. Watson and Dostoieffsky. Some of our biblical critics are there, and Emile Zola. Then, when other books failed, he fell back on the old, old story. Need I name it? He told his nurse that his enjoyment of books had begun and would end with Boswell's 'Life of Johnson'.

Intellectual life has splintered up so much more since Stephen wrote that a like-minded reader today might well feel about his world as he felt about Johnson's. By subsequent standards the Victorian intellectual aristocracy seems remarkably small and tightly-knit: everyone knew everyone else, and was somebody else's brother-in-law. But by comparison with the eighteenth century this aristocracy no longer had the stage to itself, and the days when a whole literature could be governed by the standards of an undisputed *élite* were over. Nor could it be said of Stephen's epoch with anything like as much truth as he said of Johnson's that 'the environment of the man of letters was congenial: he shared and uttered the opinions of the class to which he belonged'. Stephen acknowledges this, and then stops short; where he is disappointing is in his reluctance to apply the sociological method to his own times. Our descendants, he argued, will be able to sort us out into a coherent pattern – and 'meanwhile a Tennyson and a Browning strike us less as the organs of a society than by the idiosyncrasies which belong to them as individuals'. This is a trifle disingenuous, since it is hard to believe that Stephen didn't have *any* ideas about the social significance of his contemporaries. But if he befriended Meredith and encouraged Hardy, he never attempted to write about their work; and in his fine study of George Eliot, though he praises her ability to anatomize a changing society in her novels, he declines to treat the novels themselves as a symptom of further social change. Ultimately he prefers the simpler pieties and humours of *Adam Bede* to the complexities of *Middlemarch*, just like any conventional reviewer of the day.

In this failure to get to grips with the literature of his own time Stephen shows up to disadvantage beside the man he ridiculed, Taine. Taine's picture of nineteenth-century England is lurid and frequently grotesque, but hardly more so than the actual scenes which he was describing; if he goes quaintly wrong on points of detail, he also succeeds in conveying, with a gusto that was quite beyond Stephen, the sheer turmoil of Victorian life, its extravagance and squalor and superabundant energy. His account of the London docks, for instance, has all the murky power of a Doré engraving. And looking at the English business class from the outside, he could appreciate to the full the forces embodied, say, in the unyielding pride of a Mr Dombey. ('To find a parallel we must read again the *Mémoires* of Saint-Simon.') By contrast, Stephen was lukewarm. He had something of his brother's notorious distaste for Dickens; in his article on him for the *Dictionary of National Biography* he makes the Fitzjamesian observation that 'if literary fame could be measured by popularity with the half-educated, Dickens must claim the highest position among English novelists'. This is the son of Sir James Stephen, K.C.B., speaking, and he is *not* prepared to forgive the Circumlocution Office.

Stephen's attitude to Arnold is equally revealing. He admired him and learned a great deal from him, but he insisted on drawing the sting from his social criticism. However trenchantly Arnold had satirized the ugliness and coarseness of the Philistines, he had done so in the spirit 'of one who recognized the monster was after all a most kindly monster at bottom'. It would be difficult to put the matter more complacently. On the other hand Stephen's own 'philistinism' has its sympathetic side. Certainly it saved him from self-righteousness and the wrong kind of critical intransigence. The more irreconcilable modern opponents of mass culture are fond of quoting his remark that 'really the value of second-rate literature is nil'; they conveniently overlook the fact that on another occasion he could reflect that 'all books are good, that is to say there is scarcely any book that may not serve as a match to fire our enthusiasm'. Must one point out that neither statement is meant to be taken entirely literally, or treated as absolute dogma? Yes, I suppose one must – as though it were not the most natural thing in the world to feel in certain moods that only a handful of writers are ultimately worth bothering with, and at other times that a diet of nothing but the classics would be intolerable.

In any case, it would have been unbecoming for the editor of the *Cornhill* to have campaigned too vigorously against second-rate literature, since that, after all, was the staple commodity in which he dealt. During Stephen's term of office, which lasted from 1871 to 1882, the magazine continued to publish work by most of the leading writers of the day: Arnold, Hardy, Henry James were among his contributors. But this is very far from saying that every number contained fiction of the quality of *Washington Square* or *Far From the Madding Crowd*. Much more characteristic were such offerings as *Zelda's Fortune* and *White Wings: A Yachting Romance*. No doubt Stephen would ideally have preferred to print masterpieces, but he soldiered on; and though he might grumble about having to blue-pencil Hardy ('delete "amorous" substitute "sentimental" ') in order to placate his public, for the most part he went along quite happily with their views on the proprieties. Nor was he at all averse himself, as a reader, to a nice old-fashioned romantic wallow, with wedding-bells ringing out in Chapter the

Last. The level of non-fiction in the *Cornhill*, on the other hand, was kept as high as he could afford under the middlebrow circumstances. As high, or higher: an audience which thrilled to the fortunes of Zelda was easily bored by John Addington Symonds on Italian art or Birkbeck Hill's Johnsonian studies or Stephen's own 'Hours in a Library', and the magazine's circulation, which was around 25,000 when he became editor, had been more than halved by the time he resigned. His successor, James Payn, an old friend from Eton and Cambridge days, was a popular novelist without any intellectual pretensions who was called in by the publishers in an effort to win back lost readers.* Although the editorship had never been more for Stephen than a part-time job, a respectable source of income while he got on with his own books, he was irked at the thought of failure. True, before leaving he had at any rate managed to discover one new contributor of real promise in Robert Louis Stevenson. But even he was not an author whom he could take all that seriously. Looking back near the end of his life, he disagreed with critics like Henry James who had praised the deepening psychological penetration of Stevenson's later stories, and plumped firmly for *Treasure Island* as his finest work.

Did he recognize at the same time that the whole mainstream Victorian literary tradition was drying up? Whatever forebodings he may have had he kept to himself. For ten years, after giving up the *Cornhill*, his energies had largely been devoted to organizing the *Dictionary of National Biography*, and his thoughts largely fixed on the past. The *D.N.B.* remains his most enduring achievement. It is also a monument to the more attractive side of Victorian private enterprise: a sixty-three-volume colossus, mainly written by freelance scholars and financed by George Smith out of his own pocket. (Not that Smith didn't have the money to spare: quite apart from his publishing ventures, he is supposed to have made over £1,000,000 out of the British concession for Apollinaris.) A generation earlier, Matthew Arnold, in his essay on Academies,

---

* Payn's prosperous career might be summed up as everything that Gissing's wasn't. In the course of the literary recollections which he wrote for the *Cornhill* he remarks that there is less jealousy among authors than in any other profession – a view which has not yet been confirmed by subsequent research.

had been able to cite the shoddiness of English biographical diction-
aries as a self-evident example of how much better they ordered
these things in France. After Stephen and his team had done their
work, such a reproach would have been impossible. Scholarship is
cumulative, and inevitably the *D.N.B.* has been overtaken by
research in the course of eighty years. But it is still one of the most
serviceable of all reference-books, and – as anyone who has ever
been side-tracked by it will testify – one of the most beguiling.

For Stephen himself it represented both a triumph and a retreat.
In 1882 he had published his most ambitious book, *The Science of
Ethics*. It was not a success; and in embarking on the *Dictionary* he
was putting his gifts to more appropriate if less adventurous use.
He might preach post-Darwinian ethics, but he felt more at home
with the limited certainties of the obituary column. As Noel Annan
has pointed out, for an evolutionary thinker he was strangely indifferent to the actual mechanisms of social change; and the whole
self-defeating idea of a science of ethics, although it may have
answered the immediate emotional needs of men who had only
just shaken off their religion, seems completely at odds with his
own traditional practice as a moralist. There is nothing very
obviously scientific about the flexible common sense which
informs most of his literary work. He rode with the positivist tide,
but he was too sane to suppose that irrefutable moral judgements
could ever be arrived at by looking them up in a ready-reckoner.
Nietzsche might have had him in mind when he wrote, in *Beyond
Good and Evil*, that

moral sensibility in Europe today is just as subtle, ancient, manifold, sensitive, and refined as the 'science of morality' that goes with it is young,
raw, clumsy, and inept. This is a fascinating opposition which occasionally takes on colour and flesh in the person of some moralist.

Which is another way of saying that Stephen himself was often
more impressive than his ideas. There is a constant hint about him
of unused capacity, reserve power. Thomas Hardy sensed it when
he wrote the sonnet comparing him to the 'spare and desolate'
Schreckhorn which he had been the first to climb. Meredith
sensed it when he put him into *The Egoist* as the laconic tutor
Vernon Whitford, with his 'sunken brilliancy'. To such men he

was potentially a hero. But the hints remained hints, the reserve was never to be lowered. Fifty years after Meredith, Stephen's daughter portrayed him as Mr Ramsay in *To the Lighthouse* – a Vernon Whitford grown old and querulous and hypersensitive, a disappointed man. Mr Ramsay is the utilitarian as he appeared to a generation of aesthetes, forever going on about 'reality' as though it were a hard, angular, well-scrubbed kitchen table, blind to the flamingo clouds of the imagination. In his cut-and-dried fashion he thinks of philosophy in terms of the alphabet. He can run through the letters up to Q (and 'very few people in the whole of England ever reach Q'). But there he sticks. 'Z is only reached by one mind in a generation. Still, if he could reach R it would be something.' On then to R. But it eludes him, and by his own marking-system he is a failure. He is also the prisoner of his own critical habits of thought. When he goes to bed after the dinner-party which marks the climax of the first half of the novel, he picks up a volume of Scott. Downstairs they have been saying that nobody reads Scott any more, and all he can think of as he opens the book is that they will soon be saying the same about him. He is feeling thoroughly sorry for himself. Then, as he reads on, he is completely absorbed, slapping his thighs at the humour. The book entrances him – and 'now, he felt, it didn't matter a damn who reached Z'. He is reading for the love of it, all thoughts of the professional critic put to one side. But not for long. A few reflections about morality and English novels and French novels and the contrast between Scott and Balzac start to intrude, and though he tries to keep his mind on the story he is soon fretting again over whether or not his own books are still admired by the Young.

To the Lighthouse is a work of fiction, not an autobiography; equally, Mr Ramsay is an irritable paterfamilias seen through the eyes of childhood, not a public man studied by an impartial ob-server. Virginia Woolf herself was capable of appraising her father's character far more favourably, as she was to show in the tribute (reprinted in *The Captain's Death-Bed*) which she wrote on the centenary of his birth. Still, the fact remains that Mr Ramsay *is* Stephen, at one remove: a Stephen who could never get beyond Q. A little more personal resonance, one feels, a higher degree of social involvement, and his criticism might have ranked beside

Arnold's. As it is, he played safe: he is the Gentleman in the Library, content not to ask too many embarrassing questions. This sets a definite limit on his value to posterity. Unlike Arnold, he never seems an indispensable critic – except, that is, in the sense of there being no finer example of his type available. Without him, we should scarcely have guessed quite how formidable a Gentleman in a Library could be.

V

In their different ways Lewes and Bagehot, Hutton and Stephen were all unmistakably mid-Victorian figures; taken together, they speak eloquently for the standards of the audience which they served. But it would clearly be absurd to judge the whole of Victorian literary journalism by what they achieved: they represent the apex of the profession. Meanwhile life on the lower slopes went on much as it always has. Yet even here the high literary ideals of the age could cast an unexpected glow. Take the case of James Hannay (1827–73), in many respects a classic Grub Street casualty. Pitchforked into the world as a boy he joined the navy, quit at the age of eighteen after being unjustly court-martialled, and decided to try his luck as a writer. Obscure comic papers gave him a bare living; his nautical experiences were turned into picaresque novels; he graduated as that most forlorn of creatures, an English Humorist. 'The English humorists!' V. S. Pritchett has written. 'Through a fog compounded of tobacco smoke, the stink of spirits and the breath of bailiffs, we see their melancholy faces.' Such was the atmosphere in which Hannay moved when he first came to London, flitting from one furnished room to the next but never getting very far from Covent Garden. Then, in the 1850s, he began to prosper. An ardent Carlylean, he hired the Edwards Street Institution, where Carlyle had lectured on Hero-Worship fifteen years earlier, and scored a modest success with his own set of lectures on *Satire and Satirists*. Thackeray, his other great idol, gave him a useful introduction to the *Quarterly*, while his electioneering work for the Tories in Scotland secured him the editorship of the *Edinburgh Courant*, a post which he held for five quarrelsome years until he was invited to join the staff of the newly-founded *Pall Mall*. By this time, however, he was sinking into alcoholism, and his pen shook in his hand. His political patrons came to the rescue and had him appointed British consul in Barcelona, where he piled up debts, neglected his duties, and systematically drank himself to death. Apart from his novels he left behind a mass of uncollected journalism, a study of Thackeray, and a *Course of English Literature* which had originally appeared in weekly instalments in the *Welcome Guest*, a short-lived penny magazine published by Vizetelly and edited by George Augustus Sala.

Hannay is of course no more than a very minor period curiosity – the most curious thing about him being how naturally he fell into the tones of earnest didacticism in the midst of so much shabby dissipation. The *Course of English Literature*, which he himself described as 'an incitement to a course' rather than a comprehensive syllabus, is much more intelligently written than the average handbook. It displays considerable learning, inculcates a decent respect for historical scholarship, and makes some strenuous demands on the aspiring student. Any reader of the *Welcome Guest* who followed Hannay's instructions to the letter would have been better educated than many a modern B.A.(Hons.) by the time he was finished.

The most inveterate of Hannay's journalistic enemies, Edmund Yates (1831–94), was another humorist – and one without an ounce of earnestness in him. Yates's early background was not unlike G. H. Lewes's. He came from a well-known theatrical family, but his parents were anxious for him to follow a more settled career, and found him a position with the Post Office, where he eventually rose to become Head of the Missing Letter department. At the same time he steadily pushed his way ahead in Fleet Street. It was while reading *Pendennis* that he had first set his heart on journalism – ironically, since he was to earn his one secure footnote in literary history by lampooning Thackeray, getting himself expelled from the Garrick, and triggering off a notorious quarrel between Thackeray and Dickens as a consequence. His real forte was malicious Society chit-chat: he has a strong claim to be considered the inventor of the modern gossip-column, the spiritual great-grandfather of Paul Slickey. In his own words, the articles which he wrote as a young man under the pseudonym of 'The Lounger at the Clubs' were 'the commencement of that style of personal journalism which is so very much to be deprecated and so enormously popular'. Subsequently he ran a weekly newspaper column as '*Le Flâneur*'; later still – in 1874 – he founded the *World*, 'a journal for men and women', which meant in effect that it specialized in sailing close to the wind. One particular libel, on Lord Lonsdale, went too far, and Yates found himself in jail. But he soon bounced back again. On his release, two hundred friends gave a banquet for him at the Criterion; and the *World* remained the most popular society magazine of the period.

Anyone who thinks of journalism before Newnes and North-cliffe as uniformly dignified ought to keep a portrait of Yates near at hand – preferably the one he himself chose as the frontis-piece for his memoirs, which shows him looking up from his desk with a beady eye and a knowing leer. The memoirs them-selves are admittedly still quite readable, in their low-minded way, especially when he sets about paying off old scores – against Lewes, for example, whom he had known since the Cyder Cellar days, and whose rise in the world he plainly resented. But after a few pages one is glad to get away from him. He was a shady customer, with his tricks and schemes and smoking-room confidences; ulti-mately the thought of him rather turns one's stomach. And yet shady customers have their uses too: in the prevailing moral climate of the 1880s a more respectable editor might have hesi-tated for a very long time indeed before taking men like Shaw and William Archer on to his staff and letting them write pretty much as they chose. Shaw at any rate thought so. Some of his finest work – the articles later republished as *Music in London, 1890–1894* – originally appeared in the *World*, and he was duly if sardonically grateful. As he explained to Yates's successor:

You know exactly what Yates was; and you will see, if you consider the matter for a moment from any point of view, that he and I suited one another extraordinarily well. He felt, without perhaps knowing it definitely, that what the clubs & the country houses & the respectable middle classes want is blasphemous, seditious, licentious, completely emancipated, thoroughly human & unmoral papers, made perfectly presentable, and guaranteed as the correct social thing. . . . When Yates engaged me he did not ask me any questions as to my speculative beliefs; but the opinions of Archer, myself & Theodore Child [the Paris correspondent of the *World*, and a close friend of Henry James] were as obviously identical on leading social topics as if we had all passed a rigid test examination to qualify ourselves for entrance to hell.

Shortly after Yates's death, Shaw severed his connection with the *World*; but within a few months he was working for a man who exemplified even more strikingly the truth that brigands sometimes make the best editors. Frank Harris (1856–1931) was much noisier and more generally overpowering than Yates, much more of a blatant beast. He was, in short, Frank Harris. But the two men had their affinities, and once his heyday was past Harris took to editing scandal-sheets in the Yatesian tradition. One of them was called *The Candid Friend*; another, *Modern Society*, landed him briefly in Brixton for contempt of court – an episode he used to refer to as his martyrdom. This was in the period of his decline, however; at his zenith he reached heights which a Yates could never have scaled. After originally making a name for himself on the *Evening News*, he talked the proprietors of the *Fortnightly Review* into appointing him editor, a post which had only recently been vacated by the bleakly puritanical John Morley. An implausible conjunction, though no more implausible than most things about Harris. At any rate, he never made any secret of his contempt for his predecessor and for high Victorian journalism generally. In his autobiography he records a conversation to this effect – a characteristic Imaginary Conversation, by the sound of it – with Henry James. He alleges that James said to him, 'I regard Mr Morley and Mr Leslie Stephen as the first men of letters in England', to which he replied crushingly that, on the contrary, they were uncreative mediocrities, 'only hodmen and incapable of conception'. Whether anything remotely resembling this exchange ever in fact took place we shall never know; but by his own lights Harris did try to rejuvenate the *Fortnightly* during the eight years he remained in charge there.

It was with the purchase of the *Saturday Review*, however, that he really came into his kingdom. After the death of the original owner that paper had passed into the hands of a rich lawyer with no experience of journalism. Quick to scent an opening, Harris put in a successful bid, scraped together the necessary capital in a matter of days, and installed himself as editor. His first action on taking over was to get rid of the entire existing staff: in H. G. Wells's *Experiment in Autobiography* there is a memorable account of him summoning them one by one to his office, bawling insults at them at close range, and hustling them downstairs, never to return. Then he began building up a formidable editorial team of his own. Making Shaw his drama critic was his most inspired *coup*; other leading contributors included Wells, Cunninghame Graham, Beerbohm (who eventually succeeded Shaw) and the art-critic D. S. MacColl, then fighting the battles of Impressionism in a world still ruled by academicians. For younger readers in particular it must have seemed like a break in the clouds. No more staid men with sound views, no more suffocating gentility. And no retreat in the face of opposition pressures: when publishers, indignant at the severity of Harris's reviewers, started cancelling their advertisements, he simply made good the loss by persuading South African millionaires to publish their company reports in his columns instead. For four crowded years, he kept the sparks flying; then something went obscurely wrong, and he resigned. After his departure the paper stumbled along, changing direction several times and finally collapsing in the 1930s amid the fascistic eccentricities of its last owner, Lady Houston. It had managed to keep going for almost exactly eighty years. But it is a sign of Harris's success that if its name means anything today, except to students of Victorian history, it is on account of his brief editorship. The journal created by Fitzjames Stephen and Maine and all the other original *Saturday* reviewers survives in popular memory as a leader of the revolt against everything for which they stood.

4

SOME LIBERAL
PRACTITIONERS

I

There were closer links between literature and public life in
Victorian England that can readily be realized in our own more
complex, more compartmentalized world. Statesmen wrote
learned works in their spare time; authors were lured into party
politics. Consider, for example, how many nineteenth-century
historians also served (with varying degrees of success) as Members
of Parliament: among others, Grote, Macaulay, Acton, G. O.
Trevelyan, Lecky, Bryce. Or, from another angle, think of
Gladstone, with his *Homeric Studies*, his lifelong passion for Dante,
his unflagging literary interests. In the 1830s his first book was
praised by Wordsworth and made the occasion for a famous
Edinburgh article by Macaulay, 'Gladstone on Church and State';
fifty years later, his review of *Robert Elsmere* ('Weg on Bobbie')
was the talk of the day; in the midst of parliamentary business he
somehow found time to write about Tennyson and Leopardi.
Nor was he altogether unique. His culture was essentially traditional Oxford culture, shared (though seldom with the same
intensity) by other educated members of the governing class,
Liberal and Conservative alike. Among the Tories, Disraeli is a
case apart, but all the Conservative prime ministers of the
Victorian and Edwardian period were men of some literary or
scholarly attainment. Peel, like Gladstone, was a Double First;
Derby beguiled his leisure translating the *Iliad* into blank verse;
Salisbury was a *Saturday* Reviewer; Balfour had ambitions as a
philosopher. There were, in fact, literati (and illiterati) on both

sides of the House. Even so, it was undoubtedly the Liberals who had the stronger literary connections. They attracted idealistic support, and at the same time they offered far more scope to ambitious middle-class intellectuals. There were a good many clever Conservatives, but there was no Conservative equivalent to a career like that of Gladstone's biographer John Morley.

Morley (1838–1923) was the son of a doctor from Blackburn. He grew up in a rigidly religious atmosphere, and unlike his friend Leslie Stephen he had to pay a heavy personal price for his loss of faith. His father cut him off completely, and he left Oxford forced to make his own way in the world, without money or influence. Journalism would never have been his first choice as a profession; he had hoped to become a lawyer, but that was now out of the question. So he took lodgings in Staple Inn and went the rounds of editorial offices. The early days were difficult and obscure; then he was spotted by Cook, and enlisted as a *Saturday* Reviewer – out of tune with the paper's politics, but proud enough of his miscellaneous articles to have them collected and published (although later he was glad that he had brought them out anonymously and wanted to disown them). His years on the *Saturday* were more exciting intellectually than professionally: he became a close friend of Stephen and Meredith, while Mill and George Eliot both took a liking to him. But he was still unknown to the general public when, at the end of 1866, the intervention of an old Oxford acquaintance, Cotter Morison,* secured him the editorship of the *Fortnightly*. At the time he replaced Lewes he was only twenty-eight.

It was a gamble which paid off: his fifteen years in charge of the paper were as distinguished an editorial term of office as any in the nineteenth century. He succeeded partly on account of innate managerial prudence (that sharp face!), partly because he felt convinced that he had something momentous to say. Under his control, the *Fortnightly* quickly came to be recognized as an un- rivalled platform for the advanced thought of the period. Tighten-

---

* J. Cotter Morison (1832–88), historian, Positivist, *Saturday* Reviewer. He was the son of Morison 'the Hygeist', who made a fortune out of Morison's Universal Pill (satirized in *Past and Present*) and founded the British College of Health in New Road.

ing up the loosely liberal policies of his predecessor, but without allowing himself to be diverted into mere sectarian propaganda, he contrived to give his readers the sense that they were riding a great central wave of Progress, intellectual, scientific and political all in one. He also believed in offering value for money: the roll-call of *Fortnightly* contributors over the years includes dozens of famous or once-famous names, but it scarcely conveys how much Morley managed to pack into individual numbers. To take a random instance, the issue for January, 1873, runs to 148 closely-printed pages. It contains lengthy articles by Mill on Aristotle, by Henry Maine on Indian legislation, by Frederic Harrison on 'The Revival of Authority', and by Edmund Gosse (aged twenty-three) on 'Ibsen, the Norwegian Satirist', as well as four chapters of the current serial, *The Eustace Diamonds*, Swinburne's 'Memorial Verses' to Gautier, and an intelligent piece on *Middlemarch* by Sidney Colvin. Other items include a review of William Morris, a long critical essay on the House of Lords, and an editorial angrily denouncing the imprisonment of a group of gas-stokers who had been convicted for trying to organize a strike.

The article on Aristotle was only one of a series which Mill contributed; during the closing years of his life, in fact, he wrote exclusively for Morley. He saw in the *Fortnightly* the kind of effective spearhead for progressive opinion which he had once hoped, prematurely, to make out of the *Westminster*, and the review in turn faithfully reflected most of his own leading ideas. Another influential senior contributor was Thomas Huxley, whose paper on 'The Physical Basis of Life' (1869) created a furore when it first appeared which Morley compares in his *Recollections* to the excitement stirred up 'in a political epoch' by *The Conduct of the Allies* or Burke on the French Revolution. As this implies, initially the *Fortnightly* was famous not so much for its radicalism as for its devout rationalism, that opium of the mid-Victorian intellectuals. But every epoch is a political epoch, and the pressures of social controversy also made themselves felt from the first. The fast-ripening friendship between Morley and the slightly older Frederic Harrison counted for a good deal in this respect, especially in the early days: Harrison may not have succeeded, contrary to popular legend, in turning the *Fortnightly* into the organ of doctrinaire Positivism, but he was certainly instrumental in gingering up its politics. (It was on his account, for instance, that Morley agreed to look into the case of the jailed gas-stokers.) Even more decisive, a little later on, was Morley's alliance with Joseph Chamberlain, which dates from their first meeting in 1873, and which set the political tone of the *Fortnightly* for the rest of the decade. Militant 'anti-theology' remained the most notorious single plank of the paper's programme, and Morley himself continued to be best known to the general public as the man who spelt God with a small 'g'. The days when he was to be equally famous for spelling Gladstone with a big 'G' still lay ahead. But by the time he gave up the editorship in 1882 he had been widely marked down as somebody with an obvious future in politics, a leading spirit, along with Chamberlain and Dilke, of the powerful new radical wing of the Liberal party.

In literature as in thought the *Fortnightly* plumed itself on being the champion of the enlightened minority. The hour had come, Morley believed, for a cool reappraisal of the established great names of the previous generation: Dickens, Tennyson, Carlyle. On the other hand Browning, still scolded by most critics for his obscurity, was given whole-hearted support, and the more gifted younger writers of the day usually found a welcome. There were articles by Pater and John Addington Symonds, poems by William Morris and Rossetti, regular eruptions in both verse and prose from Swinburne. The contemporary author who meant most to Morley, though, was undoubtedly Meredith, a frequent contributor – he once deputized as editor for three months while Morley was away in America – and a lifelong friend, apart from an early quarrel triggered off by Morley's excessive touchiness. Towards the end of his career Meredith planned to write a novel called *The Journalist*, in which Morley was to have been one of the main characters, but eventually the scheme was abandoned. Something of the general flavour of high-minded radicalism around 1870 can be caught, however, in one of his best novels, *Beauchamp's Career*, which originally appeared as a serial in the *Fortnightly* (1874-5) after having been turned down by the *Cornhill*. The general flavour, and the general disarray. Nevil Beauchamp's headlong career as a Radical candidate (based on that of Meredith's old friend Commander Maxse) is ardent, idealistic, chivalrous – and ultimately futile. He revolts against the ancestral Toryism of his background, but he feels equally out of place among the Liberals, who are characterized by his mentor, the grizzled republican Dr Shrapnel, as 'Tories with foresight, Radicals without faith'. They are presented as sluggish, undependable, the party of compromise. Yet in real life where else was there for a young radical to turn, if he hoped to achieve practical results? The novel despairs of finding a solution, and Nevil plunges gallantly to his death in the closing chapter. Commander Maxse, more prosaically, lived on: he was the man responsible for arranging the first meeting between Morley and Chamberlain.

In his memoirs Morley celebrates Meredith in his best alabaster prose, as 'Phoebus Apollo descending upon us from Olympus'. The attraction which the novelist's lyrical paganism had for him is plain enough: he saw it, theoretically at least, as a desirable emotional counterpoise to the austerities of free thought. There was paganism and paganism, however, and some varieties were apparently much less acceptable than others. Almost the only piece of Morley's literary criticism at all widely remembered today is his frantic attack on Swinburne's *Poems and Ballads* in the *Saturday Review*, which led to the volume being withdrawn by an apprehensive publisher. In view of this, it may seem strange that as an editor he should have been so well disposed to Swinburne, even if it was to the barricade-storming Swinburne of *Songs Before Sunrise*. But the truth is that his outburst against *Poems and Ballads* was not really a very characteristic performance. For one thing, his language is so shrill that it often sounds like a deliberate parody of the style which is being denounced. Swinburne is 'the libidinous laureate of a pack of satyrs', in addition to being 'an unclean fiery imp of the pit' who is accused of 'tuning his lyre in a sty'. In part this is no doubt the hysterical excitement of a puritan scenting danger, comparable to Morley's revulsion from the more perfervid passages in Rousseau ('a vision of the horrid loves of heavy-eyed and scaly shapes that haunted the warm primeval ooze'). Yet by the end of the piece one is also left wondering whether he was really so very upset by 'Faustine' or 'Laus Veneris' after all, whether he didn't in fact rather welcome the chance to let himself go. A certain barely conscious cynicism, too, may have suggested to him that wielding the hatchet is one way to make your mark. At any rate, he had no permanent quarrel with Swinburne's poetry, any more than he did with the whole drift towards aestheticism, provided it kept within respectable bounds. His review of the first edition of *The Renaissance* (1873) is more representative than the *Poems and Ballads* fandango. He commends Pater for trying to drive a wedge into 'the prodigious block of our philistinism', and also for a slightly more unexpected reason:

That a serious writer should thus raise aesthetic interest to the throne lately filled by religion only shows how void the old theologies have become.

At the same time he is quick to point out that aestheticism can never hope to be more than a creed for half-days and holidays: our ordinary working lives are necessarily cut out of 'homespun substance', and Pater's gospel must be understood to apply exclusively to 'what remains seriously for a man to do and feel, over and above earning his living and respecting the laws'. It is the tired businessman who is supposed to burn with a hard gemlike flame.

Only because he thought it signalled the impending death of religion proper was Morley able to look so kindly on the religion of art. He once confided to an associate that he 'liked drab men best', and certainly it strains the imagination to picture him deciding to help usher in an era of peacocks and pomegranates as a deliberate act of policy. To some extent he was simply carried along by an irresistible tide: ideally he would no doubt have preferred to publish young poets and critics with a firm radical commitment, but fewer and fewer seemed to come forward. For his own part he remained unaffected by his juniors, holding fast to the conviction that literature was 'a weapon and an arm, not merely a liberal art', and criticism essentially a branch of intellectual history. His most ambitious literary works, the studies of Voltaire, Rousseau and Diderot, were primarily undertaken in order to extend and also to Europeanize the intellectual pedigree of Victorian liberalism; and if they are of no great interest today, at the time they represented more of an advance than a modern reader might casually assume. Voltaire was still commonly regarded as a bogeyman, an intellectual libertine with a wicked grin; the Enlightenment as a whole was still largely viewed through a haze of English – and Anglican – prejudice. As late as the 1890s Lord Acton could decide against asking Morley to contribute to the volume of the *Cambridge Modern History* covering the French Revolution because he was afraid that Bishop Stubbs would make trouble if he did. And in the 1870s not only were there ecclesiastical objections to be reckoned with; in addition, a reading public reared on Carlyle had to be persuaded to start looking at the Revolution calmly and analytically. Carlyle himself is the subject of one of Morley's more severe essays. He is given credit for rousing his readers to a justified if nebulous sense of crisis, but denied a permanent place in 'the central march of European thought and feeling': his books, which once seemed so epoch-making, are now of purely historical interest. Morley's chief complaint against him is that he has no respect for the evidence when it fails to fire his imagination. Why should society be considered an open book to a reader, however impassioned, who brought to it 'neither patience nor calm accuracy of meditation'? Why should it remain 'the one field of thought in which a man of genius is at liberty to assume all his major premises, and swear all his conclusions'?

The self-assertive prophet, it would seem, must give way to the social scientist and the trained professional historian. But not, as yet, to the practical critic: at least, Morley himself, in his essays, shows very little patience with the living detail of literature. Like many another literary ideologue, he is deeply in love with the idea of centrality. Writers are important to him chiefly in so far as they can be said to urge forward 'the central current of thought' in their society, and often he talks as though there were only room for one current at a time. Dante was the poet of Catholicism, who handed over the torch to Shakespeare, the poet of Feudalism, who passed it on to Milton, the poet of Protestantism; Byron spoke for Revolution, until he was temporarily vanquished by Carlyle, etc. The *haecceitas* of an author, the qualities which make him worth reading rather than merely worth reading about, are a secondary consideration: what really counts is his contribution o the March of Mind. For all things tend towards a final liberation of the spirit. The sun is breaking through the clouds, the cobwebs are being swept away, and Morley's favourite humanistic hymn can be heard rising in the background:

> *Edel sei der Mensch,*
> *Hilfreich und gut!*

Rationalists, too, have their prophetic moods: it was only a dream, but a potent dream while it lasted.

Not that the young Morley cherished any mystical beliefs about progress coming to pass of its own automatic accord. It took immense 'social energy' to change the world – and immense 'social patience' as well. 'The wise innovator', he wrote in his essay *On Compromise* (1874), was the man who had learned how 'to seize the chance of a small improvement, while working incessantly in the direction of great ones'. What most impressed his original readers, it is true, was his rigorous insistence on intellectual honesty at virtually any cost. Opinions were sacred. But as soon as he turned from theory to practice, he was ready to moderate his demands. The real problem, as he saw it, was how best to distinguish between the legitimate and the illegitimate half-measure; *On Compromise* has recently been described – by Alan Bullock and Maurice Shock, in the introduction to their anthology *The Liberal Tradition* – as fundamentally 'an exposition of the technique of gradualism ... pointing to the path which British politics have followed during the age of democracy'. And if this does credit to Morley's statesmanlike instincts, it also helps to explain why the book has not become the minor classic which he evidently intended it to be. There is too absolute a divorce in his mind between the worlds of belief and action, too glaring a discrepancy between his air of inflexible probity and his underlying caution. It shows up in the frigid rhetoric.

In a more general way his writing fails to convince because it is too obviously contrived, because (perhaps only with the wisdom of hindsight) one can hear behind it the steady tick of personal ambition. Before he had fully committed himself to the idea of a parliamentary career, Matthew Arnold urged him to stay on the sidelines as a political commentator – 'a proud and very useful place, where you would be more useful, happier, more yourself, than in Parliament'. For a while it looked as though he might follow Arnold's advice: in 1880 he became editor of the *Pall Mall Gazette*. But the lure of Westminster was too strong, and after two unsuccessful attempts he finally won a seat in the Commons in 1883. Three years later Gladstone appointed him Chief Secretary for Ireland.

It was not only through his own writings and through the *Fortnightly* that Morley helped to shape the literary outlook of his contemporaries. As early as the mid-1860s he had begun to act as a reader for Macmillan's, and for many years he was to be their senior literary adviser. From Hardy to *The Golden Bough*, most of the firm's major acquisitions passed through his hands, while in 1877 he was put in charge of the new *English Men of Letters* series. These were years in which sets of brief biographies were starting to appear on every side – *English Worthies, Men of Action, Famous Scots, Heroes of the Nations*; Morley himself also edited *Twelve English Statesmen* for Macmillan's. But the *Men of Letters* project was more successful than any of its rivals. The first series ran to thirty-nine titles, and at a fee of £100 per volume Morley was able to recruit most of the leading critics of the day. Admittedly the very biggest names eluded him: he failed to enlist Arnold, and George Eliot, after some hesitation, declined to take on Shakespeare – one of the more intriguing might-have-beens of criticism. (She spoke highly of the first volumes when they appeared, especially of Hutton's *Scott*, which she read aloud to Lewes.) Several of Morley's more enterprising strokes came off, however; Huxley on Hume, Sir Richard Jebb on Bentley, the relatively youthful Henry James Jr on Hawthorne.* Other contributors included various close friends, such as Leslie Stephen,

---

* It would be wrong to infer from this that Morley properly understood or appreciated James, who had in fact originally been taken on as a Macmillan author against his advice. Asked by the firm for an opinion on the essays which make up *French Poets and Novelists*, he reported: 'Of charm, delicacy, finesse, they have none.' If this had been intended as a deliberate piece of Lifemanship, it would surely have put Morley straight into the same class as Hope-Tipping, who will be remembered for his masterly strictures on D. H. Lawrence's neglect of the sexual relationship, and on 'the almost open sadism of Charles Lamb'.

who supplied studies of Swift, Pope and Dr Johnson, and Cotter Morison, who tackled Gibbon and Macaulay. Morley's old Oxford tutor, Professor Fowler, was assigned John Locke, while the Rector of his old college, Mark Pattison, agreed to write the volume on Milton – and took the opportunity to make his famous conversation-stopping remark about an appreciation of that poet being 'the last reward of consummated scholarship'.

To some extent subjects as well as authors provide an index of Morley's own personal inclinations. His basically condescending attitude towards fiction, for instance, is apparent from some of the more obvious gaps – no Richardson, no Jane Austen, no Charlotte Brontë. The dramatists, too, are neglected: no Marlowe or Ben Jonson (although Sheridan scrapes by, perhaps because he was also a politician). On the other hand philosophers and historians are comparatively well represented, while the influence of the grand old fortifying classical curriculum can be seen reflected equally in the choice of Bentley as a subject and of Pattison as a contributor. Morley also felt that it was necessary to include at least one 're-cognized divine' in his team – 'for respectability's sake' – and duly commissioned Dean Church to write on Spenser. He could have spared himself the anxiety: even without a Dean, the series would have been respectability itself. Right from the start, it was accorded semi-official status, and for a couple of generations it remained an unfailing standby for harassed teachers and conscientious students. No comparable series has ever come so close to attaining the rank of a traditional British institution. In *Some People*, the unlovable J. D. Marstock keeps a complete set on his mantelpiece while cramming for his Foreign Office examination, a long row of thin yellow Men of Letters and square red ones: ' "My tutor," Marstock would say, "told me that the examiners expect one to have read the E.M. of L.S." '

The square red volumes on which Marstock was relying were a second series, started in 1902 with Morley as adviser though no longer as editor. Commercially they were a considerable success, largely because most of the great Victorians were by now dead and eligible for inclusion. Chesterton's volume on Browning did particularly well. But on the whole the earlier series is the more distinguished. It has its duds (Principal Shairp on Burns, for instance, is more insipid than one would have thought possible), and that it should contain a study of permanent literary value in James's *Hawthorne* is only an accident. Generally, though, the level of workmanship is high. Most of the early volumes are well-proportioned and solidly constructed, and if they were partly designed with the growing demand for textbooks in mind, they manage to keep the fact decently disguised.

In so far as they *were* put to educational use, Morley himself entirely approved. He was one of the leading supporters of the campaign to secure full recognition for English as a university subject, as well as being a firm believer in evening classes and extension lectures for the under-privileged, where literature obviously had an important role to play. Properly taught, indeed, nothing could do more for the betterment of the masses. The patronizing language seems appropriate in the context: his intentions were honourable, but with the masses themselves he had very little direct sympathy. Despite its intriguing title, his lecture 'On Popular Culture' (1876) turns out to be a conventional plea for encouraging adult education: anyone hoping to hear much about folklore or craftsmanship or working-class entertainment will be sorely disappointed. (Mr Raymond Williams ought to add this particular linguistic specimen to his collection.) What Morley wanted was 'to make industrial England a sharer in the classic tradition of the lettered world', to pour academic culture down its throat. His Mansion House address 'On the Study of Literature' (1887) is equally high-minded, and equally dispiriting: it has its full share of that characteristic nagging tone which Meredith once said used to make him sound like an old maid telling off an errand boy. He deplores the spread of slang, and laments the fact that so many of the books borrowed from public libraries should be mere novels:

> Our average is about 70 per cent. . . . Do not let it be supposed that I at all underrate the value of fiction. On the contrary, when a man has done a hard day's work, what can he do better than fall to and read the novels of Walter Scott, or the Brontes, or Mrs Gaskell, or some of our living writers. . . . I only suggest that [the proportion] is much too large, and we should be better pleased if it sank to about 40 per cent. . . .

On the positive side, his arithmetic is even more precise. He calculates how much can be got through if half an hour a day is set aside for reading, and wonders whether Mark Pattison was being unreasonable when he said that no self-respecting citizen should own less than a thousand volumes. ('He pointed out that one could stack 1,000 octavo volumes in a bookcase that shall be 13 feet by 10 feet, and 6 inches deep, and that everybody has that small amount of space at disposal.') In addition, he recommends the making of abstracts and the keeping of commonplace books. The great thing about literature is that it can elevate a man's character, without in any way unfitting him for a public career: 'I venture to say that in the present Government, including the Prime Minister,* there are three men at least who are perfectly capable of earning their bread as men of letters.'

Morley was always especially resentful of any suggestion that he was a *littérateur* who was out of his element in politics. He prided himself on his realism, and he disliked the nickname of 'Honest John' which dogged him throughout his parliamentary career. Yet what else could he have expected, after so unremitting a display of rectitude? Morley the politician has his faintly absurd aspects, and his melancholy aspects, too. Always a vain man, he cut a less than heroic figure at the times when his ambition got the better of his judgement – during the Gladstone succession crisis, for instance, when he was angling ineffectually for the Foreign Office. The ironies of his term as Secretary for India (1905–10) are more painful to contemplate. The appointment seemed a promising one: he was widely admired by Indian liberals, both on his own account (enthusiasts had even translated *On Compromise* into Urdu and Gujerati), and as the heir to a great political tradition. Gokhale, the moderate Congress leader, hailed him as 'the reverent student of Burke, the disciple of Mill, the friend and biographer of Gladstone'. Here at last was a statesman capable of pushing through much-needed Indian constitutional reforms. As it turned out, the hopes which had been raised were not to be fulfilled: all that emerged was a comparative mouse, the Indian Councils Act of

---

* Salisbury, who had been a *Saturday* Reviewer during Morley's time on the paper: every week they used to sit alone together in the editorial anteroom waiting for their assignments, without once exchanging a single word.

1909, which made little more than token concessions to Indian demands. It is true that Morley had only limited room for manœuvre: he had to contend with the delaying tactics of a Whig Viceroy, Lord Minto, as well as the entrenched hostility of Anglo-Indian diehards. But when every allowance has been made, he stands convicted as timid and unimaginative. He deliberately went on record as saying that he would have nothing to do with any reform which could be construed as paving the way for the establishment of parliamentary democracy in India; and, whatever his private misgivings, he countenanced a number of severely repressive government measures, including a Newspaper Act designed to muzzle the Indian nationalist press. It was all a far cry from his championship of Irish Home Rule and his eloquent denunciation of the South African War, let alone from the ringing libertarian certainties of *On Compromise*. ('You have not converted a man because you have silenced him. . . . To think you are able by social disapproval or other coercive means to crush a man's opinion, is as one who should fire a blunderbuss to put out a star.')

At home, meanwhile, a large public had come to revere Morley as the last prominent defender of the true Gladstonian faith. He spoke with the accents of an elder statesman; his three-volume *Life* of Gladstone (subsequently re-issued in sixpenny parts) was one of the great Edwardian best-sellers; and in August 1914 he honourably rounded off his public career by resigning from the cabinet in protest against the decision to declare war. By this time, however, he had long been written off by the more radical spirits of the succeeding generation as a sententious old Polonius, Lord Morley of Borley. To Bernard Shaw, whom he had once offered work on the *Pall Mall Gazette*, he was 'the worst of all political scoundrels – the conscientious, high-principled scoundrel'. Similar jibes at Morley are dotted throughout Shaw's early letters. 'It is impossible,' he wrote to a friend in the 1880s, 'to attain even high mud mark in politics without taking that solemn literary obsolescence and shaking the starch out of him twice a week regularly.' These were the sentiments of a socialist; but there were other writers, less politically involved, who found the idea of Morley equally oppressive on quite different grounds. To Yeats, for instance, he represented everything in Victorian culture which had been most at enmity with joy, everything grey, ponderous, drearily rationalistic – and the revulsion was mutual. The elderly critic who responds to a newcomer of genius with blank hostility is a familiar enough figure, too familiar to be normally worth getting very indignant about; but Morley's adverse report on Yeats (it is quoted at length by Charles Morgan in *The House of Macmillan*) surely deserves to be put in a class by itself. When the poet's work was recommended to the firm in 1900, he turned down his thumbs as hard as he could: 'I do not say that it is obscure, or uncouth or barbaric or affected – tho' it is all these evil things; I say it is to me absolute nullity . . .' The volume singled out for special attack is *The Wind Among the Reeds*, which had been published the previous year, and which contains such poems as 'The Song of Wandering Aengus' and 'I have drunk ale from the Country of the Young': not yet Yeats at his most powerful, admittedly, but by comparison with anything that Morley ever wrote, enough to burn a hole in the page.

Morley is the kind of Victorian liberal whom later generations of social critics, whether on the Left or on the Right, have taken the greatest pleasure in unmasking. He can be presented as a humbug who skirted round the realities of power on paper, while accepting them readily enough in practice when it suited him; as a dupe who thought that he was pleading the cause of metaphysical Progress when he was in effect advancing the interests of capitalism; as a doctrinaire with a dangerously narrow view of human nature. The very purity and intellectuality of his liberalism excite a pitch of hostility which, posthumously at least, more unpretentious, run-of-the-mill politicians generally manage to avoid. Yet if we are to get down to fundamentals and final estimates, the 'negative' freedom in which he believed is the bedrock of any potentially decent society. It may be far more inadequate and unsatisfying in itself than he would have been willing to admit, it may need to be supplemented with innumerable forms of positive social action – but it comes first. Without a guaranteed minimum of freedom from coercion for the individual, 'positive' freedom is merely the tyrant's plea. And since the forces making for coercion in the world are always very strong, it is no bad thing that a man like Morley should have had his share of political cunning. As for his limitations as a literary critic, these seem to me an accident of his temperament, and his period, rather than the necessary outcome of liberalism as a political philosophy. It could easily be argued, for instance, that the most natural attitudes for a writer styling himself a liberal ought to be a relish for human diversity, and a Forsterian faith in personal relations. If Morley, on the contrary, often appears stiff, pompous and chillingly impersonal, it is not so much because he was a Mid-Victorian Liberal as because he was a Mid-Victorian, and even more because he was Morley, a self-important, watchful front-bench rhetorician.

II

Frederic Harrison (1831–1923) is a more engaging figure than Morley, and his literary essays, though far less ambitious, have more natural warmth: in particular they are enlivened, as Morley's never are, by a certain peppery informality. On the face of it, given his life-long commitment to Positivism, one might have expected him to be the more doctrinaire critic of the two; but in criticism temperament usually counts for as much as ideology, and temperamentally Harrison was impetuous, erratic, nothing if not human. Unlike Morley, he doesn't stand on ceremony. He can interrupt a formal essay on Trollope with the sudden reflection that 'good old Anthony had a coarse vein – it was in the family', and one's heart goes out to him when, for example, he breaks off in a generally favourable review of Froude's *Carlyle* to exclaim: 'This uniform brutality towards servants is a very evil sign' – a remark which in its context recalls, however faintly, the well-known passage in the *Lives of the Poets* where Dr Johnson takes the measure of Swift ('To his domesticks he was naturally rough . . .'). As for his actual judgements, they owe far more to a conventional Victorian upbringing than to Positivism; when he writes on literature, in fact, it is odd how small a part his Comtean allegiances seem to play. He might be almost any well-to-do old-fashioned radical, who just happens to have one rather large bee in his bonnet.

Still, a Positivist is what he was, for nearly seventy years, and whether he should be classed among the Liberal Practitioners at

all is highly debatable. In the 1860s and 1870s he hesitated to en-
dorse the Liberal Party even as a stop-gap, and he looked forward
to the eventual formation of a third party, a Labour party; at this
period the radical wing of English Positivism which he led,
together with E. S. Beesly, was in the forefront of the struggle to
secure the full legal enfranchisement of trade unions. For the
better part of a generation, before the coming of the Fabians, the
Positivists served, in Mr Royden Harrison's phrase, as 'Labour's
intellectuals'. If there is nevertheless a plausible case for describing
the young Frederic Harrison as a Liberal Practitioner, it is partly
because in a general way he was a progressive without being a
socialist, but much more because he was originally put into that
category by Matthew Arnold himself. As far as literary historians
go, in fact, he counts almost exclusively as one of the capering
marionettes of *Friendship's Garland* and *Culture and Anarchy*. In
other respects he is pretty much a forgotten man (not even mentioned by name in the *Concise Cambridge History*, for instance), and
even authorities on Victorian literature tend to see him through
Arnold's eyes. Such is the fate of secondary figures. He was ridiculed by Arnold for paying an extravagant compliment to the
working class – 'theirs are the brightest powers of sympathy and
the readiest powers of action' – and this is simply cited by Professor Holloway in *The Victorian Sage* as one of the 'gems' which
Arnold collected, along with the usual fatuities from Hepworth
Dixon, Sir Charles Adderley, and the rest of them. Or again,
Raymond Williams, in *Culture and Society*, after quoting Harrison's
scornful reference to 'this same *sauerkraut* or *culture*', goes on to
comment that 'the challenge of the valuations concentrated in the
idea of culture was bound to provoke hostility from defenders of
the existing system'. But, quite apart from the fact that it was a
fictitious character, 'Arminius', who was made to hold forth about
sauerkraut, it is at least arguable that the Positivist was less concerned to defend the existing system than the poet. The passage
in question comes from 'Culture; A Dialogue', a satirical rejoinder
to the early chapters of *Culture and Anarchy* which appeared in the
Fortnightly in 1867, and which Arnold himself (who was in no
danger of confusing Harrison with the Hepworth Dixons and
Adderleys) found brilliantly funny. It is a highly entertaining

burlesque, certainly; but it also raises issues which deserve a serious answer. How is Culture to work? How is it to be attained? Harrison's ironies cut quite deeply into Arnold's bland evasions. No doubt he enjoys letting Arminius overstate his case for him; but he *had* a case – and he also had the right to be in a fighting mood. These were the years in which he was in the thick of his fight for the trade unions, and he could hardly help judging *Culture and Anarchy* in its immediate political context. Arnold's attitude to the working class was, after all, more heavily authoritarian than some admirers care to recall. In the abstract, his criticisms may sound rather convincing; he depicts a Populace not yet ready to be entrusted with political responsibility, infected with the spirit of 'doing as one likes'. But it is worth reminding oneself of the kind of concrete example of this which he gives:

I remember the manager of the Clay Cross works in Derbyshire told me during the Crimean war, when our want of soldiers was much felt and some people were talking of a conscription, that sooner than submit to a conscription the population of that district would flee to the mines, and lead a sort of Robin Hood life underground.

Bearing in mind Scutari, who can blame them? It is a relief to turn from this to Harrison's conduct as a member of the Royal Commission on trade unions in 1867. Without romanticizing their virtues, he admired both the practical achievements of the unions and their underlying philosophy; when he praised the working class for its powers of sympathy and action, he was not just providing Arnold with another gem of liberal claptrap, but speaking from first-hand experience. As a member of the Royal Commission he watched over labour interests, and together with two other dissenting members he drew up a minority report which subsequently served as the starting-point for the union legislation of the 1870s – legislation which probably did more than anything else to help avert the revolution which Arnold feared. Harrison could afford to smile at the picture of him in *Friendship's Garland* as a Jacobin oiling the guillotine. He knew the leaders of the working class better than Arnold, and respected them more.

Nor should the definition of culture which originally got him

1 Lord Jeffrey

2 The Fraserians, by Maclise (Maginn standing at the head of the table)

3 Thomas Barnes

4 Thomas Carlyle, by
'Ape' (from
Vanity Fair)

5 Matthew Arnold
(from *Vanity Fair*)

6 John Stuart Mill, by G. F. Watts

7 Agnes Jervis Lewes,
George Henry Lewes and
Thornton Leigh Hunt,
from a pencil sketch by
W. M. Thackeray

8 Richard Holt Hutton

9 Leslie Stephen with his
daughter Virginia

10 Watler Bagehot

11 Edmund Yates, by 'Spy' (from *Vanity Fair*)

12 James Hannay

13 Frank Harris, by Max Beerbohm

14 John Morley, by 'Ape' (from *Vanity Fair*)

15 Frederick Harrison, by 'Ape'
(from *Vanity Fair*)

16 Augustine Birrell

17 Herbert Paul

18 J. M. Robertson

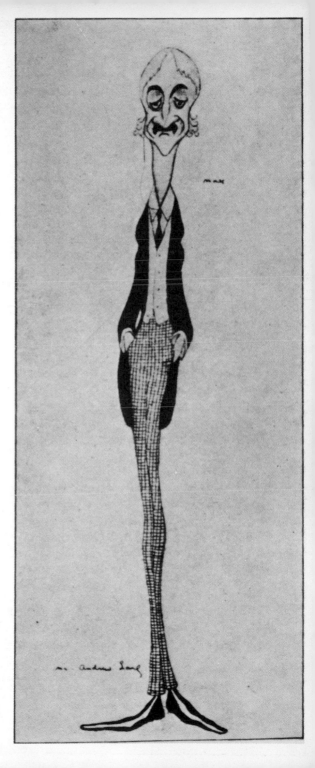

19 (opposite) 'C. F. Masterman
preserving his ideals',
by Max Beerbohm

20 Andrew Lang, by
Max Beerbohm

21 George Saintsbury, by William Nicholson

into trouble with Arnold be taken in deadly earnest. 'A desirable quality in a critic of new books,' he had called it, 'and one which sits well on a professor of *belles lettres*.' This was the momentary annoyance of a reformer impatient for results, not the considered opinion of a philistine. It is true that Harrison lacked Arnold's vision of culture as an entire way of life, and in this sense Raymond Williams is justified in finding him the less truly radical writer of the two. But he was also a highly cultivated man, in the solid Victorian fashion, and where he did see a conflict between culture and politics, it was one which genuinely troubled him: there was no question of simply paying lip-service to Art and then rushing back to stern reality. In the memoir of Harrison by his son, Austin Harrison, he can be seen passing his days in an atmosphere heavy with literature, preoccupied above all with the great contemporary critics of Victorian materialism. Ruskin, for example, whom he knew well, and about whom he wrote an excellent volume for the *English Men of Letters*, was something of an obsession: 'my father', says Austin, 'rarely got through a meal without referring to that important personage.' Nor, in spite of their clashes, did he ever doubt Arnold's commanding stature. Taking stock after his death, he saw him as the master critic of the age; indeed, he thought that modern criticism could scarcely have been carried on without the vocabulary which Arnold had bequeathed to it. But as for the question of Culture, he was impenitent: 'The mystery still remains, *what* is best, how are things to be seen really as they are, by *what* means can we attain to perfection?'

At other times, however, in more Comtean moods, it all seemed much less of a mystery. The world had long ago decided who were the authors who really counted. In his most extended literary study, *The Choice of Books* (1879), Harrison asks bluntly how a man with only twenty-four hours a day at his disposal can be expected to cope with the unprecedented torrent of modern literature. His answer is equally blunt: most new books should be thrown straight into the nearest dustbin. The classics ought to be enough for anyone – and he goes on to supply a list of standard works, English and European, ancient and modern, which would certainly keep most ordinary readers tied up for as far ahead as they could plan. Based on Comte's Positivist Library, but adapted and enlarged for the benefit of an English public, Harrison's choice is in the main sturdily conventional. 'There are no "tips" in literature,' he wrote, forestalling one of the more objectionable bits of modern critical slang; 'the best authors are never dark horses'. This was perhaps less the voice of Positivism than the growl of approaching middle age. From the 1870s onwards, he felt increasingly out of tune with the way the literary world was going. He deplored the advent of the lightning reviewer, 'the young man with a kodak', and while he conceded that not all aesthetes were poseurs, he was convinced that they had got hold of the wrong end of the stick: 'art will be beautiful when life is beautiful, and assuredly not till then'. What incensed him most of all, however, was the spread of bibliomania, the passion for resurrecting forgotten texts and dredging up minor curiosities. If there was one literary type of the period whom he thoroughly despised it was the 'book-trotter', whom he depicted wandering aimlessly from shelf to shelf and then finally settling down to write *Half-Hours with Obscure Authors*. With such men nibbling at the foundations, great books were in danger of being smothered by the sheer weight of little ones. Yet at the same time Harrison was acute enough to recognize that he was dealing with more than a passing craze, that 'at the bottom of all this lies that rattle and restlessness of life which belongs to the industrial maelstrom wherein we ever revolve'.

What then was to be done? As long as the storm still raged, the Religion of Humanity, however pitifully few converts it might attract, did at least seem to offer the advantages of a fixed point, a still centre; and after 1880 Harrison's main efforts went into running the headquarters of the independent London Positivists at Newton Hall, a dingy meeting-house tucked away in a courtyard off Fetter Lane. In the outside world a new generation of researchers were beginning to follow the lead he had set with his trade-union investigations – most notably Beatrice Webb, who acknowledged a major debt to him, and Charles Booth, who had flirted with Positivism for a time. But by now he himself had withdrawn firmly into the sectarian fold. At Newton Hall he was kept busy, delivering innumerable lectures, organizing thanksgiving pilgrimages to the graves of the illustrious dead, officiating at austere little ceremonies in honour of Humanity (as personified by a reproduction of the Sistine Madonna). It was the mildest, the least enthralling of pocket utopias, but it satisfied his emotional needs. And meanwhile Humanity, common Humanity, went its own unregenerate way.

Harrison's horizons were limited, and – unlike his Positivist colleague Professor Beesly – he was not an especially striking personality in his own right. But he raised questions which needed asking, and took on jobs which needed doing. From a literary point of view what is interesting and unusual about his work is the way in which he manages to respond so strongly to the romantic root-and-branch critics of industrialism without letting himself be completely overwhelmed by them. Certainly it would be quite false to think of him as buoyed up by a simple optimistic faith in the technological millennium. He never wrote a more powerful piece than 'A Few Words about the Nineteenth Century' (1882), in which he flays the impostures of Victorian civilization, its injustice, its huge complacency, its buried squalor. At times the vehemence which he brings to his theme almost matches that of Ruskin himself. Yet there is another side to him as well, a side which rebels against taking the easy negative way out, and makes him suddenly turn on his fellow-critics. For, in spite of everything,

the Vatican with its syllabus, the Mediaevalists-at-all-costs, Mr Carlyle, Mr Ruskin, the Aesthetes, are all wrong about the nineteenth century. It is *not* the age of moneybags and cant, soot, hubbub and ugliness. It is the age of great expectation and unwearied striving after better things.

Torn between a sense of mission and a feeling of helplessness, convinced that somehow the world *had* to be transformed, he settled in Positivism for a solution which need hardly detain us. But he is more than the sum of his eccentricities: without the quixotic impulse which made him a Positivist he might never have taken up the cause of the trade unions. It was eccentrics like Harrison who helped to save Victorian England from itself.

III

In 1887 Morley calculated that at least three members of the Tory government then in power were 'perfectly capable of earning their bread' as professional authors. A generation later, if he had carried out a similar survey among his colleagues in the Campbell-Bannerman or Asquith administrations, the score would have been a good deal higher. Edwardian Liberalism not only boasted its intellectual dreadnoughts like Haldane and Bryce; it was also exceptionally well supplied with outstanding newspapermen. Outside Parliament, there was a swarm of eminent Liberal editors and leader-writers (all of them for some reason bristling with initials) – C. P. Scott, A. G. Gardiner, J. A. Spender, H. W. Massingham, J. L. Hammond, and many others. Inside, there was a large contingent of Liberal members with journalistic experience. Asquith himself, before he made his reputation as a lawyer, had spent ten years supplementing his income as a literary man-of-all-work on the *Spectator* under Hutton and Townsend. Once again, in itself simply lumping together writers of every description under the general rubric of 'journalism' proves little or nothing. A philosopher and sociologist like L. T. Hobhouse, who wrote the classic exposition of what Liberalism meant to his generation, also deserves to be remembered, by virtue of his years on the *Manchester Guardian,* as a notable journalist. So, in his own way, does Hilaire Belloc, who sat as a Liberal M.P. from 1906 to 1910. So, for that matter, does the sometime Liberal member for South Hackney, Horatio Bottomley. In the nature of things, Liberal journalism was compounded of as many different and often discordant elements as the Liberal Party itself. Still, it undoubtedly remains true that few political parties at any period have been more hospitable to writers, or had a stronger tinge of literature about them.

Can anything else quite account for the career of Augustine Birrell (1850–1933)? Birrell was a man of letters, and that was a recommendation, even if his books had no visible connection with his political beliefs. The son of a Baptist minister from Kirkcaldy who had settled in Liverpool, he began life as a solicitor's articled clerk; then, after an unexpected legacy had enabled him to go to Cambridge, he read for the Bar and took chambers in Lincoln's Inn. From his Liverpool days he had been a zealous book-collector, but if he had any early ambitions to write himself they were well concealed, and he finally stumbled into literature almost by accident. The members of a little debating-society to which he belonged, the Sons of Ishmael, decided to put out a collection of essays 'for a lark', but when it came to it the other contributors defaulted, so he took on the job single-handed and had 250 copies printed at his own expense. The book, *Obiter Dicta* (1884), created an unexpected stir: it quickly ran through half-a-dozen impressions, and Birrell suddenly found himself a minor celebrity. In the most tremulous way possible, he had struck a responsive chord. According to the *Dictionary of National Biography*, *Obiter Dicta* appeared at a time 'when an influential section of fashionable society had become ashamed of appearing only to frequent Melton and Newmarket, and the book's fascinating style and its small bulk made it easy to carry about from country house to country house and discuss under the trees on a fine afternoon'. One wonders exactly what there was to discuss: the book opens with a few bromides about Carlyle and Browning, and then trails off into the meagrest of literary chit-chat. As for the essays in Birrell's subsequent collections, *Res Judicatae*, *In the Name of the Bodleian*, and the rest of them, they are if possible even less substantial. 'Hannah More Once More', 'Is it Possible to Tell a Good Book from a Bad One?', 'Lawyers at Play' – this is the book-trotting which Frederic Harrison deplored with a vengeance. And the manner is embarrassingly well-suited to the matter: 'Much red gold did they cost us, these portly tomes, in bygone days, and on our shelves they shall remain till the end of our time . . .', etc. The less impressionable reviewers nicknamed this kind of stuff 'birrelling', but there was an audience for it, and it had a vogue; eventually, too, it became one of the models regularly held up for the benefit of schoolboys sentenced to write whimsical 'compositions'. (The lightweight essay was something of a Liberal speciality: another favourite with the older breed of English masters was 'Alpha of the Plough' – A. G. Gardiner, editor of the *Daily News*.) It will come as no surprise that Birrell was a great admirer of Lamb, and of the whole Elian approach; he once wrote, without any hint of irony, that 'every author, be he grave or gay, should try to make his book as ingratiating as possible'. Despite such provocations, however, no one could really be irritated with him for long. He is altogether too mild and cheerful and unassuming – a benign old bookworm, meant for a quiet life.

To those who know of him only as a bellettrist, it must seem extraordinary that such a man should have been Chief Secretary for Ireland for nearly a decade, throughout the feverish years culminating in Easter Week 1916: rather as though Edmund Gosse had been made Viceroy of India, or E. V. Lucas Secretary for War. But when Campbell-Bannerman put him in charge of Irish affairs in 1907 he was already a parliamentary, if not a ministerial, veteran. He had first served as a back-bencher from 1889 to 1900, without unduly exerting himself. (In Oscar Wilde's 'The Critic as Artist' there is a passing salute to 'the author of *Obiter Dicta* – that charming and graceful writer who has lately deserted the turmoil of literature for the peace of the House of Commons'.) In 1900, at the Khaki election, he lost his seat; when he re-emerged, some five years later, it was as President of the Board of Education. He spent a year piloting a bill designed to redress Nonconformist grievances through the Commons, only to see it killed by the Lords; meanwhile Bryce had resigned as Irish Secretary, and no obvious replacement was available; so, not without foreboding, he agreed to cross what he was later to call 'that odious Irish Channel'. His predecessors included not only Morley and Bryce, but such men as G. O. Trevelyan and George Wyndham: if academic polish could have solved the Irish problem, it would have been settled long before. As it is, Ireland was the rock on which some of the greatest political careers had foundered, and in Birrell it simply claimed another, lesser victim. After the Easter uprising, he resigned; he may have been much less culpable than some who remained, but he had certainly seriously under-estimated the likelihood of violence. Two years later, he quit Parliament for good, and turned to the more congenial task of writing a biography of his father-in-law, Frederick Locker-Lampson, who had been well-known in Victorian times for his tinkling *vers de société*. No shadow of a gunman *there*.

Occasionally, during the 1920s, he would come out of retirement to perform the duties of a literary elder statesman. He was the principal guest of honour at the Marvell tercentenary celebrations in Hull in 1921 (he had written the life of the poet for the *English Men of Letters*), and in the commemorative volume got up to mark the occasion he can be seen in full frock-coated dignity, delivering an address at the Guildhall which is reprinted along with some observations by the Lord Mayor. ('Marvell little thought that 250 years after his death he would be the means of Hull receiving the biggest and cheapest advertisement that to my knowledge it has ever received.') The volume also contains, among other things, tributes from Sir Edmund Gosse and J. C. Squire, photographs of specially decorated Corporation tramcars, and an essay by 'T. S. Eliot M.A.', intended, in his own words, not as an act of piety, but in order to prompt a little serious thought about Marvell's poetry.

This might seem an appropriate point at which to take our leave of Birrell. But before doing so, it is worth reflecting that Eliot's essay not only cast a brilliant new light on Marvell; it also finally put an end to the two-hundred-year-old popular tradition – the liberal tradition – which celebrated him as above all the champion of constitutional liberty, the tribune beyond reach of a bribe. Perhaps Eliot didn't intend the piece to have this effect, but he does rather go out of his way to stress how little resemblance Marvell's liberalism bore to that of some later Liberal practitioners, to the ethos of the United Grand Junction Ebenezer Temperance Association or to the Dissidence of Dissent. This is beyond dispute; and it is equally true that there was a strong element of make-believe in the legend of Marvell the exemplary democrat. Yet the fact remains that for thousands of Victorian Liberals the seventeenth century was *alive* with an intensity that now seems hard to credit. When John Bright told an audience of working men that the author of *Paradise Lost* was 'the greatest name in English political history', he may not have been advancing the cause of literary criticism very far, but arguably he was doing more to win readers for Milton than most professional Miltonists. And Marvell's connection with the greater poet naturally added to his fame;* Wordsworth was speaking for generations of admirers when he grouped him together with

> the later Sydney, Harrington,
> Young Vane, and others who call'd Milton friend.

By the time we reach Birrell this tradition is very much weaker, but not yet extinct. He praises Marvell as 'of all public men then living [in the 1670s] the one most deeply imbued with the spirit of our free constitution – its checks and balances jumped with his humour'. A neat way of putting it. In Eliot, needless to say, there is nothing about free constitutions. Why should there be, indeed? His purposes are his own: he sets out to define the qualities of Marvell's best poetry more precisely than any previous commentator had done, and to exhibit them as the product of 'European, that is to say Latin, culture'. The result is a brilliant essay in reinterpretation, one of the classics of modern criticism. But as the hundred-thousandth undergraduate faithfully transcribes the familiar phrases about tough reasonableness and slight lyric grace, let us at least acknowledge that for the mass of ordinary readers (I don't speak of scholars) there are losses to be set against the gains; that in supplying a valuable new historical perspective, Eliot also helped to destroy a far from contemptible old one.

IV

Perhaps Liberalism has always been, as the scientists say, a false isolate, and one should only properly speak of 'Liberalisms', of a loose cluster of interests held together by expediency, local circumstances, and piecemeal humanitarian goodwill. If this is true of the party of which Gladstone took command in the 1860s, it is doubly true of the party inherited by his Edwardian successors. The 1906 landslide brought into Parliament Liberals of every stripe: imperialists, Little Englanders, aristocrats, Dissenters, trade-unionists, old-style adventurers, new-style radicals; men as

---

* In his bibliography Pierre Legouis (*André Marvell, poète, puritain, patriote*) records a public lecture on Marvell, eulogizing the *puritain*, if not the *poète*, delivered at Birmingham in 1859, shortly after Bright was elected an M.P. there.

different from one another in training and temperament – to confine ourselves to our *littérateurs* – as a thoroughbred whig like Herbert Paul, and an embattled secularist of the Bradlaugh school like J. M. Robertson.

Paul (1853–1935), a former leader-writer for the *Daily News*, had previously sat in the Commons during the 1890s. Shortly after his return, a nervous breakdown compelled him to retire; he recovered, but made no attempt to get back into politics, settling for an appointment as a Civil Service commissioner instead. His published works belong to the earlier phase of his career. They include a five-volume *History of Modern England*, biographies of Gladstone and Froude, and two collections of essays, *Men and Letters* and *Stray Leaves*. A keen party man, his Liberalism was of a purely traditional cast; his watchwords are constitutional freedom and respect for civil justice, and he sometimes gives the impression that he is still fighting the battles of 1832 or even 1688. He wrote a spirited defence of Macaulay, but the more fundamental criticisms which had been levelled against the historian simply passed him by. Within his well-defined limits, however, Paul is an attractive figure: urbane, confident, with a sense of proportion which saves him from the excesses of his bookish contemporaries. Nothing in the world would have induced him to birrel, while one of his most polished performances is a witty dissection of E. V. Lucas's overgrown biography of Charles Lamb – 'the methodical annals of a non-methodical life'. His own tastes ran to a little light cynicism – in relaxed moments, to the chaff of *The Dolly Dialogues*. At Oxford he had been president of the Union, and he never entirely lost his Union manner. The *History of Modern England* has been described as 'the *Annual Register* tempered by epigrams'. But he could be serious enough when seriousness was called for. He wrote an excellent non-epigrammatic essay on George Eliot, for instance, in the form of a review of Leslie Stephen's *English Men of Letters* monograph, protesting against that book's 'coldly judicious' estimate of *Middlemarch* with a conviction which forces one to admit that there *is* something chilling about Stephen, after all. His own enthusiasm for the novel is intense, and intelligently expressed; he even makes what was one day to become a stock comparison (had anyone made it before?) with Tolstoy. On the other hand the volume which he himself contributed to *English Men of Letters*, on Matthew Arnold, mainly serves to show up his limitations – the limitations of a solid but anachronistic country-house culture, and of long years spent being drilled in hexameters and 'longs and shorts'. He is more at home with Arnold's prosody than his poetry (he thought his finest poem was the laboured elegy for Dean Stanley, 'Westminster Abbey'); and though he scores a few debating points against his social criticism, he remains whiggishly impervious to its true implications.

Paul was an Etonian; J. M. Robertson (1856–1933) was a poor boy from Stirling who left school at the age of thirteen, found his way into local journalism, and read every book he could lay his hands on in his spare time. By his twenties he was already a walking encyclopaedia. His first great adolescent passion, which went to appropriately heroic lengths, was for Carlyle: in later life he could never quite forgive himself for the hours he had spent diligently writing out his own précis of the last and feeblest of the Master's works, *The Early Kings of Norway*, on its initial appearance. Then, by degrees, he found his true calling in secularism, a cause which he was to serve faithfully – religiously, indeed – for the rest of his days. Summoned to London by Annie Besant, he joined the staff of Charles Bradlaugh's *National Reformer*; eventually he succeeded Bradlaugh as editor, also becoming widely known in both England and America as a lecturer, polemicist and pamphleteer. A tireless debater, he gave nothing away in controversy, pursuing his opponents with the sarcasms of a prosecuting attorney and the grinding thoroughness of a German professor. Nor did he mellow with the years: as late as 1929 he produced a compendious *History of Freethought in the Nineteenth Century*, which looks as though it might have been published in the nineteenth century itself, with its pugnacious footnotes, its jargon, its sepia portraits and smudgy photographs of Colenso, Haeckel, Wellhausen. The tone is often harsh, the arguments, to a modern reader, often seem simply beside the point. But no one who knows the book will be disposed to doubt either Robertson's scholarship or his tenacity.

In addition to his Freethought propaganda, he wrote extensively on political and social questions. A staunch anti-imperialist, he was particularly active at the time of the South African war, which he whole-heartedly condemned. Later, as an M.P., he proved a loyal and energetic follower of Asquith, though without reaching the heights which some had predicted for him. He remained in the Commons until 1918; for four years, from 1911 to 1915, he was Parliamentary Secretary to the Board of Trade.

Robertson's writing has few surface charms. He insisted that the first and last duty of a critic was to be 'veridical', and at the same time hotly denounced the spread of impressionistic criticism, calling instead for stricter objectivity and a more scientific approach. In practice this largely meant a weakness for technical language, and a tendency to come up with such sentences as 'I am inclined to suspect that Pope's total cerebration would compare very well with Tennyson's, the cerebration of leading poets giving a very doubtful clue to the average cerebration of their periods'. Not that the thought of his own infelicities made him any more charitable towards those of others; on the contrary, he shared with his predecessor on the *National Reformer*, the poet James Thomson, a passion for seizing on examples of slipshod grammar and remorselessly cataloguing minor faults of style. At the least provocation, he reaches for the tawse. And yet in his laborious way he is entitled to more respect than most of the bellettrists of his period. His two volumes of collected criticisms (entitled, with true Robertsonian directness, *Criticisms*) are the work of a singularly honest man; in particular, his comments on the erosion of Scottish culture during the nineteenth century – a process of which he himself was to some extent a victim – seem, to an outsider at least, exceptionally convincing.

The same could hardly be said of the Shakespearean studies which preoccupied him during the last thirty years of his life. Elaborating the so-called verse tests which had originally been devised by the Victorian scholar F. G. Fleay, he developed in old age into the most thoroughgoing of all the 'disintegrators' of the Shakespeare canon, notorious for the abandon with which he assigned great stretches of the plays to Marlowe, Chapman and others. His arguments, as always, were forcefully expressed, but too arbitrary, too wilful, too acrimonious. They remind one of

Edmund Wilson's remark about 'the curiously un-Shakespearean atmosphere' engendered by so many of the dramatist's commentators. A writer who is habitually credited with superhuman powers is bound to attract the kind of crankiness normally reserved for the outer fringes of religion or such things as the cult of Napoleon, and though Robertson wrote a book assailing what he called the Baconian heresy, the disintegrators can surely be seen as a rival, if more rational, group of heretics. Fleay himself was an odd character, who eventually wandered off into the wilds of amateur Egyptology; while one could at least make out a case for an insistent need to strike at images of supreme authority being part of Robertson's psychological make-up. At any rate, very few of his theories, as far as I can see, have been accepted by modern Shakespearean scholars. He did win over one notable convert for a time, however, in T. S. Eliot, whose essay on *Hamlet* is partly based on his contentions. An improbable alliance, on which one hopes the full-scale biography of Eliot, when it comes, will shed some light: Robertson also wrote a number of articles for the *Criterion*.

He is obviously fated to be remembered, if at all, by his Shakespearean aberrations: a pity, because he shows up to better advantage in his two collections of essays on 'modern humanists' – Carlyle, Arnold, Mill, the usual round of major Victorian prophets. It is true that if he had any following today, one would probably want to use these books simply as texts on which to hang a few reflections about the deficiencies of ironclad rationalism. They are often pedestrian, they constantly try to explain away the life of the imagination in pseudo-physiological terms, there is a fundamental *griminess* about them. But it would be pointless to drag them from obscurity merely in order to catalogue their defects. What is admirable about Robertson is his struggle to hold on to those things which he thought were of permanent value in his humanists, without yielding an inch to their more illiberal attitudes. In this he resembles Frederic Harrison; and like Harrison, he is at his most cogent when he gets to grips with the author of *Culture and Anarchy*. There were aspects of Arnold which he found hard to forgive. He was outraged by the suggestion that Hyde Park rioters ought to be flung from the nearest available equivalent to the Tarpeian Rock, all the more so since it came from a man who had accused Bradlaugh and the other leaders of the Reform League of 'intemperate' talk. 'Need I say,' he wrote, 'that Mr Bradlaugh would have recoiled with horror from such a political counsel under any circumstances; and that never in his whole career, under the extremest provocation and excitement, did he say anything that could be compared for intemperance with the smooth atrocity of his critic.' This is Bradlaugh's disciple speaking, and doubtless it would have been possible to react to Arnold's remarks with a more polished sense of irony. But there was also something to be said, under the circumstances, for literal-minded indignation, especially since Robertson wasn't content to close on this note, as he so easily might have been. His final estimate of Arnold was a very high one: he saw him, in spite of everything, as an ally, and he recognized that whatever shortcomings he had were cancelled out twenty times over by his services 'to liberalism, to culture, to the very spirit of civilization'.

V

Dissimilar as they were in so many ways, Morley, Birrell, Paul, Robertson were all unmistakably men whose views had been formed in the nineteenth century. Meanwhile a generation of 'New Liberals' was emerging during the Edwardian period, a loosely-knit group of younger intellectuals who hoped to steer the party further to the left and adapt it to the challenge of modern conditions. Among the leaders of the New Liberalism, none was regarded as showing greater promise than C. F. G. Masterman (1873–1927). Churchill's Under-Secretary at the Home Office; the first chairman of the National Health Insurance commission; a seat in the cabinet at the age of forty – everything seemed set for a brilliant career. But Masterman was unlucky. The Opposition couldn't forgive him for his National Insurance work, while in the course of an enquiry into a reform-school scandal during his time at the Home Office he incurred the irrational and implacable enmity of Horatio Bottomley. Singled out for attack by the Northcliffe Press, hounded remorselessly by *John Bull*, he lost his seat at a by-election and was unable to find another. During the First World War he was in charge of propaganda to neutral countries; during the early 1920s he staged a brief comeback as an M.P. and then faded away, a sad and frustrated political misfit. However, he is far from being completely forgotten; his best-known book, *The Condition of England* (1909), still has many admirers.

Masterman was not just a politician who also happened to be an exceptionally well-read man; his literary tastes and his Liberalism were closely intertwined. As a schoolboy he had been passionately devoted to Henley's paper the *National Observer*, but he recoiled from the poet's sabre-rattling and from the whole turn-of-the-century imperialist mood. He used to characterize the period in which he had grown up as 'the Reaction', and it was partly to combat the reactionaries that he first went into politics. A more important driving force, however, was his Christianity. At one time he had considered taking orders; his first book was a study of Tennyson as a religious teacher; and he wrote a biography of F. D. Maurice, for whose Christian Socialism he had deep admiration. As a young man, he was active in the Christian Social Union under Bishop Gore and Canon Scott Holland, and he made his debut in journalism as the editor of the C.S.U. paper the *Commonwealth*. Subsequently he became a well-known figure in Fleet Street proper. A. G. Gardiner took him on to the *Daily News* as literary editor; he helped Massingham to get the *Nation* going; there was a time when he was Belloc and Chesterton's inseparable third musketeer (although in the end Belloc turned against him, very nastily too). One of his closest friendships was with Ford Madox Ford, who used to keep him in touch with the latest literary news and lend him books by unknown young authors like D. H. Lawrence and T. S. Eliot. The Mastermans spent the summer of 1913 touring the Rhineland together with Ford and Violet Hunt – one last civilized excursion before the bombardment. According to Ford they were followed everywhere by the German secret police, under the impression that Masterman was in fact Churchill, but the whole story sounds like a piece of fine Fordie-ish *blague*.

The war when it came was no great surprise to Masterman. Five years earlier he had rounded off *The Condition of England* with a chapter called 'The Illusion of Security', in which he allowed his melancholy to come to the surface:

The wise man will go softly all his days; working always for greater economic equality on the one hand, for understanding between estranged peoples on the other; apprehending always how slight an effort of stupidity or violence could strike a death-blow to twentieth-century civilization. . . .

These subdued tones scarcely suggest a party manifesto; and it would be hard to guess from internal evidence that at the time he wrote the book Masterman was already a junior minister. He is far more concerned in it with fundamental causes than with day-to-day politics. The title echoes Carlyle and the text echoes Ruskin and Morris, while the division of society into 'Conquerors', 'Suburbans' and 'Multitude' is deliberately modelled on *Culture and Anarchy*. But in the forty years since Arnold wrote, a great deal has changed. The Conquerors are more flashily plutocratic than the Barbarians were; the Suburbans have lost the strenuous religious faith of their Philistine fathers; the Multitude are more articulate than the Populace, and better organized. And Masterman also takes into account a fourth layer of society, which *Culture and Anarchy* had largely ignored, the world of the 'Prisoners' at the bottom of the heap – tramps, sweated labourers, small girls hired to lick adhesive labels at the rate of thirty gross a day until their tongues have hard, polished tips and are permanently coated with brown gum. His evidence is partly drawn from personal experience of 'settlement' work in the slums, partly from bluebooks and exposés of the period. Less conventionally, he also cites a good deal of contemporary or recent fiction, from Gissing and Wells to popular novelists of the day like Pett Ridge. A reference to 'the lash of Mr Galsworthy's satire' suggests that he may not have been the most demanding of critics.* But he doesn't

* He showed better taste in this respect, however, than some of his distinguished seniors, whose judgement tended to go to pieces when they picked up a contemporary novel. After a lifetime of refusing to review fiction, Birrell broke his silence in order to write an enthusiastic notice of *The Constant Nymph*. And J. M. Robertson once amazed Mrs Masterman by suddenly pouring praise on *Sanders of the River*.

pretend to offer more than social documentation, and this he does with intelligence and sensitivity. The gains are indisputable: his discussion of the retail trade, for instance, would inevitably make rather dry reading without the quotations from *Kipps*.

For all Masterman's shrewdness and depth of concern, *The Condition of England* is somewhat lacking in impact. There is an underlying feeling of lassitude about it, of helplessness in the face of events. But it is an honourable piece of work, one of the last to be written in the direct tradition of Victorian social criticism. Some fifteen years later Masterman wrote what was meant to be a sequel, *England After the War*; it has flashes of (largely pessimistic) insight, but it was not a success, and he must have known that his time had gone by. Liberalism itself was disintegrating as a political force.

One can make too much, all the same, of 'the strange death of Liberal England'. What is equally striking is the extent to which Liberal attitudes survived the debacle of the party as such, and the way in which individual Liberals continued to exercise great influence: men like Beveridge and Keynes, or, within the more limited sphere of literature and scholarship, men like Gilbert Murray, G. M. Trevelyan, H. A. L. Fisher. Throughout the inter-war period, in fact, high academic culture – what one might call Order-of-Merit culture – still had a recognisably Liberal slant. But for those who came of age intellectually after 1914, liberalism as a personal creed was inevitably something increasingly distinct from Liberalism as a political movement. And even as a literary ideal, it only retained its vitality in the hands of writers like E. M. Forster who were prepared to recognise its centrifugal tendencies and its prosaic limitations. It was no longer possible to treat 'liberalism' and 'culture' as more or less synonymous; at best, they could be seen as uneasy allies, each supplying the other's deficiencies. For as George Santayana put it in *Soliloquies in England*, if culture requires liberalism for its foundation, 'liberalism requires culture for its crown. It is culture that integrates in imagination the activities which liberalism so dangerously disperses in practice.'

5

THE BOOKMEN

I

Most Early Victorian criticism was heavily didactic in tone, uncompromisingly moralistic, political or religious in standpoint. By the end of the 1870s, however, a distinct change could be felt in the atmosphere. The winds of doctrine were dying down, the lay sermon was giving way to the causerie, the emphasis had shifted to Appreciation. And a new race of critics was beginning to come forward – book-lovers, bookmen, vignettists, gossipers in libraries, adventurers among masterpieces. Such types had long existed, no doubt, under other names, but never before in such profusion, nor with so large an audience at their command. In the past they had tended to be strictly peripheral figures, annotators and anecdotalists. Now, down at least until the First World War, they were to have a comparatively free run, to shape the outlook of the greater part of the educated reading public.

We have reached the age of what H. L. Mencken used to call 'beautiful letters', a phenomenon for which there is no one simple explanation. It can be seen, in the first place, as a straightforward swing of the pendulum, the young reacting against the sheer frumpishness of their elders; and in the second, as a watered-down version of tendencies represented more vividly by, say, Swinburne and Art for Art's Sake. The bookman was a genteel first cousin of the aesthete: he, too, had taken to heart the lessons of Pater, though he drew less dramatic conclusions from them. There is also the large, vague but very real question of the whole Late Victorian mood. Whatever one puts it down to – economic difficulties, foreign competition – it is undoubtedly possible to detect by the 1880s a widespread faltering of Victorian self-confidence, a new edginess and uncertainty about the future. Among writers, such a climate might have been supposed to favour a mood of determined realism, and so, in some cases, it did. But the commonest reaction was withdrawal, a retreat into nostalgia, exoticism, fine writing, *belles-lettres*. And at the same time there were also more immediate and mundane reasons for the changing character of literary journalism. One was the ceaseless demand for new material, as the number of magazines and publishing houses multiplied; another was the extent to which this demand was now met by Oxford and Cambridge products with smooth Oxford and Cambridge manners. Gissing shows his usual attention to detail when, in *New Grub Street*, he makes his embittered literary drudge, Alfred Yule, who has come up the hard way, complain that he can no longer hope to compete against the influx of well-connected young graduates. As they widened their horizons, the older universities were proving at least as much a training-ground for journalists as a nursery for philosophers.

For newspaper readers in the 1880s, no single journalist personified Oxford – and 'culture' – more strikingly than Andrew Lang (1844–1912). An astonishingly prolific writer, in his own time Lang enjoyed a dozen different reputations: the collections of fairy tales and the translations of Homer which keep his name current represent only a fraction of his output. He himself took most pride in his contributions to anthropology; 'I might have been a great anthropologist,' he once remarked, 'if I could have made a living out of it.'* As it is, he wrote extensively on myth, ritual and totemism. (One place where traces of his influence can still be seen is in Freud's *Totem and Taboo*.) He also turned out historical works, biographies, novels, antiquarian monographs and bushels of miscellaneous prose, while his original ambition to be remembered as a poet never quite deserted him. Caught up in the Swinburne craze at Oxford, and intrigued by intricate stanza forms, he was one of the first of the 'Rondeliers', the little group of revivalists (Henley and Austin Dobson were the best known) who kept the air humming in the 1870s and 1880s with ballades and triolets and villa-

* Quoted by J. W. Burrow, *Evolution and Society* (1966).

nelles. As early as 1872 he had published a volume of translations and original pieces, *Ballads and Lyrics of Old France*, wholly serious in spirit. Then, as the cult spread, his attitude turned self-consciously skittish: the titles of his subsequent collections – *Ballades in Blue China*, *Grass of Parnassus*, *Rhymes à la Mode* – tell their own story. The failure of his one extended effort, a miniature epic in six books on the somehow unpromising theme of Helen of Troy, confirmed him in his view of himself as a lightweight, a grasshopper. But he went chirruping on: the *Poetical Works* put together by Mrs Lang after his death run to four volumes, and they are incomplete.

The Rondeliers were born too late for one literary generation, too soon for the next. They half rose to embrace aestheticism, and then sank back; if they hankered fitfully after bohemia, it was from a respectable distance. And their verse itself is generally life-less: they used their *formes fixes* to constrict rather than sharpen the language of poetry. Even at this hour of the day it can be startling to recall that Hopkins, who detested them, was an exact con-temporary. The whole movement was wistful, ennervated, Alexandrian. Lang, at least, would have admitted as much; he was convinced that he was living in a silver age, that the springs of invention were running dry. In his own verse he mostly wavered between pastiche and parody, or took refuge in banter. The strongest personal feelings which he allowed to break through were a faint melancholy (especially when writing about Henry Brown, the friend who had died while they were both students together at St Andrews), and a limp nostalgia for the border landscapes of his childhood:

> *Bring me here, life's tired-out guest,*
> *   To the blest*
> *Bed that waits the weary rover,*
> *Here should failure be confessed,*
> *   Ends my quest,*
> *Where the wide-winged hawk doth hover!*

Meanwhile he had to earn a living. After a few years of marking time as a don, at Merton, he moved to London and became a leader-writer for the *Daily News*, and a general freelance. Before long he had established himself as one of the most sought-after journalists of the day, famous for his facility at dashing off an article in a railway compartment or a cricket pavilion or wherever he could snatch a few minutes. Dozens of books, hundreds of essays, thousands of reviews: there was no stopping him. By the end of his career, life's tired-out guest must have produced enough fugitive journalism to stock a small library.

Was he worried about frittering away his gifts? As a boy, he had picked up the familiar romantic notion of the literary life from Thackeray:

Marryat never made us wish to run away to sea. That did not seem to be one's vocation. But the story of Pen made one wish to run away to literature, to the Temple, to the streets where Brown, the famous reviewer, might be seen walking with his wife and his umbrella. The writing of poems 'up to' pictures, the beer with Warrington in the mornings, the suppers in the back-kitchen, these were the alluring things. . . .

Unfortunately, though, 'the best part of the existence of a man of letters is his looking forward to it through the spectacles of Titmarsh'; on closer inspection, most of the magic dissolves. Lang can scarcely have had many illusions about Fleet Street and its demands, after all his years on the treadmill. But if he felt the strain, or if his artistic conscience troubled him, no sign was allowed to show; the front which he presented to the world was one of un-ruffled calm. He was the droopy aristocrat of letters, slender, graceful, smiling faintly to himself. Not everyone succumbed to his spell. Max Beerbohm, whom he was unwise enough to snub, has left a savage verbal caricature depicting him as a monster of affectation and *hauteur,* 'as detached as any palm in a pot', while many others who met him were put off by his distant manner, his drawl, his elaborate old-fashioned discourtesy. But for thousands of those who knew him only in print, he was an altogether winning personality – the embodiment of high academic distinc-tion, yet at the same time casual and relaxed, his essays gliding along with a pleasant effortless ripple. Publishers courted him, journalistic tyros were exhorted to imitate his style. And he was much approved of by the tweedier sort of schoolmasters and dons, especially on account of the learned levity with which he celebrated the pleasures of cricket and angling and golf.

Whatever subject he touched on – and in theory he offered to write about everything except religion and politics – his manner was almost always that of a man living in a book-lined universe. 'This author did not, like Fulke Greville, retire into the convent of literature from the strife of the world, rather he was born to be, from the first, a dweller in the cloister of a library.' He read incessantly, and out of his reading he tried to construct an arcadia where the natives were always on friendly terms. One of his hobbies was composing letters to dead authors, chatty little missives addressed to Q. Horatius Flaccus, Maître Françoys Rabelais, Henry Fielding Esq. Another was devising encounters between fictional near-contemporaries: Christian and Piscator, Lovelace and Tom Jones, Lady Crawley (*née* Sharp) and Mrs Proudie. It all smacks of the competition-page and the Christmas quiz, but Lang would not have been unduly put out by the charge of frivolity. He clung tenaciously – and, if challenged, petulantly – to the conviction that literature ought to remain the same cheerful pastime that it had seemed when he was a boy. Not surprisingly he was also an ardent bibliophile, a snapper-up of first editions and fine bindings. Some of the poems which he wrote about the thrills of *la chasse au bouquin* are positively mawkish. At times he might have misgivings – books were not just toys. But equally, it was no use pretending to be more deeply moved by them than he in fact was. Even the heaviest guns of his youth had lost most of their thunder; yesterday's angry prophecy was now simply another collector's item:

> *Here's Carlyle shrieking 'woe on woe'*
> *(The first edition, this, he wailed in);*
> *I once believed in him – but oh,*
> *The many things I've tried and failed in!*

Hardly the most receptive state of mind for a professional reviewer. There was one type of book, however, which could be guaranteed to revive Lang's waning powers of enthusiasm: the straightforward tuppence-coloured adventure story. No one did more than this fastidious scholar to promote the turn-of-the-century vogue for Romance, for long-lost kingdoms, imitation D'Artagnans, chronicles of Ruritania and the Spanish Main. His favourite contemporary novelist was Stevenson, a friend with whom he had a good many affinities, and one whose works he was always ready to boost – even though he could detect in them the occasional unwholesome streak of subtlety which led him to make his once-notorious demand (it might have been his motto) for 'more claymores, less psychology'. Romance was a blood-thirsty business. A still more congenial spirit, at his own level, was Rider Haggard, with whom he collaborated on a novel called *The World's Desire*, a piece of gorgeous Cecil B. De Mille hokum about the adventures of Odysseus and Helen in the Egypt of the Pharaohs. He had originally helped to launch Haggard with a whole series of enthusiastic reviews of *King Solomon's Mines*, just as later he was to boost the sales of Stanley Weyman's *A Gentleman of France* and make Anthony Hope's reputation overnight by extolling *The Prisoner of Zenda* at a Royal Academy banquet. A puff from Lang usually meant that a publisher's troubles were over, and provided it had its quota of swashbuckling and high adventure he was willing to condone the trashiest melodrama. The novelist Forrest Reid, who had grown up during Lang's heyday and hung on his words, could recall reading a story called *Bail Up!*, dedicated to Lang 'by special permission', which had struck him even at the age of fourteen as pretty crude:

> The comic passages – as is usually the case – were particularly excruciating, and Lang, whose own gaiety was so charming, must have loathed them. Still he *would* have these books, and nobody dared to contradict him. His prestige, his learning, his wit and his irony were too formidable.

Few of his readers would have wanted to contradict him, in any case. For the majority, members of the great lending-library public, he brought words of comfort. At a time when the serious novel and the best-seller seemed to be drifting irretrievably apart, here was a critic who simply conjured away the whole problem of relative values. Milton was literature, and so was Stanley J. Weyman. What made this catholicity so reassuring was that Lang was indisputably the complete man of letters: you only had to follow his regular causerie in *Longman's Magazine*, 'At the Sign of the Ship', to see that. Every month for nearly twenty years he produced a dozen pages of scholarly small talk, chopped up into separate, easily digested paragraphs. *Longman's* gave him his most effective personal platform; he was able to gossip, reminisce, comment on the latest books, air his pet antiquarian theories. Towards the end his energy flagged, and he took to filling up space with scraps of Scottish local history and incredibly tedious anecdotes about psychical research. The weekly column which he began writing for the *Illustrated London News* after *Longman's* closed down in 1905 had even less to offer; by this time he was losing his touch, and everybody knew it. But in its day 'At the Sign of the Ship' was the most widely admired and talked-about feature of its kind.

Stevenson, Zenda, antiquarianism – it all sounds harmless enough. There was another side to the coin, however. If Lang had one consistent policy as a reviewer, it was to ridicule or disparage practically every truly important novel which came his way. He sniped impartially at Russians and Frenchmen, at naturalists and symbolists, at Thomas Hardy and Henry James. Tolstoy and Dostoievsky, he thought, deserved 'the punishment which Dante assigns to those who deliberately seek sadness'. Zola repelled him, *The Kreutzer Sonata* moved him to write an idiotic undergraduate squib. Forced to weigh 'the dubitations of a Bostonian spinster' against 'a fight between a crocodile and a catawampus', he voted for the catawampus. One of the distinguishing characteristics of the modern element in literature is that it disturbs. The more he recognized this, the more Lang clutched at the primitive certainties of the penny dreadful. And if novelists insisted on threatening his peace of mind, he was always in a position to retaliate. He knew how to wound: his treatment of *Tess*, for instance, drew bitter protests from Hardy.

It was left to Henry James, who had been outwardly on polite terms with him since the 1870s, to deliver the final damning verdict. Writing to Gosse shortly after Lang's death, he allowed himself to give vent to the accumulated exasperation of forty years:

Where I can't but feel that he *should* be brought to justice is in the matter of his whole 'give-away' of the value of the wonderful chances he so continually enjoyed (enjoyed thanks to certain of his very gifts, I admit!) – give-away, I mean, by his *cultivation*, absolutely, of the puerile imagination and the fourth-rate opinion, the coming-round to that of the old apple-woman at the corner as after all the good and the right, as to any of the mysteries of mind or of art. .... I perhaps throw a disproportionate weight on the whole question – merely by reason of a late accident or two; such as my recently having read his (in two or three respects so able) Joan of Arc, or Maid of France, and turned over his just-published (I think posthumous) compendium of 'English Literature'. The extraordinary inexpensiveness and childishness and impertinence of this latter gave to my sense the measure of a whole side of Lang, and yet which was one of the sides of his greatest flourishing. His extraordinary *voulu* Scotch provincialism crowns it and rounds it off; really making one at moments ask with what kind of an innermost intelligence such inanities and follies were compatible.

A stronger man than Gosse might have quailed in the face of a blast such as this (I have quoted only a specimen extract). Four months earlier he had described Lang as 'the most elegant mind that the English-speaking world has brought forth in our time'. Now he hastened to signal his agreement with James by return of post: 'His puerility, as you say, was heart-rending.'

Can anything be salvaged from the wreck? The *History of English Literature* which drew down James's wrath is unquestionably best forgotten – a solid wodge of received opinion, no better or worse perhaps than a dozen similar manuals, but coming from a man of Lang's abilities blatantly commercial in inspiration. There was a more agreeable side to his 'flourishing', however. The multicoloured succession of *Fairy Books* which he edited, *Blue*, *Crimson*, *Lilac* and the rest, are no bad monument to be remembered by. They are the product of that same instinctive feeling for legend and folktale which originally drew him to anthropology – and which can also be seen at work, however dimly, in his infatuation with cloak-and-dagger Romance. For he had a case, though it was one which he let go by default: a better critic – a Chesterton, an Orwell, a Robert Warshow – could have made it for him. Such men realized even more clearly than he did that the appeal of blood and thunder is eternal, that the roots of melodrama run very deep; they also recognized that distinctions still have to be drawn – between art and entertainment, between adult readers and children, between good bad books and bad bad books. This Lang again and again refused to do, just as he refused to think through his whole position. Whether through cynicism or fear of life, he cultivated the fourth-rate opinion almost as assiduously as James says that he did; and the result was triviality, lassitude, a final throwing-in of the towel:

> *Prince, tastes may differ; mine and thine*
> *Quite other balances are scaled in;*
> *May you succeed, though I repine –*
> *'The many things I've tried and failed in!'*

II

Lang was a don lost to journalism; George Saintsbury (1845–1933), his Fleet Street colleague and companion for twenty years, was a journalist transformed in middle age into the most venerable of professors, an academic institution in his own right. King Saintsbury, Stephen Potter called him. For generations of students he was the supreme exponent of Eng. Lit. (an objectionable term, but there seems to be no adequate alternative), and his textbooks apparently still have some wear in them even now. At any rate, his *Short History of English Literature* remains in print (in its twenty-second impression), preserving the traditions not merely of the 1890s, when it was written, but in many cases those of Oxford in the early 1860s, when he had been an undergraduate* – for if there was one thing as remarkable as the range of his learning, it was his refusal to learn.

Still, would he have been quite the same omnivorous Saintsbury, the man who had read 'everything', if he had succeeded in being elected to one of the five fellowships for which he applied and had settled down to work on his projected history of the English Scholastics? In all probability, yes: he had been a haunter of book-stalls since childhood. But it is tempting none the less to think of him being driven on to his more improbable feats of reading by chagrin at his failure, and a determination to beat the professional scholars on their own ground. Certainly the memory of his fatal

* Anyone who thinks this is an exaggeration should look up his remarks on the relative importance of Dean Mansel and John Stuart Mill.

Second in Greats was still rankling sixty years later, while it was in the period following Oxford, during his long reluctant stretch as a schoolmaster, that he must have laid down most of his great cellar of miscellaneous knowledge. In particular, half a dozen years spent in Guernsey helped to reinforce the passion for French literature with which he originally made his name. He began as a reviewer of French books for the *Academy*; then, after creating a stir with an essay on Baudelaire which Morley published in the *Fortnightly*, he decided to return to London and set up shop as a professional critic. Arnold had brought home to Englishmen the general significance of French culture; Saintsbury, with more enthusiasm and less discrimination, made it his business to acquaint them with the facts.* His first book was *A Primer of French Literature* (1880), followed two years later by a *Short History*, while he wrote copiously on French themes for the *Encyclopaedia Britannica* and in the press. At the same time he was also proud to be known as a dependable all-round reviewer, turning his hand as required to military history, cookery, mathematics (or so he says), sport, equally ready to grapple with a theologian or to wade through a mass of new novels. Reviewing was comparatively well paid: he calculated that he could average £3 10s. for an evening's reading and a morning's writing. It was also, for a man of his sanguine temper, immensely enjoyable. Like Pendennis – he was yet another idolater of Thackeray – his hand trembled with anticipation whenever he opened a parcel of review-copies, even after twenty years on the job.

To a later generation it seems strange that someone as earnest as Saintsbury should not have been more afraid of such a routine wearing him down into a hack. He himself would no doubt have snorted at the idea, or summoned up a long line of distinguished precedents. He had grown up in an age which still saw no disgrace in over-production, and he had an almost boundless faith in his assimilative powers. Equally, he makes it plain that he thought of his friends and fellow-clubmen – Lang, Dobson,

---

* 'We should recognise more fully than we do the immense importance and interest of French literature. Certain productions of this literature Mr Saintsbury may misjudge and overpraise; but he is entirely right in insisting on its immense importance.' – Arnold on Sainte-Beuve in the *Encyclopaedia Britannica* (1886).

Gosse, H. D. Traill – not simply as scholars and essayists, but, taken *en bloc*, as the most distinguished literary group of their time, the guardians of the tradition. With Lang he was especially intimate: night after night they trudged back together from Fleet Street to their homes in Kensington ('walk up the Cromwell Road until you drop and then turn right'), and it was through Lang that he was first introduced to the *Saturday Review*, a paper with prejudices exactly matching his own. In 1880 he became a permanent member of the *Saturday* staff, and he was soon writing regular political leaders as well as reviews. His particular brief was to savage Gladstone's Irish policy, a task for which he needed the minimum of encouragement – although he was cautious enough to save his editor from accepting Pigott's Parnell forgeries as genuine and falling into the same trap as *The Times*. He also wrote on Indian affairs, with equal intransigence; he was a fanatical admirer of Lord Roberts, 'Bobs', who occasionally helped him out with 'more or less confidential communications'.

Meanwhile there were books, and contributions to books. A history of Elizabethan literature. Thirty-six articles for the *Britannica*, eight for *Chambers's*. Ten introductions for Ward's *English Poets*, thirty-seven for Sir Henry Craik's *English Prose*. Compact volumes commissioned by the standard series: *Dryden* for 'English Men of Letters', *Marlborough* for 'English Worthies', *The Earl of Derby* for 'The Queen's Prime Ministers', *Manchester* for 'Historic Towns'. And every year a sheaf of prefaces, anthologies, translations, annotated editions. When he finally left the *Saturday*, at the time of Frank Harris's take-over, Saintsbury was able to contemplate earning his living as a freelance scholar. But shortly afterwards, in 1895, the Regius Chair of English at Edinburgh fell vacant: he applied, and emerged the victor from a tough contest with Henley and Walter Raleigh. In academic quarters the appointment was regarded as a gamble, and when he arrived in Edinburgh he knew that he was still on trial, that there were sceptics to be confuted. The first thing he did was to renounce journalism, without reservation. Then he plunged into his major works, histories of English prosody and prose rhythm, and above all his enormous *History of Criticism*. These were credentials which few cared to question. Mr Balfour let slip a complimentary reference in his Romanes lecture, Lord Morley paid tribute in his presidential address to the English Association, the universities began bestowing honorary degrees. Saintsbury had become generally accepted as the doyen of academic critics, the nearest thing to a Critic Laureate.

The extent of his success as a teacher is more debatable. He is said to have been stimulating, even inspiring, with individual pupils and small groups, but much less impressive on the rostrum. His lectures were too rambling from the point of view of an examination-ridden audience; and sometimes, as he girded himself for the badly-lit classrooms and the stamping feet and the strains of 'Why are we waiting?', he must surely have wished that he was back among grown men. He was generally popular, nevertheless. His students realized that they had a legend on their hands, and made the most of it. Dozens of stories circulated about his rumbustious asides, his impossible handwriting, the convolutions of his syntax.* About his personal kindness, too. The inevitable comparisons were produced: he was cast in the Johnsonian mould, he had Hazlitt's gusto, he was like something out of Peacock. He was, in short, everything that an old-fashioned professor ought to be; and with advancing years he came to seem more prodigious than ever, a gnarled and rugged piece of antiquity.

For all his weight of learning Saintsbury was not, in the modern sense, a fully paid-up professional scholar. He disliked specialization, resisted the encroachments of organized research, and laughed at the kind of fact-grubber who could get excited about whether Chaucer had been taken prisoner near Rennes or near Rheims. His ultimate philosophy was a simple one: first read all the books, and then recommend whatever you have enjoyed as forthrightly as possible. When he left Edinburgh, he slipped back easily into writing for the press. '*On revient toujours.* The Professorship ceasing, the reviewer revives.' But then as a pro-

---

* In the Saintsbury *Memorial Volume* a former student recalls learning a specimen sentence by heart: 'But while none, save these, of men living, had done, or could have done, such things, there was much here which – whether either could have done it or not – neither had done.'

fessor, too, the only audience whom he had really thought it
worth bothering with had been 'the general congregation of
decently educated and intelligent people'. An admirer like
Mencken could use him as a stick for beating the genteel academic
tradition, and picture him alarming solemn New England pedagogues with his 'iconoclastic gaiety, his boyish weakness for
tweaking noses and pulling whiskers, his obscene delight in slang'
– his hearty contempt, in fact, for Beautiful Letters. This is
Saintsbury remade a little too thoroughly in Mencken's own
image. He was, after all, a mid-Victorian, a High Churchman, a
High Tory. But it is at any rate true that there is a vigorous unacademic spontaneity about his style, with its sudden detours and
lunges, its thick peppering of jokes and reminiscences. His later
books especially are like huge monologues – interior monologues,
almost. Everything reminds him of something else, and the free
associations come tumbling out. In one of his essays he parodies
the process himself:

You have to read a novel in which somebody (*not* as somebody to be
laughed at or with) speaks of the 'Emperor August*ine*'. . . . You compare
Augustus and Augustine; and imagine what an emperor the Saint might
have made, finding it rather more difficult to make a saint out of the
Emperor. Naturally in trying to assemble favourable views of Augustus
(the gorgeous vesture of *Antony and Cleopatra* becoming a leaden cope
crushing him down for Englishmen), 'Prends un siège, Cinna!' comes
into your mind, and you giggle as that parallel passage of Crabbe's:

We saw my Lord, and Lady Jane was there,
And said to Johnson, 'Johnson, take a chair!'

follows Corneille's in your memory. Whence by natural opposition the
said mind reverts to that excessively improper but decidedly witty epigram on Fulvia which Martial attributes to the Emperor. . . .

Etcetera. This is tongue-in-cheek, but only just; even by the
standards of his book-soaked contemporaries, Saintsbury's prose
is remarkable for being such a tissue of quotations and allusions,
half of them unidentified or unexplained.

The knowingness, the mystification, can be maddening. If the
general congregation of intelligent readers are expected to be able
to catch a stray echo from the *Rolliad*, or find their way around the
novels of Theodore Hook, or recognize a minor character from

Marryat on sight, then the church will soon be empty. Undoubtedly Saintsbury was often guilty of using his learning as a bludgeon, of implying that until you have mastered everything you are incapable of passing an authoritative judgement on anything. His own single-mindedness, his stamina, his fly-paper memory, put him in a powerful position; even though his pose of omniscience may have been something of a journalist's trick, the amount of information which he did have at his disposal is staggering. Few English critics before or since can have mastered so much. But in the end all this emphasis on erudition, on sheer quantity, is a sign of weakness. 'We read Anatole France in order to find out what Anatole France has been reading' – and Saintsbury, too. One usually carries away from him a dazed impression of how much he knows about this and that, rather than anything particular which he has to say about the subject in hand. Not that he lacks insight or originality. He was capable of casually throwing out the kind of remark which would have made another man's fortune: a generation before Eliot, for instance, he suggested (in his 'Muses' Library' introduction) that there was an affinity between Donne and Baudelaire. He moves easily across great tracts of European literary history. His jokes are quite funny, his metaphors are unhackneyed. He never hedges his bets. And yet none of it seems to add up, or to matter as much as it should.

Sooner or later everyone who has written about him is moved to draw an analogy between his attitude to literature and his vast knowledge of wine. The connoisseur sips, savours, pronounces judgement. As a matter of fact he himself disliked the narrower implications of connoisseurship, and often said so. But it is true that he approached books in a frankly hedonistic spirit, determined as far as possible not to let anything interfere with his enjoyment. Throughout his career he waged a noisy war against theoreticians and system-builders:

> The Rule in Criticism brings Hell and Death; the readiness to accept the illimitable idiosyncrasy of the work for what it is in itself worth (as the advertisements say) to YOU, brings Heaven and Life.

And he was equally intolerant of any suggestion that form and content were inseparable, an idea which tended to get mixed up in his eyes with the heresy that 'you have to be able to take pleasure in the subject represented before you can take pleasure in the representation'.

The remarkable thing is not that Saintsbury should have held such views, but that he should have maintained them so rigidly, with such vehemence; and, in particular, that he should have thought it possible to draw so absolute a distinction between form and content, as though the subject of a work of art were simply an excrescence which could be lopped off at will. Even odder is the sight of the most diehard of Tories advocating, as far as literature went, an extreme form of liberalism. Indeed, one is half-inclined to see politics at the bottom of it: isolate 'form', and you can concentrate on Shelley's rhythms or Ruskin's imagery without being unsettled by their heterodox opinions. More directly, however, Saintsbury's clumsy version of aestheticism can best be accounted for as a pig-headed reaction against the equally pig-headed moralism of the previous generation (which was summed up for him by the story of Charles Kingsley's reply to his children, when they asked him who Heine was: 'A bad man, my dears, a bad man'). There were elementary prejudices to be dispelled, and if he had done no more than insist that art obeys its own laws, and has to be taken on its own terms, who but a philistine or a commissar would disagree? As it is, though, he provoked Pater himself into entering a mild protest against the excessive zeal of his devotion to Form. His theoretical devotion, that is to say; in practice he makes no attempt to conceal his extra-literary commitments. But he remains hemmed in by his doctrine of Taste as an end in itself, and again and again cut off in consequence from the true sources of a writer's greatness. (Where the question of greatness scarcely arises, with a Prior or a Praed, he is generally more successful.) The wine-bibbing analogy is, after all, a measure of his limitations; one has only to think of Wordsworth's contempt for men 'who will converse with us as gravely about a *taste* for Poetry, as they express it, as if it were a thing as indifferent as a taste for rope-dancing, or Frontiniac, or Sherry'. Saintsbury is never as superficial as that, nor are his enthusiasms factitious. But they do often seem out of all proportion to his living involvement with authors. And his catholicity, admirable up to a point, works against him in the end. His criticism is full of forthright judgements and down-right opinions, yet ultimately shapeless, a wilderness of signposts.

Even more than Lang, he is an example of what might be called a first-generation aesthete, an aesthete on paper. At no point would he have considered that his credo carried any practical implications, that it entailed adopting an exotic life-style or spurning the established social order. Hence there was nothing incongruous about a solid conservative making his critical debut with an encomium of Baudelaire: you simply praised the poet as a superlative verbal craftsman, and dismissed his obsession with evil as a pose. To Saintsbury's juniors, this was understandably an impossible attitude; in any case, they had their own Decadent axes to grind. Writing in the 1890s, Arthur Symons, while giving the older man his due for originality, complained that his essay was too sane, too English, that it ignored 'the sub-stratum of vice which unquestionably existed in Baudelaire'. Saintsbury refused to budge; there were sub-strata which were better left alone. He viewed the writers of the *fin-de-siècle* with the revulsion of some-one who had inadvertently helped to pave the way for them, rather like a Russian liberal of the Stepan Verhovensky generation confronted by a nihilist. They were prime examples of the spirit of 'rotting' which he saw coming over the horizon around 1880, and which he resisted bitterly, along with almost everything else in literature which he encountered after that date. A few later authors – Kipling, Compton Mackenzie – were allowed to slip by, and just occasionally he changed his mind: he was kinder to Zola in his *History of the French Novel* than he had been before. Mostly, though, he condemns out of hand. In the last of his books to be written in Edinburgh, *The Peace of the Augustans*, he lets fly in all directions. (Although he refrains from attacking living authors by name, many of his targets – they range from Henry James to Wyndham Lewis – can be readily identified.) Disgusted with the contemporary world, he turns back to the eighteenth century for 'rest and refreshment' – an unhappy formula which echoes through the book, as though he were proposing a picnic. Simi-larly, his talk of 'the new paradise of the novel' seems ludicrously misleading as soon as one thinks of what actually goes on in eighteenth-century fiction. He is admittedly not quite as complacent as he threatens to be. In his first chapter he takes up the challenge of Swift. A *peaceful* Augustan? Only in the sense that his despair is never shrill, that his awareness of 'the accepted hells beneath' (a phrase Saintsbury borrows from Whitman) never leads him into romantic self-pity or hysteria. This might well provide the starting point for a broad consideration of eighteenth-century clarity and decorum. But to give a coherent account of Augustan civilization, Saintsbury would need to be a far more historically-minded critic than he is, and a far more disciplined one. Despite promising to avoid what he calls a 'talkee-talkee' book, he is soon rambling off down the usual side-paths of learned gossip; essentially one can learn more about the eighteenth century from a few paragraphs of Leslie Stephen. And as the book progresses the underlying prejudices increasingly show through, until finally, in a wallow of praise for the smart young satirists of the *Anti-Jacobin*, they become almost insufferable, and one wants to rub Saintsbury's face in the *unacceptable* man-made hells which he so sturdily disregarded.

After his retirement Saintsbury moved to Bath, to a set of rooms in the Royal Crescent. One of his neighbours there was Frederic Harrison, with whom he struck up a quaint friendship, conducted with immense courtliness on either side. Living on into the 1920s, both men now seemed improbable survivors from before the flood; if anything, Saintsbury, though a good dozen years younger than Harrison, looked the more ancient of the two, with his black skull-cap and his patriarchal beard. At the same time he was far from finished. These were years during which he acquired a new public through the success of *Notes on a Cellar-Book*, which led on in turn to the founding of a club in his honour – not a very common experience for a critic. Writing still came easily to him: the *Cellar-Book* was followed by three *Scrap-Books*, while the articles, introductions, reviews kept appearing until almost the very end. Nor did he ever completely cut himself off from contemporary literature, despite his growls. He turns up in Scott Moncrieff's *Marcel Proust: An English Tribute* (1923) with a thought in passing ('Has anybody said that he partakes both of De Quincey and of Stendhal?'). Kipling visited Bath to ask his advice about the background for a story with a Jacobean setting, 'Proofs of Holy Writ'. And among younger critics – since he was still capable of springing a surprise – he commended Middleton Murry. It would be interesting to know what he thought of Eliot; he contributed to the first number of the *Criterion*, but declined an invitation from the editors of the *Dial* in New York to supply them with an article on *The Waste Land*.

For someone who was so endlessly talkative about literature, Saintsbury is oddly reticent when it comes to his own affairs. He left instructions in his will that no biography should be written, and one feels that he meant it. Even the *Scrap-Books* reveal little of the man himself, or of the motives which spurred him on through his career. What they do make plain is the full, the breath-taking extent of his Toryism. A true *Saturday* Reviewer to the last, he grows purple in the face at the mere mention of trade unions, rails against 'conshies', keeps up a sustained and tedious diatribe against virtually every enlightened measure which has been taken since 1832. One wants to be indulgent, to recall that these are the ineffectual rages of an old man of eighty. But it is still rather horrible to see him flaring up because he has just learned that some window-cleaners in an East End workhouse now earn as much as £4 a week. The most that can be said for him is that he is not afraid to stand by his bloody-mindedness in print. As Orwell remarked of the *Scrap-Books*, 'it takes a lot of guts to be *openly* such a skunk as that'.

Saintsbury's political views are not particularly interesting in themselves; for the most part they are simply the commonplaces of clubs and senior common rooms eighty or ninety years ago. What *is* interesting, however, is the extent to which he manages to overcome them when he writes about literature. Edmund Wilson, his most distinguished modern admirer, talks of a 'dramatic element' in his work provided by the clash between diehard principle and immediate critical response: 'The thrill for the reader arises from Saintsbury's displays of gallantry in recognizing and applauding the literary merit of writers whose views he abhors.' This seems to me very true; but I think that Wilson is letting his fancy run away with him when he adds that 'there are moments when one nearly suspects him of having invented the

Tory background – in the same way that a dramatist or a novelist arranges contrasting elements – on purpose so that his passion for literature might find itself pitted against this and score unexpected victories over it'. On the contrary, the whole trouble with Saintsbury's Toryism is that it is neither imaginatively satisfying nor intellectually challenging, but merely a mass of conventional prejudice. And while this may not prevent him from seeing merit in (say) Tom Paine's prose or James Thomson the Younger's verse, it does restrict the interest of his criticism in a much more fundamental way, by severely limiting the range of questions it occurs to him to ask about friend and foe alike. In paying tribute to Saintsbury's catholicity Edmund Wilson tends to project his own virtues on to him, and indeed to overrate him generally: I find it hard, for instance, to see how he can bestow unqualified praise on the 'charm' of a style which is often repulsively clotted and ungainly.* Yet if Wilson exaggerates, he hasn't chosen his hero at random. Flawed though it is, there is something impressive about the spirit as well as the scale of Saintsbury's labours: a magnanimity, an underlying belief that literature, at least, is a republic where every citizen is entitled to his rights. And he has substance. Even the clumsiest contortions of his prose convey an impression of thwarted power rather than affectation. He is a critic whom one can lose patience with completely, and then decide one has badly misjudged, and then lose patience with all over again; but at any rate, unlike the great majority of his contemporaries, a critic whom one can come back to.

III

Both Lang (whom he despised) and Saintsbury (whom he bitterly resented for having cheated him out of the Edinburgh chair) were old acquaintances of W. E. Henley (1849–1903), the most belligerent Tory man of letters of their generation. Their professional connection with him dated from the 1870s, when they were both contributors, along with Robert Louis Stevenson and Austin

---

* For a contrary view to Wilson's, see the comment by Arnold Bennett quoted on p. 217 below.

Dobson, to the first paper he edited, a little-known weekly called *London*. At this time, and for a good many years afterwards, Henley kept his politics out of his journalism. In the 1880s, his life was still dominated by the over-intense friendship with Stevenson which had begun when he was a patient in the Edinburgh Royal Infirmary, and which was to end in estrangement and bad blood, its only lasting memorial the character which he inspired, Long John Silver. During the earlier part of the decade he also made a minor reputation for himself as editor of the *Magazine of Art*, in which he championed Rodin and discovered a notable art critic in Stevenson's cousin, R. A. M. Stevenson. Then, in 1889, he accepted an invitation to return to Edinburgh and take charge of the *Scots Observer*, a new weekly journal which was being set up by a group of wealthy Scottish Tories as a rival to the *Saturday Review*. Trying to run a national weekly from Scotland proved an awkward business, and within two years the paper's name had been changed to the *National Observer* and Henley had shifted his headquarters back to London. Even so, the circulation never rose above 2,000: the paper was too Conservative for most intellectuals, and too intellectual for most Conservatives. But such readers as it did attract found it easily the most bracing and unconventional review of the day. It gave Henley a chance, too, to lord it over his 'Young Men', the loyal little band of contributors who used to meet regularly and argue into the night at Solferino's restaurant off Leicester Square. 'The Henley Regatta', Beerbohm christened them. This prosperous phase lasted until 1894, which was Henley's year of disaster. First his only child died of meningitis, a blow from which he never properly recovered; then he was forced to give up the *National Observer* when the ownership of the paper changed hands. At the end of the year he became editor of a monthly, the *New Review*, a post which he held until 1897. As far as its actual contents went the *Review* was arguably an improvement on the *National Observer*; the novels which were serialized in its pages during Henley's term of office included *What Maisie Knew*, *The Nigger of the 'Narcissus'* and *The Time Machine*. But it lacked a distinctive character of its own – and there was no Regatta. Henley, as we have seen, would willingly have given up the editorship to become a professor in Edinburgh. He was an embittered man; and on top of being beaten by Saintsbury, he acquired a new grievance when a campaign to get him appointed Poet Laureate came to nothing. There was some consolation, however, in the Civil List pension procured for him chiefly through the exertions of his friend George Wyndham, which at least prevented poverty from being as much of a burden as ill-health in his final years.

The *National Observer* played a considerable part in promoting the legends of late Victorian imperialism. It published, among other things, *Barrack Room Ballads*; and during the years when he was editing it Henley himself emerged as a Bard of Empire. Although he had long been a romantic jingo, no one could have guessed it from his first collection of poems, *A Book of Verses* (1888), which consisted partly of ballades and other rondeliering trinkets ('A dainty thing's the villanelle'), partly of powerfully realistic *vers libre* sketches of hospital life. In 1892, however, he published *The Song of the Sword*, with its famous lyric *Pro Rege Nostro* ('What have I done for you, England, my England?') and its preposterous title-poem:

> Clear singing, clean slicing;
> Sweet spoken, soft finishing;
> Making death beautiful . . .
> Arch-anarch, chief builder,
> Prince and evangelist,
> I am the Will of God:
> I am the Sword.

To which one of his reviewers, Professor Minto, retorted: 'No you're not; you're only an Ancient Pistol'. Henley's massacres all took place on paper: they were the daydreams of a frustrated cripple rather than positive calls to action. In his less feverish moods he wrote very different kinds of verse – brooding impressionistic townscapes, mostly. But the climate of the times encouraged him in his drum-and-trumpet posturings, and so did the set of journalists around him. He perpetrated some particularly fearsome doggerel at the time of the Boer War.

The favourable reception of *Views and Reviews* (1890) enhanced his standing as a literary oracle. He described this collection as 'a mosaic of scraps and shreds recovered from the shot rubbish of some fourteen years of journalism', although it was in fact much more lovingly put together than this would suggest: there were sections instead of paragraphs, each with its indented rubric and its ornamental tailpiece. It is hard to see now why his criticism should ever have created much of a stir. He was widely read, and he could turn a jaunty epigram or fondle an exotic adjective in the Stevenson manner. But his opinions are nothing more than opinions, and most of his enthusiasms come across as robustious rather than robust. An exception might perhaps be made in favour of his comparative outspokenness about sex. It is something to find a Victorian critic who is capable, for example, of describing Mr B in *Pamela* as 'a kind of Walking Phallus'. And while he may not hit quite the right note in his essay on Burns when he calls him a 'lewd peasant of genius', his account of the poet is certainly preferable to the standard nineteenth-century bowdlerization. (D. H. Lawrence praises it in one of his letters.) Then, in addition to his criticism, and more usefully, Henley was an energetic anthologist, editor, and organizer of editorial projects. His outstanding achievement here was the splendid series of 'Tudor Translations', each with an introductory essay by a leading scholar of the day. Saintsbury was allotted Florio's *Montaigne*, for instance, W. P. Ker *Froissart*, Walter Raleigh *Castiglione*.

However, it was neither as a writer nor as an editor that Henley impressed his contemporaries most, but as a personality: the zestful warrior, the 'Viking Chief of letters'. To a later generation the nature of his appeal seems impossibly remote. Not that his personality has simply faded away; far from it. He comes forcefully to life in almost every account of him – but the things of which one is made aware are his vindictiveness, his raw wounds, his rasping vulgarity. While the poems have gone flat, one can still hear him clearly enough in his letters, planning an attack in next week's *National Observer* which will make the victim 'sit up like buggeration', or gloating over the 'pleasant sight' of 'Oscar at bay'. ('Holloway and Bow Street have taken his hair out of curl in more senses than one' – this about the man who only the year before had been condoling with him on the death of his child.) And it doesn't make the thought of Henley any less depressing to recall that he had good reasons for feeling a grudge against life, that the ugliness and the pain were mixed up together. A wretched story. Yet at the same time one has to accept the fact that it wasn't only mediocrities and hangers-on who stood in awe of Henley, but men of genius as well. Yeats 'admired him beyond words', and the account which he gives of him in *The Trembling of the Veil* provides the most persuasive explanation of the ascendancy which he established. For the Irishman he was above all a great actor, cast in an inferior role, perhaps, but still able to build up an image of power 'till it became, at moments, when seen as it were by lightning, his true self'. Without opponents there would have been no drama – but it was the drama which counted, not the cause. In this passion for play-acting, for self-projection, there was an affinity between Henley and Wilde which ran as deep as their antagonism. They were in fact friends for a time, although Wilde had the prescience to remark at their first meeting that 'the basis of literary friendship is mixing the poisoned bowl'. Afterwards they went their own ways, and a violent attack on *Dorian Gray* in the *Scots Observer* (written by Henley's lieutenant Charles Whibley) set the seal on their rivalry. If Wilde cast himself as the symbolic hero of the Decadence, Henley was equally ready to figure as the hero of the Counter-Decadence. Yet he was almost as much of an aesthete as Wilde after his fashion. In poetry he had begun as a rondelier; in arranging the 'mosaic' of *Views and Reviews* he aspired to be the Critic as Artist. And his imperialism was the outcome of the search for a picturesque attitude rather than a solid political philosophy. The sword was a toy sword – which doesn't make it any the less objectionable that he should have talked as though it were a real one.

There is no compelling reason why aestheticism should be associated with a reactionary outlook in politics. It can just as easily lead on to political quietism, or liberalism, or, as it did in Wilde's case, to socialism of a sort. But in practice the aesthetes of the late nineteenth century, when their passions flowed over into politics, usually turned out to be men of the far Right. It may be that those whose first aim is to 'appreciate' the world are the natural enemies of those whose first aim is to change it; it may be that, pushed far enough, the cult of Beauty inevitably merges with the cult of Violence in a common cult of the Irrational. At any rate, Henley's progress from aesthete to belligerent nationalist was a minor local variation on a widespread European theme of the period. In France there were figures like Maurice Barrès; in Italy there was D'Annunzio, whose 'exclusive aestheticism', as Henry James put it, was 'bound sooner or later to spring a leak'. And from D'Annunzio it was only a step, if that, to the aestheticism of someone like Vittorio Mussolini, the Duce's son, who became notorious during the Abyssinian War for expressing his pleasure at the beautiful patterns – like blossoming roses – made by bombs being dropped on groups of defenceless native horsemen. By comparison with later developments, Henley's arm-chair heroics seem fairly innocent. He had his generous instincts. But it makes a big difference, too, that he lived and wrote in what was still, all said and done, an exceptionally secure society, a society in which traditional conservatism was too strong for there to be much future for doctrinaire reactionaries. In a less stable situation, he might have seemed a much more disturbing portent.

Apart from Kipling and Yeats, the members of the Henley Regatta were minor figures, often very minor figures indeed. But a few shreds of bygone renown still cling to the name of Charles Whibley, largely because he was a friend of T. S. Eliot, who devoted two separate essays to him – one in *The Sacred Wood*, placing him among the 'imperfect critics' but dealing charitably with his imperfections, and the other an extended obituary tribute, which is reprinted in *Selected Essays*. Whibley (1859–1930) was working as an editor for Cassell's when he first got to know Henley, around the time that the *Scots Observer* was being launched. He soon made his mark as the new paper's most virulent contributor: even Henley sometimes had to ask him to tone down his attacks, although he was generally prepared to overlook his faults (including his constitutional laziness) and let him have his way. Whibley was 'the Wise Youth', his favourite protégé and a partial replacement in his affections for Stevenson. This was one Henley friendship which lasted, although it was never to be quite so close again after the end of the *National*

Observer phase, when Whibley went to Paris as the correspondent of the *Pall Mall Gazette*. Here he acquired some new heroes, notably Mallarmé: he used to attend the famous Tuesday gatherings in the poet's apartment in the Rue de Rome. But when he returned to England at the end of the 1890s he settled back into the old High Tory groove. On Frederick Greenwood's recommendation he was commissioned to write a monthly feature for *Blackwood's*, 'Musings Without Method', which was to be his main occupation for the rest of his life. He also took charge of the Tudor Translations after Henley's death, and contributed to the *Cambridge History of English Literature*. The kind of things he did best were studies of literary oddities like Sir Thomas Urquhart and sketches of the literary underworld, of Elizabethan pamphleteers and Grub Street characters like Ned Ward.

The Whibley whom Eliot met when he settled in London was a chubby, middle-aged clubman with a taste for good wine, first editions and classical quotations, and a bellyful of prejudices. He had close links with the academic establishment: he was a great friend of Ker, whose essays he edited, while in old age he married a daughter of Sir Walter Raleigh. And he moved in the fashionable world. There are some interesting glimpses of him in the recently published diaries of Lady Cynthia Asquith, pawing Lady Cynthia as opportunity presents itself ('His ardour and attentions were most trying. I wish he wouldn't quote Donne and call me "his New-found-land" '), and entertaining her with stories about the war. ('An Englishman threw a bomb into a German trench, and when he went up to it, found he had killed seven out of eight Germans – "Lucky swine!" said he to the surviving German, as he firmly stuck his bayonet through his body.') No collection of Whibleyana would be complete, either, without Beerbohm's drawing of 'Mr Charles Whibley consoling Mr Augustine Birrell for the loss of the Education Bill by a discourse on the uselessness of teaching anything whatsoever, sacred or profane, to children of the not aristocratic class'. It is I suppose just possible, dipping into 'Musings Without Method', to see the point of Eliot's enthusiasm. Whibley knew how to write, after a rather ornate fashion, and his invectives at least have some bite in them. But he was not a pleasant man.

The staff of the *National Observer* took a warmer interest in the Tory hierarchy than the Tory hierarchy did in the staff of the *National Observer*. The one exception, as far as the politicians were concerned, was George Wyndham, who began contributing to the paper in the early 1890s. Wyndham (1863–1913) had a passion for literature which survived Eton, Sandhurst, the Coldstream Guards, 'the Season', and the House of Commons. He also had immense pride of caste; but on literary matters he was ready to submit to Henley's guidance, and even Henley's corrections, as meekly as any member of the Regatta. It was Henley who persuaded him to edit North's *Plutarch* for the Tudor Translations, and who encouraged him to write the studies collected after his death as *Essays in Romantic Literature*. 'Romance' was Wyndham's line – not romanticism, but adventure, chivalry, a dream of feudal honour and Renaissance courtliness which led him to celebrate Malory, Ronsard, the Elizabethan mariners, the novels of Scott. Fifty years earlier he might have found his natural place among the leaders of Young England; in his own circle it seemed almost inevitable that he should deck out the idea of imperialism in neo-Elizabethan trappings. His temperament inclined him towards the tuppence-coloured and the flamboyant. But whatever else he was, he was no dilettante. A great deal of scholarship and hard work went into the hundred pages of his introduction to *Plutarch*, and into his edition of Shakespeare's poems, where he took particular satisfaction in being able to draw on his knowledge of heraldry and field sports. He could summon up more enthusiasm for the minute technicalities of these subjects than it is given to most of us to feel, but in the context his expertise was unquestionably an advantage.

There are times, reading about Wyndham, when it is hard not to believe that he was invented by an Edwardian novelist. The family estate with the improbable name ('Clouds'); the subaltern in barracks teaching himself Italian; the best-dressed man in the House of Commons – it all seems a little too good to be true. And what adds to the air of unreality, as Eliot remarks in his note on Wyndham in *The Sacred Wood*, is that 'his literature and his politics and his country life were one and the same thing'. Naturally this limits the scope of his criticism, but his literary friends were not disposed to complain; they had found their Prince Rupert, and they were happy to pay homage. A case in point is the fulsome dedication of Raleigh's Tudor Translations edition of Hoby's *The Courtier*: 'To George Wyndham, soldier, courtier, scholar, in a year of high emotion, and the accomplishing of unimaginable destinies, this treatise of amenity in deed, this old-faced but ever lustrous mirror of the complete gentleman'. The year was 1900, and for 'high emotion' read 'Mafeking'. Wyndham was Under-Secretary for War at the outbreak of the South African hostilities; then, in 1900, he was appointed Chief Secretary for Ireland. He sponsored an important Land Act, and his term of office was widely regarded as an outstanding success, but in 1905 Unionist agitation over a proposed scheme of administrative reform forced him to resign, and his ministerial career was at an end. He remained an M.P., however, although after the Liberals had returned to power he tended to brood darkly over what he saw as the danger of the Commons being overrun by the representatives of cosmopolitan finance – 'chappies in polo-breeches', 'piebald hybrids', 'Levantine levies'. (It was around this time that he became a friend of Belloc.) Then, during the House of Lords crisis of 1911, he came forward as one of the leading diehard opponents of the Parliament Act. His immediate comment, on hearing that enough Conservative peers had voted with the Government for the Bill to get through, was: 'We have been beaten by the Bishops and the Rats.' After this he largely withdrew into private life; he seems to have felt that the Romance had gone out of politics, that the imperial spirit was dying.

IV

Most of the men of letters in the Saintsbury–Lang Savile Club circle have inevitably been forgotten, including some, like Henry Duff Traill, author of *The New Lucian* and scourge of the realistic novel, who looked formidable enough in their day. Others continue to lead at least a shadowy existence. Austin Dobson (1840–1921) was the most accomplished of the rondeliers, and a great authority on the literature and art of the previous century; his

Eighteenth Century Vignettes and similar collections are still readable, but too prettified, too placid. One can hardly expect to catch the full force of the eighteenth century from a writer who felt obliged to alter Dr Johnson's famous description of Lord Chesterfield's *Letters* so that it read: 'They teach the morals of a *courtesan*, and the manners of a dancing master'. And Dobson is always wandering off into the least enthralling kind of Eng. Lit. gossip, about Prior's Kitty and Steele's Prue.

There is one belletrist of his generation, though, whose name still means something to the world at large: Sir Edmund Gosse, his close friend and for many years his colleague at the Board of Trade. Not that Gosse (1849–1928) could be said to survive on the strength of his innumerable collections of essays – *Critical Kit-Kats, Silhouettes, Books on the Table, More Books on the Table* – or his dainty volumes of verse – *In Russet and Silver, On Viol and Flute* – or even his lives of Donne and Swinburne. But there is *Father and Son*; there is the legend of the snobbish, prickly, disingenuous literary politician; and there is the irony of the two taken in conjunction, of the career which transformed the solemn little boy – 'Papa, don't tell me that she's a Paedobaptist!' – into the elderly mandarin who prided himself on his coroneted friends and who was capable of replying, when asked whether he was interested in such-and-such a young writer, 'I have not been invited to take an interest in him'. One can easily forget, contemplating Gosse in old age, how difficult the very first steps of that career were. Certainly the Plymouth Brethren among whom he spent his childhood would have been appalled to learn that their Infant Samuel was going to grow up into a literary critic. They were deeply suspicious of the secular imagination. As a boy, Gosse had worried himself sick when he heard a preacher denouncing the Stratford Tercentenary:

At this very moment there is proceeding, unreproved, a blasphemous celebration of the birth of Shakespeare, a lost soul now suffering for his sins in hell!

and he was pathetically grateful to his father for reassuring him that the condemnation was rash, that for all they knew Shakespeare might have repented of his sins and been saved. Literature was still something to be explored surreptitiously, a fearful joy. But before long it was to provide him with an escape-route, and after that with a passport to the exalted social regions for which he yearned.

At seventeen he started work in the British Museum, as an assistant librarian. He found himself in a strongly literary atmosphere; Coventry Patmore had only just resigned from the staff, while in addition to Richard Garnett his colleagues included such minor or minimal poets as Arthur O'Shaughnessy (author of 'We are the music-makers' and *Lays of France*), Théo Marzials (who wrote the words for one of the great Victorian drawing-room hits, 'The Creole Love Song'), and John Payne, founder of the Villon Society. The Museum was a hive of rondeliering, or, as Gosse himself put it, 'a nest of singing birds'. But the pay was miserable, and at twenty-six he welcomed the chance to go to the Board of Trade as an official translator. Even here, the salary was only £400, while his literary earnings at this time amounted to not much more than £100 a year. What the Civil Service offered him, however, was the kind of leisure which an earlier generation of writers had found in the East India Office – leisure to write, and leisure to cultivate his literary connections. His most celebrated catch was Swinburne, whom he had first approached, much to his father's dismay, as early as 1867. Gradually he set about making himself indispensable to the poet, only to have the prize snatched from his hands by Watts-Dunton. But there were plenty of other prizes to be won. He dined everywhere, corresponded assiduously with leading authors, said the right things to the right people. When he applied for the post of Clark Lecturer at Cambridge in 1880, the three testimonials which he submitted, according to his cousin Arthur Waugh (but cousins sometimes exaggerate) were from Tennyson, Browning and Arnold. At any rate, he was duly elected, and his first set of lectures were well received; they were subsequently published by the University Press, under the title of *From Shakespeare to Pope: an inquiry into the causes and phenomena of the rise of Classical Poetry in England*. And then, out of a clear sky, came the biggest single setback of his career, a devastating chapter-and-verse attack on the book in the *Quarterly* by John Churton Collins. Gosse's friends rallied to his defence and turned on his assailant. Collins was churlish (he had been one of Gosse's dinner-guests), he was pedantic, crusty, unbalanced, malicious. The only trouble is that he also happened to be right, that he had no difficulty in pointing out one howler after another. It might not have mattered so much if *From Shakespeare to Pope* had simply been presented as an avowedly amateur essay in appreciation. But there were those causes and phenomena, the whole show of elaborate scholarship which went with blunders about which century an author lived in, and whether a work under discussion had been written in prose or verse. We all make mistakes, but some of Gosse's are so glaring that one half suspects him of a psychological kink, an impulse towards self-betrayal. Or it might simply be that he tried too hard, that facing a university audience he felt the need to over-compensate for his own lack of academic training. Whatever the explanation, he was deeply wounded by the consequences. He tried to extricate himself from Collins's charges where he could: he tried to eat humble pie where he couldn't; he made airy little jokes to his family about 'Shirt 'n Collars'. But the experience had shaken him badly, and it was to rankle for years.

Gradually, however, he regained his self-confidence. He pushed doggedly ahead with his books: biographies, essays, historical surveys. And if the professional scholars still looked askance at his scholarship, he could always console himself with the thought that he enjoyed the regard of literary men to whom a Churton Collins was of no account. New friendships ripened – with Hardy, with Henry James. He began to take up younger writers, and moved into a home in Hanover Terrace where he could hold court in style. To his immense satisfaction, in 1904 he was appointed librarian to the House of Lords. Here he was able to indulge to the full both his snobbishness, and his powers of feline observation; he kept a diary during his term of office, and such extracts from it as have appeared in print suggest no lack of the quality which his biographer, Evan Charteris, described as 'sparkling malice'. For he was a complicated kind of a snob, and if he loved a lord, no one could exactly accuse him of being a flunkey:

Peers frequenting the library [writes Charteris] can hardly have failed to notice that their Librarian was interested in something more than the books confided to his custody. Their going and coming was closely observed by a pair of piercing eyes which gleamed through gold-rimmed spectacles from a far corner of the Library, where the Librarian sat at his desk. Nothing escaped the observation of those eyes – they were alert to give a welcome to a friend, they were even more alert to condemn a fault. The mishandling of a volume or an aimless interference with the shelves would bring Gosse at a rapid springy trot across the floor of the Library to the side of the offender with a bitingly civil request to know if he could be of any assistance.

There were ludicrous scenes: Gosse publicly berated an elderly peer who had extinguished a small burner used for heating sealing-wax – 'If you did that on purpose I must ask you to apologize' – and when the apology was refused he complained to his superiors and kept the quarrel going for years. His touchiness was even stronger than his snobbery, and his governessy instincts were stronger than either; he was the sensitive soul who keeps proving more obstinate than ordinary thick-skinned humanity, the fragile creature who turns out to be indestructible. Although he had hoped that the retirement rules would be waived for him, he was compelled to give up his librarianship in 1914. But at the age of seventy he found a new perch as chief reviewer for the *Sunday Times*, a position which he held until his death. He remained a keen student of the literary stock market to the last, carefully advancing some reputations and nibbling away at others. Among younger writers he was chiefly interested in the poets. He approved of Edith Sitwell and Siegfried Sassoon, but drew the line at 'that preposterous American filibuster and Provençal charlatan', Ezra Pound.

His social ascendancy was reinforced by his international connections. From the early days of his career he had aspired to be a literary envoy between Britain and the Continent: the very first separate item of criticism listed in the official bibliography of his work is an article by him which somehow found its way into a Dutch magazine, *Een Nieuwe Meteoor aan Engeland's Letterkundigen Hemel: Algernon Charles Swinburne*. When he was still looking for work as a reviewer, R. H. Hutton told him that he needed a speciality, and suggested, more or less at random, the virtually unexplored subject of Scandinavian literature. It turned out to be the best piece of advice he could have been given. Spending his vacations in Norway and Denmark, charming his way into the company of Scandinavian authors, he was able to bring back to England the earliest news of Ibsen, and to set himself up as an authority in a field where there were as yet no real rivals. He also prided himself on his work as a popularizer of French literature. It was through a common enthusiasm for French verse-forms that he first became friendly with Austin Dobson, while as a critic he claimed to be the disciple of only one man, Sainte-Beuve. On the other hand until he was middle-aged he had little more than a tourist's knowledge of France, while his views on French literature were conventional and staid: he much preferred the Parnassians to the Symbolists, for example. But he made a useful public figurehead, especially during the period of the *Entente* and the First World War, when he was fêted by the French Academy and accepted in France as virtually the official representative of English literature. He was on particularly close terms with André Gide, who liked him but noted in his *Journal* that all too often he seemed animated less by genuine feeling than by '*une sorte de self-respect*'.

Gosse would make a good subject for a new biography. Charteris's official life was necessarily circumspect; there is no hint in it, for instance, of the Gosse who can be encountered in Phyllis Grosskurth's biography of John Addington Symonds, attending Browning's funeral service in Westminster Abbey and constantly taking furtive glances at the photograph of a comely youth which Symonds had just sent him from Italy. A biographer would also be able to draw on the numerous descriptions of Gosse which have been left by his contemporaries. By all accounts, he had an exceedingly sharp tongue – 'a man whom one would prefer to survive', according to Henry James, which didn't prevent the two of them remaining friends for over thirty years. Beerbohm was another intimate; he and Gosse once composed a sonnet about James, sending each other alternate lines on postcards –

> You stand, marmoreal darling of the Few,
> Lord of the troubled speech and single eye.

Gosse also retained the friendship of figures as different as Lord

Haldane and Chesterton. Maugham described him as the most amusing talker he had ever met. Yet when all the tributes have been added up, the impression which remains longest is one of artfulness and calculation, of literature subordinated to petty social ends. And one portrait of Gosse which his hypothetical biographer should be careful not to overlook is the account given in his memoirs by Evelyn Waugh, who as his kinsman had known him since early childhood:

> Unlike Desmond MacCarthy, who succeeded to his position, he had little natural amiability or generosity. I was early drawn to panache. I saw Gosse as a Mr Tulkinghorn, the soft-footed, inconspicuous, ill-natured habitué of the great world, and I longed for a demented lady's-maid to make an end of him.

The minor departments of literature tend to defy generalization no less than the major. There were critics in Late Victorian England who had as little in common with the Gosse circle as they did with one another – Alice Meynell, who wrote one of the best Victorian appreciations of Dickens; F. W. H. Myers; Havelock Ellis, who originally came before the public not as a sexologist but as the editor of the invaluable Mermaid Dramatists series, and the author of *The New Spirit* (1890), a collection of essays on Ibsen, Tolstoy and other controversial topics which was a clarion-call in its time. And even among more conventional men of letters there were naturally marked differences of temperament and widely varying degrees of talent. Richard Garnett, for instance, had a number of links with Gosse. They were colleagues at the British Museum (where Garnett remained for nearly fifty years, eventually becoming Keeper of Printed Books); they were the joint authors of *English Literature: An Illustrated Record*, a sumptuous four-volume affair published by Heinemann in 1903. But any comparison between them as scholars would be cruelly unfair to Gosse. Garnett was a prodigy of learning; he also had a quite un-Gosse-like vein of spirited 'pagan' scepticism which came out in his collection of stories, *The Twilight of the Gods*. Other scholars had their own whims and specialities. Nevertheless, viewed from a distance the orthodox Late Victorian literati do seem to merge into an unusually compact group – the Courthopes and the Mackails, the

Sidney Colvins and the Sidney Lees. On the whole they were probably more erudite than their modern successors; they were often civil servants, and they had the Civil Service virtues; they were nothing if not in earnest about their responsibilities as the custodians of tradition. But they were also stuffy, conventional, sedate, out of touch with the growing points of literature in their time; and a modern reader who ventures into their world soon finds himself struggling for lack of oxygen.

One reason for the broad similarities of outlook among Victorian men of letters was that most of them were children of the business or professional class, with little if any first-hand knowledge of working-class life or of the industrial regions. To take some of the figures who have been mentioned in this chapter, Lang was the son of a lawyer from Selkirk; Saintsbury's father was secretary of the Southampton docks; Henley's father was a bookseller from Gloucester; Whibley's, a merchant from Sittingbourne in Kent. The elder Gosse was a naturalist who lived in London and Devonshire; Richard Garnett senior was a clergyman and, like his son, on the staff of the British Museum; Mackail was a son of the manse from a village in Buteshire. It is of course simple-minded to suppose that a writer's opinions can be directly accounted for in terms of his social origins; yet it would be hard to imagine a critic with a working-class background writing in the style of, say, Lang, or playing down politics quite as much as Mackail does in his otherwise admirable life of William Morris.

Not that there were many Victorian critics with a working-class background in the first place. Under nineteenth-century conditions an occasional genius might overcome extreme poverty, but for mere talent the obstacles were immense. In later as in earlier Victorian times the few critics of working-class origins tended to be Scotsmen, like the poet James Thomson (1834–82), who was brought up in the Royal Caledonian Asylum, an orphanage for the children of poor Scottish soldiers and sailors, and who himself served for some years as an army schoolmaster, before being discharged for a minor breach of discipline. Thomson survives as the author of *The City of Dreadful Night*, but he was also a critic of considerable gifts. After leaving the army he

worked mainly as a journalist, although he was too uncompromising (and cantankerous) to make much of a living at it. His poems
give one some idea of his grim lodging-house existence, dogged
by alcoholism, suicidal depressions, insomnia –

The city is of Night, but not of Sleep

– and contemporary memoirs help to fill out the picture. Thomson
tramping through the rain and slush to George Eliot's funeral,
unable to see anything when he finally got there except a mass of
dripping umbrellas; Thomson in jail, after setting fire to his land-
lord's kitchen; Thomson on his death-bed, in the throes of his last
terrible haemorrhage – far more than Gissing, he was the gaunt
outcast of Victorian letters.

Until 1875, when he quarrelled with Bradlaugh, his principal
outlet was the secularist *National Reformer*; from then until shortly
before his death, he wrote chiefly for *Cope's Tobacco Plant*, a trade
magazine published in Liverpool. Here, apart from being expected
to provide a certain amount of straight sales talk, such as his
causerie 'Stray Whiffs from an Old Smoker', he was allowed to
write at length about whatever he chose – Rabelais, Whitman,
Ben Jonson – although not unnaturally Cope's encouraged him to
work in as many references as possible to the beneficial effects of
tobacco. The results were often bizarre; and it is unfortunate that
the selection of his essays compiled after his death by his friend
Bertram Dobell* should have drawn so heavily on his contributions to the *Tobacco Plant*. Recently, however, a new selection of
his prose (edited by Professor W. D. Schaefer) has given him a
chance to live down his nicotine-stained reputation. It would be
pointless to claim too much for him, or to pretend that he wasn't
handicapped by his early lack of opportunities. In verse he has a
weakness for the would-be Sublime, for words like 'tenebrous'
and 'vastitude'; in prose he often lapses into pedantry or laboured
sarcasm. But in neither case can his faults altogether obscure an
essential power and originality. The tone of his criticism is often
harsh, but not without justification: it is a relief to find someone

---

* Dobell (1842–1914) was a Charing Cross Road bookseller and antiquarian,
largely self-educated, who is chiefly remembered for having discovered and
identified the works of Thomas Traherne.

ready to pay back the hatchet-men of the *Saturday Review* in kind. And, given the period at which he wrote, it at any rate makes a change to find someone who is prepared to cast a dissenting vote against Tennyson: 'When wax flowers are oracular oaks, Dodona may be discovered in the Isle of Wight, but hardly until then . . .' On the positive side, Thomson was well ahead of his time in his enthusiasms, and cosmopolitan in his outlook. He was one of the first English critics to comment intelligently on Blake; he felt sure that much the greatest American writer, apart from Whitman, was 'the author of *The Whale*' (*Moby Dick*); his renderings of Heine won him praise from no less a person than Karl Marx. And no Victorian had a deeper admiration for Swift, whom he described as 'too strong and terrible for Macaulay and Thackeray'. His finest piece of prose is a Swiftian satire on the dream of human perfectibility and indefinite moral progress, *Proposals for the Speedy Extinction of Evil and Misery*. Needless to say, he falls far short of his model; but at the same time the *Proposals* are very much more than a pastiche. There was a well-spring of authentic existential bitterness in Thomson which set him as far apart from Victorian radicals as from Victorian conservatives, and further apart still from contemporary men of letters who were trying to 'revive' the eighteenth century. How odd to think of this proud, lonely, saturnine figure living and writing in London at the same time as Austin Dobson and Edmund Gosse.

6

EARLY ENGLISH

I

At the beginning of the nineteenth century, and for at least a generation after that, the idea of a university offering to teach 'English' would have seemed ludicrous – except in Scotland, where the standard English authors still enjoyed something of the academically privileged status of foreigners. The general growth of Victorian higher education, however, was inevitably accompanied by an expansion of organized English studies, of *Anglistik*. How could it have been otherwise? English was an obvious popular substitute for the classics; it was well suited to the needs of training colleges and public examination boards; the Romantic movement had invested it with unprecedented moral prestige, and at the same time it could be put across to practical men as the most serviceable, the least abstruse of the Humanities. A highly patriotic subject, too. Then again the literature was quite simply *there*, as they say, on the printed page, or better still in manuscript, a goldfield waiting for scholars and commentators to stake their claims. Under the circumstances, the only surprising thing is that progress should have been as slow as it was. There were delays to be endured, prejudices to be overcome; and even when English departments were finally established, the first results – in terms of published work at least – were generally unimpressive. Until the closing years of the century the notion of a *critique universitaire* scarcely existed in England, while even the labours of exhuming and annotating texts were as often as not performed by private enthusiasts far from the universities – by a country gentleman like

Whitwell Elwin, the editor of Pope, or a clergyman like Alexander Grosart, the Nonconformist minister from Blackburn who was responsible for the Fuller's Worthies Library and scores of other useful reprints. Despite an occasional exception, such as Masson's voluminous life of Milton, the same is no less true of literary biographies. It was left to a busy journalist and man of affairs like John Forster, for instance, to undertake the standard lives of Goldsmith, Landor and Swift.

One by one, however, the citadels fell, until by the 1890s even Oxford was ready to capitulate. The story of how the battle was fought has been told more than once, most notably by Stephen Potter in that entertaining book *The Muse in Chains*. (Why doesn't some Grosart reprint it?) It is a chastening story, on the whole, in spite of the comedy which Mr Potter manages to extract from it, a chronicle of obstinate last-ditch stands and bungled opportunities. The philologists tugged this way, the bibliographers tugged that. Mistakes were made in devising curricula for which we are still paying the price. Institutions failed to adapt to changed circumstances, and only the specialists seem to have had any very clear idea of where they were going. The subject grew, but it didn't thrive.

Before assigning blame with too liberal a hand, one must concede that the difficulties, the inherent difficulties, were immense. How do you organize the wholesale teaching of imaginative literature, without putting the bird in a cage? How do you construct a syllabus out of the heart's affections, or award marks for wit and sensitivity? Candidates will be expected to show a knowledge of human nature – which, human nature being what it is, represents an open invitation to wander on at random, to drain the subject of intellectual content. And since nobody wants that, a strong countervailing current is inevitably set in motion. Teachers turn with relief to the small, hard, ascertainable fact; they become preoccupied with sources, or analogues, or backgrounds, or textual cruces, or other interesting but secondary considerations. Such problems are of course by no means unique to English studies. They exist in many other academic fields as well. But they do present themselves with peculiar force and intimacy when studying the literature of one's native language, and it could be argued that, armed as we are with microfilm and computer, we have not entirely solved them even now. For the pioneers, it was harder still.

When all the allowances have been made, however, there seems no inescapable reason why the early development of English teaching should have been as stunted as it was. If only a sufficiently commanding and adult personality had concerned himself with the subject. . . . Leslie Stephen would have been the ideal man: he wrote an admirable paper (originally delivered as a lecture at St Andrews) on 'The Study of English Literature' which reveals as sane and realistic a grasp of first principles as one would expect. It suggests that any English department planned by him would have struck as harmonious a balance as humanly possible between the rival claims of criticism, scholarship and pleasure. He understood how to make creative use of social and intellectual history; he knew that auxiliary studies were to be neither superstitiously over-valued nor despised; he had, in short, a keen sense of the appropriate. But no one asked him to put his ideas into practice, and the specialists went on their way unheeding.

Professional English studies as they actually developed drew their inspiration from two main sources: the new scientific philology (scientific, but with a romantically 'Saxon' tinge), and the movement for adult education. Sometimes these two streams would converge, most turbulently in the person of F. J. Furnivall (1825–1910). Furnivall helped to found the Working Men's College, together with F. D. Maurice, and lectured there on the English Poets from Chaucer to Tennyson; he was also, besides being a redoubtable scholar himself, one of the great rock-blasting entrepreneurs of Victorian scholarship, the kind of man who if his energies had taken another turn might have covered a continent with railways. As secretary of the Philological Society, he spent twenty years amassing materials for the *New* (Oxford) *English Dictionary*, of which he was one of the first editors; as founder of the Early English Texts Society, he performed an indispensable service for medievalists. Societies were his natural element. Apart from the E.E.T.S., he also founded the New Shakspere Society, the Ballad Society, the Chaucer Society, the Wycliffe Society, the Shelley Society, the Browning Society. It is a measure of his optimism that he even tried to start a Lydgate Society, though it failed to get off the ground.

Of all these organizations, the most ambitious was naturally the New Shakspere. (New, to distinguish it from the original Shakespeare Society, which had been discredited by the forgeries of its founder, John Payne Collier; Shakspere, because Furnivall insisted on spelling it that way.) Its activities were a curious mixture of genuine scholarship, pseudo-science, and richly embroidered speculation, while its guiding policies turned out to be more contradictory than Furnivall seems to have realized. On the one hand, he decreed that the first aim should be to establish the exact chronology of the plays, which in practice meant having recourse to his colleague F. G. Fleay's metrical tests: that way Disintegration lay. On the other hand, he urged members to study the essential unity and organic growth of Shakespeare's achievement, which in effect meant weaving garlands of imaginative biography. Edward Dowden's *Shakspere: His Mind and Art* was the best-known product of this approach, but Furnivall himself was never reluctant to let his fancy wander:

So our chestnut-haird, fair, brown-eyd, rosy-cheekt boy went to school. . . . Taking the boy to be the father of the man, I see a square-built yet lithe and active fellow, with ruddy cheeks, hazel eyes, a high forehead, and auburn hair, as full of life as an egg is full of meat, impulsive, inquiring, sympathetic; up to any fun and daring; into scrapes, and out of them with a laugh. . . .

In its more sober moments the Society encouraged a good deal of serious research and sponsored numerous valuable reprints. Even the verse-tests, applied in moderation, had their undoubted uses. But in the eyes of at least one contemporary – Swinburne – they amounted to sacrilege, and he let fly at Furnivall in the press. The public controversy which ensued was one of the most infantile of the century. The scholar nick-named the poet 'Pigsbrook'; the poet, with equally devastating philological wit, nick-named the scholar 'Brothelsdyke'. Any layman who followed the affair hoping for enlightenment must have come away feeling that he had strayed into Bedlam by mistake.

Some of Furnivall's other outbursts were better suited to the occasion. When the odious Whibley attacked him in the *Scots Observer*, he immediately dashed off an appropriate reply. ('Send him up to Barnum's as the champion skunk of Scotland.') There are times when it is impossible not to applaud his fighting spirit, or marvel at his vitality. Like the young Shakespeare, he was a lithe and active fellow; at the age of seventy he had enough sur-plus energy left to found the Hammersmith Sculling Club for Girls and Men, and he was still turning out with them on the river every Sunday at the age of eighty-five. He was also an ardent old-fashioned socialist, who refused to be bound by snobbish conven-tion. It is characteristic that the memorial volume published after his death should have contained, along with contributions by scholars from all over the world, a simple tribute from a waitress in the ABC tea-shop in Oxford Street where he used to hold court.

Only a man of Furnivall's obstinacy could have accomplished what he did, when he did. Unfortunately, however, the same blunt qualities which made him an effective pioneer also served to cramp and coarsen his imagination: a subject dominated by Furnivalls was a subject for the emotionally retarded. Comparable limitations, though less drastic ones, mark the career of Henry Morley (1822–94), the first Englishman to make the academic teaching of English his full-time profession. Morley was another heroic primitive, a true early Victorian. He originally qualified as a doctor, but after being swindled and bankrupted by his partner took up school-teaching instead. It was while running a school in Manchester that he first discovered his prowess as a public speaker. Desperate to supplement his income, he advertised and delivered a short course of lectures covering an impressive range of topics: 'The Crust of the Globe', 'The Human Body', 'The Human Mind', 'Sanitary Law', and 'A Critical Analysis of the *Faerie Queene*'. The response was encouraging enough for him to persist, and to try his luck at journalism. At first there was more interest in his views on Sanitary Law than on the *Faerie Queene*. John Forster commissioned him to write a series of articles on domestic hygiene for the *Examiner*; then Dickens offered him five guineas a week, which he accepted, to come to London and join the staff of *Household Words*. He might easily have remained a professional author; during his years on the paper he also found time to publish a number of books, the most successful of them being a life of the French potter Palissy (a favourite hero of Samuel Smiles). Gradually, however, it was borne in upon him that his true mission was to teach English literature, to show how English authors had written a collective biography of the national mind. After lecturing for some years at King's College, in 1865 he succeeded David Masson as Professor of English at University College, a position he was to hold for quarter of a century. He also flung himself into extension lecturing, especially in the North of England, hurtling round Yorkshire and Lancashire with an hour on the Jacobean drama here, an hour on the Caroline poets there, an hour on the eighteenth-century novel somewhere else. His diaries read like a cross between Bradshaw and the index to Legouis and Cazamian; his constant complaint was that railway compartments were too dark to read in. No one who was not driven on by a burning belief could have kept up the pace. For lecturing was only half the story; he was simultaneously editing innumerable reprints of the classics for Routledge and Cassell, and manufacturing a long succession of textbooks. His *First Sketch of English Literature* (1873) sold getting on for 40,000 copies; his *English Writers*, though unfinished at the time of his death, already ran to eleven volumes; Baron Tauchnitz in person requested him to write a survey of Victorian literature as Volume 2000 in the Tauchnitz series. With legitimate pride in his labours, he used to refer to his house as 'Inky Villa'. No other teacher of his generation had worked harder to popularize his subject.

Morley was entirely devoted to literature, and utterly unpretentious as an individual. Life at Inky Villa must have been a curious blend of the homely and the exotic: he records in his diary how he casually spent an evening 'reading to the missus as much as she could bear of the last half of the *Duchess of Malfi*. Horrors upset her.' When he eventually retired, and went to live in the Isle of Wight, he simply redoubled his scholarly efforts. At the same time he developed a passion for fruit-growing; his garden, he claimed, was 'one of the fruitiest bits of England'. Not a particularly subtle man – and yet he succeeded where subtler men would have failed. One need only recall Arthur Clough, who preceded him briefly as professor at University College in the early 1850s. Clough was the original Poet in the English Department, and he was thankful to get out of it as quickly as possible; Morley by contrast completely identified himself with his job. He really cared for his students (he even used to treat their minor medical ailments, gratis), and he tried to make them feel that what they were studying was the subject of subjects. Nor could anyone have made much headway in those bleak early days without the kind of rough self-confident energy which he possessed in such abundance. He believed in it all – the *Ormulum* and Martin Marprelate, *Pharonnida* and John Philips (not to be confused with John Phillips). The prospects for English studies seemed boundless. But English studies meant *Anglistik*, meant drawing maps or piling up information. As for delicacy, depth, the creative transforming surge of life – these things were not Morley's business, and he would never have pretended that they were.

II

Resistance to the introduction of English was naturally strongest at Oxford and Cambridge. Everything about the subject was suspect: it was modern, it was enticing, it was bound to be the softest of soft options. Most of all, it was unnecessary. A self-respecting undergraduate simply picked up his native literature as he went along; he no more had to be instructed in Milton and Fielding than he had to be taught the basic outlines of English history or the best-known parts of the Bible. For much of the century, indeed, this was the common assumption of educated men. It was not some arch-reactionary don, but John Stuart Mill, who gave it as his view (in his St Andrews inaugural) that Latin and Greek were the only languages which should be allowed a place in the curriculum, and that 'the leading facts of ancient and modern history should be known by the student from his private reading'. How many students actually lived up to this counsel of perfection is another matter. One suspects that even at the best of times they never amounted to more than a small minority; and as the university system expanded, it became obvious that much of the future necessarily lay with the study of modern languages, modern history – and modern English. Modernity: that, for Oxford and Cambridge at least, was the major stumbling-block. But happily a way round soon suggested itself. What was modern English without Middle English? What was Middle English without Old English? What did any of it mean without Gothic, Frisian, Old Norse, High German, Middle Dutch? From which it followed that when literature *was* finally smuggled into the older universities, it came heavily disguised as philology. At Cambridge the great man was Skeat, the professor of Anglo-Saxon. There were some distinguished post-medieval scholars in the university as well, such as Aldis Wright, librarian of Trinity and co-editor of the *Cambridge Shakespeare*, but they took no part in teaching; and English, in so far as it existed as a subject at all, was tacked on to the Medieval and Modern Languages Tripos. A separate chair of literature (endowed by the future Lord Rothermere in memory of King Edward VII) was not established until 1911. At Oxford, the pressure for change was felt earlier, not least on account of the campaign mounted from outside by Churton Collins, and resistance was more devious. In 1885, bowing, as it at first seemed, to the inevitable, the authorities set up the Merton Professorship of English Language and Literature. A chair of Anglo-Saxon had existed in the university since the eighteenth century, so it might reasonably have been concluded that the new professor's qualifications were to be literary rather than linguistic. Working on this assumption, some half a dozen prominent critics allowed their names to go forward as candidates, Saintsbury, Dowden and, of course, Churton Collins among them. They should have known their Oxford better. The successful applicant was an Englishman who up until then had been teaching at the University of Göttingen, A. S. Napier, a deeply obscure specialist in Germanic philology.

This was the signal for Churton Collins really to move into action. The necessity for an English School and the sins of the Oxford anti-literary establishment became an obsession with him. He bombarded the newspapers, lectured, harangued, wrote a book, enlisted the support of leading public personalities. No cause could have been closer to his heart. From his Balliol days, his passion for expounding poetry had been a byword. He was acknowledged to be the most successful of the extension lecturers. His scholarly publications covered an unusually wide field. He loved literature, and, despite the rebuffs he had received, he loved Oxford. But he was also a hustler, a trouble-maker; and his attack on Gosse merely confirmed suspicions that he was not the type of man that Oxford wanted. It would be wrong to suppose that he was simply banished to outer darkness on account of his tactless behaviour. He had influential friends, such as Mr Asquith. The Duchess of Teck attended a course of his lectures. Like Gosse, he was frequently invited to give talks on literature in smart Mayfair drawing-rooms, as a kind of intellectual cabaret-turn. But in the academic world he had got himself an irretrievably bad name, and it was in spite of his advocacy rather than because of it that Oxford eventually agreed to set up an English Honours School in 1893. Even so, he still had wild hopes of the new Merton professorship of literature (just literature) when it was instituted ten years later. But the job went to the younger, more polished, altogether more eligible Walter Raleigh, and Collins had to content himself with accepting the offer of a Chair at the University of Birmingham.

Had he been elected instead of Napier in the first place, and then been given a chance to create the English School of his dreams, the whole subsequent development of the subject at Oxford would certainly have been very different in at least one fundamental respect. By training he was a classicist, and every bit as strong as his belief in English studies was his conviction that they had to be indissolubly bound up with a study of Latin and Greek. Homer and Virgil, he argued, were indispensable for a decent knowledge of English literature. *Beowulf* was almost totally irrelevant. True to character, he overstated his case. There is a good deal of English literature, after all, especially fiction, on which the Classics have no bearing whatever. And even where there is a direct debt to the Latin or Greek, a knowledge of the original model, however much it may add to a reader's appreciation, is by definition not absolutely essential. As Leslie Stephen remarked, in a passage referring obliquely to the whole Churton Collins controversy, you can admire a girl without having to find out first whether or not she gets her looks from her grandmother. The study of literature is one thing, the study of literary genetics is another. Collins himself did not always distinguish between them: he had first come into prominence with a set of articles (published by Stephen in the *Cornhill*) on Tennyson's borrowings from other poets, and tracking down sources was his speciality. Naturally he attached too much importance to it. All the same, his general position on English studies was clearly a more tenable one than that of the compulsory-Gothic brigade. An English school as he envisaged it might have developed into something really impressive; and, to put the case at its crudest, one would rather carry away from a university a smattering of Catullus than a few garbled memories of the *Finnsburh Fragment*.

If only he had kept his temper, if only he had known when not to labour the point. But diplomacy was an art he had no use for, and the frustrations of academic politics were the occasion of his boiling rages rather than the cause. On the face of it, he was a conventionally unconventional don, of the sort one expects to meet in detective stories (and indeed, he once wrote a detective story himself). He was a keen amateur criminologist, a railway enthusiast who liked to ride on the footplate, a dabbler in psychical research. He got to know the Tichborne Claimant, and went down to Whitechapel to join in the hunt for Jack the Ripper. He had a passion for graveyards: whenever he arrived in a strange town, the first place he visited was always the local cemetery. He used to go for regular swims in the Serpentine at seven in the morning. An ebullient, rather boyish extrovert, it seemed, with a wide-ranging curiosity. And then every so often his spirits would slump, and he would be seized by the most paralysing black suicidal depression. These moods often came on for no apparent reason, and sometimes lasted for months at a time; the doctors, lacking any alternative explanation, put them down to overwork, but they plainly argue a severely disturbed personality, a bottled-up aggression which found partial relief in the licensed ferocity of Collins's work as a critic. This is not to say that his more damaging reviews were merely 'neurotic'. On the contrary, most of the errors to which he drew attention ought not to have been let pass, and other reviewers in the same situation might well have delivered equally unfavourable verdicts. But he did bring to the task of demolition a peculiar intensity, which was over and above the call of scholarly duty, and which suggests the brooding assassin rather than the judge. Gosse was merely the first of his victims; during the course of his career, especially after Frank Harris had encouraged him to speak his mind in the *Saturday Review*, he succeeded in savaging a fairly representative cross-section of his fellow-critics, from Aldis Wright ('dilettantism, pedantry') and Stopford Brooke ('twaddle') to the great Saintsbury himself ('seems to take a boisterous pride in exhibiting his grossness'). To read through the reviews which he thought it worthwhile reprinting in *Ephemera Critica: or Plain Truths about Current Literature* (1901) is still a bracing experience. It is true that at times he lacks all sense of proportion, that he can work himself into a lather because some forgotten eighteenth-century poetaster has accidentally been referred to as John when it should have been James. Once he was really on the warpath, any piece of ammunition would do. But by no means all the blunderings which he condemns were trivial ones. How odd, for instance, that Saintsbury should have persisted in placing *Measure for Measure* among Shakespeare's early plays and bracketing it with *The Two Gentlemen of Verona*. And as for the more pretentious belletrists, they simply played into Collins's hands. Poor Gosse is given another going-over, this time for his *Modern English Literature*, with its unhappy attempts at phrase-making – e.g. the description of Keats's odes as 'Titanic and Titianic'. Richard Le Gallienne, as a first offender, is let off with a caution; but Collins cannot resist quoting from his review of Pater's *Plato and Platonism*: 'The temperate beauty, the dry beauty beloved of Plato, finds expression in the sweet and stately volume itself, with its smooth night-blue binding, its rose-leaf yellow pages, its soft and yet grave type.'

This was the kind of verbal upholstery which could be passed off as serious criticism in those days without too much trouble, and Collins's open displays of animus at least make an invigorating contrast. Judged by less parochial standards, however, he is liable to seem a mere irritable chalkdusty pedagogue – certainly not the man to give the cause of English studies an imaginative new lead, as opposed to a useful polemical push. He had little interest in contemporary literature; when he did praise a living author, it tended to be someone like William Watson (who wrote an ode to him) or Stephen Phillips. And his passionate belief in the scholarly virtues went with an arrogance which allowed him to assert dogmatically, for instance, that the Elizabethan dramatists,

although their bread depended on the brutal and illiterate savages for whose amusement they catered, still talked the language of scholars and poets, and forced their rude hearers to sit out works which could have been intelligible only to scholars and poets.

After this, it is rather sad to reflect that he should have lived long enough to see his own reputation as a scholar heavily undermined. The first number of the *Modern Language Review* (1905) contained a review by W. W. Greg of his edition of Robert Greene, dismissing it as the work of 'an arm-chair editor' – a coldly efficient piece of analysis, with none of Collins's *ad hominem* huffing and puffing, clearly marking the advent of a rigorous new professionalism to which he could lay no claim.

His closing years in general were rather overcast. At Birmingham he embarked on one last crusade, and began agitating for the establishment of a university school of journalism. But it was not quite the same thing as campaigning single-handed against the Gosses and Napiers and their friends in high places, and much of the old fight had gone out of him: there were to be no more explosive letters to the papers from 'Oxoniensis' or 'A Lover of the Truth'. He died in 1908, under circumstances which have never been properly cleared up. While visiting Oxford, he was seized by an acute depression, and decided to spend a month with a doctor friend in Lowestoft trying to recuperate. His stay there apparently did him good, but on the day he was due to leave he was found drowned in a stream on the outskirts of the town. The coroner's jury returned a verdict of accidental death; as far as could be ascertained, he had succumbed to the effects of a sleeping-draught and somehow lost his footing. Among the documents found on his body were a few notes for a speech on Dr Johnson which he had been invited to deliver in Lichfield, and a sheet of paper on which he had written down some lines from *Piers Plowman*:

I was wearie of wandering and went me to reste
Under a brod banke by a bourne side,
And as I lay and lenede and lokede on the waters,
I slumbered in a sleping, hit sownede so murie.

III

Churton Collins was held at bay by Oxford for a generation; Walter Raleigh (1861–1922) had to be positively cajoled into going there. When the Merton Chair was offered to him in 1904, his first response was to turn it down flat: he was only just beginning to settle in to a professorship in Glasgow, he felt duty-bound to stay. But eventually the electors prevailed on him to change his mind. It was now accepted that 'English' meant English literature, and Raleigh seemed the right man to set the subject on its feet. He had already acquired a high reputation as a teacher. He was enthusiastic without being fanatical, elegant without being frivolous. He had star quality, and by comparison his rivals looked like a group of honest workaday drudges. The *moment*, the *milieu* demanded him.

He reached the top by a circuitous route. First, University College, London, where Henry Morley pounded the facts into him. Then, Cambridge, where he read History and got a Second, but without shedding any tears over it. A period as professor of English at the Mohammedan Anglo-Oriental College, Aligarh, was cut short by an attack of dysentery, and he was sent back to England – to extension lecturing, to Owens College, Manchester, to Liverpool, where he succeeded A. C. Bradley as professor. At the time of his appointment, his list of publications consisted of a paper which he had read to the Browning Society while he was an undergraduate. The Liverpool years were rather more fruitful. He published his first books, or booklets – on the English Novel, on Stevenson, on Style; edited Castiglione for the 'Tudor Translations'; gave the Clark Lectures, on Milton. Finally in 1900 he went to Glasgow, once again taking over from Bradley.

Raleigh's earliest books are, in their disagreeable way, *fin-de-*

siècle curiosities. He was on the outer fringe of the Henley–Stevenson circle, and had managed to pick up some of their worst mannerisms; he was also enslaved to a tortuous private ideal of Fine Writing. *Style*, in particular, must be one of the most stilted books ever written, with every sentence straining to be brilliant. A characteristic flourish is the description of the teacher of writing as

a Professor of eloquence and thieving, his wingèd shoes remark him as he skips from metaphor to metaphor. . . . From his distracting account of the business it would appear that he is now building a monument, anon he is painting a picture (with brushes dipped in a gallipot made of an earthquake). . . .

We look up Churton Collins's comments in the *Saturday Review*, and we are not disappointed:

This is the most intolerable piece of literary coxcombry which it has ever been our irritating ill-fortune to meet with. It may be described as the reductio ad absurdum of the preciosity of Pater and Stevenson. The one endeavour of the writer appears to be to avoid simplicity and to juggle alternately with paradoxes and platitudes. All is spangle, tinsel, paste. . . .

Raleigh's acrobatics were not entirely senseless, however; indeed, he took to them on principle. Touched by the spirit of his period, he was insistent that all art, as he wrote in his essay on Stevenson, was 'play of a sort; the "sport-impulse" (to translate a German phrase) is deep at the root of the artist's power'. For a critic, this is the beginning of wisdom – though admittedly no more than the beginning. How the impulse to play combines with the truth-telling functions of art, how it expresses itself most effectively or economically in terms of the medium, how it both submits to established conventions and breaks them down: these are the really interesting questions, and it would be useless to pretend that Raleigh, trapped by a rudimentary aestheticism, gets very far with them. However, he had at least grasped a vital principle which eludes the Churton Collinses of every generation, and once he had discarded the spangle and the paste he showed himself capable of writing genuinely original, genuinely helpful criticism. He had, in particular, a strong feeling, quite exceptional in those distant pre-Empsonian days, for the plasticity of language, the serious creative possibilities of word-play. Even amid the lush undergrowth of *Style* there is an occasional insight lurking – the suggestion, for example, that

where words are not fitted with a single hard definition, rigidly observed, all repetition is a kind of delicate punning, bringing slight differences of application into clear relief.

In *Milton* (1900) this kind of subtlety is harnessed to an appropriate theme; and the *Shakespeare* (1907) which he was persuaded to contribute to 'English Men of Letters', if not perhaps the book which George Eliot might have written, is as debonair a performance as anyone who wants a 200-page introduction to Shakespeare has a right to expect.

Raleigh's contemporary fame hardly rested on his writings, though. Once installed at Oxford he published very little, and the one book which, to judge from scattered hints, he owed it to the world to write – the study of Chaucer which would have rescued him from the clutches of the professional Chaucerians – was permanently set aside. Instead, he devoted himself to building up the English Faculty, more by force of personality than anything else. He administered, and haggled with bursars, and achieved the kind of success as a lecturer which is even harder to explain to posterity than an actor's – especially when the lectures are largely taken up, as they were in this case, with reading out favourite passages from the authors under discussion. One doubts whether a later, sterner generation of undergraduates would have been quite so easily impressed. However, at the time, in an Oxford bathed in the golden glow of *Sinister Street*, Raleigh's panache seems to have done the trick: Stephen Potter gives a persuasive account of how he used to send his audiences away tingling with a sense of the unique value of the particular writer he had been expounding, eager to find out more on their own account. Not every professor can claim to have accomplished as much. But he himself felt dissatisfied: it was humiliating to make a career out of praising other people's books, and his talent for self-dramatization required a wider stage than a university. Asquith offered him a seat in Parliament, but that was not really his line either. What he craved most of all was the life of action, and when war came his only regret was that he was over military age. Still, he could always do his bit as a cheer-leader. He turned to pamphleteering, and got his reward when he was appointed official Air Force historian. His new duties took him, romantically, to Baghdad, where he contracted a fever; he flew home, but within a matter of days he was dead. At Oxford, his students were shaken by the news. One of them, Robert Graves, has recorded how much it saddened him, and made him feel as though his connection with the university was at an end.

The discontent which gnawed at Raleigh can be seen most plainly in the two volumes of his correspondence which were edited by Lady Raleigh and published after his death. They show a man horribly ill at ease in his chosen role, twisting this way and that in his efforts not to become identified with it too closely. Taking these letters as her main text, Mrs Leavis has written a sharp attack on Raleigh, in which she condemns him as 'the most dangerous kind of academic, the man who hasn't enough ability to set up on his own as a creative artist and bears literature a grudge in consequence'. The comparison which places him most effectively, she suggests, is with Leslie Stephen. But it could be argued that this particular conjunction of names is not quite as devastating as she supposes, since Stephen, who generally had little use for academic English scholars, went out of his way to make an exception for Raleigh:

> The critic who can be subtle and delicate without losing touch with Johnsonian common-sense would represent the ideal eclecticism. Professor Raleigh approximates at least to that desirable combination; and he has also the merits of an admirable style. . . .

Stephen is commenting on *Milton*, a book which it took rather more than a 'grudge' to write. As usual, Mrs Leavis exaggerates and over-simplifies. However, once it has been toned down most of her indictment can be allowed to stand; and in point of fact Leslie Stephen's daughter put much the same case with a good deal more finesse in a paper (reprinted in *The Captain's Death-Bed*) which effectively crystallizes what was wrong about Raleigh. As Virginia Woolf says, he was a Professor of Literature who decided to transform himself into a Professor of Life; and the result was a peculiarly jarring clever man's philistinism, a dishonest philistinism. The letters are a perfect symphony of false notes in this respect. There is no need, perhaps, to pull a solemn face over Raleigh's pseudo-heartiness, or his misplaced slang, or his plain blunt man's expostulations – 'My Gawd! the eunuch was the first modern critic' (though if this last is true, it was hardly for another eunuch to do the My-Gawding). But the volley of cheap little jokes about 'Bill' Wordsworth and 'Bill' Blake are really too bad. Apropos of Blake, for example: 'Do you suppose Bill had a pain? Is anything known about his kidneys?' And there is a vein of sheer malice which comes out whenever Raleigh gets round to a modern author who displeases him. The note which he sent to a friend, together with two postcard photographs of the writers to whom he refers, is entirely in character:

I send you Zola and Ibsen, an admirable pair.... Look at them and think of Shakespeare's face, even in the Stratford bust. Or of Claverhouse's. Or of Robert Louis Stevenson's. Or of any decent midshipman. They both have bad mouths. I think we must frame them with the legend 'Modern Pigs' underneath. Myself I think their portraits an absolutely convincing and final criticism on the faults and merits of their works: discussion is impossible after seeing them.

The critic as physiognomist – one can see how the idea must have appealed to Raleigh, who was never slow to judge people by their looks. To judge them, and find them wanting. Appropriate, really, that the one scrap of his writing which has passed into general circulation should be the lines provoked by an Oxford garden-party. *I wish I loved the Human Race, I wish I loved its silly face. . . .* As funny poems go, quite a good one. But one doesn't warm to the man who could also quote, with evident relish, Schopenhauer's aphorism to the effect that 'a new face is almost always a shock, from the surprising resource Nature shows in combining unedifying elements'.

Raleigh is one of the earliest native examples, in the literary field at any rate, of the anti-academic academic, a type which, for reasons which do not have to be spelt out, English departments are naturally bound to attract. If he had been a pure scholar or a dedicated teacher, if he had been a relatively simple organism like Furnivall or Masson or Henry Morley, he would never have felt the frustrations which he did. But as it is, he was a man with at least a touch of baffled creativity, a man with more taste and intelligence than his professional predecessors; and the very qualities which up to a point made him better equipped to understand literature than they were, also made him inwardly more reluctant to teach it. He had a nagging sense that it was impossible to reconcile the inhibitions of academia with the energies of art, a suspicion that it might be difficult to lecture on the same poems or novels year after year without turning into an automaton. However, plenty of teachers, good teachers, have had the same misgivings and spent their careers trying to come to grips with the problem. Raleigh, by contrast, responded with little more than self-contempt, of the kind which soon spills over into contempt for others. His faith in what he was officially supposed to be doing ebbed away, and he seems to have found his keenest satisfaction in simply doodling in the margins of literature – in playing elaborate nonsense games, making up stories composed of words with the same number of syllables ('literary professorships undoubtedly remunerate occupancy . . .'), writing parodies of Mr Gladstone and the ballad of Sir Patrick Spens and, of course, Bill Blake –

> *If you try to do what's right*
> *You pass your life in a horrible fright,*
> *And your Emanation – Lord protect her!*
> *Commits adultery with your Spectre . . .*

It is true that Raleigh's disillusionment was very much his own affair. As far as his undergraduates were concerned, he remained a stimulating lecturer; and on the principle that all sensible students get most of their education from one another between classes, there was a lot to be said for his informality. Still, no one could claim that he bequeathed Oxford an English Faculty in perfect working order. When he died, T. S. Eliot, writing in the *Dial*, proposed that Irving Babbitt should be brought over from Harvard as his successor, which might have proved rather too drastic a remedy. But clearly some sort of new broom was urgently needed: a professor with a constructive educational policy, or a post-Victorian literary outlook, or both. Instead, the electors played safe and appointed George Gordon, a placid traditionalist who subsequently became known to a wider public as chairman of the selection committee of the Book Society – very much a man of the Baldwin Age. Naturally no great changes were to be looked for from such a quarter. Raleigh had at least chafed at the accumulated clichés of his subject; Gordon was content to go through the orthodox motions like a sleepwalker, to reassure his readers that

the old masterpieces and ancestral favourites – the plays of Shakespeare and the Waverley novels, Don Quixote and the Vicar, Elia and honest Isaak, the world of Dickens – are not shaken from their place in the chimney corner of our leisure when the door opens to admit the fresh arrivals and newcomers of our own time.

IV

Oxford had Raleigh; Cambridge had the comparable though more attractive figure of Sir Arthur Quiller-Couch (1863–1944), who was appointed King Edward VII Professor in 1912 ('tax not *that* royal Saint with vain expense', as he once murmured). An astonishingly unacademic choice, all the more so when one considers the mistrust with which English studies were still commonly regarded. The first holder of the Edward VII Chair – he died only a few months after being elected – had been a classicist, the famous Greek scholar A. W. Verrall. Yet Q himself, at the time he took up his position, was known almost solely as a journalist and popular novelist; he had no learned publications to his credit, unless you count *Adventures in Criticism* and the *Oxford Book of English Verse*, and no experience of teaching. Politics are said to have been behind the appointment: according to a story recounted by the late E. M. W. Tillyard, in *The Muse Unchained*, Asquith had originally intended to offer the job to Grierson, fresh from his edition of Donne, but Lloyd George persuaded him that it might as well go to a good party man. And one thing which was never in doubt was the soundness of Q's Liberalism. He had worked hard for the party in Cornwall, both at the county level, especially in the field of elementary education, and closer home, in Fowey, where at one time or another he held most of the main public offices, from harbour commissioner to mayor. The knighthood bestowed on him in 1910 was primarily an acknowledgement of his services as a local political chieftain: when he returned to Fowey from the investiture he was greeted by a crowd of supporters and the town brass band playing 'A Fine Old English Gentleman'. All very rousing, but not necessarily a guarantee that he would make a satisfactory professor – and in Cambridge the news of his appointment provoked more than one disapproving sniff.

However, his lectures were an immediate success. He turned them into social occasions, and, more important, he left no doubt about his conviction that English deserved a place of honour in English universities. Admittedly he seldom did much more than ramble cheerfully round the subject, shedding a vague glow of enthusiasm. Most of his views on literature, and for that matter on life, were the sturdy commonplaces of a fine old English gentleman who also happened to worship at the shrine of Romance (in the Andrew Lang sense), and who had begun his career writing adventure stories in the manner of Robert Louis Stevenson. Judged by subsequent Cambridge standards, he often seems impossibly florid, and on the whole his critical methods are what can only be described as under-ingenious. But in 1912 the world was younger, and professors could still talk about criticism in terms of an adventure, and there was an audience eager to be shown the shining prospects – an audience whose requirements he suited admirably.

The First World War helped to consolidate his position as a public figure. He had never been a rabid militarist: his anti-jingo attitude at the time of the Boer War (during which he took the chair at one of Lloyd George's protest meetings) makes an agreeable contrast to Walter Raleigh's Henleyesque exultation. He was, on the other hand, intensely patriotic, and indeed his whole conception of English literary history was bound up with a romantic notion of thatched-and-timbered Englishry. One negative way in which this manifested itself was in a thorough dislike of the German quasi-scientific approach to English. In the heat of 1914 he allowed his antagonism to take some pretty childish forms, assuring a Cambridge audience, for instance, that no Hun, however learned, could possibly hope to do justice to the lines

> *At eve the beetle boometh*
> *Athwart the thicket lone.*

But he had expressed more measured hostility to *Anglistik* long before that. He also had a strong prejudice against Anglo-Saxon (partly, perhaps, on account of his Celtic loyalties); in one of his pre-war novels he had dragged in an attack on *Beowulf* as 'a blown-out bag of bookishness'. Consequently he was more than willing for compulsory philological work to be excluded from the English Tripos when it was finally established in 1917. The actual planning of the Tripos he left to others. He did have one pet scheme, however – a paper on 'the English Moralists'. His colleagues blocked the plan, and when he persisted, tried to talk him out of it; a subtler man might have been convinced by the thoughtful objections they raised. But for Q, the Moralists were simply an essential part of the splendour of the subject, and not to be abandoned, whatever the technical difficulties. When he was asked what exactly he meant by English Moralists, and how he proposed to teach them, his usual retort, according to Tillyard, was 'a lyrical outburst on the glories of their writings issuing into a roll-call of the great names: "Hooker – Hobbes – Locke – Berkeley – Hume"; and ending with an exhausted "my God", as emotion got the better of him'. Eventually he carried his point, and in practice he turned out to have been justified.

His broad, frank, splashy approach had other advantages as well. He was never afraid to begin at the beginning – to insist that students of literature should learn how to write decently; to point out that in any half-way adequate English course *something* had to be done about the Authorized Version; to remind Cambridge undergraduates that 'the real battle for English' was being fought in the elementary schools, and that the new reading public whose tastes they were being asked to deplore was mostly made up of ordinary hard-pressed working men and women with nothing much to look forward to. There was a chivalrous side to him which is pleasant to contemplate. (It showed itself, for example, in the spirited campaign which he conducted against the Liberal Government's Mental Deficiency bill, with its provisions for locking up the feeble-minded as well as the insane.) And he had style: he brought a touch of the *grand seigneur* to the rather fiddling world of examination boards and statutory requirements. Initially, at least, he helped things to go with a flourish. But as time passed, he came to count for less and less in the life of a Faculty which was being stirred up by I. A. Richards and *Scrutiny* and *Seven Types of Ambiguity*. Indeed the whole idea of him officially presiding over 'Cambridge English' right through the inter-war period has its surrealist aspects. Understandably he felt more at home in Fowey, organizing the Silver Jubilee celebrations or carrying out his duties as commodore of the Yacht Club.

Most modern literature grated on him much as one would expect. On the eve of the Second World War, *aet.* seventy-six, he brought out a new edition of the *Oxford Book of English Verse*, with a wonderfully plangent preface expressing his bewilderment ('it were profane to misdoubt the Nine as having forsaken these so long favoured islands'), and calling the poets to order. ('Agincourt, Agincourt, know ye not Agincourt?') On other occasions he could be merely peevish; it is a pity, for example, that he allowed himself to describe Hopkins as a 'precious, priestly, hothouse darling'. But in at least one of his quarrels with an approved modern master he deserves to have the last word. When he encountered Eliot's notorious remark about contemporary society being 'worm-eaten with liberalism' he was suitably outraged, and his indignation spilled over into an essay, 'Tradition and Orthodoxy' (1934):

> This 'Liberalism' which Mr Eliot arraigns as a worm, eating itself into the traditions of our society, reveals itself rather as Tradition itself, throughout Literature. . . . What is the alternative? What the dirty trump card ever up dogma's sleeve to be slid down and sneaked, upon opportunity? It is suppression; tyranny; in its final brutal word – force. Look around Europe today and consider under what masks dogma is not feeling for, or openly shaking, this weapon to cow the minds of free men. . . .

Q's prose may not be quite so elegant, so intelligent as Eliot's. But on the essential point he is in the right and Eliot is in the wrong. And if anyone protests that Eliot was merely teasing, or playing a game, or that his judgements were only meant to apply in some special apolitical realm of literary theory – then they are in effect accusing him of being flippant where Q was being serious.

Both Raleigh and Quiller-Couch, one feels, could only have occurred when they did. They were as much ambassadors as heads of departments; they belong to a unique phase when the academic study of English had clearly outgrown its poky anti-quarian beginnings, but was not yet fully professionalized and trade-unionized. A generation later, an appointment like Raleigh's at Liverpool would have seemed reckless, one like Q's at Cambridge almost inconceivable. Yet given the openness of the situation, were they such very daring choices after all? Supposing a university had had the courage to offer a post to a really outstanding writer. Not a full-dress professorship, perhaps; when the University of Birmingham, an enterprising exception, invited G. K. Chesterton to apply for the Chair which eventually went to Churton Collins, he had the good sense to refuse. No author wants to be sucked into a lifetime of teaching and administration if he can help it. But there were so many compromise arrangements which could have been tried out – part-time jobs, temporary lectureships, occasional seminars. They might not always have worked; as whole shelfloads of American novels testify, a writer in residence is often a fish out of water. But the risk was worth taking. However, funds were limited, and imaginations were more limited still, and nobody wanted to experiment. By the 1920s, a mood of sombre professionalism had set in, best exemplified by the founding of the *Review of English Studies* in 1925. The academic *apparatchiks* were in full command, and it was too late to change the patterns which had been laid down.

7

POPULAR
APPROACHES

I

The squabbles of dons naturally meant nothing to the Victorian
reading public as a whole. Most ordinary readers of Dickens and
Tennyson and Carlyle had better things to do with themselves
than worry about Shaksperian verse-tests and Merton professorships. This is not to say, however, that many of them were not
extremely interested in literary history or eager for critical
guidance through its labyrinths. And guidance, in the earlier half
of the nineteenth century at least, was still fairly hard to come by,
even at the level of basic information. The first general history of
English literature, a brief survey by Robert Chambers, did not
appear until as late as 1836. No doubt enterprising students, given
enough leisure, were able to piece together the story for themselves
from Dr Johnson, Hazlitt and other standard critics. No doubt
intelligent readers, irrespective of social class, were able to find
their way around tolerably well without the help of guidebooks.
'There's nothing in my trade,' a street bookseller told Henry
Mayhew, 'that sells better, or indeed so well, as English classics.'
But there was also a large public which, emerging from a domin-
antly religious culture, both believed in the importance of
literature and felt uneasy with it, which venerated the printed
word and yet at the same time hardly knew where to begin. A
public even less sure of itself when the claims of contemporary
authors were canvassed. A public which could be led grotesquely
astray.

Consider the career of the Reverend George Gilfillan (1813–78).

If he is ever allowed his two lines in the textbooks today, it is simply as an obscure idiot who was snuffed out by a now almost equally obscure satire, William Aytoun's *Firmilian*. But there was a time when thousands of readers were happy to be swept along by his dogmatic, wildly emotional judgements and his strange billowing style. A Dissenting minister from Dundee, he first broke into print with a series of literary portraits contributed, free of charge, to the *Dumfriesshire and Galloway Herald*. Christopher North gave him a certain amount of mild encouragement (or in Gilfillan language, he was 'no niggard encomiast'), and Carlyle was sufficiently impressed to recommend his work to the *Quarterly*, though without persuading Lockhart to take him up. For the time being he had to content himself with holding forth in local papers and minor periodicals. But not for long; his fame spread quickly, and a collection of his essays, *A Gallery of Literary Portraits*, sold well enough for the publishers to bring out *A Second Gallery*, and then *A Third*. Part of the appeal of these volumes lay in their topicality, since as well as setting up as an educator Gilfillan took pride in being known as a fearless champion of the poetic *nouvelle vague*. He was particularly drawn to grandiose spiritual epics of the type best exemplified by Philip James Bailey's *Festus*, and it was almost inevitable that he should have appointed himself critic-in-chief to the newly emerging school of 'Spasmodic' poets – Alexander Smith, author of *A Life Drama*, J. Stanyan Bigg of Ulverston, author of *Night and the Soul*, and above all Sydney Dobell: 'Bailey must look after his laurels; Tennyson, Bigg and Smith are in danger of being eclipsed by Yendys.' ('Sydney Yendys' was Dobell's palindromic pseudonym.) The tormented fustian of these writers went straight to his heart – their nonsense suited his nonsense – and he flung himself into persuading the world of their immense merits, with evident success. Then in 1854 came *Firmilian, A Spasmodic Tragedy*. Ridiculing the antics of Gilfillan and his protégés was no very hard task, and in addition Aytoun had the weight of Establishment opinion on his side; an old *Blackwood's* veteran, he was Professor of Rhetoric at Edinburgh University, and also, by an unkind stroke, Christopher North's son-in-law. Gilfillan fought back, raging against 'that tissue of filthy nonsense, which none but an ape of the first magnitude could have vomited, yclept *Firmilian*'. But the party was over, and though he toiled on for another twenty-five years – his later publications include *Night*, a poem in nine books – his reputation never really recovered. He managed to drum up 7,000 subscribers, however, for his annotated edition of the British Poets in forty-eight volumes; while among less sophisticated readers there was a continuing underground demand for the *Literary Portraits*. A selection of them appeared in Everyman's Library as late as 1908, and was reprinted in the 1920s. (The subjects, it should be said, include Shakespeare and Burke as well as J. Stanyan Bigg.)

Gilfillan is the MacGonigall of criticism: any page of his work, opened at random, will yield its crop of absurdities. And yet if he was a preposterous figure, he was not exactly a contemptible one. He throbbed with the libertarian idealism of the Mazzini–Kossuth epoch (in America he would surely have found his niche as an Abolitionist), and he refused to be intimidated by great names when his beliefs were at stake. Although he had wept over *Sartor* – it reminded him of Bunyan's *Grace Abounding* – he drew the line firmly at the gospel of Hero-Worship, while he was exasperated by Macaulay's whiggishness: it seemed that Liberty was 'no more the mountain nymph, but the highly accomplished daughter of a nobleman living in Grosvenor Square'. The critic whom he most wanted to emulate was Hazlitt, and he could at least reasonably claim to have inherited some of his hero's fighting spirit. Still, there is no getting away from the bombast. It can be simply prodigious: even Francis Jeffrey, who was seldom immune to flattery, must have been taken aback when he was informed that by collecting his contributions to the *Edinburgh Review* he would be 'rearing a monument which shall only perish when the steam-engine, which he has eulogised, has ceased its titanic play'.

The nineteenth-century taste for the tumid died hard. A generation earlier, at a guess, the kind of people who listened respectfully to Gilfillan would have been queuing up to buy Robert Montgomery's poem *The Omnipresence of the Deity*; a generation later, it might have been Sir Lewis Morris's *Epic of Hades*. Such readers were generally at the mercy of newspaper puffs, especially in the religious press, and often quite beyond the reach of serious criticism: as Dr Kitson Clark has pointed out, *The Omnipresence of the Deity*, which was only in its eleventh edition when Macaulay delivered his famous broadside and supposedly extinguished Montgomery for ever, actually went on to its twenty-eighth edition. Gilfillan, too, partly belongs outside literature proper, in a world of tracts and Sunday School prizes. His most popular book was called *Bards of the Bible*; he wrote for an audience which still tended to think of poetry chiefly as an adjunct of religion, which frowned on fiction, and which in the not very distant past had been opposed to the idea of secular literature altogether.

A great deal of Victorian writing about literature was, like Gilfillan's, vaguely inspirational – 'spilt religion', as T. E. Hulme said of Romanticism. Equally active, however, were the campaigners for adult education and the apostles of Self-Help: men like George Lillie Craik, author of *The Pursuit of Knowledge under Difficulties* and a mainstay of the Society for the Diffusion of Useful Knowledge, who later became Professor of English at Belfast and produced a heavily factual literary history, with an eye on the burgeoning textbook market. For many of Craik's readers the study of literature must have seemed simply part of the general ethos of getting ahead. It paid dividends. But there were also an impressive number of ordinary Victorians who saw the pursuit of knowledge in terms of liberal curiosity, and for whom self-help meant something more than material advancement. They were the audience catered for by Charles Knight, at one time publisher to the Society for the Diffusion of Useful Knowledge, who spent a long and honourable career trying to provide good literature at reasonable prices. They were also the readers who bought well over 100,000 copies of Robert Chambers's *Cyclopaedia of English Literature* (1843–4) within a few years of its first publication. The *Cyclopaedia*, which went on selling well in revised editions right through the century, was an elaborate guide-cum-anthology based on Chambers's earlier outline history; students may have found it handy for reference purposes, but it was primarily intended to be read for pleasure, not just as a textbook.

Almost all subsequent Victorian literary histories, however, were textbooks plain and simple. From around 1860 a spate of manuals, surveys and primers began to appear: according to

Professor Altick, the expert on such matters, by 1887, the year of jubilee, there were no less than forty-four on the publishers' lists. The schoolmaster was abroad, and the crammer – for these books were symbols of the homage which bureaucracy had been induced to pay to virtue. They were partly designed for use in colleges and schools, but even more for the benefit of candidates hoping to pass Civil Service, I.C.S. and other public or professional examinations, most of which included an English paper. Austin Dobson actually wrote a *Civil Service Handbook to English Literature.** It need hardly be stressed that the cramming system was deadly, the very opposite of everything that a literary education ought to be. A student who has grudgingly learned to reel off a few unrelated facts about Dryden and Pope represents only a marginal advance on a boy who has been taught to describe a horse as a graminivorous quadruped. Not that guidebooks as such are necessarily to be despised; it is only that most Victorian specimens were dreary beyond belief. Probably the best of them were Henry Morley's *First Sketch* and Stopford Brooke's *Primer of English Literature*, and even they were not very satisfactory. Matthew Arnold reviewed the *Primer* at length when it first appeared, speaking as kindly as he could of its mild virtues, and then gently pointing out just a few of its ineptitudes. No quality counted for more in such an undertaking, he suggested, than brevity, and in a future edition the author might perhaps consider making some cuts – e.g. the opening pages, in which it is explained to students that literature has two main divisions, poetry and prose. The whole review (it can be found in *Mixed Essays*) is a neat example of Arnold's lucidity and deftness of touch, his cool diagnostic skill. It leaves one reflecting on how well he could have carried out the operation himself. But Matthew Arnolds, unlike Stopford Brookes, are not sent into the world to write primers.

It is curious, all the same, that the pedagogues should have had the field to themselves, that no history of English literature aspiring to be anything more than an elementary résumé should have been

* One should perhaps add that there was a period, later on, when the Civil Service examiners used to set far more enlightened English papers than the universities – largely thanks to Stanley Leathes, who became secretary to the Civil Service Commission in 1903, and who was an important backstage influence on the founders of the Cambridge English Tripos. See Tillyard, *op. cit.*

available until the very end of the century. Why was no one moved to attempt, say, the literary equivalent of John Richard Green's *Short History of the English People?* (Green, incidentally, devotes proportionately more space to figures such as Chaucer and Spenser than almost any modern general historian would.) And why was there no native counterpart to Taine? The *Histoire de la littérature anglaise*, which appeared in an English translation in 1871, enjoyed considerable popularity – more, one suspects, as a broad historical fresco than on account of the author's deterministic theories. An English work conceived on the same scale, minus the scientific pretensions, would obviously have been assured of a larger audience still. Once again one's thoughts turn to Leslie Stephen, who toyed with the idea of embarking on just such a history when he gave up the editorship of the *Cornhill*. An attractive possibility. But then the *D.N.B.* intervened, the project had to be shelved, and it was eventually left to the professors of the following generation – Saintsbury, Oliver Elton and the rest – to fill the gap to the best of their abilities.

II

The chief practical purpose of literary histories is to teach us something about books which we have never read and probably never will. Nobody quite likes admitting it, and most historians proceed on the unspoken assumption that sooner or later one can get round to reading everything. But the ordinary reader, at least, knows that life is short; and if he is at all conscientious, there are bound to be times when he feels simply oppressed, when all the major masterpieces and minor masterpieces in the world seem to fly in his face like Alice's cards. So much to do, so little done. And it gets worse all the time. Early in the nineteenth century, Jeffrey observed plaintively that if authors insisted on turning out books at the rate that they did, within a mere two hundred years or so it would be necessary to invent 'some sort of *short-hand reading*', if the whole system were not to break down. A generation later, as the avalanche really gathered force, two hundred years must have looked like an absurdly optimistic estimate.

There were powerful voices raised throughout the Victorian age, inveighing against the pursuit of second-rate novelty, exhorting readers not to waste their time on anything less than the best, the *very* best, that had been thought and said in the world. Carlyle, in his Rectorial address at Edinburgh, urged his audience never to forget that books were 'like men's souls: divided into sheep and goats [*Laughter and cheers*]'. A few led up towards the light, a frightful multitude led down towards the nameless depths. 'Keep a strict eye on that latter class of books, my young friends!' Ruskin preached on the same theme, more melodiously, in an equally famous lecture, 'Of Kings' Treasuries'. (It later served as the opening section of *Sesame and Lilies.*) He conceded that there was such a thing as 'a good book for the hour', but – 'will you go and gossip with your housemaid or your stable-boy, when you may talk with queens and kings?' Even those who could lay their hands on their hearts and say 'no' still had to face the problem of sheer numbers, however. There were simply too many kings and queens to get to know in a single lifetime. Suppose, for example, one tried to follow the advice of Frederic Harrison, who very reasonably maintained, in *The Choice of Books*, that nobody's literary education was complete unless he was familiar with Lucretius and the *Nibelungenlied* and Calderon and Ariosto and . . . Mere skimming, moreover, was worse than useless. The masters had to be read and re-read, pondered and scrutinized, before they began to yield up their true significance.

The burden was more than ordinary flesh and blood could bear, and in the later years of the century many suggestions were made for substituting a crash-course. The best-known of these schemes, widely discussed at the time, was Sir John Lubbock's List of 100 Books (1886), originally the substance of an address delivered at the Working Men's College. As a close friend and leading disciple of Darwin, Lubbock* insisted that the laws of natural selection applied every bit as much to literature as to life. There was a struggle for existence and a survival of the fittest among books, as well as among animals and plants. On the other hand he didn't pretend that his choice had been in any way systematically or

* Later Lord Avebury (1834–1913), M.P., banker, social anthropologist, entomologist, archaeologist, geologist, botanist, etc.

'scientifically' arrived at – which is just as well, in view of the fact that it included *Self-Help, The Last Days of Pompeii* and Southey's *Curse of Kehama*. He also allowed himself the luxury of counting Scott's complete novels as a single item, because they happened to be his particular favourites. However, incidental aberrations of this kind hardly matter, since such lists are in any case basically self-defeating. Any reader capable of profiting from them is *ipso facto* perfectly capable of compiling a list of his own – and also of recognizing how preposterous the whole idea is, except as a parlour game. Happily a game is what it largely remained, on this side of the Atlantic at least. In America, where they order these matters more spectacularly, the pursuit of Greatness led on to President Eliot's Harvard Classics – the 'Five-Foot Shelf' of culture – and then, in the fullness of time, to the Chicago Great Books, complete with Dr Mortimer Adler's definitive index of Great Ideas, the Syntopicon. But no comparable chimera has ever been dreamed up over here. When Oxford began publishing 'The World's Classics' in 1901, for instance, it was without any suggestion of them being *the* world's classics. On the contrary, the label was an agreeable anomaly, and there has always been a disarming indifference to Greatness about a series which confers world-classical status, if only by name, on *The Kellys and the O'Kellys* and *Sir Harry Hotspur of Humblethwaite* and *Is He Popenjoy?*

It was easy for disciples to come away from Ruskin, or a score of lesser prophets, thinking of literature as an unfailing source of life, which simply had to be turned on in order to irrigate the waste lands of society. But the ground was often stonier than they had bargained for, and they could be cruelly disappointed. Gissing made the discomfiture of one such idealist a major theme in his early novel *Thyrza* (1887). It is not one of his better books, but wedged in the interstices of a melodramatic plot it contains a good deal of sober and convincing social observation. The idealist, Egremont, is the son of a wealthy manufacturer of oil-cloth with 'extensive works in Lambeth', a self-made Midas who started out from nothing. The younger man, by contrast, has had an opportunity to acquire second-generation culture and a second-generation conscience. Just down from Oxford, deeply impressed by *Sesame and Lilies*, he goes back to Lambeth determined to spread sweetness and light among the workpeople there as best he can – in the first quixotic instance by giving a course of public lectures on the Elizabethan poets. He manages to collect an audience of eight or nine – an intelligent radical, a cantankerous freethinker, the inevitable toady, a few nondescripts – but only one of them, a workman called Gilbert Grail, shows any real feeling for the subject. Grail has the temperament of a student, and ever since the age of twenty, when mere chance led him to pick up a volume by Isaac D'Israeli, he has been trying to explore the English classics on his own account. As far as the others are concerned, however, 'English literature did not hold the average proletarian mind', and Egremont reluctantly decides to devote his second course of lectures to a series of miscellaneous 'Thoughts for the Present'. In the end his efforts come to nothing, and the only one of his students left facing the future with much confidence, the radical Ackroyd, achieves personal salvation by rejecting the gospel of Ruskin and Arnold and concentrating on scientific work instead: 'Ackroyd had never cared much for literature proper; his intellectual progress henceforth was to be in the direction of hostility to literature.' Under the circumstances, who can altogether blame him? When he and his assistant, a cheerful, remarkably Wellsian youth, experiment with ways of producing a new improved type of candle, they are not simply hoping to make their fortunes; it matters quite as much to them that they are doing something which feels satisfyingly relevant to their lives, something purposeful. Candles are real, oil-cloth is real, the bricks and mortar of Lambeth are reality itself – and by comparison Elizabethan poetry seems like a remote tedious dream. Near the end of the book Egremont recognizes that at least he would have made more headway if he had had the sense to start off with a contemporary author; he wishes he could begin all over again with Whitman, whose poetry he has just discovered. But this is the one feeble ray which is allowed to penetrate the encircling pessimism. Gissing's general position is characteristically bleak. Very few members of any class genuinely care about literature, and among the poor there is only an occasional Gilbert Grail, who has 'conceived his passion by mere grace'. Education can ultimately do little or nothing to help the others: lovers of poetry are born, not made.

The temptation is to shrug all this off as typical Gissing morbidity. As usual, he loads the dice against any real possibility of change for the better; as usual, he is mawkishly obsessed with the plight of the sensitive misfit. G.G. stands for George Gissing as well as Gilbert Grail. Yet however crudely, however priggishly, *Thyrza* does raise an awkward question for anyone who believes (*a*) that literature ought to play a major part in education, and (*b*) that only a relatively small number of people at a given time are likely to have the necessary maturity, or the requisite sensibility, or the 'mere grace' to form literary judgements of any value. Much of the finest modern criticism, after all, says by implication what Gissing rather tactlessly spells out: that there can be no half-measures or middlebrow compromises, that in literature *Le mieux est l'ennemi du bien*. And this is perfectly fair. A critic's first duty is to stick by the standards he believes in, and he must be allowed the right, on paper, to banish anyone who falls short of them to outer darkness. But what teacher, faced with the flesh and blood actualities of the classroom, could afford to do the same, or would want to?

III

Few of Gissing's literary contemporaries shared his dour misgivings; the majority were content to see the future in terms of expanding markets, fresh opportunities, a steady extension of the reading public as universal compulsory education began to have its full effect. Certainly the statistics looked rosy enough. The census returns for 1881 listed some 3,400 'authors, editors and journalists'. In 1891 there were nearly 6,000; in 1901, around 11,000; in 1911, nearly 14,000. At the same time there was an equally rapid increase in the number of new outlets available to writers. Magazines and periodicals sprouted up as never before in the 1880s and 1890s, while by the end of the century the London Directory contained the names of over four hundred separate publishing houses. Obviously a high proportion of the census-taker's 'authors, editors and journalists' were totally obscure penny-a-liners, while at the same time the average publisher was mainly on the look-out for the guaranteed commercial success. But the literati had a chance to bask in the general sunshine as well. Such, at least, was the view of Sir Walter Besant, who as founder of the Society of Authors knew as much as anyone about the economics of literature at that time. In his manual for aspiring writers, *The Pen and the Book* (1899), Besant depicted

the kind of life led daily by the modern man of letters – not a great genius, not a popular author: but a good steady man of letters of the kind which formerly had to inhabit the garrets of Grub Street. This man, of whom there are many – or this woman, for many women now belong to the profession – goes into his study every morning as regularly as a barrister goes to chambers. He finds on his desk two or three books waiting for review: a MS sent him for opinion: a book of his own to go on with – possibly a life of some dead-and-gone worthy for a series: an article which he has promised for a magazine: a paper for the *Dictionary of National Biography*: perhaps an unfinished novel to which he must give three hours of absorbed attention. There is never any fear of the work failing as soon as the writer has made himself known as a trustworthy and attentive workman. The literary man has his club: he makes an income by his labour which enables him to live in comfort, and to educate his children properly. Now this man a hundred years ago would have been an object of contempt for his poverty and helplessness: the cause of contempt for Literature itself.

When Gissing was persuaded to attend a Society of Authors banquet, he thought that it was 'a mere gathering of tradesmen', while Besant himself struck him as 'commonplace to the last degree: a respectable draper'. One can see why. But if the shop-keepers bred and multiplied, so did their clientele, and Besant's well-groomed, well-organized, well-provided-for man of letters, however much of a clockwork dummy he may sound in the abstract, was at least as representative a figure of the period as Henry Ryecroft or the casualties of *New Grub Street*. Between 1880 and the First World War there must have been proportionately more popular interest in authors and the world of authors than at any time before or since. A large middle-brow public, with a limited range of other amusements available, asked to be painlessly instructed in what might be termed the folklore of literature; and there were plenty of instructors happy to come forward and satisfy the demand.

The most influential of these mass-circulation mandarins was probably Sir William Robertson Nicoll (1851–1923), a Free Church minister from Aberdeen who in 1886 became the first editor of the powerful Nonconformist paper the *British Weekly*. For over a generation Robertson Nicoll delivered his literary judgements week after week, under the pseudonym of 'Claudius Clear', and they were accepted whole-heartedly by the bulk of his readers. According to the critic Dixon Scott, writing in 1913,

every Thursday, in *The British Weekly*, Sir W. Robertson Nicoll addresses an audience far more numerous, far more responsive, far more eagerly in earnest, than that controlled by any other living critic. He praises a book – and instantly it is popular. He dismisses one, gently – and it dies. He controls the contents of the bookshelves of a thousand homes – they change beneath his fingers like bright keyboards – and every alteration means the modification of a mind. What Claudius Clear reads on Wednesday, half Scotland and much of England will be reading before the end of the week.

Scott had been one of Claudius Clear's discoveries, and his tribute has to be taken with a grain of salt – indeed, stylistically, since he was a clever man, he provides rather more than a grain himself. But even Robertson Nicoll's enemies testified to the loyalty which *The British Weekly* inspired, and not only in Scottish manses, either. It penetrated deep into the English suburbs, where there were thousands of readers like Mr Polly's lugubrious cousin, a railway booking-clerk, who never missed a number.

Robertson Nicoll saw himself as a follower of George Gilfillan, but he was both very much worldlier (much more sapient, he might have said) and far less tempestuous than his predecessor. Instead of cosmic drama, he specialized in serving up thick dollops of kailyard sentimentality. Barrie was one of his early protégés – he ran *When a Man's Single* as a serial in the *British Weekly* – and he was the friend and biographer of 'Ian Maclaren', the author of *Beside the Bonnie Brier Bush*. On the other hand the level of his taste could fluctuate wildly, and he also, for example, championed the novels of Mark Rutherford in season and out. Dealing with the literature of the past he was mild, discursive, anecdotal, deeply versed in the lives of the illustrious obscure, and at the same time always ready to address himself to such familiar problems as What Would We Think of Johnson without Boswell? and Was Thackeray a Cynic? Dealing with the literature of the present, he was bland; his principal advice to prospective reviewers was that they should 'leave the bitter word unspoken'. This is not quite the whole story, however. He was also a notorious, an incorrigible gossip: H. G. Wells put him into *Boon* as 'Dr Tomlinson Keyhole'. And he had his reserves of ruthlessness: John Buchan portrayed him in *Castle Gay* as the self-made newspaper magnate 'Thomas Carlyle Craw', a character also partly based on Rothermere. There was nothing very incongruous about bracketing him with a Fleet Street millionaire. He was perfectly at home with them in real life: *A Bookman's Letters*, his selection of Claudius Clear essays, is dedicated to his friend George Riddell, owner of the *News of the World*. Like Riddell, he was a confidant of Lloyd George, and one feels that under other circumstances he might well have become a politician himself. As it is, much of his energy spilled over into literary politics: he was a leading impresario, publishers' reader, tipster, busybody, maker of reputations.

One important source of his influence was the *Bookman*, the monthly which he founded in 1891. To give it its full sub-title, it was 'a journal for Bookreaders, Bookbuyers and Booksellers', and no English paper can ever have been more cosily, more lavishly, more exclusively devoted to the spirit of *belles-lettres*. At the head of each number, by way of a war-cry, stood James Russell Lowell's ringing affirmation: 'I am a Bookman'. Inside, along with the usual sheaf of reviews, interviews, reminiscences, trade notes, there was paragraph after paragraph, page after page of the latest Paternoster Row small talk. Mr Kipling is off on his honeymoon; Mr Barrie has (we understand) turned down an honorary degree; Mrs Humphry Ward is coming back from Cannes to negotiate with her publishers; Miss Beatrice Harraden has gone to Lucerne to recuperate; Mr J. B. Pinker has acquired an important new client; Mr William Le Queux's next offering is tentatively entitled 'If Sinners Entice Thee'; an Edinburgh firm will shortly be offering for sale attractive bronze statuettes of R.L.S. in

Samoan garb. How Robertson Nicoll must have enjoyed pasting
his snippets together. The first issue of the *Bookman* sold 15,000
copies, and its success was assured. Illustrations were added, a
Bookman Illustrated History of English Literature was published in
monthly parts, and the magazine continued on a prosperous
course which only came to an end in 1935. Just how prosperous
can best be gleaned from the special numbers brought out every
Christmas, which have to be seen to be believed: thick folios of
three or four hundred pages, swollen with advertising, studded
with photographs, embellished with woodcuts, linotypes, red
chalk portraits of famous authors (J. D. Beresford, say, or
Humbert Wolfe) and colour plates from current gift books – as it
might be, Brangwyn, Lewis Baumer, a nursery frieze of Fairy-
land, a roguish chocolate-box Becky Sharp, a turkish-delight
Rubaiyat, a luscious travel poster or two. On the whole, the
cornucopia overflows with kitsch. But some unexpected things
turn up as well. There are contributions from Hardy and Yeats.
Henry James is pronounced (by Dixon Scott, in 1913) the greatest
of all living artists. A comparatively young and as yet little-known
F. R. Leavis takes stock of the year's work in criticism for 1931,
explaining the significance of *Seven Types of Ambiguity*, com-
mending *Axel's Castle* (especially the chapters on Proust and
Joyce). And even Samuel Beckett makes an appearance, with a
short story. Towards the end, in fact, there was a determined
effort, under the editorship of Hugh Ross Williamson, to drag the
paper right into the twentieth century.

Claudius Clear was the most popular of the popularizers, but he
had a good deal of competition. There were, for example, the
weekly literary letters in the *Sphere* by his friend 'C.K.S.' –
Clement Shorter (1857–1926), whose career, even more than
Robertson Nicoll's, took him through that curious borderland
between new-style mass journalism and old-style belletrism which
existed around the turn of the century. A Londoner who left
school at fourteen, Shorter began life as a junior clerk in Somerset
House. His earliest literary efforts were a selection of Wordsworth
and an edition of *Wilhelm Meister*, both commissioned by an
Oxford Street bookseller; his first journalistic job of any consequence was that of book critic on the *Star* under T. P. O'Connor.

This in turn brought him into contact with the proprietor of the *Illustrated London News*, who offered him the editorship in 1890. It was a period in which the line-block and other photo-mechanical innovations were beginning to transform the possibilities of pictorial journalism, and Shorter was quick to seize his opportunity. Before long he was editing no less than five separate picture papers: the *Illustrated London News*, the *Sketch*, the *English Illustrated Magazine*, the *Album*, and *Pick-Me-Up*. But literature, he let it be known, remained his first allegiance. In the office he might spend the day dreaming up eye-catching graphic novelties; at home he worked industriously on his study of *Charlotte Brontë and her Circle*. He even thought it worth his while taking advantage of the Diamond Jubilee to compile a reverential patchwork history of Victorian literature ('Sixty Years of Books and Bookmen'). Then, in 1900, with the encouragement of Northcliffe, he started the *Sphere* – a name which had occurred to him, he said (and he was not a man much given to irony), while reading Emerson:

> *I am the owner of the sphere,*
> *Of the seven stars and the solar year,*
> *Of Caesar's hand, and Plato's brain,*
> *Of Lord Christ's heart, and Shakespeare's strain.*

Messages of congratulations on the first number were somehow coaxed out of Swinburne, Meredith and Hardy; and 'C. K. S.' was fairly launched as a literary panjandrum. For the next twenty-five years he was free to gossip, preach, extol the English classics, puff his friends, sneer at his enemies. And quite apart from the *Sphere*, Shorter had his finger in almost as many pies as Robertson Nicoll. He wrote copiously on the Brontës, and turned himself into the foremost living authority on George Borrow. Through his wife, the poetess Dora Sigerson, he had contacts with the Irish literary revival. He founded the latter-day *Tatler*. He was a great man for centenaries, introductions, literary souvenir-hunting, Omar Khayyam Club convivialities. It may be a mere overlap of Christian names – the most successful of the careerists in that novel is called Clement Fadge – but he sounds like somebody waiting to be put straight into the more satirical pages of *New Grub Street*. And yet he was also one of the very few editors of the period who gave Gissing any encouragement, commissioning sketches and short stories from him for his magazines in the 1890s. All in all, Meredith's description of him can stand as a reasonably charitable epitaph: 'The type of literary man who would print a famous writer's blotting-pad in a limited edition if he could get hold of it, though according to his lights and limitations he did his best to further the appreciation of good literature.'

Viewed as anything more than tourist guides or publicists for a deserving cause, the Robertson Nicolls and Shorters had little to recommend them in the eyes of discriminating contemporaries. Arnold Bennett used to assail them regularly in the days – his best days – when he was writing for the *New Age* as 'Jacob Tonson', and showing how a literary column really ought to be run. He complained of their stuffiness, their log-rolling, their lax middle-brow standards, their utter provincialism. But he recognized the need for popularizers, and in other moods he was only too glad to take on the role himself. Claudius Clear published *A Library for £5*; Arnold Bennett published *Literary Taste* (1909), explaining, with a fine disregard for round numbers, how to build up an adequate library for £28 0s. 1d. The 350-odd volumes which he lists represent a fair basic selection of standard English literature, although some of the nineteenth-century items disclose a surprisingly mid-Victorian streak – he even casts his vote for *Festus* – and others sound at least as peculiar as anything that Robertson Nicoll might have recommended. Who, for instance, was Eric Mackay, author of *The Love-Letters of a Violinist*? (Research reveals that he was Marie Corelli's half-brother.) The whole book in fact has an old-fashioned home-brewed flavour, of a kind which would never have done for 'Jacob Tonson': the only example of literary excellence discussed in detail is Lamb's essay 'Dream Children'. But then Bennett was hoping to convert the readers of the *Daily Mail* rather than the readers of the *New Age*. Fundamentally *Literary Taste* belongs with his various exercises in practical philosophy; and although, if only by virtue of its subject-matter, it is much less Babbittish than *How to Live on Twenty-Four Hours a Day* or *Mental Efficiency*, it proved equally popular. Thirty years after its first appearance it bobbed up again, in a revised edition, as one of the earliest Pelicans.

IV

The most impressive aspect of *Literary Taste* is simply the range of pocket editions on which Bennett was able to draw when compiling his reading-lists: the Temple Classics, Everyman, the Mermaid, the Muses' Library, the Canterbury Poets, Newnes' Thin-Paper Classics, the Globe, Methuen's Little Library, a dozen others besides. He and his generation were much better off in this respect than any of their predecessors. Not that the cheap reprint was anything new in itself. In the late eighteenth century there had been the celebrated series of standard authors issued in weekly parts by John Bell, John Harrison and John Cooke; in the early Victorian period there had been the Aldine Poets, the Bohn Library (neither of them as cheap as all that), and their competitors. Charles Knight's efforts have already been mentioned. But the average nineteenth-century popular reprint, of the kind displayed in Booksellers' Row, was shoddily produced, poorly edited, and printed in what Dwight Macdonald once described in another context as retina-detaching type. It was only during the 1880s and 1890s that there began to be a substantial improvement, only during the Edwardian decade that the best-known of the reprint series – the World's Classics, Everyman, Nelson's, Collins' – made their appearance.

A full history of the reprint movement would feature a very mixed assortment of heroes. There was Henry Morley, finding time on top of all his other activities to edit Morley's Universal Library (which sold at a shilling a volume) for Routledge, and the National Library (threepence in paper covers, sixpence in cloth) for Cassell's. There was the Tyneside publisher Walter Scott, with his Camelot series and his Canterbury Poets, which were originally edited by another Northumbrian, the poet Joseph Skipsey, who had started life as a coal-miner. There was John Buchan, who initiated several highly successful series when he went to work for Nelson's in 1907. But one enterprise plainly stood out by itself. *Everyman, I will go with thee and be thy guide, In thy most need to go by thy side.* Other reprint publishers merely published reprints; Everyman's Library was an institution, a benign presence, a crusade. And as the first editor, Ernest Rhys, explained in the little homily which used to be printed at the back of each volume, it was also 'an act of faith': faith on the part of Rhys himself, and equally on the part of the publisher, J. M. Dent, 'the Chief'.

A book-binder's apprentice from Darlington who came up to London in the 1860s with half-a-crown in his pocket, Joseph Dent (1849–1926) was a classic Victorian autodidact. In his memoirs he describes how at the age of fifteen he joined a Mutual Improvement society attached to the local chapel, and how he was allotted the task of preparing a paper on Dr Johnson, a subject of which he knew nothing. By the time he had finished reading Boswell, his fate was settled. Literature became a second religion to him, and though he recognized that he would never be an author himself, he determined at any rate to serve 'as a door-keeper of the Temple'. In the first instance that meant book-binding, and it was not until the close of the 1880s that he felt confident enough to venture into publishing on his own account. He began in a small way with the Temple Library, so called because the first volumes were by writers with Inns of Court associations: *Elia*, edited by Augustine Birrell, and Goldsmith's poems and plays, edited by Austin Dobson. The books were well produced, the great Quaritch signified his approval, and Dent was encouraged to range further afield. His first major commercial success was the Temple Shakespeare. a set of dapper little volumes edited by Israel Gollancz, using the Cambridge text, and stylishly got up, with emblems designed by Walter Crane, rubrics giving the act and scene printed in pillar-box red at the top of every page, and other carefully chosen adornments. Partly inspired by Charles Knight's Cabinet Shakespeare (Knight was one of Dent's principal professional heroes) but reaching a much wider audience, in its early years the Temple edition sold something like quarter of a million copies annually. Other ambitious projects followed: the Temple Classics, the Mediaeval Towns series, forty volumes of Balzac with introductions by Saintsbury, *Morte d'Arthur* in monthly instalments with illustrations by the nineteen-year-old Aubrey Beardsley, editions of Scott, Landor, Peacock, Thackeray, and then, in 1906, the unveiling of Everyman. A thousand of the

Best Books, published in batches of fifty, and selling at what Dent fondly referred to as the Democratic Shilling – such was the original scheme, though the coming of the 1914 war meant that it had to be substantially modified. Dent was lucky with his timing: for one thing, many important Victorian copyrights had only just expired. And he was luckier still with his editor. Ernest Rhys (1859–1946) was a mining engineer by training, who had given up his profession as a young man in order to devote himself to writing. He was a founder-member of the Rhymers' Club, one of the less accident-prone of Yeats's companions of the Cheshire Cheese; he also had wide editorial experience, dating from his connection with the Camelot series in the 1880s. By chance he had been quite independently brooding over the need for a series like Everyman at the same time as Dent, and when he was appointed editor he was willing to slave away zealously, sustained by a strong sense of mission, with only a British Museum forager or two to help him out. At an absurdly meagre salary, too, since Dent, whatever his other qualities, could be as tight-fisted as a peasant when it came to dealing with his staff.

The series itself, on the other hand, was planned on a quixotically generous scale. Grote's *History of Greece*, in twelve volumes. Hakluyt (with introductions by Masefield) in eight. A new translation of Livy in six. Plutarch, Motley, Hallam, three volumes apiece. The sheer scope of the Library would have been enough to put it well ahead of its competitors. But even more important was the special Everyman aura. There was the name of the whole enterprise, at once picturesquely medieval and hopefully democratic. (It was hit on by Rhys, who described it as dropping from heaven 'like a good lyric'.) There was the decision to break the series up into thirteen separate compartments, each with its own distinctive coloured binding. Fiction was carmine, Theology and Philosophy were purple, Reference was maroon, Science was fawn. Oratory – it would be an almost inconceivable category in a comparable modern series – was bound in brown. There were the gilt trellis-roses running up the spine, and the allegorical end-papers: a heavily draped handmaiden representing Good Deeds, her robes caught up in a fantastic sinuous arabesque of branches and tendrils representing the Tree of Life. Then the title-page, with an even thicker tangle of foliage; and facing it, an appropriate flower-embroidered motto. Those Everyman mottoes! *Precious life blood of a master spirit ... holdeth children from play ... unacknowledged legislators ... for that they come home to men's business and bosoms.* ... Selections of Oratory were introduced with a quotation from Homer: *When he sent his great voice forth out of his breast and his words fell like the winter snows, nor then would any mortal contend with Ulysses.* Volumes in the Reference section led off, inevitably, with *I will make a prief of it in my notebook.* And there was a special motto For Young People, too: *This is fairy gold, boy, and 'twill prove so.*

Not all Young People were suitably stirred. Humphry House once wrote an amusing essay on 'The Art of Reading', in which he recalled the 'feelings of distress and shame' which Everyman books had aroused in him when he was a boy. Distress, because of the 'Everyman, I will go with thee' formula: better call a book a feast, or an adventure, anything rather than a constant companion whom he could never hope to get rid of. Shame, because of the mottoes with their impossible demands. It was a standing reproach to be reminded every time he opened a rather useful Latin crib that *The Sages of old live again in us*; it was appalling to think that he might fall asleep and spill the casket of precious life blood on the floor. Books were only one extension of life among many; and he thoroughly resented Everyman's 'heavily ornamented, factitious reverence for literature'. From a detached adult standpoint, it is hard not to agree. But to each his own childhood experience. Personally I used to find the elaborate Everyman trademarks intriguing rather than intimidating; like the M-G-M lion or the Twentieth Century Fox searchlights, they were all part of the occasion. And surely it is true that for most children the trimmings of a book simply add to its impact. I am reminded of the passage in Leigh Hunt's *Autobiography* where he pays tribute to John Cooke, the J. M. Dent of the 1790s, recalling just how avidly he had pored over Cooke's sixpenny editions of the British Poets as a schoolboy: 'I doated on their size; I doated on their type, on their ornaments, on their wrappers containing lists of other poets, and on the engravings from Kirk ...'. A child can be as greedy as a bibliophile when it comes to such details.

In any case, the Everyman embellishments, sound commercial proposition though the Library was always meant to be, were something more than routine window-dressing. Dent set new standards of format for popular reprints, while there was nothing calculating about Rhys's personal reverence for literature. In his memoirs and elsewhere he writes about Everyman's as though he were discussing a religious movement. The labyrinth had a plan; ideally one author led on to another, all the compartments interlocked. When he really got carried away with himself, Rhys summed up his feelings about the Library with a quotation from Blake:

> *I give you the end of a golden string*
> *Only wind it into a ball*
> *It will lead you in at Heaven's gate*
> *Built in Jerusalem's wall.*

And he spoke about literature as 'the City of Books', making it sound like a cross between a secularized *Civitas Dei*, the great library of Alexandria, and his other favourite cause, the League of Nations. (He was the first treasurer of the League of Nations Union.) Floating around in his mind, too, was the idea that literature was somehow bound up with freedom, if not positively with the English constitution: one of the volumes which he contributed to Everyman's himself was 'a source-book of English history', *The Growth of Political Liberty*. He also encouraged Dent to start a weekly journal, *Everyman*, primarily designed, in Dent's words, 'to foster a taste for books among the proletariat'. Launched in 1912, with an initial circulation of over 100,000, it ran for about eighteen months. Shaw, Chesterton and Wells were among the contributors.

Although the Jerusalem-building phase of Everyman's really came to an end in 1914, as long as Rhys was connected with it the Library retained some of its original messianic glow. Gradually, however, the mottoes and decorations were shorn away, until the series developed into the useful but relatively featureless affair which it is today. By the 1940s the foliage and the precious life blood had gone for good.

8

EDWARDIANS

I

In the 1890s big papers grew bigger and brasher while small papers grew more exclusive, more stylized, more flamboyant. If it was Northcliffe's decade it was also Aubrey Beardsley's, a decade of coteries and collectors' items, ornate periodicals and exotic reviews – not only the *Yellow Book* and the *Savoy*, but the *Dome*, the *Pageant*, the *Quarto*, the *Hobby Horse*, the *Chameleon*, the *Rose Leaf*, and others so exquisitely obscure that, like the works of Enoch Soames, there is no mention of them to be found even in the index to Holbrook Jackson's *The Eighteen Nineties*. The little magazine, comparatively unknown in England before, was as much an expression of the *fin-de-siècle* spirit as the limited edition; both were symptoms of the splintering-up of Victorian culture, of a process of fragmentation which might well have been expected to go even further in the years which followed. What actually happened was something quite different, however. There are false dusks in literature as well as false dawns, and the mauve and yellow Decadence was one of them. The 'Nineties', after all, were only a very small part of what was in fact going on in the 1890s. They led on to a period dominated by writers who were closer to the Early Victorians than to their immediate predecessors in their readiness to enter the public arena as preachers, debaters, entertainers. However critical of the established order, men like Shaw and Wells, Bennett and Chesterton, put their trust in a popular audience; they might promulgate minority opinions, but not the idea of a minority culture.

Even so, for a serious writer coming to the fore in the 1900s worldly success was certainly a more ambiguous goal than it would have been two or three literary generations earlier. Nothing illustrates this more clearly, or indeed more notoriously, than the career of Arnold Bennett. It is a neat piece of inadvertent symbolism, as Walter Allen has pointed out, that Bennett should have made his journalistic debut by winning a competition in *Tit-Bits*, and then followed this up by publishing a short story in the *Yellow Book*; from the very outset he was disconcertingly ready to switch roles, to appear now as a tradesman, now as a dedicated artist. His first novel, *A Man from the North* (1898), shows him scrupulously pursuing the 'high aesthetic line', carefully modelling himself on George Moore and George Moore's masters, Flaubert, Turgenev, Maupassant. The story of a young clerk who drifts into marriage with the wrong girl and fatalistically abandons his literary ambitions, it is a novel about not writing a novel, an exercise in grey, muted realism which one respects rather than admires – respects chiefly, as Joseph Conrad wrote, on account of the author's uncompromising artistic conscience. A critic with nothing else to go by could hardly have doubted Bennett's intense seriousness. But he might well have hesitated to predict a flourishing future for him as a novelist. Wasn't he by the sound of it altogether too diffident, too withdrawn? The quickest way to dispel any such illusion would have been to glance at the other book which Bennett published in 1898, *Journalism for Women: A Practical Guide*. It was a very practical guide indeed. ('Do not disdain to write mere paragraphs. The present is an era of paragraphs, and they form a most marketable commodity . . .') And it bore the evident stamp of authority – for the disciple of Flaubert and the Goncourts, the painstaking student of *écriture artiste*, had been earning his living for several years past as the editor of *Woman*, scribbling fashion notes under the name of 'Gwendolen' and romantic idylls under the name of 'Sal Volatile'.

Bennett not only rather gloried in contradictions like these; when it offered itself he also seized the chance to turn them to profitable journalistic account. One evening – once again in 1898 – he suggested to C. Lewis Hind, the editor of the *Academy*, that the paper needed a sensational serial to liven it up. Hind immediately replied by commissioning him to write his literary autobiography, which appeared anonymously later that year as *The Truth About an Author*. 'Sensational' would be too strong a word, but the book did succeed in provoking a minor outcry at the time. Bennett energetically sets about blowing the gaff, high-lighting the part played in his career by chance, opportunism and plain effrontery. He draws a defiantly worldly picture of the professional author who 'labours in the first place for food, shelter, tailors, a woman, European travel, horses, stalls at the opera, good cigars, ambrosial evenings in restaurants; and gives glory the best chance he can. I am not speaking of geniuses with a mania for posterity; I am speaking of human beings.' The tone is often flippant, the bouncy narrator represents only one side of Arnold Bennett. But when it deals with the mechanics of literary life – reviewing, reading for publishers, the toil of composition – the book is unusually honest, sometimes too honest for comfort.

Bennett meant to give offence, and the reviews which he received in papers like *Blackwood's* and the *Athenaeum* were as indignant as he could have wished. For older, more conservative readers, it must have seemed an additional scandal, a sign of the degenerate times, that *The Truth About an Author* should have appeared in a journal which had once been such a bastion of scholarship and good taste. What would Mark Pattison or Charles Appleton have said if they could have seen what their austere plans had come to? It was almost as deplorable as Frank Harris's blitzkrieg on the *Saturday Review*. By the time Bennett wrote, however, the *Academy* had irretrievably changed its character. In 1896 it was taken over by an American patent-medicine tycoon, Morgan Richards, who bought it as a present for his daughter, Pearl Craigie (the novelist 'John Oliver Hobbes'). She in turn called in Lewis Hind, a semi-popular journalist of much the same stamp as Clement Shorter, who had previously been working as editor of the first English illustrated weekly to introduce colour, the *Pall Mall Budget*. By his own candid admission Hind had nothing very pressing to say (except about painting – he was later one of the first Englishmen to write appreciatively about the Post-Impressionists, especially Matisse). But he knew how to put together a readable paper, and under his guidance the *Academy* quickly cast off its gloom. There is a satirical echo of the whole episode in *Tono-Bungay*, where Uncle Ponderevo acquires control of 'a representative organ of British intellectual culture', *The Sacred Grove*. To show what he means by British intellectual culture, Wells reproduces a specimen contents page:

A Hitherto Unpublished Letter from Walter Pater.
Charlotte Brontë's Maternal Great Aunt.
A New Catholic History of England.
The Genius of Shakespeare.
Correspondence: – The Mendelian Hypothesis; The Split Infinitive; 'Commence' or 'Begin'; Claverhouse; Socialism and the Individual; The Dignity of Letters.
Folk-lore Gossip. The Stage: the Paradox of Acting. Travel, Biography, Verse, Fiction, etc.

This is scarcely a caricature of the real thing – and it is a useful reminder of just how moribund the tradition against which men of Bennett's generation were rebelling had become. Under the circumstances, even the bold-as-brass assertiveness of *The Truth About an Author* seems pardonable, a kick in the right direction.

Or it would do, if one had no idea how the story ended, if one could simply forget about the yacht and the ritziness and the reputation-mongering at a hundred pounds a thousand words in the *Evening Standard*. In his later years Bennett came to epitomize the gaudiest notion of literary success, and he is still paying the price. Admittedly, there is something disarming about his un-inhibited pursuit of ambrosial evenings in restaurants and all the rest of it: today he would no doubt have taken care to maintain an anti-Establishment pose in the midst of his opulence. But there is no getting round the fact that he let his commercial instincts drag him down, that he systematically manufactured a succession of mediocre best-sellers. Ezra Pound's lampoon in *Mauberley* has stuck:

> *In the cream gilded cabin of his steam yacht*
> *Mr Nixon advised me kindly, to advance with fewer*
> *Dangers of delay. 'Consider*
>   *Carefully the reviewer.*
> *'I was as poor as you are . . .'*

There is truth in the picture, certainly, but what its easy accept-
ance reveals most clearly is our need to construct a literary mythology, in which writers act out exemplary roles. It is as though we
required symbolic sacrifices on the altar of artistic integrity,
authors weighed down with all the sins of lusting after wealth and
fame which we are anxious to disown in ourselves. (At the
opposite mythological extreme are the martyrs, characters like
Reardon, the novelist in *New Grub Street* who makes a career out
of preserving his professional honour: what he does with it, what
he actually writes, is of secondary importance.) It could even be
said that Bennett, in his more truculent moods, took the role of
the irredeemable materialist on himself. But no one should confuse
the two-dimensional Mr Nixon with the real, complicated, inconsistent Arnold Bennett – and indeed, no one who knew anything
of his best work possibly could. The psychology of an artist cannot
be reduced to the simple contrasts of a morality play. Bennett's
naked careerism may have done him lasting damage as a writer,
yet without it, would he have had any career at all? *Psychologiser,
c'est tout pardonner* – but there is surely a very good case for supposing that Bennett's cruder ambitions were bound up with his
stamina, his curiosity, his appetite for experience, with qualities
which were indispensable to him as a novelist.

The novels themselves are what count in the end, and for
practical purposes that means *The Old Wives' Tale*, *Clayhanger*,
and five or six others. Although they are not as underrated as they
were a few years ago, when critics were simply inclined to blame
Bennett for not being Virginia Woolf, they still tend to get
treated rather condescendingly. But perhaps it is inevitable that
books should be taken for granted, when they are so heavily
steeped in prosaic everyday realities. If one wanted to explain to a
ghost what it felt like to be alive – on the whole, by and large –
Bennett is the English novelist one would turn to first. He is a
master of the middle range, almost unsurpassed at showing how
everything goes on as usual and nothing remains the same. And
the themes which engage his imagination most deeply are the very
opposite of those one associates with his public career. The man
on the make is fascinated by passive endurance. The social lion
thinks his way back into the mind of the fumbling novice. The

bon viveur finds his inspiration among servants, misers, small shop-keepers. Bennett is a standing argument, in fact, against rigid views of human nature, a striking example of how people can develop on different levels at once. On the strength of his early journalism a purist might easily have assumed that he would dwindle into a middlebrow entertainer within the first few years of his career. Yet it was not until he was into his forties, with plenty of pot-boiling work behind him, that he reached the summit of his powers. A creative talent may not be able to survive indefinite punishment, but it is usually more resilient than over-scrupulous critics will allow.

So is critical ability, when it springs from a basically creative impulse, at any rate. In the years around 1910 Bennett not only wrote his finest novels; he also kept up a sustained flow of critical comment, marked by a vigour – yes, and a delicacy – which few of his squeamish detractors have ever approached. The ruminations of 'Jacob Tonson', which appeared in the *New Age* from 1908 to 1911, could still serve as the model for what a good literary column ought to be. Perhaps 'criticism' gives the wrong idea. Although Bennett's own aims as a novelist did lend a fair degree of consistency to his views, he was not concerned with abstract theory, still less with minute analysis. Instead, he talked at large about the literary climate, the current publishing season, neglected authors, foreigners, censorship, reading habits, rates of pay. His comments were blunt, personal and succinct. He named names. He didn't hesitate to set down immediate and not always purely literary impressions. Going to hear H. G. Wells give a talk to the Times Book Club, for instance, what struck him as much as the lecture itself were the women in the audience, 'women certainly deeming themselves to be elegant':

Being far from the rostrum, I had a good view of the backs of their blouses, chemisettes and bodices. What an assortment of pretentious and ill-made toilettes! What disclosures of clumsy hooks-and-eyes and general creased carelessness! It would not do for me to behold the 'library' public in the mass too often!

There spoke the ex-editor of *Woman* – and Jacob Tonson was nothing if not a journalist. He brought his readers news about literature.

The same could no doubt be said of the Bennett who wrote a column in the *Evening Standard* nearly twenty years later, the difference simply being one of quality. It is remarkable how often the *New Age* articles hit the nail on the head, how decisively Bennett grasped the significance of writers who were still unknown or underrated in England at the time. He helped to create an interest in Chekhov and *The Brothers Karamazov* where there had been virtually none before,* sang the praises of *La Chartreuse de Parme*, defended Conrad against the obtuseness of the reviewers. Many other distinguished names, French names especially, which were hardly to be heard of again until the 1920s, are sprinkled about his pages. And he was more than a mere astute tipster: his praises have the ring of authentic excitement.

Today it is hard to appreciate how bold they must have seemed to his original readers until one recalls the atmosphere in which he was working. The destructive side of his campaign was directed in the first instance against 'the Mudiesque middle class' and its moral preceptors, such as the cleric who announced that he would send his daughter to a house infected with diphtheria or typhoid fever just as soon as put a copy of *Ann Veronica* in her hands. Then there were the Hall Caines and Corellis, the reviewers who boosted them, the corrupters of taste. But the writers who received the most slashing treatment at his hands were the academics. 'Sterile', 'pretentious' and 'tedious' were the favoured adjectives. Churton Collins had 'an agreeable face, with pendant hair and the chin of a fighter; on literature he was probably the most learned man in the British Isles'. But the root of the matter was simply not in him. Saintsbury, that 'Albert Memorial of learning', had equally little true feeling for literature: 'Professor Saintsbury may be as loudly positive as he likes – his style is always whispering "Don't listen".' Raleigh, Dowden and the rest were guillotined with even less ceremony. None of these men, as far as Bennett was concerned, counted as a writer; they didn't know how to judge literature because they hadn't been there. On the other hand, with the example of the French from Sainte-Beuve to Rémy de Gourmont in front of him, he guarded against making a fetish of artists being

* Strange as it may seem, an English translation of *Karamazov* (1880) did not appear until 1912.

the only properly qualified critics. The trouble lay with the practitioners themselves rather than with their profession. 'I wish,' he once wrote at the end of one of his onslaughts, 'that some greatly gifted youth now aged about seventeen would make up his mind to be a literary critic and nothing else.' Did he know what he was saying?

Academic tradition has taken its revenge on Bennett. The Jacob Tonson articles (a selection of them were published in 1917 as *Books and Persons*) are rarely mentioned in literary histories or handbooks of criticism. And perhaps there is nothing very much to say about them, except to record that they have *impact*, more impact than a lot of the things which do get mentioned. Abrupt enthusiasm, the unconsidered opinion, the conversational zig-zag: these are what open readers' minds to books, at least as often as the formal critique.

By the time of the First World War, Bennett was on the slippery slope. In *The Author's Craft* (1914) he is tetchier than ever with that objectionable dilettante spirit which refuses to see the connection between art and money, and with those irritating creatures who make a literary virtue of unpopularity. He lays about him pugnaciously, calling unexpected witnesses to back him up in his views about hard cash (Meredith rather than the inevitable Trollope), snapping impatiently at the semi-demi-Flauberts. ('Nobody has any right to be ashamed of human nature. Is one ashamed of one's mother? Human nature *is* . . .' etc.) Impossible not to feel a twinge of sympathy. But the whole argument, for a man of Bennett's intelligence, is conducted at an absurdly low level: difficulties are dodged, issues are blurred. He is too busy, one feels, justifying his own bank-account, and the essay reads like a prologue to his final gilded Beaverbrook phase. And yet. . . . Anyone who wants to moralize over his decline still has to account for *Riceyman Steps* (1923), which is as austere and concentrated a work of art as any he produced. The longer one looks at his career, in fact, the less tempted one is to read it as a plain cautionary tale. The pursuit of money corrupts: it led Bennett into writing some trashy books, and into delivering some outrageous verdicts. But creative self-renewal remains a more mysterious thing than the history of a man's opinions.

II

'The world was very old indeed, when you and I were young.'
Of all the Edwardians, G. K. Chesterton, who was still only a
schoolboy at the beginning of the 1890s, was the one who felt the
Decadence most directly as a personal burden. By contrast, Fleet
Street seemed to offer hope and freedom. He began his literary
career as a journalist, and a journalist he remained. This, for some
people, has been enough in itself to condemn him outright; but
even the most zealous Chestertonians must often have wished that
he had not written so much, so fast, under such pressure. He was
a man of remarkable gifts, far more remarkable than his present
overclouded reputation would suggest. At his finest, for instance,
he was a wittier writer than Oscar Wilde or Max Beerbohm (as
Beerbohm himself readily acknowledged): wittier because he
had a deeper understanding of life. But as he turns the barrel-
organ, and the paradoxes come thumping out, the wit can easily
pall and the profundity can get completely overlooked. The best
is so very good, the worst is so flashy and cheap. And in between
there is that great sprawl of ready-made Chesterton humour,
amusing, readable, but never saying quite as much as it seems to,
and easy to forget.

Confronted with an output of such variable quality, admirers
have naturally sometimes tried to boil Chesterton's work down in
an attempt to isolate its essential virtue. The most determined effort
along these lines of which I know is Hugh Kenner's *Paradox in
Chesterton* (1948). Kenner has very little use for what he calls the
toby-jug side of his hero; the Chesterton who counts in his eyes
is the writer who was a Neo-Thomist by instinct long before he
had actually read Aquinas, whose paradoxes and analogies, far
from being mere verbal conjuring-tricks, expressed a consistent
vision of the paradoxical nature of reality itself. A traditional
Christian vision, which would have been wholly intelligible to
such masters of paradox as the Church Fathers, the Schoolmen,
the Metaphysical poets. If he had been born in a better age, the
author of *Orthodoxy* and *The Everlasting Man*, instead of dissipating
his energies in ephemeral newspaper work, might have been 'a

principal ornament of the medieval Sorbonne'. Kenner's position is stated even more sternly in the essay by Marshall McLuhan which serves as an introduction to his book. According to McLuhan, we must abandon the literary and journalistic Chesterton to his fate, and forget about his idiosyncrasies, his day-to-day interests, the accident of his having happened to grow up in Late Victorian England. The only claim he finally has on our attention is his achievement as 'a metaphysical moralist'. Few things could be more misleading, it would seem, than the genial popular legend of G. K. C. Inside him all the time there was a very thin man indeed struggling to get out.

Whether or not one accepts the Kenner–McLuhan thesis is ultimately a question of religious belief, but there are aspects of it with which one does not have to be a Catholic to agree. Chesterton's paradoxes usually make a serious point, and the best of them often have the quality of theological wit. When he protested that he disliked nothing more than light idle sophistry, he was not being sophistical. Nevertheless, Kenner's portrait seems to me to misrepresent the essential Chesterton. It turns him into the kind of solemn theoretician whom he would have been the first to find irksome. It gives no real idea of his recklessness, his lightheartedness, the extent to which he was immersed in the present. Above all it leaves out of account his democratic temper. Many other English writers have preached Democracy in the abstract; Chesterton is one of the very few who genuinely liked the common man (because he was sure there was no such thing). And then, like any writer, he has his own rhythm. When one actually reads him, his strengths and weaknesses are mixed up together – it is impossible to prise the pearl from the oyster. Moreover, as Kenner makes clear, Chesterton's philosophy is based on celebrating the uniqueness of things, and it is a contradiction to celebrate *him* by draining his work of its precise flavour and individuality.

Had he been meant by nature for a theologian, he could have become one, even without the medieval Sorbonne at his disposal. He dissipated himself in journalism because he wanted to. Originally, it is true, he had vague hopes of becoming an artist, and he studied at the Slade for several years, without making much headway. While there, he also attended lectures at University College, where he met Ernest Hodder Williams, whose family published the *Bookman*, and he began by reviewing art books for that magazine:

I need not say that, having entirely failed to learn how to draw or paint, I tossed off easily enough some criticisms of the weaker points of Rubens or the misdirected talents of Tintoretto. I had discovered the easiest of all professions; which I have pursued ever since.

It was his work for the *Speaker* which first made his reputation, however. This was a weekly which, after J. L. Hammond took over as editor in 1899, became for a time the leading paper of advanced young Liberal intellectuals. And it was on another, much more popular Liberal paper, the *Daily News*, that he reached his largest audience, writing a regular Saturday article from 1903 to 1912. This was his best-known platform, but he wrote for dozens of other papers as well. In the years before 1914 he was one of the sights of Fleet Street. He was also one of the great exponents of the Fleet Street myth. He habitually portrayed it as a larger-than-life bohemia, a haunt of self-destructive minor genius, a warren of grotesques; and he could be as romantic as Pendennis about the grandeur of the Press:

A poet writing his name upon a score of little pages in the silence of his study may or may not have an intellectual right to despise the journalist: but I greatly doubt whether he would not be morally the better if he saw the great lights burning on through darkness into dawn, and heard the roar of the printing wheels weaving the destinies of another day. Here at least is a school of labour and of some rough humility, the largest work ever published anonymously since the great Christian cathedrals.

By the time of the First World War, however, the intoxication had worn off. From 1911 onwards, although he still contributed to many other periodicals, he became increasingly associated with his brother's paper the *New Witness* – originally the *Eye Witness*, and continued by him after Cecil Chesterton's death in the War as *G. K.'s Weekly*. This withdrawal was a result, first of his bitter falling-out with the Liberals, brought to a head by the Marconi affair, and then of his disillusionment with the party system itself.

Chesterton's hatred of capitalism and his dread of the monolithic state were the generous responses of a man who saw the sickness of his society far more clearly than the ordinary Liberal and felt it far more deeply than the self-confident Fabian social engineers. Unfortunately, though, a sense of outrage often proved as bad a counsellor in his case as it had in Carlyle's. His diatribes against usury and corruption were those of a man on the edge of hysteria; his anti-semitism was an illness. Despite this, his fundamental decency is never obscured for long. He hated oppression; he belonged to the world before totalitarianism. But the positive side of his politics – Distributism, peasant smallholdings, Merrie Englandism – led him into a hopeless cul-de-sac.

All this is now a matter of history. His critical writings, on the other hand, are still widely known, although they have long been excluded from the official canon of modern literary criticism. The reasons are plain enough. His methods are everything that our schoolmasters have brought us up to abjure. He wanders from the text and generalizes lavishly. He is too excited by large conceptions to pay very much attention to accuracy in small ones. He is often content to make his point through a mere phrase, or a joke, or an unexpected adjective. He would hardly have known how to begin 'erecting his impressions into laws'. He is extravagant, and he relished extravagance in others. Much of what he wrote was unashamed popularization. He is casual, unguarded, unsystematic. He plays with words, and he would rather parody an author than tabulate his faults. He contradicts himself. While he is working out his own ideas he is never afraid to get in the way of his author. In a word, he is a stimulating and at times an inspired critic.

What exactly do we learn from him? A Chesterton essay is a performance, a furious display which is meant to leave us with a warm diffuse feeling that life has more possibilities than we had realized, or that a familiar author is more interesting, or that an unfamiliar author is more enticing. He does not so much make out a case as work himself up, and his enthusiasm is usually intelligently enough expressed to carry the reader along with him. For the time being, at least. The overall effect is to animate rather than inform, and it is an effect which can easily wear off. But the sum of the parts is often greater than the whole: Chesterton's incidental remarks are more important than his grand conclusions. They are also more startling, not because they are unexpected – anyone can stand a platitude on its head – but because they are unexpectedly true. And a good Chesterton paradox is the reverse of a neat self-contained epigram: it suggests ideas rather than clinches them. When he says, for instance, that Herbert Spencer's closed intellectual system made him more truly medieval than Ruskin, he is starting a train of thought which may not necessarily take in Spencer *and* Ruskin *and* the Middle Ages, but which does cut provocatively – 'bisociatively' – across conventional assumptions. He once described Shaw's plays as expanded paradoxes, and his own paradoxes have the power to gather force and expand in the mind.

Few charges have been levelled at him more frequently than that of verbalism. He himself would hardly have come to the defence of every last pun and quibble in his work, but while pleading guilty on minor counts he would probably have added something to the effect that taxing a writer with verbalism was like reproaching a painter for pigmentism: his whole business was with words. And it could fairly be claimed that his excess ingenuity represents the overflow of a remarkable insight into language and its workings. William Empson has commented on his great powers as a verbal critic, and as with Empson the ambiguities which he unravels are functional rather than decorative. He focuses on a cliché or a battered simile until it begins to recover its original brightness. He brings out the wealth of implication in everyday speech, and also its inadequacy: we habitually say more than we realize, but less than we intend. And he scrapes away some of the prejudices that have accumulated around the big abstract words. True imagination, he reminds us, is intensely materialistic; a sentimentalist is in a sense more realistic than a scientific enquirer, because, though he may distort situations, he is incapable of reducing them to statistics. A master of language himself, Chesterton is exceptionally alive to verbal felicity in others. He also has an outstanding talent for clear exposition. Many of the mots which he flings out – 'Tennyson could not think up to the height of his own towering style', 'the fighting of Cobbett was happier than the feasting of Walter Pater' – are perhaps only neat journalistic devices, though they are very effective ones of their kind; but where he comes into his own is in describing the effect of an author evocatively – and his comments are no less critical for being picturesque. On the contrary, a serious judgement on a serious author was too subtle a thing to be definitively summed up in a formula. Judgements, like scenes, had to be *rendered*. George Eliot, for instance:

> In her best novels there is real humour, of a cool sparkling sort; there is a strong sense of substantial character that has not yet degenerated into psychology; there is a great deal of wisdom, chiefly about women; indeed there is almost every element of literature except a certain indescribable thing called *glamour*; which was the whole stock-in-trade of the Brontes, which we feel in Dickens when Quilp clambers amid rotten wood by the desolate river; and even in Thackeray when Esmond with his melancholy eyes wanders like some swarthy crow about the dismal avenues of Castlewood. Of this quality (which some have called, but hastily, the essential of literature) George Eliot had not little but nothing. Her air is bright and intellectually even exciting; but it is like the air of a cloudless day on the parade of Brighton. She sees people clearly, but not through an atmosphere. And she can conjure up storms in the conscious, but not in the subconscious mind.

He makes elaborate judgements, and at the same time he responds to simple qualities. His writings on Dickens are the most notable example here. What he is best at is rejuvenating the original popular idea of Dickens, the Dickens whose characters have escaped from literature into folklore and whose jokes are self-explanatory. Everyone now recognizes that he makes far too much of the Christmassy Dickens, and modern critics have revealed levels of symbolism and psychological depths of which he was very largely unaware. But arguably he was doing something more difficult than his successors. Most of them in fact agree that within his limits he was concerned with essential aspects of Dickens – aspects which they seldom try very hard to convey in their own words. One suspects that they are secretly rather grateful to him for having saved them the task. His strength was that he was unembarrassed by the childish element in art, and would no more have condescended to it than he would have condescended to an actual child. He acknowledged the primary claims of myth:

'art is a luxury, fiction is a necessity'. And he was able to deal uninhibitedly (*not* indiscriminately) with popular literature because he believed that everything should be judged first as an example of its own kind. Tom Hood was no more to be blamed for not being Wordsworth than Gilbert and Sullivan were to be criticized for having failed to grapple with the ethical problems of Norwegian idealists. A writer's chief duty was to obey that most difficult of injunctions and to be himself. Possibly this large tolerance of Chesterton's is a fault in him as a critic. But it is one of the things that helps to make him a popularizer of genius. How pale and constricted most professional advocates of literature seem by comparison.

Like all platform performers, he runs a constant risk of being trapped by his own style. Opinions get fed into the machine, and what emerges is not so much inaccurate as inappropriate. Everything takes on the same slightly hectic tone. But this is as much a basic characteristic of Chesterton's imagination as the result of journalistic habit, an aesthetic rather than an intellectual defect. He sees the world in terms of loud contrasts and garish colours; the picture has the boldness of a cartoon, but it lacks light and shade.

And yet though these are faults, they are the defects of his qualities, of an approach which is admirably personal and direct. Looking back in his autobiography on his first critical study, *Browning* (1903), Chesterton ruefully recalled all the errors of fact which it contained – 'but there is something buried somewhere in the book; though I think it is rather my boyhood than Browning's biography'. What this means in practice is that though his comments are often technically irrelevant, unlike more single-mindedly 'responsible' critics he moves easily on the same emotional level as his poet. And when he digresses – talking about a stanza from 'Childe Roland', for instance – he does not simply wander off, but looks to a larger context:

This is a perfect realization of that eerie sentiment which comes upon us, not so often among mountains and water-falls, as it does on some half-starved common at twilight, or in walking down some grey mean street. It is the song of the beauty of refuse; and Browning was the first to sing it. Oddly enough it has been one of the poems about which most of those pedantic and trivial questions have been asked, which are asked invariably by those who treat Browning as a science instead of a poet, 'What does the poem of "Childe Roland" mean?' The only genuine answer to this is, 'What does anything mean?' Does the earth mean nothing? Do grey skies and wastes covered with thistles mean nothing? Does an old horse turned out to graze mean nothing? If it does, there is but one further truth to be added – that everything means nothing.

These are the words of the potential convert to Catholicism, but one hardly has to share Chesterton's doctrines to be stirred by his questions.

Living on into a vastly altered post-war world, he declined the consolations of old fogeydom. But while his comments on Eliot, Aldous Huxley and other writers whom he saw emerging in the 1920s are respectful, and even friendly, he couldn't pretend that he felt at home with them. In a broadcast talk which he gave shortly before his death in 1936 he summed up the whole trend of the times as 'intellectually irritated'. And he could equally have characterized the Edwardian age, or at least the Edwardian literary scene, by its comparative lack of irritability. For better or worse, the writers who held the stage before 1914 were thicker-skinned than their successors. They were expansive; they believed (not too fanatically) in their schemes for saving the world; they didn't feel compelled to write as though they were always on oath. If there was such a thing as a dominant Edwardian note, it was one of confident give-and-take. It is a note which has largely disappeared; but the fact that it would ring false if anyone tried to revive it today shouldn't mislead us into supposing that it was not once natural and spontaneous.

III

The Edwardian era was an age of great journalists rather than great journals. True, the bookstalls were crowded with periodicals as never before. Almost all the major Victorian reviews still appeared, along with such newcomers as H. W. Massingham's weekly the *Nation* (eventually to be swallowed up by the *New Statesman*) and the *Saturday Westminster* (a literary offshoot of the

Liberal evening paper the *Westminster Gazette*). *The Times*, after experimenting unsuccessfully with a magazine called *Literature*, began publishing the *Times Literary Supplement* in 1902. There were a flurry of smaller papers besides, while in addition serious writers contributed to the popular press more frequently than is sometimes supposed. Max Beerbohm, after drawing up a long list of acknowledgements to editors at the beginning of one of his collections of essays, remarked that he had had no idea that he had put his eggs into so many baskets, and many other authors of the period could have echoed him. On the face of it, both readers and writers were extremely well provided for. But magazines consist of more than paper and ink, and Edwardian intellectuals were dissatisfied with the situation. In particular, most of the older journals had lost their dynamism. Of the weeklies, only the *Spectator* continued to show a profit, but during the long editorship of J. St Loe Strachey it increasingly lost its hold on younger readers, and among the *avant-garde* it became a byword for stuffy gentility. (*Malheur à la malheureuse Tamise/Qui coule si près du Spectateur* . . .) The *Athenaeum* and the *Saturday Review* were in the doldrums; the *Academy*, after Hind's departure and Mrs Craigie's death, passed into the hands of Lord Alfred Douglas and his obnoxious henchman T. W. H. Crosland. The monthlies were even more moribund. By today's standards, admittedly, there is something impressive in the mere fact that so many papers existed at all, and however dull the established reviews might be in general, at any rate they offered an outlet to some individuals of talent. But only two journals of the period really count as creative forces in their own right. One was the *English Review*, which during the year (1908–9) in which it was edited by Ford Madox Ford was as brilliant a literary magazine as there has ever been in this country: its contributors ranged from Hardy and H. G. Wells to D. H. Lawrence and Wyndham Lewis. (Subsequently, under the editorship of Austin Harrison, it settled down to a respectable but unsensational existence.) The other was A. R. Orage's *The New Age*.

Orage (1873–1934) was at once a rather mysterious figure, around whom innumerable legends gathered, and a fairly typical self-made provincial intellectual of his generation, the Arnold

Bennett generation: extremely independent-minded in some respects, extremely gullible in others. A poor boy from a village in Huntingdonshire, he would probably have had to leave school to start work on the farm, if it had not been for the patronage of a local landowner, which enabled him to go to a teachers' training college. He first appeared in print in the 1890s, writing 'A Bookish Causerie' for Keir Hardie's weekly paper the *Labour Leader*. At this time he was an elementary school-teacher in Leeds, equally active on behalf of the Independent Labour Party and the Theosophical Society – a foretaste of divided aims to come. He was also a leading member of a philosophical discussion club, the Leeds Plato Group, where he got to know an architect, A. J. Penty, who converted him to the arts and crafts movement; while under the influence of another friend, Holbrook Jackson, he added Nietzsche to the brew. In the early 1900s Orage, Penty and Jackson all settled in London, where Orage tried to find a foothold as a freelance journalist and wrote two books on Nietzsche which won him a minuscule reputation. All three men were romantic socialists who were dismayed by the dry and bureaucratic outlook of orthodox Fabianism, but at first Orage and Jackson were nevertheless ready to agitate for change from inside the Fabian Society. They helped to establish the Fabian Arts Group, and when they took over *The New Age*, an insignificant Liberal weekly which the owners were forced to sell in 1907, it was Shaw who put up half the money they needed. (The other half came from a wealthy Theosophist.) In the early years of Orage's editorship – Jackson dropped out after a few months – the paper acted as a general clearing-house for radical ideas, with special emphasis on the cultural aspects of Socialism: Shaw, Wells, Chesterton and most of the other major Edwardian controversialists were among the (unpaid) contributors. As time passed, however, Orage found it harder and harder to hide his disagreements with the Fabians, until finally, together with Penty, he took his stand as one of the leading advocates of Guild Socialism. From the point of view of Shaw and the Webbs this meant that *The New Age* now had to be written off as a political force – one of the reasons which prompted them to found the *New Statesman* in 1913.

On its literary side *The New Age* looked towards the future. In the early days of Orage's editorship debate inevitably centred around the Shavian drama, realism in the novel and other staple Edwardian themes, but before long more modernistic and more outlandish topics were claiming attention. By 1911 Ezra Pound was a regular contributor, the verslibrists were arguing their case, Imagism was already in the air. Orage's policies favoured experiment, iconoclasm, and curiosity about foreign literature; in particular, he helped to spread the 'Russian fever' which raged among intellectuals just before the First World War. His readers were kept informed, too, not only about current literary innovations, but about a whole swarm of new philosophies and new movements of which the first rumours were reaching London in those intoxicating days: Cubism, Bergsonism, Futurism. And articles on psycho-analysis began appearing in 1912, at a time when Freud's theories were still a taboo subject in the medical profession, and very few laymen had even so much as heard of them. It was not until the following year, in fact, that Ernest Jones founded an English Psycho-Analytical Society. The secretary of the Society, David Eder, was a close friend of Orage, and a frequent contributor to *The New Age* – although the credit for writing the very first pieces on psycho-analysis which Orage published must go to one of his journalistic henchmen, an embittered and otherwise obscure freelance called A. E. Randall, who also contributed ferocious theatre criticisms to the paper under the pseudonym of 'John Francis Hope'.

For many of Orage's contributors *The New Age* was an informal club, almost a second home, as well as a magazine. They would spend long hours thrashing out ideas with him in his office in Tooks Court, off Chancery Lane, or in the basement of the ABC restaurant near-by where he could always be found with a band of the faithful on appointed afternoons. There is an excellent account of these sessions in Paul Selver's memoir *Orage and the New Age Circle* (1959). Some of the hard-core members of the circle, like Randall, were comparatively unknown apart from their connection with the paper – J. M. Kennedy, Tory intellectual and translator of Nietzsche, rumoured to be a member of the secret service; the ultra-temperamental Beatrice Hastings, who ended up by publishing defamatory pamphlets about Orage after his death;

C. H. Norman, described by Selver as 'a malcontent of malcontents', a tireless sniffer-out of scandals and injustices. Others made names for themselves (of very different kinds) elsewhere: Pound, Eder, Cecil Chesterton, the Australian cartoonist Will Dyson, Clifford Sharp, who later became the first editor of the *New Statesman*. And coming and going on the fringe of the group there were Orage's latest discoveries, who might range from Katherine Mansfield to Michael Arlen (or Dikran Kouyoumdjian, as he then was). For Orage, in the words of his biographer Philip Mairet, was 'a great artist in literary encouragement'. He was open to new ideas and on the alert for new talents; he was ready to tire himself out working over manuscripts inch by inch, weeding out faults, suggesting improvements, helping writers to realize their half-formulated intentions. Edwin Muir, Herbert Read and dozens of others have described how much they looked up to him, how much they valued his encouragement and admired his editorial integrity. With a circulation of a few thousand, *The New Age* could seldom afford to pay its contributors even a nominal fee, but they were eager to write for it just the same. What it did offer them was the stimulus of a serious audience, an attentive hearing, a sense of being in touch.

Orage was an editor first and foremost – the most brilliant editor for a century past, according to Shaw. He had the right mixture of qualities, a personality at once pertinacious and self-effacing. When somebody asked him why he didn't devote himself to writing his own books, he replied, 'I write writers'; although in fact he was also a prolific contributor to *The New Age*. He was responsible for most of the paper's political notes, and after Jacob Tonson's demise he also undertook (over the initials 'R.H.C.') a weekly column called 'Readers and Writers', which ran from 1913 to 1921. It was largely on the strength of 'Readers and Writers' that T. S. Eliot described Orage – has any other editor ever been garlanded with such compliments? – as 'the finest critical intelligence of our day'. This is an obituarist's *nihil nisi bunkum* exaggeration, but Orage's essays certainly reveal an original mind, playing over the whole field of literature, endeavouring to judge books by what he believed to be permanently valid standards of criticism. He was a literary moralist – that is to say, he insisted that the more successful a work of literature, the more closely its moral and formal qualities would coincide:

> Words and phrases are more than notes of music: they must express ideas as well as create the atmosphere in which the ideas can be conveyed. And the smallest error is sufficient to destroy the intended effect.

Style was essentially an instrument for getting at the truth, and one of the peculiar tasks of criticism was 'ministering to a style diseased'. Whether he was analysing the rhythms of a passage by De Quincey, or taking apart a piece of high-flown rhetoric from *The Times*, Orage shows the same scrupulous attention to verbal detail. But his general judgements on authors are much less interesting, and often seem merely perverse.

Along with his gifts there went, not exactly a streak of charlatanism, but a knack of gathering charlatans around him, and ultimately, as it turned out, succumbing to their influence. Guild Socialism had never entirely satisfied him as a political creed, and after the War, when it became apparent that it had no immediate prospect of success, he shifted his ground again, enthusiastically taking up Social Credit and the funny-money theories of Major Douglas. Ordinary readers of *The New Age* might have borne with one such aberration; but at the same time his interest in the occult had revived, and he was becoming more and more absorbed in the quest for esoteric 'wisdom'. First he came under the influence of Dmitri Mitrinović, an attaché at the Serbian Legation in London who peddled his own cabbalistic doctrine of Panhumanity; together the two of them collaborated on a column in the paper under the pseudonym of 'M. M. Cosmoi', speculating obscurely about the meaning of the World-Process. Then Mitrinović was ousted by the more aggressive personality of Ouspensky, who was in London preaching the gospel according to Gurdjieff. In 1922 Orage resigned the editorship of *The New Age* and entered Gurdjieff's institute at Fontainebleau as a neophyte. For whatever psychological reasons he was willing to submit to the gruelling physical labour and the constant humiliations which Gurdjieff imposed on his followers. Years later he told a friend that an unfavourable review could never have upset him now: after Gurdjieff, he knew what it was to be insulted by a real expert.

On graduating from Fontainebleau, however, he soon had a chance to reassert himself. At the end of 1923 he went to New York, where he spent the remainder of the 1920s as Gurdjieff's chief representative in America. How could he have fallen for such mumbo-jumbo? He was a man with a craving for the absolute, and although he described himself as an agnostic during his time on the *New Age*, one can see that the pressure of a religious impulse was at work behind his achievements. As Mairet says, everything he took up was half-way towards a religion. But the thought of him spreading the word of Gurdjieff among rich discontented New Yorkers is a profoundly depressing one. And what is the point of having the finest critical intelligence of the day, if you devote it to expounding the cosmology of *All and Everything: Beelzebub's Tales to his Grandson*?

In the end he broke with Gurdjieff (though not with Major Douglas) and returned to England, where in 1932 he started a new magazine, the *New English Weekly*. He was soon writing criticism again and back at his trade of discovering young writers: he was the first London editor to publish a poem by Dylan Thomas – 'And Death shall have no dominion'. Despite its Social Credit eccentricities, the *New English Weekly* was an excellent paper on its literary side; and perhaps the chief moral to be drawn from the last phase of Orage's career is that high literary ability can co-exist with the most dubious doctrines, and survive exposure to the most extravagant kinds of nonsense.

9

MODERN TIMES

I

Modern literature has gone on being modern for a very long time. On a historical chart we are as far away from *Ulysses* as *Ulysses* was from *Daniel Deronda*; as far away from *Prufrock* as *Prufrock* was from Swinburne's *Poems and Ballads*; as far away from *Sons and Lovers* as *Sons and Lovers* was from *A Tale of Two Cities*. Since the 1920s, the cycle of literary fashion has accelerated and the world has changed at an unprecedented rate, yet the modernity of the great pioneers of modernism has proved remarkably hard-wearing. Of these figures Eliot, though not necessarily the greatest, is the most decisive historically. His double role of poet and critic has given him a unique position in the evolution of literary modernism.

His critical authority derives in the first place from his achievement as a poet and the force of his actual judgements. But these are not enough in themselves to explain the peculiar intensity of his influence. There is also a quality of extreme deliberation which had hardly been seen in English criticism since Arnold. What makes his poetry so memorable (literally memorable) is that each line seems to have been looked at for six months, and the same is true of his best essays. Every effect has been carefully scrutinized, every aside has been pondered. There is no slack in his criticism. And this tension is intimidating – it convicts the reader of lazy-mindedness, as the Edwardians never did. The most glancing opinion is charged with significance; every topic he touches on demands to be explored. Undoubtedly his impact is heightened by the fact that he expresses himself through short self-contained essays. The hierarchy of values behind his work involves us all the more deeply because it is never made fully explicit, because we have to piece it together for ourselves from hints and suggestions. He implies a re-reading of the entire course of English literature, but he leaves it to others to fill in the details.

Given his boldness, his wholly modern timbre, this preoccupation with the idea of order was one of the things which recommended him most strongly to his early admirers. At a time when established standards seemed to be dissolving on every side, here was an innovator who insisted on the need for fixed values, a traditionalist who saw tradition in terms of a perpetual struggle: 'It cannot be inherited, and if you want it you must obtain it by great labour.' His fascination was that he both embodied and resisted the disintegrating tendencies of the age. And there are other, equally tantalizing contradictions. His tone is at once cautious and dogmatic, evasive and precise. He advocates an impersonal art, and at the same time succeeds in making one more curious about his own personality than he would have done if he had been a whole-hearted Romantic egoist.

For readers who had been brought up on *The Golden Treasury*, coming to grips with Eliot for the first time could be a disconcerting experience, something which involved more than adjusting one's opinions and assimilating unfamiliar techniques. It was almost like having to learn a new moral code, in which the most elusive and most desirable virtue was the possession of 'a superior sensibility'. A rather mysterious concept, this sensibility, not to be equated with sensitivity, or delicacy of feeling, or the ability to co-ordinate fragmentary impressions, though it includes elements of all three. The underlying image often seems to be that of a kind of sieve: the finer it is, the more it rejects. And despite the immense positive impetus which Eliot gave to criticism, especially through the manner in which he re-directed attention to the seventeenth century, his over-all influence was as much restrictive as liberating. He taught readers to mistrust their own judgements. Possibly he played on feelings of uncertainty that were already there; in the aftermath of the First World War, nothing seemed as dependable as it once had. At any rate, he effectively put paid to the mixture of historical survey and slapdash impressionism which had largely done duty for criticism up till then. His whole appeal was directed towards a tiny hypothetical *élite* of readers who had outgrown their textbooks – 'the few people who talk intelligently about Stendhal and Flaubert and James'.

At the same time, it has proved easy to exaggerate in retrospect the extent to which he broke with his seniors, and the violence of the resistance which he encountered. Naturally there were angry protests – one can hardly expect to go around killing off reputations without inviting reprisals. Second-rate conservative critics were still growling at the mention of his name in the 1930s or even the 1940s, and academic orthodoxy scarcely budged for the better part of a generation. There were learned attempts to snub 'Mr T. S. Eliot, an American critic' ridiculously late in the day. Because of this, other academics have been able to portray themselves as putting up a heroic struggle to obtain recognition for Eliot twenty years after *Prufrock*. In fact the remarkable thing is how quickly he conquered literary London, or the parts of it which probably mattered to him most. By 1920 he was treated with respect by someone like Arnold Bennett; he had many affiliations with Bloomsbury; his essays were being published in the *Times Literary Supplement*. A passage by Desmond MacCarthy, written in 1921, gives some idea of how his reputation stood at that date:

When two people are discussing modern poetry together, the name of T. S. Eliot is sure to crop up. If one of them is old-fashioned, and refuses to see merit in the young poets who refuse to do more than retail 'the ancient divinations of the Muse,' the other is sure to say sooner or later: 'But what about Eliot? You may dislike *vers libre* (I admit it is easy to write it badly) and dislike attempts to manipulate modern experience in verse; still, what do you think of Eliot? You cannot dismiss him.' And the other will reply: 'Well . . . yes . . . Eliot . . . I grant you there seems to be something in him.'

Given this degree of interest in his work, what difference did it make if the Squirearchy closed their ranks against Eliot or Arthur Waugh compared him to a drunken helot? On the contrary, a supply of badly-aimed insults helped to keep up the sense of excitement.

Eliot's own occasional comments on the men of letters of the previous generation are for the most part unexpectedly mild – a good deal milder than some of his comments on poets and novelists. The essay on Charles Whibley is a special case (Whibley was a friend, who had helped the *Criterion* over a bad patch with financial support), but it is generally true that you are more likely to find Eliot being complimentary about W. P. Ker than about Hardy or Meredith. He was deferential towards good scholars, and in his essays he makes a considerable show of his own technical scholarship. This in itself was a striking contrast with Shaw, Wells and the other leading Edwardians, who had very little connection with the academic literary tradition (and have never quite been assimilated to the 'official' canon of Eng. Lit.). In fact poets are more liable than novelists or dramatists to have a strong historical sense of the tradition behind them, and, apart from anything else, Eliot was the first poet for well over a generation to count as the dominant literary figure of his day. The general effect of his approach was to confer new prestige on the whole activity of criticism. It is true that he sometimes talked as though only poets were really competent to judge their own craft, but there was a secure if modest place in his scheme of things for the 'second-order' critic who provided the climate in which creative writers could work to the best advantage. As he wrote in the introduction to *The Sacred Wood*:

. . . the great bulk of the work of criticism could be done by minds of the second order, and it is just these minds of the second order that are difficult to find. They are necessary for the rapid circulation of ideas. The periodical press – the ideal literary periodical – is an instrument of transport; and the literary periodical press is dependent upon the existence of a sufficient number of second-order (I do not say 'second-rate', the word is too derogatory) minds to supply its material. These minds are necessary for that 'current of ideas', that 'society permeated by fresh thought', of which Arnold speaks.

What exactly is the role of the second-order critic, beyond elaborating and making better known the conclusions of first-order minds? The tools of criticism, Eliot declares more than once, are comparison and analysis. He himself was a master of comparison, of the significant juxtaposition, but he never makes it very clear what he means by analysis. Characteristically, he deals mainly in negatives, warning against fanciful or undisciplined interpretation. The general stance, however, counts for more than the lack of examples: he readily persuaded disciples that they could find a worthwhile vocation in analysing works of literature. To adapt his own phrase about Arnold and criticism, one might say that he was not so much an analyst as a propagandist for analysis. If he cast out the old-fashioned man of letters, he called into being the New Critic.

From 1922 he also had an opportunity to demonstrate how his ideal literary periodical ought to be conducted. *The Criterion* ran for seventeen years, for all but one of them (1927–8, when it came out every month) as a quarterly. It was produced at leisure; for most of its existence it was comfortably subsidized; and there was no undue worry about circulation figures, which are said to have hovered around 400. Here, if anywhere, was the chance to create a magazine of the highest possible intellectual distinction. The reality turned out to be very different, as is generally acknowledged – although out of respect for Eliot critics still find it hard to admit just how disappointing *The Criterion* actually was. Naturally there were good things in it. In the beginning Eliot tried to fulfil his ideal of Europeanism; towards the end he started drawing fairly regularly on gifted contributors of the Auden generation. But more typically there were long level stretches of tedium. How many of the 400 subscribers really felt much enthusiasm for all those right-wing calls to Order and all those exercises in para-theology? Eliot's original statement of aims sounded promising enough. Steering a middle course between sectarianism and shapelessness, he wanted to bring together a group of writers who were 'in communication' – though not necessarily in agreement – about the ways in which tradition could be developed and reaffirmed in the modern world. A reasoned conservative journal on the lines he indicated would have performed a valuable service for opponents as well as supporters, by clarifying the issues and raising the level of debate. The trouble is that so much of what went into *The Criterion* was irrelevant logic-chopping, only tenuously linked with social realities. Even on the purely literary side the paper was strangely out of touch. To take a single instance, the treatment of contemporary fiction was completely arbitrary: there was not a word about the novels of, say, Waugh or Isherwood. And Eliot fell short of his own polemical ambitions. The full-scale studies in which he promised to expose the errors of popular prophets like Shaw and Wells never appeared; instead there were only petulant asides. Petulance, indeed, was one of the hallmarks of *The Criterion*, and more especially of Eliot's own regular editorial commentaries. The frivolity, the failure to confront his enemies squarely, can be quite startling. Freud, for example – *The Future of an Illusion* gets sneered at on account of its 'stupidity', *Civilization and Its Discontents* is brushed aside as 'an innocent prank'. It is when he reflects on public affairs, though, that Eliot is capable of his silliest flights. 'I cannot believe in over-population so long as there is room in the world for everyone to move about without suffocation.' Did Chesterton or Shaw at their most perverse ever say anything quite as inane? It would be easy to compile a fair-sized sottisier of such remarks, but not very amusing. They make rather ugly reading in the light of the paper's whole political record, particularly in its later years. Digging through the bound volumes of *The Criterion* in the 1930s is not a very edifying experience. What is even creepier than the occasional tenderness shown towards Nazism is the wilful determination to ignore or gloss over the plainest facts of political life at the time. Human kind, it seems, cannot bear very much reality.

For readers today, the chief interest of the paper must inevitably lie in what it reveals about Eliot himself – not only about his editorial policies and his milieu (to judge by their contributions, incidentally, some of the second-order minds he surrounded himself with seem to have been very second-order indeed), but also about the accumulation of themes which were to bear fruit in his later poetry. Easily the most instructive account of *The Criterion* which has appeared so far is that by Herbert Howarth in his book *Notes on Some Figures Behind T. S. Eliot* – an account mainly devoted to showing how much Eliot learned from his contributors, how often an article or a review (on *Alcestis*, on Indian mysticism, on Beethoven, on St Thomas à Becket) would give him a cue which he followed up in *Four Quartets* or his plays. And what is true of his editing applies to his criticism as well.

Increasingly, as time goes on, the best of his critical work comes to seem an annexe of his poetry. In his early essays he was working out his position, seizing on those qualities in other poets which he could make use of himself, creating the taste by which he was to be enjoyed. Once he had done this, most of the fire went out of him. As a critic, that is: contrary to the usual rule, the major poet (the poet who wrote the *Four Quartets*) survived a good deal longer.

II

The end of the First World War saw a new crop of little maga-zines, flauntingly experimental and aggressively anti-tradition-alist. By the time of the Armistice, literary hostilities had already broken out with the appearance of the Sitwells' yearbook *Wheels* (1916–22) and Frank Rutter and Herbert Read's periodical *Arts and Letters* (1917–20). Eliot became assistant editor of that curious Imagist-cum-feminist paper *The Egoist* in 1917, while two years later Middleton Murry was appointed editor of the *Athenaeum*. A general determination to 'make it new' was in the air, together with a revulsion from the literary establishment which had been intensified by disgust at the shams of conventional war poetry. The most immediate objects of this animosity were the circle of writers around Edward Marsh, the editor of *Georgian Poetry* and chief sponsor of Rupert Brooke, but it was not so much Marsh himself as J. C. Squire (1884–1958) who was soon to be cast as the leading villain of the piece. During the war Squire and his friends, notably W. J. Turner and Edward Shanks, had begun building up a network of contacts which gave them a considerable say in the review pages of at least half a dozen papers, including the *Observer* and the *New Statesman*. In addition, from 1919 Squire had his own journal, the *London Mercury*, which provided him with an influ-ential platform from which he could damn the dangerous literary bolsheviks of the period. And damn them he did. The printing of *The Waste Land* was 'scarcely worthy of the Hogarth Press'; Wilfred Owen's 'Strange Meeting' was dismissed out of hand; there were innumerable sarcastic flights about pretentious and incomprehensible highbrows. Squire's belligerence naturally provoked equally violent counterblasts, and his positive ideals aroused just as much antipathy. He and his friends were associated with everything that an intellectual of the day was liable to wince at most – cricketing week-ends, foaming tankards, Sussex-by-the-sea, pale green pastorals, thigh-slapping joviality. It only needed someone to have the bright idea of christening them the Squirearchy, and the legend was complete.

Before the war Squire had been comparatively unknown outside a small literary circle. He had had to make his own way in the world (his father, who was an unsuccessful veterinary surgeon – and a drunk – had walked out on the family when he was a child), and after leaving Cambridge he went back to his home town, Plymouth, to start work as a newspaper reporter. Then in 1907 he decided to try his luck in London. At this time he was an enthusiastic Fabian, and the first editor who took him up was Orage. He became a regular contributor of criticism and verse to the *New Age*, which may seem rather improbable in the light of his subsequent Squirearchical persona – though no more improbable than the fact that his earliest books should have been an essay called *Socialism and Art*, which appeared with a preface by Walter Crane, and a volume of translations from Baudelaire. It was as a neat, better-then-*Punch* parodist that he first began to attract attention, but the real turning-point in his career came in 1913, when he was made literary editor of the *New Statesman*. Here, for the next half-dozen years, he laid down the law in a widely-read column written under the name of 'Solomon Eagle'. He also published a good deal of verse: one of his contributions to the third volume of *Georgian Poetry*, a tropical fantasy called 'The Lily of Malud', was interestingly enough singled out by Eliot in a review as 'an original and rather impressive poem which deserves better company'. These were years when he struck all his friends as someone who knew where he was going. And he acquired some powerful patrons, in particular Gosse, who described him as 'that peach of a man' and saw him as his own eventual successor.

The dynasty was running out, however. As Eliot wrote in the *Criterion* after Gosse's death, 'the place that Sir Edmund Gosse filled in the literary and social life of London is one that no one can ever fill again, because it is, so to speak, an office that has been abolished'. True, Squire was a considerable social force throughout the 1920s. In addition to running the *London Mercury*, he was reviewer-in-chief to the *Observer*. He edited a new series of *English Men of Letters* for Macmillan's, and acted as literary adviser to Longman's – Andrew Lang's old position. He was a reputation-maker, an anthologist, a committeeman, a promoter of good causes. But none of this, in the new climate, was enough to transform a literary politician into a literary statesman; and though a cultivated middlebrow public remained loyal to the *Mercury* (it reached a sale of about 10,000), even Squire's friends were forced to admit that it mostly made tepid reading, that the real action was going on elsewhere. His own enthusiasm seems to have waned after the first few years; he was more interested in his cricket eleven, his work for the Stonehenge Protection Committee, his admirable campaign against architectural vandalism. And there was a moment of boyish glory when he gave the first B.B.C. commentary on the Boat Race.

The last third of his life was a sad affair, with something of the macabre overtones of an Angus Wilson short story. In 1933 he was knighted: to his enemies – or at any rate to those of them who did not know his personal circumstances – it must have sounded like the final apotheosis of the Squirearchy. In fact by this time his world was beginning to fall apart, and he was well on the way to becoming an alcoholic. After giving up the editorship of the *Mercury* in 1934 he drifted further and further into a semi-vagrant existence; he was saved from the worst by his work as a reader for Macmillan's and a reviewer for the *Illustrated London News*, and by the kindness of various women friends, but for the most part his life was a chaos of unpaid bills and unfulfilled commitments. (He was once reduced to telling an editor that his manuscript had been blown out of the window of a taxi while he was on his way to deliver it.) For a time he lived in a suburban hotel, and having grown a straggling beard took to describing himself as the Sage of Surbiton – although he also insisted on being addressed by all but his oldest friends as 'Sir John'. His appearance meanwhile became steadily more decrepit: there is an account in his biography of one occasion when he showed up at the Athenaeum wearing 'white flannels, black evening slippers, a badly moth-eaten, blue, high-necked pullover, a wing collar, and an old Blundellian tie'. In his final years he lived in the country; he was less harassed, and he had the consolation of knowing before he died that Macmillan's were planning to publish his collected poems. They appeared shortly after his death in 1958, with an introduction by John Betjeman.

If anyone could be said to have succeeded to Gosse's position it was Desmond MacCarthy (1877–1952), who replaced him as resident chief reviewer of the *Sunday Times* after his death. MacCarthy had a much more open, less calculating personality than Gosse, however, and he was a very different kind of man from Squire. Half Irish, quarter German, quarter French, wholly Etonian, a favourite disciple of G. E. Moore at Cambridge, he began his journalistic career on the *Speaker*, writing mainly about the theatre. Dropped by Massingham when the paper was amalgamated with the *Nation*, he joined the *Eye Witness*, working alongside of Belloc and the Chesterton brothers. His closest links, though, dating back to Cambridge days, were with the original members of the Bloomsbury group. He helped Roger Fry to organize the first of the Post-Impressionist exhibitions, and contributed an anonymous preface to the catalogue which he later remarked was far more widely quoted from than anything he was ever destined to write again. Observations such as 'A good rocking-horse is more like a horse than the snapshot of a Derby winner' provoked almost as much laughter as the pictures themselves. Then, when the *New Statesman* was started, he was offered the post of drama critic (supposedly at Shaw's suggestion), and in 1920 he succeeded Squire as literary editor, replacing the reflections of 'Solomon Eagle' with those of 'Affable Hawk'. From 1928 to 1934 he also edited the miscellany *Life and Letters*.

Among his friends, especially among his Bloomsbury friends, MacCarthy was famous as an unfulfilled writer, the author of an unspecified, eternally postponed masterpiece, the brilliant conversationalist who could never manage to get it all down on paper. Something of him, or of his quandary, went into the character of

22 George Wyndham, by 'Spy'
(from *Vanity Fair*)

23 Charles Whibley, by Gerald Kelly

24 W. E. Henley, by 'Spy'
(from *Vanity Fair*)

26 James Thomas the Younger

25 'The Birthday Surprise', by Max Beerbohm. The presentation of the bust now
in the London Library to Sir Edmund Gosse (12), 1 G. K. Chesterton,
2 George Moore, 3 Rudyard Kipling, 4 Lord Curzon, 5 Arnold Bennett,
6 Joseph Conrad, 7 Thomas Hardy, 8 Lord Morley, 9 Lord Haldane,
10 Austin Dobson, 11 Lord Balfour

27 Henry Morley

28 F. J. Furnivall

29 Churton Collins

30 Sir Walter Raleigh

Sir Arthur Quiller-Couch

32 George Gilfillan

33 Sir William Robertson
Nicoll, by Max Beerbohm

34 Clement Shorter, by 'Spy'
(from *Vanity Fair*)

35 J. M. Dent

36 Ernest Rhys

Arnold Bennett

37 Arnold Bennett, by David Low

38 G. K. Chesterton, a self caricature done when he was a student at the Slade

39 A. L. Orage

40 T. S. Eliot, by David Low

41 John Middleton Murry, by William Rothenstein

42 Desmond MacCarthy

43 Sir John Squire

44 Christopher Caudwell

45 George Orwell

46 Goeffrey Grigson
(photograph from *New Verse*)

Bernard in *The Waves* – Bernard, whose mind hums with phrases and images going to waste, who spends a lifetime hankering after the one irresistible story which will bind together his momentary inspirations. 'I keep my phrases hung up like clothes in a cupboard, waiting for someone to wear them.' But Bernard is no more to be literally identified with Desmond MacCarthy than Bergotte is with Anatole France; and indeed, like Bergotte he reveals at least as much about his creator as about his original. For a straightforward portrait one must turn to Leonard Woolf's memoirs, where there is a drily sympathetic account of MacCarthy's non-working habits. The blank moods which compel a writer to potter around, stare out of the window, read last week's *Radio Times*, do anything rather than actually get on with his writing – these onsets of paralysis are common enough, but MacCarthy seems to have suffered from the disease to a quite exceptional degree. 'Disease' was his own word for it: he told Leonard Woolf that the moment he knew that he ought to be doing something, no matter what it was, no matter how much he really wanted to do it, he felt absolutely driven to think about doing something else. A man with a temperament like this plainly needed the goad of a weekly deadline to give of his best. But whatever inhibitions held him back from writing the novels he dreamed of carried over into his criticism as well, to the extent that he was mistrustful of a strongly subjective approach, as he readily acknowledged:

When I come across some profound piece of criticism into which the critic has, I feel, been led by surrendering to his own temperament, I wonder if my own method of criticizing is not mistaken. One cannot get away from one's own temperament any more than one can jump away from one's own shadow, but one can discount the emphasis which it produces. I snub my own temperament when I think it is not leading me straight to the spot whence a general panorama of an author's work is visible. This point is often some obvious little knoll or terrace, which almost everyone would mount to get a view. Perhaps the other kind of criticism is more valuable, in which the critic wanders down a vista which he is impelled by a personal impulse of curiosity to explore, ignoring what lies to the right or left of him, or what others see when they just look around them. But again how often the most alluring and mysterious little path in a garden leads only to the gardeners' privy!

If he had grown up in a world more permeated by Freud, MacCarthy might have hesitated over the possible implications of his metaphor. But this passage does suggest his self-awareness, and the urbanity with which he accepted his own limitations. Elsewhere he described the critic, his kind of critic, as 'a creature without a spiritual home', who made it a point of honour never to seek one.

His essays are far less highly coloured and highly wrought than those of Virginia Woolf or Lytton Strachey, but they do have the advantage of making one think about the books he discusses. The typical Virginia Woolf essay by contrast is a brilliant circular flight, which, as criticism, leads nowhere. And for his own purposes MacCarthy writes well enough. He was a skilful reporter, in the ordinary sense of the word, with the knack of turning out a swift clear sketch of a trial, a boxing-match, a political rally, a theatrical occasion, and he always tried to see works of literature embedded in their living context. Naturally he made no pretence of academic thoroughness, but he could draw unostentatiously on a wide range of European reading, and he had the great virtue of being inquisitive – I wonder, for example, how many other reviewers of *For Lancelot Andrewes* actually went away and read Andrewes's sermons, instead of taking Eliot on trust. Nor did catholicity and an even temper make him any the less a moralist. On the contrary, his interest in books was overwhelmingly in the lessons they had to teach – provided that they were lessons which had stood the test of experience. And there was nothing of the Axel's Castle aesthete about him. If he had a watchword as a critic, it was that 'a work of art whatever its theme must somehow, somewhere, suggest the desirability of life'.

MacCarthy was a man of his time and, up to a point, of his class; he could be blandly conservative in some of his judgements, and by modern standards his wisdom seems too courtly, too mellow. But it is real wisdom as far as it goes, based on a knowledge of human limitations (the knowledge which made him respond so strongly to Chekhov). Based, too, on an abhorrence of bullying and regimentation and what he once called 'beaked and clawed humanity'. Of course, this firm fair-mindedness, so admirable in the man, can be a disadvantage for the critic. It lowers the temperature of his writing, and exposes him to the beaks and claws of his colleagues. Mr Geoffrey Grigson, for instance, has recently been apologizing in the *Times Literary Supplement* for the 'triviality' which led him when he was editing *New Verse* to 'go for the Desmond MacCarthy streak in English letters'. In a sense he is right: MacCarthy was not a strikingly original critic, nor even, in himself, a particularly important one. His importance was simply that of someone who helped to keep alive a tradition of breadth, enlightenment, rational sociability, civilized forbearance. Despite the *Criterion* and *Scrutiny* and Geoffrey Grigson and Geoffrey Grigson's hero Wyndham Lewis, it is not a tradition which was entirely superseded, even in the baton-swinging 1930s – though no doubt we should all be much more rigorous and exacting today if it had been. Those of us, that is, who survived to tell the story.

III

If MacCarthy had been asked to give an example of his antithesis, the critic who surrendered to his temperament, he could hardly have found a more striking one among his contemporaries than John Middleton Murry (1889–1957). Eventually Murry's introspective depth-soundings were to carry him beyond criticism altogether, and from early on there were signs that he was looking to literature to supply him with a more-than-literary faith. But initially he made his name as a critic, and a very good one, if somewhat erratic. As an enterprising editor, too. His first magazine, which he started together with Michael Sadleir* in 1911 when they were both still undergraduates at Brasenose, was *Rhythm*. Its inspiration was cosmopolitan, mainly French: both Murry and Sadleir had stayed in Paris and become passionately enthusiastic about the Post-Impressionists, some of whose works they reproduced in their pages. Editorial pronunciamentos proclaimed the dawn of a new, dynamic, boldly exploratory age in the arts; as Frank Swinnerton, who was connected with the paper, has pointed out, the whole idea of treating 'rhythm' as a general

* Later well known as biographer, bibliographer, Trollopean, and author of *Fanny by Gaslight*.

aesthetic (or synaesthetic) principle was still a novelty in England at the time. Murry himself thought of the magazine as potentially 'the *Yellow Book* of modernism', and from another angle it can be seen as a 1920s-style little magazine born a decade too soon. But its modernism was a vague aspiration rather than a distinct doctrine; Murry drew on all kinds of non-modernistic contributors, from Hugh Walpole to Frank Harris, and after Edward Marsh had put up some money to pay off the printer's debts there was an influx of Georgian poets. By this time Katherine Mansfield had become co-editor (she and Murry lived together in a flat attached to the editorial office in Chancery Lane – just down the road from Orage, her original mentor), and the paper had been transformed from a quarterly into a monthly. It ran until early 1913, when it was metamorphosed into *The Blue Review*, which started off ambitiously, but only survived for three issues.

It was while editing *Rhythm* that Murry first became embroiled with D. H. Lawrence. It would be absurd to discuss as though it were primarily a matter of intellectual indebtedness the relationship between these two men, with all its storms and conflicts – Lawrence's angry demand for a pact of *Blutbrüderschaft*, the tensions which were dramatized in *Women in Love*, the near-hysterical ebb and flow of sympathy which continued to the last. But equally it would be futile to consider Murry's sense of his own role as a writer without recognizing how deeply it was coloured by the impact of Lawrence. From Lawrence's point of view, he was submissive, but not submissive enough, a John the Baptist who was liable to prove a Judas. The 'very essence of his malady', Lawrence wrote, after Murry had shown him the manuscript of his first novel, was that he was 'utterly unwilling to take himself for what he is, a clever, but non-original, non-creative individual'. Instead, he felt he had to 'assume himself the equal of the highest'. It is not hard to guess exactly who Lawrence had in mind when he spoke about 'the highest'. But whether inspired by resentment or not, there was obviously a strong element of truth in his diagnosis. Certainly, after having failed as a novelist and poet, Murry was to seek a kind of vicarious creativity through entering into the work of others.

This is to anticipate, however. Until the early 1920s he was content to practise literary journalism as an end in itself. His editorship of the *Athenaeum* (with Aldous Huxley as one of his assistants) was an outstanding success. Not financially: the paper was too good to last, and after less than two years, in 1921, it was absorbed by the *Nation*. But he managed to enlist an astonishing array of contributors, from Eliot to Bertrand Russell, from Valéry to Santayana. And at the same time his own essays gained him the reputation of being one of the two or three leading critics of the day. Probably the best-known of them were his attacks on the hitherto undented image of the Georgians: there was a standing feud between the *Athenaeum* and the *London Mercury*. But Squire and his friends were too easy a target, and I am inclined to agree with Murry's biographer, F. A. Lea, that the feud probably did more harm than good – it tended to put people off poetry altogether, not just off Georgian poetry. The important Murry essays were his positive ones. He chose major subjects, and ranged widely. His illustrations were freshly chosen, his comments were acute. And there was a quality of unyielding seriousness which commanded respect. He already tended to write about authors in terms of their existential struggles: his Baudelaire, for instance, was neither Saintsbury's master of word music nor the theatrical satanist of the 1890s, but a suffering spirit – 'the fox of disillusion and disgust really tore at his vitals'. Already, too, there was a measure of self-projection in his portraits. The 'critical credo' at the end of *Countries of the Mind* (1922) is unambiguous: 'The function of criticism is primarily the function of literature itself, to provide a means of self-expression for the critic.' But his eye was still kept firmly on the object, and his private preoccupations, though they lent his writing power, were not yet allowed to obtrude. Traditionalists as well as modernists were impressed. Raleigh invited him to Oxford to give the course of lectures which he published as *The Problem of Style*. And the *Athenaeum* was only one of the papers for which he wrote. In particular, like many other writers of his generation, including Eliot, he received a great deal of encouragement from Bruce Richmond, the editor of the *Times Literary Supplement*.

After Katherine Mansfield's death, however, Murry felt the need of his own magazine, to express a growing sense of personal mission. When he founded the *Adelphi* in 1923 he saw it as a vehicle for his own cloudy vision of universal harmony – and even more as a platform for Lawrence, to whose views he had been violently re-converted after reading *Fantasia of the Unconscious*. In the first number he protested that he was not an editor – 'I would do anything, I verily believe, rather than be an editor any more. . . . I am only a *locum tenens* for a better man.' The better man urged him to use the magazine to 'attack everything', and characteristically found its contents 'weak, apologetic, knock-kneed'. It was at any rate consistently Murryish in spirit. Katherine Mansfield was commemorated in practically every number, while Murry's own commentaries and essays were unrestrained exercises in self-exposure. Few people would have predicted that such a paper would have had the success which it did (over 15,000 copies of the first number were sold), but the affirmations of faith in life and the open avowal of spiritual yearnings struck a responsive chord with readers trying to escape from the post-war mood of disenchantment. What Murry offered was not so much a creed as a constant incitement to introspection. As far as literature went, this meant that he was always saying things like, 'These last years I have been haunted by two mysteries: the mystery of Shakespeare and the mystery of Tolstoi'. More immediately, he saw himself defending romanticism against the classicism of the *Criterion*. Romanticism was, he argued, the central tradition of English literature: even our classics were romantic. This was a romanticism which was palpably not bound down by time or place or textbook definitions. Rather, it was a perpetual quest for inner values, a striving towards 'the unknown God'. The basis of his thinking was now quite explicit: 'There is no escape. Religion and Literature are branches of the same everlasting root.'

We are back with Carlyle and his one green bough – and there are indeed some obvious parallels between Murry and Carlyle in their whole approach to literature. Both of them use criticism as a means of conducting an extended public self-therapy; both of them read their own conflicts into the careers of other writers; both of them value an author chiefly in so far as they can treat him as an allegorical figure. 'He is a symbolic man, one of the world's great exemplars of what a man may be; one of the chief of those who bring men to a consciousness of their own strange destinies.' This is Murry on Lawrence, but it could easily be Carlyle on the Hero as Man of Letters. The difference between the two men is primarily one of creative power – Carlyle can objectify his feelings in images or mould them into narrative, Murry can only talk about his intuitions and keep reaffirming that there *is* a mystery, that life *is* rich, that what he tells us three times must be true. It is as though Carlyle had remained shrouded in Immensities and Infinitudes, without venturing into history or satire or portraiture. His greater creativity, one feels, was bound up with his more outward-looking cast of mind, the qualities which made him so trenchant a social critic. Admittedly Murry, during the second half of his career, was deeply preoccupied with politics, as a Christian (*more suo*), as a Christian Communist, and finally as a Pacifist. By the beginning of the 1930s he had come to believe in 'the complete moral demand of conscious politics upon the modern man' (something which he said Lawrence had already reluctantly sensed in *Kangaroo*). But even in his most politically militant moods he tended to be self-absorbed, strangely insensitive to the reality, the otherness of other people. Somehow he contrived to be both weak and fanatical – a grating combination. Compare him with Carlyle again. The posthumous cult of Jane, as it shows itself in Carlyle's *Reminiscences*, may have been fuelled by self-pity, but it was also informed by emotional tact, whereas Murry's cult of Katherine Mansfield makes one want to look the other way. There was a creepy side to him which laid him open to being lampooned as Burlap in *Point Counter Point*. And the egoism with which he commandeered the masterpieces that he wrote about is too undisguised for comfort. In his hot youth, when he was editing *Rhythm*, he had once described Frank Harris as 'the greatest creative critic whom the world has known', and though it was an opinion which he was quick to retract, it is a suggestive one: his Shakespearean commentaries do have a partial precedent in *The Man Shakespeare*.

Nevertheless he was not Frank Harris, and he was emphatically not Burlap. Modern English criticism owes more to him than is readily acknowledged nowadays. He helped to give it its direction, and even, to some extent, its vocabulary: at least, one is struck, going back to the early essays, by the characteristically modern value which he assigns to such terms of praise as 'sensuous' or 'disturbing'. Again, the few brief remarks on Shakespearean metaphor in *The Problem of Style* are a signpost pointing forward to the whole subsequent exploration of Shakespeare's imagery. It is interesting to note that in the course of his discussion he speaks slightingly of those critics who go to Shakespeare 'to find something he has not got – a philosophy'. Within a few years this is exactly what he was to be doing himself. Yet would he have written so perceptively in the first place if he had not already been working towards a private religion of Shakespeare? (The parallel case of Wilson Knight comes to mind.) And although, I suppose, few readers, once they are past adolescence, are likely to be unreservedly carried along by Murry's more nebulous speculations about Keats, he does succeed in persuading one that he has caught the essential feel and tempo of the poet's inner development in a way that is denied to more detached or circumspect commentators. It is easy to sympathize, too, with his struggle to transcend the role of critic altogether, his sense of the discrepancy between a formal judgement and the actual experience of a major work of art. If he frequently ignores the kind of facts which most criticism respects, he also asks questions which criticism usually avoids. The patterns of self-annihilation and renewal, of self-division and reintegration to which he again and again recurs when writing about literature are no less real for being vague in outline. But they are psychological realities, not ones which can be explained in terms of 'metabiology' or home-made metaphysics. Had he been born a generation or two later, Murry might well have found his vocation working on the wilder frontiers of psychology; the very titles of the works of such writers as Norman O. Brown and R. D. Laing – *Life Against Death*, *The Divided Self* – are ones which he could easily have chosen for books of his own. (Mr Brown, incidentally, while he has some hard things to say about the insufficiently excremental tenor of Murry's life of Swift, does give him due credit for coining the actual phrase 'the excremental vision'.)

In an earlier age, on the other hand, Murry would almost certainly have been, as F. A. Lea says, the founder of a dissident, millenarian sect. His career after 1930 consisted mainly of a series of frustrated attempts to achieve his own ideal of Christian brotherhood, either through political persuasion or through setting up egalitarian farming communities. It makes a rather lugubrious story, complicated by the strains of a disastrous third marriage and by an autocratic element in his character which made it harder for him to accommodate himself to communal action than he admitted. Nor do his descents into everyday politics improve the picture. One can put aside as the incidental aberrations of a visionary such oddities as the hope which he expressed (in 1931) that Fenner Brockway would prove 'an English Stalin'. But his wartime pacifism seems exasperatingly wrong-headed – not necessarily as an ideal, but because it was based on a refusal to look at facts and consequences. Murry was once again wrapped up in his own situation as the leader of an unpopular minority; and Mr Lea makes the interesting point that his fanaticism and his sense of 'destiny' engendered 'a certain sympathy for Hitler (his exact contemporary, whose early struggle with his father to escape a civil service career somewhat resembled his own)'. There are times when one wishes that Murry had been a little less concerned with Symbolic Men, and a little more with real men.

In the 1930s Murry's popular reputation slumped. He handed over the *Adelphi* to his friends Max Plowman and Sir Richard Rees; and apart from *Shakespeare* his later books, although they contain a good deal of incidental literary comment, were largely ignored by the general intellectual public. Until 1954, that is, when he sprang a surprise with his admirable biography of Swift. For those who regard him primarily as a prophet, it is not part of the essential Murry canon – he deliberately schooled himself to write about an author as remote from him in spirit as possible – but it does have a more-than-scholarly vitality. So do the best of the miscellaneous essays which he continued to write from time to time for his own amusement. His study of Gissing, for instance, shows his ability to enter the emotional world of another writer undiminished. He disregards most of the sociological aspects of Gissing on which discussion usually centres, and concentrates instead, as no previous critic had done, on the currents of sexual hostility running through the novels. It is a narrow interpretation, but a compelling one. Once again Murry succeeds in giving some idea of his author's creative *daemon*; from the sociologists it would be hard to gather why Gissing went on writing novels at all. *Unprofessional Essays*, Murry called one of his last collections, and until the end he continued to display, above all in his willingness to let himself go, the advantages of the unprofessional essayist.

IV

In the 1920s the dominant characteristic of modern literature was felt to be a bringing to light of hidden areas of the personality, an enlarging and refining of consciousness. Joyce's interior monologues, Lawrence's insistence that 'you mustn't look in my novel for the old stable ego of the character', Virginia Woolf's flow of tremulous imagery, whatever the differences between them, could all be taken as pointing in broadly the same direction – towards a picture of individual experience as more fluid, denser, more disorderly, less subject to rational control than earlier generations had dared to admit. A picture which was easier to accept after the upheavals of war, and one which found confirmation in the rapid if confusing spread of what used to be known in those days as Depth Psychology. The Freudian ideas which were an unheard-of novelty when they were discussed in *The New Age* in 1912 had became common knowledge among most educated people a dozen years later. It might reasonably have been assumed that they were also bound to have a revolutionary effect on literary criticism, but this is not what actually happened. As George Watson writes in *The Literary Critics* (1962), 'the almost total absence of psychological criticism is the most astonishing negative fact of all English criticism in the twentieth century'. Mr Watson makes this observation in the course of discussing the work of I. A. Richards, and he is certainly right in pointing to the paradox that Richards, though often thought of as a psychologist, played a major role in directing attention away from psychological interpretation towards the notion of poems as detached, self-explanatory artefacts. But Richards's negative influence was obviously only one of many. Eliot's was even more powerful; 'Tradition and the Individual Talent' lay like a boulder blocking the path. Equally, there were plenty of examples of cheap mis-applied psychological criticism to which serious critics could point if they wanted an apparent justification for their resistance; mechanical debunkings often made all the more objectionable by being served up with would-be Stracheyan irony. And undoubt-edly it requires exceptional tact for a critic to make effective use of psychological concepts – although one would have thought that this was a challenge rather than a deterrent. Again, the fact that theoretically psychology only offers interpretations, not value-judgements, has often been used as an excuse for writing it off as irrelevant by critics who are themselves quite prepared to inter-pret works of art as well as evaluate them. There is the added complication that in practice many psychologists do tend to start off by assuming the positive literary merit of works which they discuss, and their judgement can be as fallible as anyone else's. A critic coming across Ella Sharpe's psycho-analytical study of Francis Thompson, for instance, might well recoil on being told in the opening sentence that Thompson was probably 'the greatest religious poet of the nineteenth century'.* If, on the con-trary, he regards Thompson as thoroughly mediocre, Ella Sharpe's comments are plainly of no professional interest to him. But that is hardly a valid reason for ignoring her remarkable paper 'From *King Lear* to *The Tempest*', which as far as I can see has been passed over in complete silence by the standard Shake-spearean editors and commentators. American critics have, of course, proved far more receptive to psycho-analytic ideas, and the ultimate explanation for this kind of neglect must lie beyond literature, in the pattern of English culture as a whole.

Nevertheless the picture is not quite as bleak as George Watson makes out. He was writing mainly with academic criticism in mind; outside the universities, on the other hand, a good many English critics have learned something from the doctrines of psycho-analysis. This is most obviously true of the Auden genera-

---

* In fairness one should point out that Ella Sharpe (who incidentally taught English literature for many years before becoming a psycho-analyst) was born in 1875.

tion (and the Empson generation: *Seven Types of Ambiguity*, as the author acknowledges in his preface to the second edition, would never have been what it is without the influence of Freud). But there were certainly stirrings before that, even if one discounts as mere curiosities such extravagant performances as Robert Graves's *Poetic Unreason* (1925). Herbert Read was advocating a subtle and flexible use of psycho-analytic concepts – not entirely exemplified, unfortunately, by his own study of Wordsworth – in theoretical essays such as 'The Nature of Criticism', written in the mid-1920s. And a less well-known though no less interesting case is that of Edwin Muir, whose early collection of essays, *Latitudes* (1924), contains an explicit plea for psychology in literary criticism. Muir began his career as a critic writing for *The New Age*, and it was Orage who arranged for him to be psycho-analysed by Maurice Nicoll, one of the earliest English Jungian analysts (and the son of Sir William Robertson Nicoll). Not that he ever subscribed dogmatically to any one set of doctrines. He believed that any critical method was justified if it was applied skilfully – 'the criticism that's best administered is best'. Still, it took a psychologist, in the widest sense, to penetrate to the heart of a book. The essays in *Latitudes* are often awkward or naïve, but there are some fine flashes: a comparison between Milton and Nietzsche; an attempt, far less affected than Raleigh's in *Style*, to explain art in terms of play. Two years later Muir published a collection of essays on contemporary writers, *Transition*, which attempts to relate the new inwardness of twentieth-century literature to the flux and uncertainty of the age. It suggests that he had the makings of a notable critic. But his criticism was a by-product of his development as a poet, and although he was to prove an outstanding reviewer, especially during his twelve-year stint reviewing novels for the *Listener*, he wrote few extended critical studies after the 1920s.

Muir was a leading contributor to *The Calendar of Modern Letters* (1925–7), which, if not quite as brilliant a production as its subsequent underground reputation suggests, was certainly one of the most ably conducted reviews of the period. The editors – Edgell Rickword, Bertram Higgins, Douglas Garman – were all recent Oxford or Cambridge graduates who admired Eliot but had been disappointed by the *Criterion's* brand of neo-classicism and what they regarded as its lack of critical rigour. Instead they proposed their own version of classicism, which depended solely on trying to establish an agreed set of high critical standards. The *Calendar* published work by Lawrence, Wyndham Lewis, Forster, Graves, but its most distinctive feature was the series of 'Scrutinies' of elderly established authors, from Barrie to Wells, written mainly by the editors themselves. 'Scrutiny' – a name with possibilities; and Dr Leavis was to acknowledge his general sense of indebtedness to the *Calendar* in his introduction to a selection of articles from its pages published in 1933. Predictably he emphasized the editors' concern with standards, their belief in paying close attention to the text and their anti-middlebrow intransigence. There were good grounds for doing this. In one direction the *Calendar's* policy led towards treating criticism as though it were an ideology complete in itself. No earlier review had attached such moral prestige to the very adjective 'critical', and editorial commentaries were sometimes contorted to the point at which it could be declared that

It is no longer useful to distinguish between an act of imagination and an act of criticism, where the first may, for all real purposes, be demoded by the second. Thus it is possible to say that the criticism in Mr Eliot's 'Sacred Wood' not only is a more valuable work than Mr Lawrence's latest novel, but takes precedence of it, makes it obsolete.

But the editors were not entirely satisfied with this attempt to construct an *élite* in a political vacuum. There was also a recurrent *communisant* strain in the magazine. Trotsky's polemics against British socialists were praised for their 'clear-sightedness':

On every side, the slug humanitarianism leaves its slimy trail, obscuring the function of intelligence and atrophying emotion – and it is only such politics as can assure the demolition of the existing ideology that are of interest.

And a discussion of literary values could suddenly break off, in the midst of the usual attacks on Edward Marsh and Squire, with the thought that 'a regeneration of intelligent sensibility may only be possible after a devastating and bloody revolt against the sickly, bourgeois, animal consciousness of our age'. Despite these portents, however, it would be just as misleading to think of the *Calendar* as a forerunner of the *Left Review* as to picture it simply as an *Ur-Scrutiny*. In practice the editors never allowed the paper's criticism to swamp its fiction and poetry; they opened their columns to a wide range of interests and opinions; and their own Scrutinizing was carried out with a general lack of rancour. There were no slabs of pre-cast jargon, no rigid dogmas. The *Calendar* was a notable magazine partly because it insisted on high standards, but partly also because it was none the less a product of the free and adventurous spirit of the 1920s.

10

CROSS-CURRENTS
OF THE THIRTIES

I

That writers should have been politically conscious in the 1930s was inevitable; the only puzzle is why they should have been quite as apolitical as they were in the 1920s. How slight an imaginative impact the Russian Revolution had at the time, for instance, how few English poets (if any) felt that Lenin's mind was cutting through history like an oxy-acetylene burner while he was actually still around. During the years when communism was becoming a central issue for French or European intellectuals, when it was attracting leading European writers from Barbusse to Brecht, the English *avant-garde* simply ignored it, and the Communist Party of Great Britain was notorious for the low proportion of intellectuals in its ranks by comparison with the international Communist movement as a whole. Whatever the reasons for this placid state of affairs, it made the sudden swing leftwards at the beginning of the 1930s seem all the more of an invigorating shock to those who took part in it. The literature of the 1920s had been peopled by largely passive figures: Tiresias, Mrs Dalloway, a succession of sensitive introverts, amused observers, melancholy pierrots. Now was the time to act; and if there was one thing which excited writers in the 1930s it was the idea of themselves as men of action. *We're Not Going to do Nothing* was the title of a characteristic tract of the period (by Cecil Day Lewis) – and indisputably there were things, plenty of things, which needed to be done. When all the blunderings of the period have been taken into account, all the fatuities, all the deceptions, can anyone doubt that it was nevertheless honourable to protest and dishonourable to lie low?

One speaks of protest, but the literary movement of the 1930s was very far from being a simple matter of pamphleteering and verse-propaganda. Few writers were willing to sacrifice modern techniques on the altar of proletarian naturalism; few found it easy to slough off such bourgeois habits as an interest in individual psychology. And then there was the complicated and compli-cating genius of Auden. There would certainly have been a school of political poetry in the 1930s without him, just as there would have been an aesthetic revolution in the 1920s without Eliot, but in both cases the results would have been incalculably different. Auden's compelling personal vision, his willingness to cross-pollinate Marxism with psycho-analysis, his ability to invest the familiar middle-class English landscape of tennis courts and minor public schools and by-pass roads with the qualities of myth – all this made him not only a direct influence on his contemporaries, but also a powerful focus for their diffuse revolutionary attitudes. On balance, he can be seen less as an ally of the Marxists than as a counter-attraction; without him, younger writers would pro-bably have been much readier than they were to toe the party line.

If most of the poets of the Auden circle were not as red as they were painted, neither were their best-known critical impresarios. Michael Robert's two anthologies, *New Signatures* (1932) and *New Country* (1933) did as much as anything to establish the public legend of a specifically 1930s movement, but although the political emphasis of the second collection was a good deal sharper than that of the first, the politics themselves – as expressed in the editor's introductory comments – were heavily romantic, con-sisting mainly of a generalized call for an end to capitalism and a fresh start, with Roberts's passion for mountaineering providing the central image of challenge and endurance. He was very much his own man. In the mid-1920s he had been a Communist for a few months, before being drummed out of the party for devia-tionism. In the mid-1930s, readers who had been expecting him to keep them happy with clenched-fist propaganda began to complain as they found him trying to fit his politics into a Christian framework, developing his own historical perspective, devoting an extended study to the ideas of T. E. Hulme. Similarly, *New Verse* (1933–9) was often attacked by militants for being insufficiently committed, which did not make it any less the most notable little magazine of the period, far more significant than such partisan efforts as *Storm* ('the only magazine of Revolutionary Fiction') or *Poetry and the People* or the literary pages of the *Left Review*. Its character was shaped partly by the influence of Auden, partly by the prejudices of the editor, Geoffrey Grigson (who for much of the time he ran it earned his keep as literary editor of the true-blue *Morning Post*). When ex-Prince Mirsky, the scourge of the British intelligentsia,* accused it of having 'lost every semblance of a genuine left-wing journal ... becoming a cesspool of all that is rejected by the healthy organism of the revolutionary movement – a sort of miniature literary Trotskyism', Grigson retorted that it was 'never left wing or right wing. It was not founded as a wing journal.' Nevertheless in practice his Audenesque enthusiasms and his anti-fascism meant that he kept the magazine on a generally leftish course – although just how irregular a course can be gathered from his adulation of Wyndham Lewis, Lewis the incorruptible. A Lewis, it should be recalled, who had come back from Germany in 1931 enthralled by the Brownshirts – 'hefty young street-fighting warriors' with clear blue eyes, 'straight-forward young pillars of the law' – and who was disenchanted with Nazism after Hitler came to power chiefly because it turned out to be too much of a popular mass movement, not aristocratic enough. Admittedly *New Verse* would never have propagated such views itself, but it took them manfully in its stride. Its real enemies were the writers of whom the editor happened to disapprove: most notoriously Edith Sitwell, but also Bloomsbury, the Book Society, Laura Riding, Michael Roberts (naturally), a long procession of Georgians, academics, *New Statesman* reviewers, middlebrow pundits, neo-romantics. This list is far from being complete. Wyndham Lewis had taught Grigson something about invective, but the pupil was determined to outblast his master. In a pseudo-mellow passage in his autobiography, *The Crest on the Silver*, Grigson remarks that he can no longer bear to read the old

* Later denounced as a 'filthy Wrangelist' and murdered during the Purges.

numbers of *New Verse*. The newspaper assaults on young poets in those days, he explains,

> were an irritant to reply in kind, to slash with the billhook, which was far too much my weapon and which I endeavoured to keep sharp, wiping off the blood from time to time – when it happened, that is, to catch someone in whom any blood was flowing. But the tactic was wrong. . . . The tactic was too uncharitable, and dust lies down sooner or later of its own accord. . . . I could no longer, now, billhook my victim and sit on his corpse enjoying a glass full of blood.

And more recently he has written that 'the tone of *New Verse*, strictly the tone, I regret'. As though the tone were something that could simply be peeled away. The polemics were an integral part of the magazine; they were also an indirect product of the Brownshirt 1930s and the Mirsky 1930s in their feverishness, their violence, their death-dealing rhetoric. Rivals had to be dehumanized, treated as corpses or monsters; local quarrels had to be turned into verbal holocausts. But it would be Grigsonian not to add that *New Verse*, chiefly through the Auden connection, stood for much that was liberating and positive as well; that it was prepared to publish writers whom it had savaged (and *vice versa*); that the majority of its attacks had at least a grain of justification; and that Grigson himself, when he isn't drinking his glass of blood, sometimes writes excellent and enlivening criticism.

Big menacing words came easily in the 1930s, even if they did not always match the big menacing facts. It is no secret that for many English left-wing intellectuals at the time the Revolution was not so much a practical proposition as a boy's own adventure, a way of revenging themselves on the Headmaster, a bogey for frightening liberals who wouldn't join the big parade:

> *Something is going to go, baby,*
> *And it won't be your stamp-collection.*
> *Boom!*

Even those writers who took their Marxism seriously were inclined to water it down, and to protest against any suggestion of encroaching on their own artistic independence. But there were some, at least, who were prepared to go the whole way, to submit to party discipline, to applaud when Edward Upward asserted in

The Mind in Chains (1937) that henceforth the only good books could be those written from a basically Marxist point of view. That much of what these militants wrote themselves should have taken the form of criticism was natural enough. It is not only that newly acquired intellectual convictions are more easily expressed through an essay than through a novel or a poem, nor that England, unlike America, lacked a tradition of populist fiction into which proletarian novelists could fit. (For every one English John Sommerfield there must have been a dozen American Robert Cantwells or Jack Conroys.) More important is the fact that Marxism as a creed favours critics – demands them, indeed, since it seeks to explain literature to a large extent in terms of latent social tendencies and implications. One need only consider the importance for Marxists of a man like Lukács, or for that matter the importance which Lukács himself attaches to Belinsky and the radical Russian critics of the nineteenth century. Not even sympathizers, however, are likely to want to resurrect the English Communist criticism of the 1930s, and at this hour in the day it would be pointless to rake up the dogmatic pronouncements of Alick West, Philip Henderson, Jack Lindsay or the firing-squad of the *Left Review* (edited by, among others, Edgell Rickword, his *Calendar* days well behind him). One might reasonably single out as an example, though, Ralph Fox's *The Novel and the People* (1937), which is milder than most – the Popular Front campaign was under way – but essentially an excursion along the usual tramlines, ending up with the text of a grimly sentimental speech which had originally been delivered at the Gorki memorial meeting in Conway Hall ('... this love which was shown to Gorki will be fertile for the future of the Soviet Union, will create many more and greater Maxim Gorkis for the first Socialist State, master engineers of the human soul'). Fox, who had originally become a Communist while on a Quaker relief mission to Russia after the Revolution, was the party's leading literary theoretician. He was killed in the Spanish Civil War.

The one English Marxist critic of the period with serious claims to be considered as anything more than a pamphleteer is 'Christopher Caudwell' (1907–37). Whatever else he may have been, Caudwell – *né* Christopher St John Sprigge – was certainly some kind of prodigy. Leaving school at sixteen, he worked first as a reporter and then for an aeronautical publisher. He wrote a succession of novels, detective stories and engineering textbooks (as well as inventing a new type of gear), and finally, at the age of twenty-seven, began exploring the Marxist classics. Two years later he was dead, killed manning a machine-gun in Spain, but in the intervening period he had written several books, including *Illusion and Reality*, which was with the printers at the time of his death, and his two posthumously published series of *Studies in a Dying Culture*. For Caudwell art was to be understood as a way of mastering the inner world, just as science was a way of mastering the outer. *Illusion and Reality* is less concerned with the socio-economic matrix of literature than it is with perception, cognition, causality, and although he tries to tailor them to his Marxist requirements Caudwell draws freely on 'bourgeois' scientists and psychologists. This is one reason why the book has been discounted by many Marxists, and also why it was seized on so gratefully when it first appeared by left-wing intellectuals who could get nothing out of the average Marxist critic. (Auden wrote an immensely enthusiastic review of it for *New Verse*, for instance.) But has Caudwell had any really lasting influence, except possibly among fellow-theoreticians? I can't pretend to be able to assess the value of his theories myself, although I must admit that my suspicions are aroused by the rather Colin Wilson-like barrage of poly-math erudition, the loose scientific analogies, the peculiar little diagrams illustrating the relationship of mind and matter, ego and reality. Arguably, too, something has gone wrong with the rhetoric of a writer who can say (1946 edition, p. 167) that 'the tremendous and elaborate superstructure of society' includes not only religion, art, laws, science, ethics and so on, but also 'life itself'. What is not in doubt, however, is that Caudwell's specific literary judgements are often extremely crude, and that his potted social history of English poetry is a comic-strip travesty. Does anyone gain anything by being told that *The Tempest* 'retains an Elizabethan reality' – Caliban is a serf, and Ariel the 'apotheosis of the free wage-labourer'? Perhaps it is just as well for Caudwell's reputation that he was generally reluctant to get down to literary detail. Even the individual case-histories of *Studies in a Dying*

Culture are heavily swathed in theory. Only about a quarter of the essay on D. H. Lawrence is devoted to Lawrence himself, for example, and not a single one of his novels is so much as mentioned by name, while the central argument simply dissolves into a flamboyant call to arms. ('Against the sky stands Capitalism without a rag to cover it, naked in its terror . . .') *Illusion and Reality*, too, is more of a tract than is immediately apparent. There are all those tell-tale asides, like the description of Byron as a potential counter-revolutionary who would have become a Danton or a Trotsky if he had lived. And after winding through his labyrinthine arguments, Caudwell emerges with a plain conclusion which might be said, in the language of the period, to be what the whole book was 'objectively' about:

It is no accident that the final period of bourgeois culture, which raised individuality to its height, produced no 'heroes', no great authors, artists, actors or poets. The great man is not just an individuality but an individuality given a collective embodiment and significance. The shadow is so enormous because it is cast over the whole of society. Bourgeois culture mocked the proletariat because it had in its first struggles produced Marx Lenin and Stalin, while according to bourgeois culture communism 'does not believe in great men' or in 'the individual' and so had here contradicted in its own teaching. In this mockery bourgeois culture only exposes its own conception of the relation of the individual to society.

The most valuable sociological studies of literature which appeared in the 1930s, such as Humphry House's *The Dickens World* and L. C. Knights' *Drama and Society in the Age of Jonson*, owed little or no direct debt to Marxism, however much they may have been affected by the prevailing radicalism of the decade. If one thinks of the impact which Marxist ideas have had on modern English historical writing, it is odd that their influence on literary criticism should have been so negligible. As it is, the comparative handful of rewarding Marxist literary essays which have been produced in this country have tended to be the work of historians proper rather than critics – Christopher Hill's studies of Marvell and *Clarissa Harlowe*, for example, which are a good deal more accomplished than anything of the same kind to be found in Caudwell or Fox.

II

The left-wing intellectual climate of the 1930s may not 'explain' George Orwell, but it certainly explains the direction which he took. The single most decisive step in Orwell's development as a writer was his revulsion from Communism and the fellow-travelling intelligentsia. A few years ago this would have been too obvious to need stating, but as the Orwell period recedes, as his propaganda-value to the Right rebounds, there are signs that the obvious is in danger of being overlooked. Raymond Williams's account of him in *Culture and Society*, for instance, is reasonably sympathetic, but it would be impossible to gather from it that there was ever a man called Stalin, or that Orwell wasn't reacting against very specific lies and atrocities. Instead, we are asked to consider him in the semi-abstract as an 'exile' who made an admirable attempt, recorded in *Homage to Catalonia*, to 'become part of a believing community', but rather mysteriously failed. Furthermore, when he drew back 'he did not so much attack socialism, which was safe in his mind, as socialists, who were there and might involve him. What he did attack, in socialism, was its disciplines, and, on this basis, he came to concentrate his attack on communism'. The issue could hardly be blurred more thoroughly than this. It is true that Orwell was a complicated man, with some dubious axes of his own to grind, and his anti-Communism reveals a good deal about him as well as about Communism. But he was responding to realities, not to private frustrations.

Before he went to Spain, he had already picked a violent quarrel with the intellectual Left in *The Road to Wigan Pier*. They were bureaucrats, technocrats, fruit-juice addicts, and so forth; but what annoyed him most about them was their ignorance of what working-class people were really like, and their assumption that they could abolish class-distinctions without at the same time 'abolishing part of themselves'. His exasperation led him into some characteristic melodramatic flourishes. Middle-class socialists saw the proletariat through the wrong end of the telescope: 'force them into any *real* contact with a proletarian – let them get into a fight with a drunken fish-porter on Saturday night, for instance – and they are capable of swinging back to the most ordinary middle-class snobbishness'. Not exactly a fair test case, as Orwell himself would no doubt have acknowledged in his calmer moments. Elsewhere in the book he takes a much less belligerent view of working-class life. In particular, there is nothing morbid or overdrawn about the mixture of admiration and guilt which he admits to feeling in the company of coal-miners. But the miners themselves, as he describes them, remain types rather than individuals, while the final hope of a Socialist millennium which he holds out makes it sound a glum prospect. With any luck, 'we of the sinking middle class .... may sink without further struggles into the working class where we belong', a fate which will probably turn out to be 'not so dreadful as we feared'. Perhaps; but the talk of 'sinking' suggests less a manifesto than a reversion to the strong vein of social masochism which can be found in *Down and Out in London and Paris, A Clergyman's Daughter, Keep the Aspidistra Flying.*

After the Spanish Civil War it was different, however. As Orwell's friend Sir Richard Rees has written, he came back from Spain both more of a pessimist and more of an optimist, with a sharper awareness of totalitarian methods and a new belief in individual decency. The immediate outcome of his experience was *Homage to Catalonia*; then in 1939 he began writing the remarkable series of essays later published in *Critical Essays* (and in one or two cases, although it mostly consists of work from a later, post-war period, in *England Your England*). Orwell followed his curiosity wherever it led him, but the best-known of these essays all ultimately turn on the nature of English society, and taken together they represent a distinct if unsystematic challenge to what were then the standard assumptions of the intellectual far Left. In *Some Versions of Pastoral* (1935) William Empson, discussing proletarian literature, had remarked that 'people who consider the Worker group of sentiments is misleading in contemporary politics tend to use the word "romantic" as a missile; unless they merely mean "false" this is quite off the point; what they ought to do is produce a rival myth'. Which, it seems to me, is exactly what Orwell did in his studies of Dickens, Donald McGill, boys' comics, etcetera; at least, it would be hard for anyone who went along with the main drift of these essays to respond with much conviction to the square-jawed stereotypes of a revolutionary poster. This is not to say that there is anything perfunctory about Orwell's radicalism. In one part of his mind, as many passages in his correspondence and his more ephemeral journalism make clear, he clung to the idea of revolution being both imminent and desirable, while his analysis of the class-feelings at work in literature could be extremely trenchant. Innocuous-seeming comics are shown to be 'sodden in the worst illusions of 1910'; funny postcards are used to document class attitudes to marriage; a good deal of the Dickens essay is devoted to examining the novelist's *petit-bourgeois* limitations, and those of his admirers, such as Chesterton, who gets rapped over the knuckles for having treated Sam Weller, who was a valet, as a symbol of the populace. Yet there is obviously very little that is Marxist about Orwell's underlying purpose. He may call for boys' comics with a progressive slant, but, as John Wain has said, can anyone suppose that he would have studied them with the same affection which he showed towards the *Magnet* and the *Gem*? And one of the great points of the essay is that the Greyfriars stories were mainly read by working-class or middle-class boys who had never seen the inside of an actual public school. Orwell takes a more sardonic view of the role of deference in English life than Bagehot did, but he accepts it as a potent factor. Similarly the closing paragraphs of the article on Donald McGill are a moving statement of his belief that ordinary people can be extraordinarily heroic 'at a pinch', but not all the time, nor in the way that official propaganda demands. And his view of Dickens is really much closer to that of Chesterton than at first appears. He admires the same artistic qualities, and the same moral generosity: 'From the Marxist or Fascist point of view, nearly all that Dickens stands for can be written off as "bourgeois morality". But in moral outlook no one could be more "bourgeois" than the English working classes.' In which case it is not entirely misleading to take Sam Weller as a symbol of the common people.

Orwell himself had no qualms about making an Everyman out of a *petit bourgeois*. George Bowling, the hero of *Coming Up for Air* (1939) is a middle-aged insurance clerk, a suburbanite of suburbanites, and *Coming Up for Air* is a novel in which Orwell tried to say many of the same things about England that he says in his criticism, though hardly with as much success. Like all his novels it is alive and kicking, but disconcertingly uneven. He lacked patience with the contraptions of fiction; it was in his essays (and in *Homage to Catalonia*) that he found it easiest to express himself with full Orwellian directness. Good prose, he once wrote, should be 'like a window pane'. Of course his critical style is not quite as transparent as this suggests, nor would it be as powerful if it were. Orwell the critic is as imaginative as Orwell the novelist. He puts across his points with a cartoonist's pictorial shorthand; he has a fondness for what he praised in Dickens, the graphic, not-strictly-necessary detail. To say that his criticism is imaginative is no doubt also to say, by definition, that it is highly selective. There are blunt generalizations which need to be argued out (Raymond Williams has collected some glaring examples) and obsessions which have to be discounted. But how few flaws there were in that window pane, if you compare him with any of his contemporaries who wrote about politics with the same degree of anger and intensity.

In his last years he was inclined to be much gloomier about ordinary people and their potentialities: the proles of *1984* are a thoroughly debased version of the common man invoked in essays like 'Donald McGill'. And his later criticism tends to be narrower, more rigidly polemical. Even the famous essay on 'Politics and the English Language', effective though it is as a protest against the cruder kinds of ideological claptrap, takes rather too black-and-white a view of language in general. A single example must serve. Orwell hoped it would be possible to 'laugh the *not un*-formation out of existence', and suggested that one way to do it was to memorize the sentence 'A not unblack dog was chasing a not unsmall rabbit across a not ungreen field'. But the whole point about the idiom is that it applies to qualities which are debatable or not immediately apparent. When Sir Richard Rees, for instance, refers to a 'not unsympathetic critic' of Orwell, what he means is something like 'a critic who is not basically hostile, as you might assume from the extract I am about to quote, although at the same time he is not entirely friendly in all other respects either'. This is not using two words where one would do, but using two to do the work of thirty.

In spite of *1984*, however, the picture which political enemies have circulated of Orwell finally sinking into misanthropic despair is a false one. The clearest proof of this are the admirable essays, written in the last three years of his life, on Gandhi and on 'Lear, Tolstoy and the Fool'. Various critics have rightly pointed out that both these essays show how strongly Orwell was drawn towards an ascetic or other-worldly ideal, more strongly than he was willing to admit. But the terms in which he rejects such an ideal seem to me ultimately of more significance. He admires Gandhi, admires him in spite of himself – but still, 'sainthood is a thing that human beings must avoid'. And he ranges himself squarely on the side of Shakespeare, and Shakespeare's 'interest in the actual process of life', against the life-denying Tolstoy of the final religious phase. Like Tolstoy, he was haunted by the idea of renunciation; unlike Tolstoy, he didn't under-estimate the difficulties. The chief moral of *King Lear*, as he saw it, was that 'if you live for others, you must live *for others*, and not as a roundabout way of getting an advantage for yourself'. This is not so very different from the warning he gave to social reformers in *The Road to Wigan Pier*: 'Ultimately you have got to drop your snobbishness, but it is fatal to pretend to drop it before you are ready to do so.' Orwell's interpretation illumines only one facet of *Lear*, and when the Campbell and Quinn *Shakespeare Encyclopaedia* says that 'like much of his literary criticism it contains elementary blunders in scholarship and reveals an insensitivity to many aspects of the play', the *Shakespeare Encyclopaedia* is no doubt correct. The only thing one must add is that like much of Orwell's criticism the essay also makes an important and original point in a way that nobody could ever forget, because it is the outcome of deeply-felt experience, not of academic debate.

III

'Not of academic debate' – but it is also true that by Orwell's time academic debate itself was no longer the same drowsy business which it had once been. More than anything else the advent of F. R. Leavis had seen to that. Until the 1930s, whatever the occasional intramural disputes about syllabuses and personnel, the actual judgements passed on literature by academic critics were scarcely a source of much controversy even inside the universities, let alone in the world at large. Admittedly during the 1920s I. A. Richards had begun tracing out suggestive theoretical prolegomena to all future criticism, and at the end of the decade Richards's pupil William Empson, the most brilliant English critic of his generation, had written *Seven Types of Ambiguity*. But Richards was more concerned with method than substance, and Empson was supersubtle – it took time for his work to sink in, and the academic establishment didn't notice that anything had happened, or at least pretended not to. (Incredible as it may sound today, *Seven Types*, as Christopher Ricks has pointed out, was not even given a review in the *Review of English Studies*.) In any case, at the beginning of the 1930s Empson took himself off to the Far East, and Richards, already more interested in general problems of language than in criticism, eventually went to America. Leavis, however, was another proposition. He was blunt, he was unambiguous, he simply wouldn't go away. From 1932 he had his own regular platform in *Scrutiny*. And his programme was a doubly ambitious one. In the first place, he saw himself as the heir of Arnold and the great nineteenth-century critics of industrial society, but confronting a situation which, chiefly on account of the spread of commercialized mass culture, was worse than anything that the nineteenth century had foreseen. Secondly, he set out to clarify the literary revolution which had taken place in the previous ten or fifteen years, primarily as a result of Eliot's achievement, and to reinterpret the whole course of English poetry in the light of modern, post-Eliot conditions.

The dissection of mass (and middlebrow) culture is best exemplified by Leavis and Denys Thompson's *Culture and Environment* (1933) and Mrs Leavis's *Fiction and the Reading Public* (1932), although there are numerous other related writings by the Leavis group as well. That this campaign has had at least a certain negative usefulness, few educated readers would want to deny. The points which it made against advertising and the popular press were fairly familiar ones, but it made them very forcibly. It exposed the flabbiness of the best-seller, Book Society world as never before. It encouraged teachers to discuss and criticize popular culture with their classes. Beyond this, however, there seems to me little that deserves praise. The trouble starts, as far as I am concerned, on the first page of *Culture and Environment*, where Leavis and Thompson ask what effect the training of taste and sensibility can have 'against the multitudinous counter-influences – films, newspapers, advertising – indeed, the whole world outside the class-room'. I leave aside the apparent implication that films and newspapers are uniformly harmful. But *the whole world*? A piece of rhetoric, perhaps, but an indicative one: it points forward towards a state of mind in which only those in the 'class-room' are regarded as having any chance of salvation – a class-room where increasingly only one subject is taught, and there is only one real teacher. From the very beginning, in fact, the Leavis view of culture was heavily over-simplified; it concentrated on symptoms (like advertising) rather than social causes or possible political remedies; and it depended on a highly dubious reading of modern history. Since the Industrial Revolution, it was assumed, there had been some kind of absolute deterioration in the prevailing quality of life, as the organic society of the past had disintegrated and a healthy natural *Gemeinschaft* had been replaced by a mechanical *Gesellschaft*. The most striking literary consequences of this catastrophe are supposedly set forth in *Fiction and the Reading Public*. One is tempted to dismiss Mrs Leavis's thesis merely on account of the obtuseness with which she brushes aside Dickens ('emotionally uneducated', 'immature'). But more significant is her quite unfounded central assumption that in the eighteenth century there existed a unified reading public with common critical standards. Richard Mayo, in *The English Novel in the Magazines 1740–1815*, and following him Christopher Ricks, have shot this argument to pieces. Professor Mayo concludes his exhaustive survey by observing that

almost any volume of the *Monthly* or the *Critical* from their earliest years will show that vulgar romances, scandalous histories, and trashy pseudo-biographies outnumbered the acceptable novels by two or three to one – and later the ratio became even more unfavourable. This literature was different in many respects, naturally, from modern best-sellers, but not superior in literary quality. In some respects it was worse.

He also notes that critics were showing concern at the spread of shoddy sentimental fiction as early as the 1690s. I suppose that Mrs Leavis might try to salvage something of her case by retreating back to Shakespeare. The Elizabethan groundlings, she writes, 'had to take the same amusements as their betters . . . to argue that they would have preferred Tom Mix or *Tarzan of the Apes* is idle. Happily they had no choice.' One short answer to that is that they did at any rate have the choice of crossing the road to see animals being tormented; all Mrs Leavis has to say here is that the bear-pit is 'beside the point for the purposes of the student of cultural history'. But even if the argument is confined to literature, there were certainly Elizabethan authors with no particular regard for the Elizabethan reading public – Thomas Nashe, for instance, whom Mrs Leavis singles out for special praise, complained in *Pierce Penilesse* that the most idiotic pamphlets and 'treatises of *Tom Thumme*' were being 'bought up thick and threefold, when better things lie dead'. And the Middle Ages? They don't come within Mrs Leavis's purview; but when I turn to *Culture and Environment* and read the idyllic account, quoted without quali-fication, of life in a self-sufficient, 'organic' fourteenth-century Rhine village, I am afraid my first impulse is to recall that the fourteenth-century Rhineland also means the Black Death and misery and pogroms. The truth is that the search for a golden age always has to be pushed further and further back in time, until we reach the Garden of Eden. This is not to substitute a myth of steady improvement for one of uninterrupted decline, nor to take shelter behind a myth of *plus ça change*. Only the most com-placent philistine could doubt that material progress has often been accompanied by cultural impoverishment. But the profit-and-loss account of cultural history is an immensely complicated one, and a thousand different factors – non-literary factors, for the most part – have to be taken into consideration in working it out. What is galling about the Leavises and their followers is not that they are altogether wrong, but that they give a cause which deserves a wider hearing a bad name through distortion, omission and strident over-statement.

Leavis on literature is a great deal more illuminating than Leavis on society, even if the originality of his early criticism was less a matter of ideas and technique than of marshalling the evidence more systematically and coherently than any previous modern critic. To students, especially, *New Bearings in English Poetry* and *Revaluation* were a godsend. They put modern poetry into an easily-mastered perspective; they reduced a bewildering mass of the literature of the past to manageable proportions. How much they have to offer readers who go back to them today is another question. *New Bearings* is heavily indebted to 'a certain critic and poet', as Leavis scrupulously concedes in the preface – although one wonders what quirk makes him want to put it so cryptically. In fact the influence of Eliot is almost everywhere apparent, and the longest section of the book is devoted to his work. In a curious way (it was to be seen later with Lawrence) Leavis is very *uncritical* about his major heroes. He may sharply reject parts of their work as inferior, but he finds it hard not to take what he admires about them on their own terms. His essay on Eliot doesn't succeed in seeing the poet in the round as well as Edmund Wilson's, published in *Axel's Castle* the previous year. On the other hand he is more pertinacious than Wilson, and he does give beginners a better idea of how to set about getting the hang of Eliot. It is remarkable, though, how little he has to say about the content of the poetry, or even, when you get down to it, about points of poetic detail. He repeatedly gives the impression of being engaged in analysing what in reality he is merely paraphrasing. The chapter on Pound is even thinner: it is largely given over to an account of *Mauberley* which does little more than keep protesting about the poet's delicacy and subtlety. The section on Hopkins is much better: Leavis had Robert Bridges to use as a foil, Empson to learn from, and his own considerable feeling for what he calls the Shakespearean quality of Hopkins's language to guide him. But then comes the incredible epilogue ignoring Auden and Graves and bestowing superlative after superlative on the poetry of the unfortunate Ronald Bottrall – 'magnificent', 'very considerable indeed', 'differs from the Eliot of *The Waste Land* in a certain positive energy' – a performance made all the more grotesque by the addition of the 'impenitent' 1950 retrospect, with its complete silence about American poetry, its patronizing nonsense about Auden's development, its dismissive sneers about Dylan Thomas, MacNeice, etc. This is jumping ahead, however. In the 1930s Leavis still had some important things to say about poetry, and *Revaluation* (1936) seems to me much his best book. Once again, given the scope of his pretensions, the actual range of topics covered is surprisingly narrow; he sometimes leans quite heavily on earlier criticism (the chapter on Pope, for instance, owes a considerable debt – duly acknowledged – to both Middleton Murry and Empson); and there is something slightly comic about his frequent air of having triumphantly demonstrated what has merely been strenuously asserted. Occasionally, too, his close readings of the text are so close as to be almost indistinguishable. It may conceivably be an advantage to have it pointed out that in the closing stanza of Keats's ode 'To Autumn' the 'stubble plains' are 'appropriately unvoluptuous in suggestion', but I find it hard to imagine the reader who needs to be told (and this is all we are told, about a wonderfully subtle piece of writing) that the rest of the stanza

is full of the evocation of thin sounds – the gnats 'mourn' in a 'wailful choir', the lambs bleat, hedge-crickets sing, the red-breast 'with treble soft' whistles, and gathering swallows twitter in the skies.

Yet at the same time many of Leavis's comments – on the 'not-too-particularized images' of Johnson's poetry, for example – are exceptionally acute, while his over-assertiveness is made easier to bear by the number of his assertions which quite simply strike one as true. And where he is wrong (most notoriously, on *Paradise Lost*) he at any rate usually sets a challenge which demands to be met.

Nor are these casual or isolated virtues. They spring from a consistent view of life, a passionate conviction of the moral basis of literature coupled with a no less passionate insistence that in a work of art morality only counts to the extent that it is vividly enacted, brought to life with the appropriate resources of the medium. Passion alone would obviously not be enough to explain the nature of Leavis's influence: he also has sound judgement, within the limits of his taste, and he can be relentless in argument. But the intensity is what finally counts, the feeling he gives that he is ready to answer with his reputation for every word he writes, and that he expects others to do the same. Without this degree of seriousness he could never have attracted so many disciples, or made the difference which he has to so many readers. But in itself seriousness, like energy, is a morally neutral quality: its value entirely depends on the uses to which it is put. Dr Leavis being serious about *The Prelude* (serious, not conventionally solemn); Dr Leavis refusing to be frivolous *à la* Lytton Strachey about Pope's satires – these are things we can be grateful for. But unfortunately there has long been a heavy price to pay for his virtues in terms of narrowness, spitefulness, dogmatism all the more pernicious for masquerading as flexibility. And it is a price which has grown heavier across the years. You only have to compare the very earliest numbers of *Scrutiny* with the later ones. The scope was much wider, the contributors more varied (in the first volume they include Lowes Dickinson, Auden, Blunden, Herbert Butterfield), there was even some poetry. Equally, the best of Leavis's original *Scrutiny* colleagues, notably L. C. Knights and D. W. Harding, were critics with sufficient independence of mind to learn from him without being intellectually flattened out. As one goes through the files, however, the magazine increasingly gives the impression of being written by yes-men. Everything about it becomes narrower, more predictable. Is this Leavis's fault? Karl Marx said that he wasn't a Marxist, and I suppose Leavis might argue that he wasn't responsible for the average Leavisite's conformism. But he would be disingenuous if he did. His whole rhetorical manner and method of approach have tended, certainly since the late 1930s, towards the setting-up of a closed system.

How do you maintain such a system and make it look plausible, if as Leavis does you always claim to be proceeding, in Dr Johnson's phrase, 'not dogmatically but deliberately'? Various techniques suggest themselves. While protesting that you are open to argument, you habitually use the language of intimidation, language which brooks no opposition ('irrefutable', 'obvious and unanswerable', 'indubitable', 'has no claim to be treated as a critical authority on the verse of the period – or any verse').*

---

* This is Leavis writing about Sir Herbert Grierson and the seventeenth century. No claim at all? Any verse whatever?

Without totally condemning an author in so many words, you effectively slam the door on him by implication. You keep repeating yourself. You dispose of writers you dislike simply by citing the adverse opinions of writers you admire. (A little judicious selection and omission may come in useful here, if you want to strengthen your case.) By giving minimal credit, if any, to critics who may have anticipated you, and by exaggerating the neglect which books that you praise have previously suffered, you create an impression of absolute originality. You attribute low motives to your opponents – if they are unnamed, so much the better. You lump together secondary and third-rate writers, as though they were equally negligible. Leavis resorts to all these stratagems, and others too – but perhaps I had better give some examples. Leavis's widely-read study of the English novel, *The Great Tradition* (1948, but individual chapters had been appearing in *Scrutiny* since 1937), seems to me a reasonable testing-ground. On the first page he boldly announces that the great English novelists are Jane Austen, George Eliot, James and Conrad (he later adds Lawrence), and then remarks, with a sarcastic reference to the way in which his earlier books have been misinterpreted by his less intelligent critics, that he will probably be accused of having said that there are no other novelists in English worth reading. This is a red herring, however. What is likely to be called into question is the *manner* in which he allows that other novelists may be worth reading. Half a dozen or so he actively recommends. But to say that 'all that needs to be said' about Defoe as a novelist was said by Leslie Stephen (in 1868) is either to say that his novels are dead or else – since Leavis adds vaguely that he was 'a remarkable writer' – to imply a theory of fiction so narrow that it needs to be justified at some length rather than left as a bare assertion.* To bundle Trollope and Mrs Gaskell indiscriminately into a list of minor Victorian novelists which also includes Charlotte M. Yonge,

---

* More fundamentally, it is also to reject the idea – which Leavis sometimes concedes, but only when it suits his purpose – that our response to a work of art can be affected by historical experience. Leslie Stephen's excellent essay may possibly have said all the things that needed saying about Defoe a hundred years ago, but how could 'his' *Robinson Crusoe* (a book for boys rather than men, he calls it) be the *Robinson Crusoe* which Camus quotes on the title-page of *La Peste*, or which Malraux said was one of the very few books in the world to retain its

Charles and Henry Kingsley, and Shorthouse, without subsequently making amends (but on the contrary, going on to talk about 'the ruck of Gaskells and Trollopes') is to rob them of all individual distinction. To say that a comparison between *The Portrait of a Lady* and *The Egoist* 'should dispose of Meredith's pretensions for ever' *may* only mean Meredith's pretensions to be as good as Henry James, but it looks suspiciously like his pretensions to be worth reading at all. Nor is one's suspicion allayed when Leavis praises Forster for having done 'the necessary demolition-work' on Meredith in *Aspects of the Novel*. As a matter of fact Forster talks of Meredith being 'in the trough', a somewhat less drastic metaphor than 'demolition'. And it would surely have been appropriate to mention at this point how much Forster's early novels owe to Meredith: a novelist dissociating himself from an influence he has outgrown is not, after all, in quite the same position as an ordinary critic weighing up his verdict. In fact the whole practice of taking over one artist's judgement of another calls for more discrimination than anyone would gather from the way Leavis sets about it. I suppose he might, if pressed, be able to explain on what basis one decides that a letter in which Henry James attacks a late and (by common consent) inferior novel by Meredith is a highly relevant piece of evidence, while ignoring, for instance, James's long, brilliant and generally laudatory essay on the despised Trollope – an essay written, moreover, when on Leavis's own reckoning James was at the height of his powers. What seems to me inexcusable, though, is that Leavis should sum up Hardy by saying that James struck 'the appropriately sympathetic note' when he wrote that 'the good little Thomas Hardy has scored a great success with *Tess of the d'Urbervilles*, which is chockfull of faults and falsity, and yet has a singular charm'. Possibly this was the appropriate note for James himself to strike, writing as a major novelist. Possibly Leavis feels that his own achievements entitle him to pat the good little Thomas Hardy on the head. But

***

truth for those who had seen the inside of prisons and concentration camps? (See Ian Watt, *The Rise of the Novel* – a book which itself adds a great deal to our understanding of Defoe.) I doubt whether Stephen himself would have disagreed with this point: he makes it clear, for instance, that his own response to the *Journal of the Plague Year* was sharpened by seeing photographs of the American Civil War.

that anyone should propose that this is the appropriate way for Hardy to be talked about in general is almost beyond belief. It is not only novelists, by the way, whom Leavis finds it convenient to turn to for confirmation of his views. Discussing the wealth of social observation in *Middlemarch*, he very reasonably cites what Beatrice Webb wrote in *My Apprenticeship*: 'For any detailed description of the complexity of human nature . . . I had to turn to novelists and poets. . . .' Only, what the dots conceal is that there is nothing about George Eliot at this point, and that the novelists she actually goes on to mention include Fielding, Thackeray and Balzac, all of whom get soundly snubbed elsewhere in *The Great Tradition*. With most writers, an omission like this would be trivial; with Leavis, it all helps to screw things into place.

As for the rhetorical tricks, they can be found on every other page. A random example is the parenthetical remark about fiction that is only good for killing time – 'which seems to be all that even some academic critics demand of a novel'. There have been some very bad academic critics of the novel, but has there ever been one whose attitude could fairly be described in these terms? I doubt it; but meanwhile an impression is being built up of a literary world full of twittering playboys, where only Leavis and a few others really *care*. And, at the same time, of a world where no one before Leavis has really seen the light. The most striking instance of this is his notorious chapter on *Hard Times*. Dickens was a great genius, he concedes, but his genius was that of a great entertainer. *Hard Times* alone has the sustained seriousness of a major work of art. Why, then, he asks

has it not had general recognition? To judge by the critical record, it has had none at all. If there exists anywhere an appreciation, or even an acclaiming reference, I have missed it.

He can't have looked very hard. Ruskin's acclaiming references are well known; and even if Leavis had forgotten them, he need have gone no further than House's *The Dickens World* (1941) to have his memory refreshed. But in fact he pays no attention in his essay to any previous critic (apart from Santayana), nor to a single one of Dickens's other novels – which makes it somewhat easier

for him to maintain the unique excellence of *Hard Times*. It is difficult to see, for instance, how anyone who bore in mind *Great
Expectations* could say that between them Bounderby, Mrs Sparsit
and Harthouse suggest 'the whole system of British snobbery'.
The Dickens chapter represents *The Great Tradition* at its most
vulnerable, however. To redress the balance as far as possible, one
might consider Leavis's treatment of Conrad. Here he has a
genuine and important claim to originality. No earlier writer, as
far as I know, had asserted as decisively or convincingly that the
novels of Conrad's middle period are what matter most, that
Nostromo rather than *Lord Jim* is his masterpiece. Had Leavis
simply taken the credit for this, no one could object. But when he
goes on to state flatly that Conrad's major achievements 'went, the
evidence obliges us to conclude, without recognition', and more
in the same vein, it must be said that the evidence (which he
doesn't give) obliges us to conclude nothing of the sort. The
recognition may have been inadequate, and it may have been
inadequately expressed. But recognition there was, on a substantial scale. Frank Swinnerton can serve as a representative witness;
in *The Georgian Literary Scene* (1935) he records that 'at the time of
its publication and for a long time afterwards it was usual to say
that *Nostromo* was Conrad's greatest book'.

Finally, and most important, there is the whole concept of the
Great Tradition itself. Roughly speaking, a literary tradition
means one of two things. There is the loose broad historical continuity provided by the common culture shared by writers of the
same language or region or social class. Leavis's Great Tradition is
obviously not of this type. Alternatively, there are specific
relationships between a group of writers in terms of influence,
direct borrowing, strongly marked affinities, the use of similar
forms and themes, and so on. Given that only five authors qualify
for an assured place in the Leavis tradition, the comparative
tenuousness of such relationships between them is rather striking.
Jane Austen, for a start. We are told by Leavis that she was the one
predecessor whose work 'had any bearing on George Eliot's
essential problems as a novelist'. This is a complete exaggeration.
George Eliot certainly admired Jane Austen – her connection with
Lewes would have been enough to see to that – but I doubt

whether she learned much more from her than, say, from Mrs Gaskell (with whom she acknowledged an affinity). In any case, there is the major influence of the Waverley novels: if you look up the index to George Eliot's essays, for instance, there is not a single entry under Jane Austen, although there are more than twenty under Scott. Similarly, in his introduction Leavis speaks of the 'obvious' influence of Jane Austen on Henry James, 'which can be brought out by quotation'. But he doesn't in fact offer a single quotation, nor, when he gets round to his chapter on James, does he make any further reference to this influence. Perhaps he thought it was too obvious. He also speaks of James's great admiration for her novels, although anyone who takes the trouble to look up James's remarks about them in 'The Lesson of Balzac' will see how qualified that admiration could be. With George Eliot's influence on James, Leavis is on much firmer ground: his drawing attention to it is one of the really valuable things about *The Great Tradition*, even if it involves playing down more important Continental influences. But then what about the influence of James on Lawrence, or of Jane Austen on Conrad? No wonder Leavis, after hinting at debts wherever he can, is forced to insist, with italics for emphasis, that he is not concerned to establish *indebtedness*. I quite agree that it is a relief to get away from influence-mongering: it is mostly an academic pastime, not very closely related to the way novels actually get written. But we are talking about tradition; and if tradition is not a matter of historical continuity, nor of indebtedness, then what exactly is it? A question of affinities? But the novelists in the Great Tradition have no monopoly of the common qualities, such as 'a profoundly serious interest in life', which Leavis claims for them. I can see how one might feel that Hardy was a less profound novelist than George Eliot (not everyone would agree); but in what possible sense could he be said to take a less profoundly serious interest in life? Finally, in fact, all Leavis can point to is what he calls the 'apartness' of his chosen novelists. Quite so; he thinks they are immeasurably better than other novelists, and he is fully entitled to say so at the top of his voice. But to dress up a list of one's preferences as a *tradition* is another matter altogether. It is to confer a false objectivity on them; to imply that they rest on far stronger social and historical

[handwritten marginal note: NOT TRUE]

foundations than is actually the case; to construct, in short, a closed system. And once the system has been set up, there is a constant temptation to assume that assertion will do the work of argument. If Leavis claims, for instance, that there are only four or five other English novelists in the same class as Conrad, that nevertheless much of Conrad's better-known work has been seriously overrated, and that *Under Western Eyes* 'must be counted among those [books] upon which Conrad's status as one of the great English masters securely rests', he certainly owes it to the reader to discuss that by-no-means simple novel at reasonable length, instead of dealing with it in exactly two pages, mostly made up of plot-summary and quotation.*

Leavis's writings since *The Great Tradition* exhibit all the characteristics already described, in more extreme forms. This is not to say, of course, that there is nothing of note in *Scrutiny* once one gets past the early volumes. Mrs Leavis on Jane Austen is well worth reading, for instance (though I must admit that given the choice I would rather read Jane Austen on Mrs Leavis), and Leavis's own later criticism still has traces of his former strength. His ambitious study of Lawrence, however, is severely handicapped by a reluctance to face fundamental issues (made plain at the outset by the manner in which he sneers at Desmond MacCarthy for having compared Lawrence to Carlyle), and also by residual Great Traditionalism: it is not very profitable to keep harping on the similarities – or differences – between Lawrence and George Eliot, while never once considering him in relation to, say, Dostoievsky. True, one or two subsequent essays, such as the note on *Adam Bede* which reasonably enough stresses George Eliot's 'very deep affinities' with Scott (and doesn't breathe a word about Jane Austen), suggest that the basic scheme of the Great Tradition may have been quietly abandoned. Rather too quietly,

---

* One curious minor feature of the system which is often overlooked is that lesser figures, once they are admitted to the fold, tend to be extravagantly overpraised – perhaps to compensate for extravagant underpraise in other directions. Thus, we can all agree that Peacock's novels are delightful, but even a blurb-writer might hesitate before describing them as *indefinitely* re-readable. And Disraeli's novels are certainly very interesting; but even someone who confined his reading to the ruck of Gaskells and Trollopes and Merediths might wonder whether they are really the work of a *supremely* intelligent politician.

when one thinks of how stridently it was originally proclaimed. For it is not so much that Leavis finds it impossible to change his mind as that he is unable to admit what a change of mind may involve. This becomes particularly apparent in the case of his more recent comments on Eliot. The language which he uses is extremely uncompromising. 'Tradition and the Individual Talent', he concludes, 'is notable for its ambiguities, its logical inconsequences, its pseudo-precisions, its fallaciousness, and the aplomb of its equivocations and its specious cogency.' The standing of Eliot's criticism 'depends as little on his penetration and sureness in the more important kinds of value-judgment as on his powers of sustained coherent and trenchant thought'. *The Cocktail Party* exposes not merely Eliot's limitations, or the extent of his decline, but 'shocking essential ignorance of the possibilities of life'. And it would be easy to multiply examples. Well and good: Leavis may be right. Let us at any rate assume that he really means what he says. But then where does that leave *New Bearings in English Poetry*, with its large indebtedness 'to a certain critic and poet', or *Revaluation*, explicitly planned as a sequel to *New Bearings*? It may be that Leavis now feels that his early books were irreparably damaged by Eliot's influence. It may be he feels that he was somehow able to squeeze all the goodness out of that influence while rejecting all the poison. But he ought to say something.

The nature and extent of his own influence would make an interesting study for a sociologist. Many of his followers obviously have a strong need, which his teachings fulfil admirably, for a doctrine which sees the established order as hopelessly corrupt but in no way pledges them to try and replace it. (This is one reason, it seems to me, why his influence was particularly strong during the early Cold War years, when the intellectual appeal of active radical movements was at its lowest.) And however much one may agree with some of the specific criticisms which he levels at the literary world, however much one may deplore the cheap tactics to which some of his victims have resorted in self-defence, the over-all effect of his teaching has plainly been calculated to produce, at any rate among his more extreme adherents, many of the characteristics normally associated with a religious or ideological sect. There is the effective demand for unqualified allegiance; the ritualistic use of approved or disapproved names; the need to exaggerate the outside world's hostility or neglect. (If Carlyle compressed his Gospel of Silence into thirty-five volumes, the final monument to Leavis's martyrdom might be said to be *Scrutiny* reprinted in twenty volumes by the Cambridge University Press.) As for the charismatic quality of Leavis's leadership, it reminds me of what Bryan Wilson writes in *Sects and Society* about those sects where the leader's personality is built into the movement:

> The leader is responsible, at least initially and in part, for the precepts and example which his votaries accept, and for the primary articulation of values to which they subscribe: his self-interpretation conditions their behaviour and beliefs.

Equally salvationist is the habit of confronting the reader with absolute choices. (If you accept Lawrence, you can have no further use for Joyce.) And, most significant of all, there is the attempt to deny essential merit (with one or two trivial exceptions) to any English creative writer who has made his appearance since the early 1930s. This is very different from saying that our literary standards have declined, or that we no longer have any writers as good as the ones we had forty or fifty years ago. Those are propositions which could be discussed (and, if true, accounted for) in ordinary critical and cultural terms. But a sudden and complete drying up of creative talent can surely only imply that human nature has been overtaken by some inexplicable catastrophe. The oddity of the picture is reinforced by continuing references to Lawrence (d. 1930) as, not just our last great writer, but as the great writer *of our time*. And meanwhile we are also asked to accept that the change of climate which finally killed off the novelists and poets nevertheless permitted the emergence of a major critic.

In case anybody suggests that I am simply trying to bracket Leavis's followers with the Christadelphians or the Elim Foursquare Gospel Church, I had better make it quite clear that I am only talking about *tendencies*, not about articles of faith. Whatever his restrictive practices, formally Leavis has always allowed for rational discussion and individual freedom of choice – and this is a matter of more than formal importance. It means that anyone who is strong-minded enough can learn from his work without having to take over his view of the world. Along with his brainwashed disciples, after all, he has had a good many distinguished admirers. But one can only speak for oneself, and in my own view he is a teacher who is liable to do more harm than good. He asks to be judged as a moralist, and it is his whole moral stance which I find repugnant. Not of course the actual values which he proclaims: indeed, how could anyone be against 'life' or 'health' or 'seriousness'? But it seems to me that ultimately he is preoccupied with the value of Value, that he makes the critical act an end in itself. The more he talks about life and health, the more he is really trying to find an impregnable position. Which means that opponents, or those he sees as opponents, have to be not merely attacked, but annihilated. The rancour infects the whole vision. A good example of this can be found in the in many ways excellent essay 'Tragedy and the "Medium" ', where, trying to define the profounder levels of experience on which tragic art insists, Leavis cites a passage from one of Lawrence's letters 'that came into my mind when this point was under discussion':

I am so sick of people: they preserve an evil, bad, separating spirit under the warm cloak of good words. That is intolerable in them. . . . What does [Bertrand] Russell really want? He wants to keep his own established ego, his finite and ready-defined self intact, free from contact and connection. He wants to be ultimately a free agent. That is what they all want, ultimately – that is what is at the back of all international peace-for-ever and democratic control talks: they want an outward system of nullity, which they call peace and goodwill, so that in their own souls they can be independent little gods, referred nowhere and to nothing, little mortal Absolutes, secure from question. That is at the back of all Liberalism, Fabianism and democracy. It stinks. It is the will of a louse . . .

Etcetera. The subject may be tragedy, but what seems to be on Leavis's mind is something more like destructiveness. And, since he *does* claim to be a moralist, it is this kind of self-deception which in the end makes his work depressing.

One would no doubt feel very differently about him if he were not a university teacher, and a potent influence in the educational world. After all, there have been critics with strong views before. Carlyle was far more bigoted, but at least he didn't have his critical opinions inculcated in teachers' training colleges. Arnold had his prejudices, but I doubt whether many Victorian sixth-formers were encouraged to reproduce them in their essays. And coming down to our own time, and to someone more comparable to Leavis in intellectual stature, supposing, say, Geoffrey Grigson had been able to inflict his views on generations of freshmen. Certainly the element of legerdemain in a book like *The Great Tradition* would matter very much less if one could feel sure that a large proportion of its readers weren't likely to be comparative beginners. And though Leavis has great things to his credit as a teacher – he woke his audiences up, he gave them a sense of direction – there is another side here, too. Good students welcomed him as an emancipator, and then found they had to spend years trying to escape from his liberating influence. Not-such-good students were given a new highfalutin alibi for their purely traditional laziness: they knew that Milton had been dislodged, even if they had never actually finished reading *Paradise Lost*. Perhaps it wouldn't have been so bad if there had been a countervailing force somewhere in the academic world, a Shem to Leavis's Shaun. (I suppose C. S. Lewis comes closest, but not close enough.) And, who knows, perhaps Leavis himself would have written better books if he had spent his career in the literary-journalistic world which he despises. But these are speculative thoughts indeed. What seems certain is that any future critical *chef d'école* will be more likely than ever to be an academic.

ADDITIONAL NOTE: Leavis's most recent book, *Lectures in America* (1969), contains an essay on 'Eliot's Classical Standing' which, while reiterating his objections to 'Tradition and the Individual Talent' (though in much more guarded terms), is mainly devoted to celebrating Eliot's creative career as 'a sustained, heroic and indefatigably resourceful quest of a profound sincerity of the most difficult kind. The heroism is that of genius.' But how are we to reconcile this with, for example, 'shocking essential ignorance of the possibilities of life'? Once again, Leavis doesn't explain and doesn't apologise, any more than he refers back to *The Great Tradition* when in the course of another Lecture in America he pays tribute to Dickens as 'a great novelist and, as such, an incomparable social historian' – the Dickens of *Dombey* and *Little Dorrit*, not merely of *Hard Times*. So much, at all events, for the legend of Dickens the great entertainer, who 'had for the most part no profounder responsibility as a creative artist than this description suggests'.

11

EPILOGUE

Cultural change is seldom straightforward. Successive periods overlap; progress is ragged; within a prevailing climate of opinion there can be innumerable variations. It takes a major social catastrophe for the main outlines of a culture to be rapidly and radically transformed, and even then old habits are liable to prove remarkably persistent. If the present sketch offers no account of individual writers who have emerged since the 1930s, then, it is not because I suppose that the literary situation was altered beyond recognition by the Second World War. Critics occasionally advance some such apocalyptic thesis, but it will hardly survive serious consideration. Certainly as far as literary journalism goes, a magazine like *Horizon* could bear comparison with all but the very best periodicals of the past, while, if we are thinking in terms of numbers, there must be as many critics in practice today as in any previous generation. Yet at the same time it is plain that the role of the literary man, and more particularly of the unattached literary man, has changed a great deal in recent years, chiefly as a result of broad social forces which are bound to make themselves felt even more strongly in future. On the whole it has diminished.

It is critics and reviewers whom I have in mind, not creative writers, but if one asks why their role should have been reduced, one must first ask whether literature itself doesn't seem less important than it once did. After the horrors of the last war, with the continuing horror of lesser wars ever since, and above all with the thought of nuclear war always there at the back of our minds, perhaps the whole thing no longer matters all that much.

These, of course, are shadows which hang over everything else as well, but even if they didn't there would still be the question of whether literature hasn't come to count for less in relation to intellectual life as a whole. The immense growth of science is the most obvious transforming factor here. Since the Two Cultures episode we have all been rather chary of suggesting that there is any antagonism between scientific and literary culture, or have chosen – understandably, in view of the way in which that particular controversy was conducted – to regard the subject as a bore. Yet the strenuous attempts which have been made all round to reaffirm that there is only one real culture are not entirely convincing, and genuine conflicts persist. Conflicts of social priority and prestige, that is. The days of intellectual collision are largely a thing of the past: science has simply left its critics behind, and no modern writer would be likely to get very far with the flatly anti-scientific thinking of a Yeats or a Lawrence. But a strong element of moral rivalry persists. If Lord Snow's view of the matter seems too crude, consider, for example, the more elegant formulations of Sir Peter Medawar:

> The scientist values research by the size of its contribution to that huge logically articulated structure of ideas which is already, though not yet half built, the most glorious accomplishment of mankind. The humanist must value his research by different but equally honourable standards, particularly by the contribution it makes, directly or indirectly, to our understanding of human nature and conduct, and human sensibility.

The humanist's standards are equally honourable, and glory isn't everything, but the message is clear. In a science-dominated world the writer can no longer hope for the same degree of intellectual authority which he enjoyed in the past. Naturally this is not going to deter a novelist or poet of genius from pursuing his vocation. It could, however, be argued that, at all but the highest creative levels, talent is a good deal more malleable than we customarily assume, and that just as up till now the humanities have tended to deflect potential scientists, in future, although there may be temporary periods of reaction, it is much more likely that potential humanists will be deflected by science.

If this is true, it is obviously especially true of the social sciences, which in any case, unlike other branches of science, do present writers with something of a direct intellectual challenge. Once again, it is not the creative writer who is in the line of fire. Some years ago, for instance, there was a fashion among critics for saying that many of the functions of the novel were being usurped by sociology. They should have been worrying about their own situation, though, rather than that of the novelist. A novel which can largely be reduced to the sum of its sociological constituents could never have been much of a novel in the first place. But the intellectual status of criticism is quite another matter, and to the extent that they have traditionally taken broad social questions as well as narrowly literary ones for their province, critics must be prepared for the sociologist to challenge them on their own ground. Not just the sociologist, either, but a whole battery of specialists: the social anthropologist, the linguist, the psycho-analyst, the social historian, the historian of ideas, indeed historians of almost every variety. Encircled by all this expertise, a critic may well protest that his main business is still simply to give a reasoned (or unreasoned) account of his feelings about a book in the language of everyday life. He may take a certain pride in being the last amateur in a world of professionals. But all the same, he knows that there are people who know more than he does about things which he is supposed to know about, and if he has any professional pretensions at all, it is hardly a thought calculated to raise his self-esteem.

The impact of the mass media on literature is both a cliché and a source of bitter controversy. Whether the essential nature of our response to the written word has been radically, McLuhanishly transformed by advances in technology is, to say the least, open to question. What no one is likely to dispute, however, is that other media are constantly competing for attention with books, and that as often as not they tend to win the competition. This is not a point which needs to be laboured, so I will confine myself to a single instance, the cinema. Nowadays when literary people get together they are at least as likely to argue or reminisce about films as about novels. (I say nothing of poems.) Nor is this simply on account of the increased artistic and intellectual ferment among film-makers in recent years. It also reflects the degree to which, for a very long time now, the experience of the cinema has been woven into most people's lives, usually since childhood. The question of childhood is particularly relevant here, since one will never do justice to many of the literary enthusiasms of the past unless one bears in mind how deeply they were implanted either before or during early adolescence. This especially applies to the novelists whom Victorian schoolchildren read (or had read to them) in bulk. It is curious to see, in this respect, how the same psychological characteristics repeat themselves in altered cultural circumstances. When Andrew Lang, for example, takes pleasure in recalling the mere names of minor characters in Scott, or Saintsbury refers lovingly to some obscure incident in Thackeray, they are liable to strike almost anyone today as impossible old fossils; but their enthusiasm is not really so very different in kind from the widespread contemporary nostalgia for the Hollywood pictures of twenty or thirty years ago. And the stern young *cinéaste* who has seen every one of Howard Hawks's films at least three times: the chances are that in an earlier age he would have been a member of the Browning Society, or an authority on Dickens's London. It doesn't follow from this that people in general are reading less; if anything, the full potentialities of a mass reading public are only just beginning to be grasped. The point is rather that the highly literate have proportionately less time to devote to literature than they did: there are too many other things for them to think about. How far, beyond this, their actual reading-habits have changed is a matter of speculation, although my own guess would be that everyone's attention-span is a little shorter than it used to be. At any rate, I can understand the point of view of the character in the Kingsley Amis novel: 'If there was one thing which Roger never felt like, it was a good read.'

Science, sociology, the cinema – the kind of forces which have been mentioned so far are at work throughout the entire more-or-less civilized world. But there is one further development which affects English critics specifically. Since the war it has inevitably been brought home to them far more forcibly than ever before that there are many other authors writing in English besides Englishmen. In practice that means, overwhelmingly, Americans. But in addition writers from Commonwealth or ex-Commonwealth countries – figures as different as A. D. Hope and Chinua Achebe – are at last beginning to count for English readers in their own right, not as curiosities or poor relations, and this is going to be more and more the case as time goes on. The English literary scene itself, too, would be noticeably poorer if it were not for some of the Commonwealth writers who have settled here in recent years. At first sight it may not seem as though all this has any particular bearing on the role of the critic. Nor does it, perhaps, in immediate practical terms. But I think it is true to say that in the past most English critics have been fortified by the idea, whether explicitly formulated or not, that by right of birth they are the guardians and interpreters of one of the world's great literary traditions. Put that bluntly, it may make them sound as though they were the custodians of the Crown Jewels, and no doubt a good deal of inferior criticism has often been a form of patriotic advertising. But the question goes much deeper than that. One need only consider the part played by the idea of English tradition in the thought of Leavis, or, more recently, Raymond Williams. Or take F. W. Bateson, a critic who certainly qualifies, both in literature and politics, as a progressive. In *English Poetry: A Critical Introduction*, (which in general seems to me an admirable book) he observes that 'in modern times a society, in the sense of a linguistic unit, rarely overflows the boundaries of the nation-state'. Our own borderline cases, he explains, are the Scotsmen, the Anglo-Welsh and the Anglo-Irish, and a footnote adds:

The important difference between the native English writer and the *métèque* (the writer with a non-English linguistic, racial or political background) is the latter's lack of respect for the finer rules of English idiom and grammar. This allows the Anglo-Irishman (like George Moore) or the Anglo-Scot (like Stevenson) to attempt effects of style, sometimes successfully, that the English writer would feel to be a perverse defiance of the genius of the language. . . . In second-rate writers on the linguistic fringe – Anglo-Jews like Guedalla, Anglo-Scots like Compton Mackenzie, Anglo-Welshmen like Emlyn Williams – there is a particular temptation to bogus slickness. On the other hand, the disregard of the organic overtones of the language often enables the *métèque* to achieve a peculiar lucidity in prose.

English Poetry was originally published in 1950. It would surely be impossible for anyone to write in this vein today, as though the 'linguistic unit' could be identified with the British Isles, and as

though the question of the 'fringe' (some fringe!) could seriously
be discussed in terms of Emlyn Williams and Philip Guedalla. Yet
the underlying assumption, that American literature is somehow
as foreign as German or French, is one which has been shared by
most English critics – academic critics, at least – until quite recently.
It might have been justified, if the mass of English readers had felt
the same way, if they hadn't been perfectly well aware of
American literature in 1950, or for that matter in 1850. Complaints about the purely academic neglect in England of 'American
studies', which we have only lately begun to wake up to, give a
very false impression when they are extended to cover the general
public. They ignore the sheer scale of earlier American inroads:
in all probability more copies of Longfellow were sold in
Victorian England than of any other living poet, not excluding
Tennyson, and more copies of *Uncle Tom's Cabin* than of any
other novel. They ignore the extent to which Tom Sawyer,
Uncle Remus and the rest were incorporated into the folklore of
English childhood. They ignore the kind of prestige enjoyed by
most major American authors among serious English readers
from the days of Emerson onwards. A man like Saintsbury, to
take a random instance, was a great admirer of Whitman –
although at the same time he would never have thought it necessary to explain why he didn't deal with American authors in his
Short History of English Literature. Arguably he was right (as regards
the actual exclusion, not as regards his lack of explanation); the
problem is an intricate one, and Matthew Arnold was being extremely short-sighted when he told the Americans that there
could be no such thing as American literature, there was only
English literature which happened to be written by Americans.*
The truth is, of course, that for Englishmen American literature
both is and isn't a foreign literature, with all the affinities, dis-
crepancies, intimate links and misunderstandings which that
entails. How far it should be studied in the universities in conjunction with English literature is an open question. One thing is

---

* Admittedly this point of view looked superficially more plausible at a time
when most American writers were either New Englanders or of predominantly
English stock. Arnold would probably have revised his opinion if he could have
lived long enough to see the emergence of, say, Dreiser.

certain, however: no English critic today can remain unaware for very long of how heavily the *métèques*, so to speak, outnumber the natives, nor of how much they have to offer the natives. This is not to say that we should simply sink all our differences in the mid-Atlantic. A uniquely English literary tradition, or complex of traditions, still exists, and is likely to go on existing for as long as anyone can foresee. But it is becoming less and less the central tradition of literature written in English.

None of the tendencies which I have been discussing is a purely post-war phenomenon, and some of them have been apparent for generations. It is simply that they have been gaining ground at an unprecedented rate in recent years. And meanwhile new social institutions have sprung up, and there has been a major shift in the way literary people earn their living.

Readers of Cyril Connolly's *Enemies of Promise* will remember that otherwise forgotten author Walter Savage Shelleyblake, who on the strength of his first book, *Vernal Aires*, was invited to become a reviewer for the *Blue Bugloss* by the literary editor, Mr Vampire. At first it was two thousand words on the Nonesuch *Boswell* ('Expatriate from Auchinleck'); then a slightly less sparkling piece on a new life of Erasmus Darwin ('Swansong at Lichfield'); then, by degrees, the slow decline into Shorter Notices of books about the secrets of Maya jungles and Kenya game-wardens and famous Royal Mistresses. It is not quite clear from Mr Connolly's account how Shelleyblake actually managed to stay afloat. Possibly he had a small private income, which went much further in those days. Possibly when funds ran out he taught for a while in a boarding school, like so many of his 1930s contemporaries.* But the probability is that by augmenting his earnings from the *Bugloss* through reading for publishers and taking on literary odd jobs, he was just about able to survive as a freelance, like his ancestors before him. For Walter Shelleyblake was a wholly traditional figure. His grandfather had been a founder member of the Neophyte Writers' Society, and later became a

---

* *To many an unknown genius postmen bring*
  Typed notices from Rabbitarse and String.
  – Letters from Iceland.

regular contributor to at least a dozen leading Victorian literary reviews. His father, after starting out as one of Henley's Young Men, scored a modest success writing a column about books and bookmen for an Edwardian weekly. And despite all the new technology and ideology, it still seemed perfectly natural in the 1930s for Walter to conform to the family pattern. Nor has the succession of Shelleyblakes failed: both Walter's sons, as their headmaster used to say on their school reports, have 'a real flair for literature'. The great difference is that so far they have been able to pursue considerably more prosperous careers than their father. It is true that in the mid-1950s the older boy initially had some trouble in getting his first academic appointment, but he is now a Senior Lecturer in English at a new university, with excellent prospects of promotion. His first book, originally his B.Litt. thesis, was a study of Boswell's imagery, his second, on which he is still working, is a reconsideration of Erasmus Darwin. His younger brother, off to a quicker start, was marked down for success from the moment he went into television. Today he is probably best known to viewers as the anchor-man of a weekly satirical review of the arts, although he also turns up regularly in paperback symposia, at Happenings, in the colour supplements, and indeed throughout the media generally. His chief current enthusiasms are John Cage, Marshall McLuhan, David Mercer, Paul McCartney and Claude Lévi-Strauss. Both he and his brother, in their different ways, have, I think, turned out reasonably typical of their generation. They both occasionally review for the *Blue Bugloss*.

Most English literary critics and scholars are already academics by profession, and in the nature of things the proportion is going to grow. The universities are expanding, and English as a subject is expanding with them. What exactly this will involve it is hard to say, although it might be a little easier if more serious thought were being given in this country to the implications – the cultural implications – of university growth in general. Expansion itself is inevitable: what we should be thinking about are the kind of *educational* (as opposed to organizational) changes which it will entail. A start has been made, especially at the new universities, but the basic issues involved are national rather than local. They affect school syllabuses, the status of university degrees, the relationship between individual universities and the system as a whole. And although the American experience of the past twenty or thirty years can serve as a useful analogy, there are too many cultural and economic differences for it to provide a straight-forward blueprint. In any case, even without the current bitter-ness and unrest it would be obvious that the next thirty years are not going to be like the past thirty years, either here or in America.

Yet despite all the imponderables, many of the actual problems seem plain enough. Some of them are bound to be simply old problems writ large – as far as English studies go, very old problems indeed. For the fundamental uncertainties about what the subject is, and how it should be taught, have not by any means been dispelled by the increase in academic numbers or by advances in scholarship. On the contrary, most critics with any life in them must surely be visited by moods of *Selbsthass* in which every additional learned article, every new critical theory, seems just another nail in the coffin. What is it ultimately all for? How can anyone who tries to keep up with Wordsworthian studies find time to read Wordsworth? It was in such a mood, or one very like it, that Randall Jarrell wrote his celebrated essay 'The Age of Criticism'*– an essay which ought to be even more celebrated than it is. Jarrell says most of what needs to be said about the over-production of criticism; his comments deal, naturally enough, with a specifically American situation, but if we are going to learn from American achievements, as we should have done long ago, we ought to take care that we also learn from American mistakes.

Of course modern advances in scholarship have been immense, and should not be taken for granted: an edition like the Twicken-ham *Pope*, for instance, is a superb piece of work, not just a monu-ment to professorial industry. And of course a great deal of academic criticism is of a much higher order than most literary journalism, past or present. Criticism may not be progressive, in the sense that a Dr Johnson or a Coleridge can ever be superseded; but that is very far from saying that good critics are incapable of learning from and improving on their less-than-Johnsonian pre-decessors. The problem, indeed, is as much one of quantity as of

* Reprinted in *Poetry and the Age*.

quality. To stick to the example of Pope: a generation or so ago very little of real note had been added to what the eighteenth-century critics had to say. Today there are, I suppose, at least half-a-dozen full-length critical studies which are worth reading, while a leading American scholar has edited an anthology entitled *44 Essential Articles on Pope*. None of this represents wasted labour. But what are we all going to do when there are forty-four essential *books?*

Perhaps that day will never come. And yet logically it should, if we accept the logic on which English studies are at present based. For it is taken for granted, by a false analogy with science or perhaps with history, that the very heart of the subject is research. From this it follows in turn that there is a heavy bias in favour of editorial work and the narrower kinds of factual enquiry. That these have their place, and, in the hands of a first-rate scholar, even their grandeur, goes without saying: there is a world in which Sir Walter Greg is legitimately a more important figure than Edmund Wilson. But it is not the world of most people who want to study literature, nor of most people who are best equipped to teach it, and there is no reason why it should be. You don't have to be a mechanic in order to drive a car. Textual and literary-historical scholarship are ancillary matters, something to be made use of but not something to be dominated by. As for purely literary research, nobody knows quite what it means. The truth is that unless you are either a critic of the first rank, or lucky enough to be caught up in a major revolution in taste, there are unlikely to be more than a limited number of original things which you have to say about any author who has been widely discussed already. But dissertations have to be submitted, and (where promotion is at stake) books have to be published. There are various possibilities open. You can spread your insights thin (many a long-drawn-out thesis could be compressed into a tolerably interesting article). You can choose an unexplored subject – and as time goes on, those that remain are bound to be more and more trivial. Or you can strain after false originality. One way or another, the books which result, and which multiply at an increasing rate, are likely to mean as little to posterity as most nineteenth-century collections of sermons do to a modern reader.

It may be asked whether any of this matters very much, except to students who have been side-tracked into reading the stuff, when they might have been reading better things. But if we adopt a full-scale American Ph.D. system we are going to hear a lot more from students who have been compelled to *write* the stuff, and from junior academics as well. It seems peculiarly perverse that the heaviest demands for research should fall on people in their early twenties, at a time when they are generally full of un-impaired enthusiasms and still working out their ideas. It is also rather questionable from the purely academic point of view, since the 'research' which counts most in literature is simply reading a great deal, far more than anyone except an occasional Macaulay can manage in his undergraduate years. Admittedly there are some students who know from the very outset that they want to be editors or philologists – W. W. Skeat began compiling Shakes-pearean glossaries at the age of sixteen – and naturally they shouldn't be discouraged. But it might not be a bad idea if no one under thirty was allowed to undertake original research without special permission. Nor does it seem to me unduly cynical to suggest that at that age most people would be more willing to settle for a limited, manageable subject than they would have been seven or eight years earlier. I agree with Hazlitt's dictum that 'he who is not in some measure a pedant, though he may be a wise, cannot be a very happy man'. But the pedantry ought to be allowed to develop in its own good time, and it ought not to be made the cornerstone of the whole academic system.

Much of the over-emphasis on secondary scholarship, like the earlier preoccupation with philology, springs from the need to prove that English is as 'professional' a subject as any other, and to remove any lingering taint of *belles-lettres*. There is far more to be said for the third method of stiffening the subject, which is likely to be the predominant one in future: 'interdisciplinary' study or, as they sometimes say, 'cross-fertilization'. Although this may sound intimidating it often implies nothing more than plain common sense. For example, in *Theory of Literature* Wellek and Warren quote from a German historian, Kohn-Bramstedt, to the effect that 'only a person who has a knowledge of the structure of a society from other sources than purely literary ones is able to find out if, and how far, certain social types and their behaviour are reproduced in the novel'. This might seem too obvious to need saying, to anyone who hadn't seen what actually goes on, to anyone who hadn't, for example, come across students praising *Hard Times* for the deadly accuracy of its satire on Utilitarianism, a subject on which it turned out most of their ideas derived from – *Hard Times*. Yet these are questions of general education rather than of literary understanding. It is perfectly possible to appreciate Gradgrind and Bounderby without knowing very much about Jeremy Bentham; and indeed, if one examines them too closely in a Benthamite context, one's enjoyment may well be rather damped down, since this almost inevitably leads on to treating the novel as though it were a none-too-accurate historical document. From the point of view of the historian, most authors – even novelists with a purpose, let alone lyric poets – are slippery customers. The evidence which they provide is too fragmentary, too oblique, simply too imaginative. There is a very strong case for studying English in *conjunction* with history. But to *correlate* the two subjects, except at a fairly rudimentary level, is an extremely arduous business; and if there is a loser in the transaction, the likelihood is that it will be literature. It is much easier to sacrifice the subtleties of a book to the demands of a broad historical thesis than *vice versa*. All interdisciplinary studies, in fact, necessarily involve seeing literature in terms of something else, rather than as an end in itself. This is even true of comparative literature, which beyond a certain point becomes self-defeating. There is no higher praise for an artist, after all, than to say that he is incomparable.

The problem of cross-breeding academic disciplines shouldn't be confused (as it often is, by optimistic university planners) with the more elementary question of whether or not the B.A. should be a general rather than a specialized degree. Here, given the fact of expansion, the arguments in favour of the general degree seem to me overwhelming. An 'honours' degree in English only makes sense on the assumption that students already possess a context of general information into which they can fit what they read – at least a nodding acquaintance with the Bible, classical mythology, the main outlines of English history, etc. This may have been a reasonable assumption in the past, but it is a highly dubious one

today, and likely to be increasingly untrue in future. It may be
objected that I am taking up the old anti-expansionist cry of
More means Worse, and so in a sense I am. The slogan is one
which ought to be heavily qualified in several respects. More
should mean Better in the long run. More may mean education-
ally Worse, but it is socially imperative. More need not mean
uniformly Worse. Nevertheless it seems to me utterly sentimental
to suppose that, in the world as it is at present, educational standards will not be adversely affected by the doubling or quadrup-
ling of the student population. Or of the teaching population, for
that matter, especially if a Ph.D. comes to be regarded as the be-all
and end-all. Goethe says somewhere that few things in the world
are more dreadful than a teacher who knows nothing except the
books which he has to teach. We may have to resign ourselves to
the prospect. But what about the good teacher, the teacher who
really cares about the wider implications? Faced with a mediocre
student, his position has always been a difficult one. He can only
simplify so far; beyond that he must either lower his standards, or
keep up the pretence that insight, imagination and literary sensibility are more evenly distributed than he knows they actually
are. Faced with a succession of mediocre students, the pressures on
him to adopt an 'egalitarian' approach are going to be heavier than
ever. This may not be altogether a bad thing: certainly one wants
to believe that the greatest literature is also the most universally
accessible. There is a beautiful line at the beginning of *The
Excursion*, singled out for praise by Matthew Arnold, about the
poet bringing news

> *Of joy in widest commonalty spread.*

That might seem to sum it all up. And yet half a dozen lines later
Wordsworth is invoking Milton's 'fit audience though few'. For
in some respects literature is fundamentally *in*egalitarian; or, to
put it as democratically as one can, not everyone has an aptitude
for it.

In the end one comes back to the most obstinate question of all.
Isn't there a certain basic antagonism between the very nature of a
university and the very spirit of literature? The academic mind is
cautious, tightly organized, fault-finding, competitive – and

above all, inordinately aware of other academic minds. Think of the atmosphere of suspicion implied by the habit of fitting out the most trivial quotation with a reference, as though it were applying for a job. Think of the whole idea of regarding literature as a *discipline*. Literature can be strenuous or difficult or deeply disturbing; it can be a hundred things – but a discipline is not one of them. Discipline means compulsion, and an interest in literature thrives on spontaneity, eager curiosity, the anticipation of pleasure; it is unlikely that a reader who comes to a book under duress, or weighed down with a sense of duty, will ever really *read* it at all, however much he may learn about it. Even the most intensely serious literature needs to be approached with a certain lightness of heart, if it is to yield its full intensity. Of course these are generalizations: there is no one collective Academic Mind, any more than there is a universal Spirit of Literature. Some authors lend themselves more appropriately to academic study than others. The idea of a graduate seminar on Ronald Firbank would be Firbankian. Conversely, hundreds of academic books have nothing inhibitingly academic about them. In the end one judges by results, and what does it matter whether, say, Ellmann's life of Joyce or *The Allegory of Love* or *The Liberal Imagination* were written in a university or not? The important thing is that they were written at all; and if it was under academic auspices, then so much the better for academic auspices. In any case, we live in a world of increasingly huge centralized institutions, and the literary tradition quite simply needs the protection of the universities. But it would be a sad day if it ever came to be positively identified with them.

No doubt there is very little danger of this happening. However much the universities grow, they are hardly going to establish an outright monopoly over high culture; and even if they did, in some science fiction future, authors would be among the last to capitulate. In reality the creative writer will no doubt keep on fending for himself, as essentially he always has, and the commercial writer will no doubt find that the rewards are getting bigger all the time. But what about the in-between, the near-creative writer, the man of letters? For the past two hundred years his chief resource has been journalism, and literary journalism is likely to go on being with us for a long time to come. Nor has there been any marked decline in quality; today, in fact, the general level of reviewing is probably a good deal higher than it was thirty or forty years ago. But the over-all situation is changing. There are fewer papers than there were, and the chances are that before very long there will be fewer still. In particular, there are far fewer 'thick journals', which in practice means principally monthlies. (For some reason English readers have always had an aversion to fortnightlies – the *Fortnightly* itself soon had to be turned into a monthly; while so many things happen in a quarter nowadays that a new quarterly would seem more like a year-book.) One need only consider how few places there are in England today where a writer can publish a serious short story or a long general article with any prospect of reaching more than a handful of readers. As for the weeklies and the newspapers, the competition for space is fierce, and literature is only one contender among many others. And meanwhile the quality press as a whole is subjected to increasing pressure – often intermittent and oblique, but no less effective for that – to get a little younger every day, and a little cooler, and a little closer to the top of the pops. Nor can this be accounted for simply by the struggle for circulation. It is part of the spirit of the age as well, or of what people have been talked into thinking of as the spirit of the age. And it also reflects the spirit of the mass media, invading every department of life.

In recent years intellectual critics of mass culture have found themselves in a completely new situation. Originally most of them took a wholly negative line, on the assumption that the cheaper the product, the wider the appeal. Subsequently they shifted their ground, and concentrated their attacks not so much on the shamelessly lowbrow aspects of the mass media as on the more insidious threat of the *faux bon*, the middlebrow travesty of high culture. As for outbursts of middlebrow anti-intellectualism, they could be laughed off or brushed aside; unless it was a question of actual censorship, they were far less of a nuisance than middle-brow artistic aspirations. Lately, however, critics have found themselves confronted by a more sophisticated and a more aggressive counter-attack on traditional literary standards in the name of the media. It can be seen most notoriously in the cult of Marshall McLuhan, although if McLuhan hadn't existed it would have been necessary to assemble the parts: by and large he has simply acted as a rallying-point for assumptions and prejudices which were already beginning to take shape long before his work became generally known. Some of the hostility towards literary intellectuals is no doubt amply justified. Most of them were slow to concede the creative possibilities of the cinema, of the positive social effects of television, while they often remain insensitive to questions of presentation and design. Equally, at least some of McLuhan's argumentative 'probes' are probing in the right direction. But few of his admirers seem particularly interested in the job of sorting out the insights from the verbiage. In practice he attracts his most devoted following among those whose pretensions he automatically flatters: 'creative' advertising men, television boy wonders, 'communicators' with nothing but their own vanity to communicate. Whatever McLuhan's own intellectual convolutions, McLuhanism as a social phenomenon is a relatively simple affair. It is part of the same pattern which can be seen in the television documentary which turns an artist's life into an excuse for fancy camerawork, in the gossip column which treats the arts as though they were a branch of show business, in the paper where lay-out takes precedence over the text. Let us honour, where we can, the new preoccupation with appearances. But let us also recognize how often, among those who proclaim it most vociferously, it goes with a feeling of deep resentment towards literature, and even towards intelligence itself.

There are critics – literary critics – intelligent literary critics – who will find nothing very objectionable about this. Aren't we dealing, after all, with a revolution in sensibility which goes far beyond local advances in gadgetry and technique? Doesn't the characteristic art of our time variously aspire towards a condition of silence, or chaos, or schizophrenia, or randomness, or impermanence, or polymorphous perversity? Haven't the Young already begun living in a post-humanist, anarchic, hallucinogenic future? Resisting for the moment the temptation to murmur 'no, they have not', we may at any rate ask whether critics who subscribe to such doctrines aren't effectively putting themselves out of business. Leslie Fiedler, never the last man to clamber aboard a band-wagon, asserts in his well-known essay 'The New Mutants' that 'even essayists and analysts recommend themselves to us these days by a certain redemptive nuttiness'. Other writers have called, less jauntily, for a new apocalyptic style of criticism to match new apocalyptic forms of art. And certainly a critic who fails to respond to the elements of disorder and irrationality in all imaginative literature, not just that of the present, is not going to get very far. But on the other hand the act of criticism itself, if it means anything more than awarding marks, presupposes that there is some point in trying to clarify disorder or in trying to render irrationality a little more intelligible. The critic who wants to abandon his traditional role of interpreter completely is in effect offering to set up as a special type of creative writer. Alternatively, all he can do is keep repeating that art defies explanation, and keep touting for his latest discoveries. He must resign himself to being the doorman at the discothèque, the assistant in the boutique. I can't see this happening myself, any more than I can see much future for the fruitcake school of criticism acclaimed by Professor Fiedler. Apocalyptic fashions come and go, especially fashions which draw their main strength from that most wasting of all assets, Youth. Yet they have their significance, too, and it would be foolish for anyone who believes in the continuity of culture not to recognize how far the values of our society are working against him. The rate of change keeps accelerating; each new artistic mode is expected not so much to supplement the last as to replace it and go one better.

To a Marxist, these are doubtless characteristics of life under 'late' capitalism, which will disappear when a more rational social order is established. Whether or not that day ever comes, the evidence at present certainly suggests that Marxist or semi-Marxist ideas are going to gain ground in the immediate future. As far as English literary criticism is concerned one inevitably thinks of Raymond Williams, whose influence will, I believe, prove much longer-lasting than that of Caudwell or any of the Marxist critics of the 1930s, because it is much more securely rooted in the realities of English culture and English tradition. (He could not in fact be called a Marxist in any formal sense.) One can easily imagine an entire school of revisionist literary history developing out of his work, and out of the work of a New Left historian like E. P. Thompson. But how far Williams's influence will eventually extend outside academic circles is another matter. When he affirms that culture is 'ordinary', one may applaud his attempt to strip the word of its snobbish or daunting connotations, and yet feel impelled to add that in literature, at least, ordinariness is a very limited virtue, and that for most readers nothing could be more disheartening than the prospect of a new race of critics who

> *crave in books*
> *Plain cooking made still plainer by plain cooks.*

Except, perhaps, the prospect of a political system under which the critic becomes an *apparatchik*, enforcing standards of cultural uniformity.

Whatever the future holds, the first qualification for being a good critic will always be an interest in literature for what it is, rather than for the ends which it can be made to serve. But the second qualification, no less essential, will be a commitment to the life which lies beyond literature, by which it must finally be judged. Criticism remains the most miscellaneous, the most ill-defined of occupations. At any given moment it is liable to start turning into something else: history or politics, psychology or ethics, autobiography or gossip. In a world which favours experts and specialists, this means that the critic is increasingly liable to be dismissed as a dilettante or resented as a trespasser. But if his uncertain status often puts him at a disadvantage, it also makes possible, ideally, the breadth and independence which are his ultimate justification. In this sense, at least, however archaic it may seem in other respects, the idea of the man of letters has a place in any healthy literary tradition.

SELECTED
BIBLIOGRAPHY

Place of publication London except where indicated.

1   The Rise of the Reviewer

On Jeffrey and the *Edinburgh Review*: Lord Cockburn, *Life of Lord Jeffrey* (Edinburgh, 1852); James A. Greig, *Francis Jeffrey of the Edinburgh Review* (Edinburgh, 1948); John Clive, *Scotch Reviewers* (1957); David Craig, *Scottish Literature and the Scottish People 1680–1830* (1961).

On Jeffrey and Scottish education, see: G. E. Davie, *The Democratic Intellect: Scotland and her Universities in the Nineteenth Century* (Edinburgh, 1961).

Bagehot's views on Jeffrey can be found in 'The First Edinburgh Reviewers' (*Literary Essays*); Leslie Stephen's in 'The First Edinburgh Reviewers' (*Hours in a Library*); John Morley's in 'Memorials of a Man of Letters' (*Studies in Literature*). There is a selection of Jeffrey's criticism by David Nichol Smith (1910).

On Lockhart: Andrew Lang, *Life and Letters of John Gibson Lockhart* (1897). There is a selection of his criticism by M. C. Hildyard (1931) and an essay by Virginia Woolf in *The Moment* (1947). For more sympathetic views of Christopher North than mine see the essays in Malcolm Elwin, *Victorian Wallflowers* (1934) and David Daiches, *Literary Essays* (1956). See also John Wain, *Contemporary Reviews of Romantic Poetry* (1953).

On the *London Magazine*: Josephine Bauer, *The London Magazine 1820–9* (Copenhagen, 1953); Humphry House, 'A Famous Literary Periodical' in *All in Due Time* (1955). See also Edmund Blunden, *Keats's Publisher: A Memoir of John Taylor* (1936) and J. C. Reid, *Thomas Hood* (1963). Stendhal wrote for the *New Monthly* and the *Athenaeum* as well as the *London*; there is an anthology edited by Geoffrey Strickland, *Selected Journalism from the English Reviews by Stendhal* (1959). On Wainewright; Jonathan Curling, *Janus Weathercock* (1938).

On Leigh Hunt as an editor: Edmund Blunden, *Leigh Hunt* (1930) and *Leigh Hunt's Examiner Examined* (with selections; 1928); William Marshall, *Shelley, Byron Hunt and 'The Liberal'* (Philadelphia, 1960).

On *Fraser's* and Maginn: Miriam Thrall, *Rebellious Fraser's* (New York, 1934); Elwin, *Victorian Wallflowers*; Logan Pearsall Smith, *Reperusals and Re-Collections* (1936). See also: Matthew Arnold, *On Translating Homer*; Augustus Ralli, *A History of Shakespearean Criticism* (Oxford, 1932). There is a selection of Maginn's writings edited by R. W. Montague (1885). For Maclise's drawings see *A Gallery of Illustrious Literary Characters. Drawn by Daniel Maclise with Notices chiefly by William Maginn*, edited by W. Bates (1873).

On Thackeray's early journalism: Gordon Ray, *Thackeray: The Uses of Adversity* (1955); *Contributions to the Morning Chronicle*, ed. Ray (1955).

On Barnes: Derek Hudson, *Thomas Barnes of The Times* (1943; with a selection of Barnes's work by Harold Child); *The History of The Times*, vol. i, *The Thunderer in the Making* (1935).

See also: A. Aspinall, 'The Social Status of Journalists at the Beginning of the Nineteenth Century' (*Review of English Studies*, xxi, 1945); Leslie Marchant, *The Athenaeum: A Mirror of Victorian Culture* (Chapel Hill, North Carolina, 1941); Sir William Beach Thomas, *The Story of the Spectator* (1928).

2   Heroes and Men of Letters

On Carlyle: J. A. Froude, *Thomas Carlyle* (1882–4) – generally underrated; David Wilson, *Carlyle* (1923–34); Emery Neff, *Carlyle and Mill* (New York, 1924) and *Carlyle* (New York, 1932); Julian Symons, *Carlyle: The Life and Ideas of a Prophet* (1952); G. B. Tennyson, *'Sartor' called 'Resartus'* (Princeton, N.J., 1964). Of Carlyle's correspondence, see especially *Letters to Mill, Sterling and Browning*, ed. A. J. Carlyle (1923). See also: Eric Bentley, *A Century of Hero Worship* (1944). On Carlyle's and Macaulay's interpretations of Dr Johnson, see Bertrand Bronson, 'The Double Tradition of Dr Johnson' (*English Literary History*, June 1951). On Carlyle and Lagarde, see Fritz Stern, *The Politics of Cultural Despair* (Berkeley, California, 1961).

On Mill: Michael Packe, *Life of John Stuart Mill* (1954); *Letters of John Stuart Mill*, ed. Hugh Elliot (1910); Alexander Bain, *James Mill* (1882). On Mill's literary criticism see especially: Mark Abrams, *The Mirror and the Lamp* (New York, 1953); Walter J. Ong, 'J. S. Mill's Pariah Poet' (*Philological Quarterly*, 1950); Edward Alexander, *Matthew*

Arnold and John Stuart Mill (1965). See also the introductions to Mill's *Essays on Literature and Society*, ed. J. B. Schneewind (New York, 1965) and *Essays on Politics and Culture by John Stuart Mill*, ed. Gertrude Himmelfarb (New York, 1963).

On Arnold see especially: Lionel Trilling, *Matthew Arnold* (1939); E. K. Brown, *Arnold; A Study in Conflict* (Chicago, 1948); and among recent more specialized studies: Frederic Faverty, *Matthew Arnold: The Ethnologist* (Evanston, Ill., 1951); Patrick McCarthy, *Arnold and the Three Classes* (New York, 1964); Edward Alexander, *op.cit.*; J. Hillis Miller, *The Disappearance of God* (Cambridge, Mass., 1963) – on the poetry. Arnold's article on Sainte-Beuve is reprinted in *Five Uncollected Essays of Matthew Arnold*, ed. Kenneth Allott (Liverpool, 1953).

3   The Higher Journalism

M. M. Bevington, *The Saturday Review*, 1855–68 (New York, 1941).

D. Roll-Hansen, *The Academy 1869–79* (Copenhagen, 1957).

On the *Nineteenth Century*: *Nineteenth Century Opinion*, ed. Michael Goodwin (1951) and Alan Willard Brown, *The Metaphysical Society* (N.Y., 1947).

J. M. Robertson Scott, *The Story of the Pall Mall Gazette* (1950) and *The Life and Death of a Great Newspaper* (1952) – includes material on Sir Edward Cook and Cust; on Cust see also Sir Ronald Storrs, *Orientations* (1937).

Sir Edward Cook, 'Fifty Years of a Literary Magazine' (the *Cornhill*) in *Literary Recreations* (1918).

E. E. Kellett, 'The Press 1830–65' in *Early Victorian England*, ed. G. M. Young (1934).

R. G. Cox, 'The Reviews and Magazines' in *The Pelican Guide to English Literature*, ed. Boris Ford, vol. 6 (1958).

The George Eliot Letters ed. G. S. Haight (New Haven, 1954–6) and *George Eliot* (1968).

G. S. Haight, *George Eliot and John Chapman* (New Haven, 1940).

Essays of George Eliot ed. Thomas Pinney (1963).

A. T. Kitchell, *George Lewes and George Eliot* (New York, 1934).

M. Greenhut, 'Lewes and the Classical Tradition in English Criticism' (*Review of English Studies*, xxiv, 1948). On Lewes and Pavlov: Y. P. Frolov, *Pavlov and his School* (English translation, 1937).

Of the standard general studies of Bagehot, the one which deals most thoroughly with his literary criticism is William Irvine's *Walter Bagehot*

(1939). See also the introductory essays to vol. i of *Collected Works of Walter Bagehot*, ed. Norman St John Stevas (1965) and Gertrude Himmelfarb, *Victorian Minds* (1968).

On Hutton: Anon, *Richard Holt Hutton of the 'Spectator'* (Edinburgh, 1899); Sir W. Beach Thomas, *op. cit.*; G. C. Leroy, 'Richard Holt Hutton' in *P.M.L.A.* (1941).

On Stephen see Maitland's *Life* (1906) and Noel Annan, *Leslie Stephen: His Thought and Character in Relation to his Time* (1951). Stephen's essay on Taine can be found in *Men, Books and Mountains*, ed. S. O. A. Ullmann (1956). Mrs Leavis's essay on Stephen is reprinted in *A Selection from Scrutiny*, vol. i (Cambridge, 1968); Virginia Woolf's centenary tribute is reprinted in *The Captain's Death-Bed* (1950).

On Hannay: G. J. Worth, *James Hannay: His Life and Works* (Lawrence, Kansas, 1964). There is nothing of note on Yates.

On Frank Harris: Hugh Kingsmill, *Frank Harris* (1932).

4   Some Liberal Practitioners

John Morley, *Recollections* (1917). D. A. Hamer, *John Morley* (1968). F. W. Hirst, *Early Life and Letters of John Morley* (1927).

Warren Staebler, *The Liberal Mind of John Morley* (Princeton, 1943).

On the *Fortnightly Review*, see Edwin Everett, *The Party of Humanity* (Chapel Hill, 1939); on 'English Men of Letters', see Charles Morgan, *The House of Macmillan* (1943); on Morley and Henry James, see Leon Edel, *Henry James: The Conquest of London* (1962); on Morley and the Cambridge Modern History, see Gertrude Himmelfarb, *Lord Acton* (1952); on Morley and India, see M. N. Das, *India under Morley and Minto* (1964), and R. J. Moore, *Liberalism and Indian Politics 1872–1922* (1966); on Morley and the succession to Gladstone, see Robert Rhodes James, *Rosebery* (1963).

Frederic Harrison, *Autobiographic Memoirs* (1911).

Austin Harrison, *Frederic Harrison, Thoughts and Memories* (1926).

On the political influence of Positivism: Royden Harrison, *Before the Socialists* (1965). W. M. Simon, 'August Comte's English Disciples' (*Victorian Studies*, December 1964).

Augustine Birrell, *Things Past Redress* (1937).

There is no general account of either Herbert Paul or J. M. Robertson; but on Robertson's Shakespearean theories see Sir Edmund Chambers, 'The Disintegration of Shakespeare', in *Shakespearean Gleanings* (1944). See also David Tribe, *A Hundred Years of Free Thought* (1967).

Lucy Masterman, *C. F. G. Masterman* (1939).

There is a good modern edition of *The Condition of England*, ed. J. T. Boulton (1960). For a collection of Masterman's minor literary pieces, see *In Peril of Change* (1905). On Masterman and Bottomley: Julian Symons, *Horatio Bottomley* (1955). There is a useful account of Masterman in Samuel Hynes, *The Edwardian Turn of Mind* (Princeton, 1968).

5   The Bookmen

Roger Lancelyn Green, *Andrew Lang* (Leicester, 1946).

On Lang see also G. S. Gordon and others, *Concerning Andrew Lang* (1949), the Andrew Lang lectures delivered at St Andrews; Malcolm Elwin, *Old Gods Falling* (1939); Forrest Reid, *Retrospective Adventures* (1941). On Lang and Beerbohm, see David Cecil, *Max* (1964).

On the Rondeliers, see James K. Robinson, 'A Neglected Phase of the Aesthetic Movement: English Parnassianism' (*P.M.L.A.*, September 1953).

George Saintsbury: The Memorial Volume (1945). With tributes from various friends, and a biographical memoir by A. Blyth Webster.

George Saintsbury: A Last Vintage (1950). With further tributes, and a bibliography.

Dorothy Richardson, 'Saintsbury and Art for Art's Sake in England' (*P.M.L.A.*, 1944); on Saintsbury see also Stephen Potter, *The Muse in Chains* (1937).

Edmund Wilson's two essays on Saintsbury can be found in *Classics and Commercials* (1950). Orwell's comment on the *Scrapbooks* is in *The Road to Wigan Pier*. On Saintsbury, Eliot and the *Dial*, see William Wasserstrom, *The Years of the Dial* (Syracuse, N.Y., 1963).

John Connell, *W. E. Henley* (1949).

Jerome Buckley, *William Ernest Henley* (Princeton, 1945). For Yeats on Henley, see *The Trembling of the Veil* (1922).

There is nothing of interest on Whibley apart from Eliot's essays, but there is scattered biographical information in John Connell, *op.cit.*

On Wyndham: J. W. Mackail and Guy Wyndham, *Life and Letters of George Wyndham* (1925). See also Whibley's introduction to *Essays in Romantic Literature* (1919).

Alban Dobson, *Austin Dobson: Some Notes* (Oxford, 1928) – includes memoirs by Saintsbury and Gosse.

Evan Charteris, *Life and Letters of Sir Edmund Gosse* (1931). There are numerous reminiscences, e.g., Osbert Sitwell, in *Noble Essences* (1950);

Alec Waugh, in *My Brother Evelyn* (1967). Gosse's correspondence with Gide has been edited by L. F. Brugmans (1959). On Gosse and French literature, see Ruth Zabriskie Temple, *The Critic's Alchemy* (New York, 1953).

On Richard Garnett and his progeny, see Carolyn Heilbrun, *The Garnett Family* (1961).

On James Thomson, see H. Salt's *Life* (1898); Bertram Dobell, *The Laureate of Pessimism* (1910); William David Schaefer, *James Thomson (B.V.): Beyond 'The City'* (California, 1965). For modern selections see poems and letters, ed. Anne Ridler (1963) and, for the prose works, *The Speedy Extinction of Evil and Misery*, ed. W. D. Schaefer (California, 1967).

6   Early English

Stephen Potter, *The Muse in Chains* (1937).

D. J. Palmer, *The Rise of English Studies* (1965).

E. M. W. Tillyard, *The Muse Unchained* (1958).

F. J. Furnivall: *A Volume of Personal Record* (with a biography by J. Munro) (1911).

There is an amusing sketch of the New Shakspere Society in F. E. Halliday, *The Cult of Shakespeare* (1957).

H. S. Solley, *The Life of Henry Morley, LL.D.* (1898). See also Morley's *Early Papers and Some Memories* (1891).

L. C. Collins, *Life and Memoirs of John Churton Collins* (1912).

Letters of Sir Walter Raleigh, 1879–1922, ed. Lady Raleigh (1926). See also Raleigh's *Laughter Through a Cloud* (1923); Virginia Woolf, 'Walter Raleigh' (now reprinted in *Collected Essays*, Vol. I); Q. D. Leavis, 'The Discipline of Letters', reprinted in *A Selection from Scrutiny*, Vol. I (Cambridge, 1968). There is a sympathetic sketch of Raleigh in Michael Holroyd, *Lytton Strachey*, Vol. I (1967).

The Letters of G. S. Gordon, 1902–42 (Oxford, 1943).

Arthur Quiller-Couch, *Memories and Reflections: An Unfinished Autobiography* (Cambridge, 1944).

F. Brittain, *Arthur Quiller-Couch* (Cambridge, 1947).

7   Popular Approaches

Richard D. Altick, *The English Common Reader* (1957).

Amy Cruse, *The Victorians and their Books* (1935).

R. K. Webb, *The British Working Class Reader, 1790–1848* (1955).

On Gilfillan, see R. A. and E. S. Watson, *George Gilfillan, Letters and Journals* (1892); Robertson Nicoll's introduction to *Gilfillan's Literary Portraits* (1909); and Jerome Buckley, *The Victorian Temper* (1952).

Walter Besant, *The Pen and the Book* (1899); *Autobiography* (1902).

T. H. Darlow, *Life and Letters of William Robertson Nicoll* (1925). See also Nicoll's *A Bookman's Letters* (1913); Dixon Scott, *Men of Letters*, with an introduction by Max Beerbohm (1916); George Blake, *Barrie and the Kailyard School* (1951).

C. K. Shorter, *Autobiography*, ed. J. M. Bullock (1927).

J. M. Dent, *Memoirs* (1928).

Ernest Rhys, *Everyman Remembers* (1931). On Everyman's see also Frank Swinnerton, *Swinnerton: An Autobiography* (1936). On Nelson's classics, see Janet Adam Smith, *John Buchan* (1965).

8 Edwardians

Frank Swinnerton, *The Georgian Literary Scene* (1935).

Derek Hudson, 'Reading', in *Edwardian England 1901–14*, ed. Simon Nowell Smith (1964).

C. Lewis Hind, *Naphtali* (1926); on the *Academy* see also *Life of John Oliver Hobbes* (1911).

Two books which give an excellent glimpse of turn-of-the-century and Edwardian publishing are Grant Richards's reminiscences – *Memoirs of a Misspent Youth* (1933) and *Author Hunting* (1934).

Reginald Pound, *Arnold Bennett* (1952). See also George Lafourcade, *Bennett: A Study* (1939); Walter Allen, *Arnold Bennett* (1948); and John Wain, *Preliminary Essays* (1957).

Maisie Ward, *Gilbert Keith Chesterton* (1944). See also Chesterton's *Autobiography* (1936); Maurice Evans, *G. K. Chesterton* (1939); Hugh Kenner, *Paradox in Chesterton* (1948); and A. L. Maycock's introductory essay to his selection of uncollected writings by Chesterton, *The Man Who Was Orthodox* (1963). For an example of how virulent Chesterton could be on the Marconi case, see 'An Open Letter to Lord Reading', reprinted as an appendix in Frances Donaldson, *The Marconi Scandal* (1962).

My account of Orage is largely based on Philip Mairet, *A. R. Orage: A Memoir* (1936; second edition with new preface, New York, 1966); Wallace Martin, *The New Age under Orage* (Manchester, 1967); and Paul

Selver, *Orage and the New Age Circle* (1959). There is a selection of Orage's essays, ed. Herbert Read and Saurat (1936). J. M. Kennedy wrote a disappointing history of *English Literature* 1880–1905 (1912).

9   Modern Times

Herbert Howarth, *Notes on Some Figures behind T. S. Eliot* (1965).
Robert Ross, *The Georgian Revolt* (1967).
Patrick Howarth, *Squire; Most Generous of Men* (1963).
F. A. Lea, *Life of John Middleton Murry* (1959); see also Philip Mairet, *John Middleton Murry* (British Council Booklet) and Rayner Hepenstall, *Middleton Murry* (1934). On Murry and Lawrence, see, among much else, Harry T. Moore, *The Intelligent Heart* (1955).

Desmond McCarthy, *Criticism* (1932); *Portraits* (1931); *Experience* (1935); *Humanities* (1953), with a preface by David Cecil; *Memories* (1953) with forewords by Cyril Connolly and Raymond Mortimer. On McCarthy see also Leonard Woolf, *Beginning Again* (1964).

Ella Sharpe's Shakespeare papers can be found in her *Collected Papers on Psychoanalysis* (1950). For English psycho-analytically-orientated criticism in general see Stanley Edgar Hyman, *The Armed Vision* (1948).

Peter Butter, *Edwin Muir: Man and Poet* (Edinburgh, 1966).

On the *Calendar of Modern Letters*, see Malcolm Bradbury's introductory 'Review in Retrospect' to the 1966 reprint.

10   Cross-Currents of the Thirties

Julian Symons, *The Thirties; A Dream Revolved* (1960).
Neal Wood, *Communism and British Intellectuals* (1959).
Michael Roberts, *Collected Poems* (1958), with an introductory memoir by Janet Adam Smith.
Geoffrey Grigson, *The Crest on Silver* (1950).
On Caudwell see George Thomson's introductory biographical note to *Illusion and Reality* (1946).
Christopher Hollis, *George Orwell* (1956).
Richard Rees, *George Orwell* (1961).
For more favourable accounts of Leavis than mine see, for example, 'Dr Leavis and the Moral Tradition' in Lionel Trilling *A Gathering of Fugitives* (1957); D. J. Enright, 'Thirty Years On: Reflections on the Reprinting of *Scrutiny*' in *Conspirators and Poets* (1966); W. W. Robson,

Critical Essays (1966). See also *The Importance of Scrutiny*, ed. Eric Bentley (1948).

11 Epilogue

Leslie Fiedler's 'The New Mutants' is reprinted in *Innovations*, ed. Bernard Bergonzi (1968).

General

Dictionary of National Biography.

Asa Briggs, *Victorian People* (1954); *The Age of Improvement* (1959).

W. L. Burn, *The Age of Equipoise* (1964).

G. Kitson Clark, *The Making of Victorian England* (1962); *An Expanding Society: Britain 1830–1900* (Cambridge, 1967).

R. C. K. Ensor, *England 1870–1914* (1935).

Élie Halévy, *A History of the English People in the Nineteenth Century* (English translation, 1924–48).

A. J. P. Taylor, *English History 1914–45* (1965).

G. M. Trevelyan, *British History in the Nineteenth Century* (1928).

E. L. Woodward, *The Age of Reform* (second edition, 1962).

G. M. Young (ed.), *Early Victorian England* (1934).

George Saintsbury, *A History of English Criticism* (1911).

George Watson, *The Literary Critics* (1962).

René Wellek, *A History of Modern Criticism* (1955–).

René Wellek and Austin Warren, *Theory of Literature* (1949).

W. K. Wimsatt and Cleanth Brooks, *Literary Criticism: A Short History* (1957).

Crane Brinton, *English Political Thought in the Nineteenth Century* (1933).

Jerome Buckley, *The Victorian Temper* (1952).

Oliver Elton, *A Survey of English Literature 1830–1880* (1920).

John Holloway, *The Victorian Sage* (1953).

W. E. Houghton, *The Victorian Frame of Mind* (Yale, 1957); *Ideas and Beliefs of the Victorians* (1949).

Ian Jack, *English Literature 1815–1832* (1963).

Holbrook Jackson, *The Eighteen Nineties* (1913).

George Levine (ed.), *The Emergence of Victorian Consciousness* (1967).

D. C. Somervell, *English Thought in the Nineteenth Century* (1929).

Geoffrey and Kathleen Tillotson, *Mid-Victorian Studies* (1965).

Basil Willey, *Nineteenth Century Studies* (1949); *More Nineteenth Century Studies* (1956).

Raymond Williams, *Culture and Society* (1958); *The Long Revolution* (1961).

G. M. Young, *Victorian Essays* (1964).

A. S. Collins, *The Profession of Letters, 1780–1832* (1928).

Alvar Ellegard, *The Readership of the Periodical Press in Mid-Victorian Britain* (Gothenburg, 1957).

George Ford, *Dickens and His Readers* (1955).

Walter Graham, *English Literary Periodicals* (New York, 1930).

James Hepburn, *The Author's Empty Purse* (1968) – contains an invaluable bibliography of works dealing with the conditions of authorship.

Q. D. Leavis, *Fiction and the Reading Public* (1932).

Stanley Morison, *The English Newspaper 1622–1932* (Cambridge, 1932).

J. W. Saunders, *The Profession of Letters* (1964).

INDEX

NOTE: Book titles are entered under their authors' names, except anthologies
Publishers' Series are entered under the series' titles
Newspapers are listed together under 'Newspapers'
Periodicals are listed together under 'Periodicals'
★ refers to footnotes on page referred to